**INDIVIDUAL
DIFFERENCES IN
CHILDREN**

WILEY SERIES ON PERSONALITY PROCESSES

IRVING B. WEINER, *Editor*
Case Western Reserve University

INTERACTION IN FAMILIES
by Elliot G. Mishler and Nancy E. Waxler

SOCIAL STATUS AND PSYCHOLOGICAL DISORDER: A Causal Inquiry
by Bruce P. Dohrenwend and Barbara Dohrenwend

PSYCHOLOGICAL DISTURBANCE IN ADOLESCENCE
by Irving B. Weiner

ASSESSMENT OF BRAIN DAMAGE: A Neuropsychological Key Approach
by Elbert W. Russell, Charles Neuringer, and Gerald Goldstein

BLACK AND WHITE IDENTITY FORMATION
by Stuart Hauser

THE HUMANIZATION PROCESSES: A Social, Behavioral Analysis
of Children's Problems
*by Robert L. Hamblin, David Buckholdt, Daniel Ferritor, Martin Kozloff,
and Lois Blackwell*

ADOLESCENT SUICIDE
by Jerry Jacobs

TOWARD THE INTEGRATION OF PSYCHOTHERAPY
by John M. Reisman

MINIMAL BRAIN DYSFUNCTION IN CHILDREN
by Paul Wender

LSD: PERSONALITY AND EXPERIENCE
*by Harriet Linton Barr, Robert J. Langs, Robert R. Holt,
Leo Goldberger, and George S. Klein*

TREATMENT OF THE BORDERLINE ADOLESCENT: A Developmental
Approach
by James F. Masterson

PSYCHOPATHOLOGY: Contributions from the Biological, Behavioral, and
Social Sciences
edited by Muriel Hammer, Kurt Salzinger, and Samuel Sutton

ABNORMAL CHILDREN AND YOUTH: Therapy and Research
by Anthony Davids

PSYCHOTHERAPY WITH CHILDREN
by John M. Reisman

AVERSIVE MATERNAL CONTROL: A Theory of Schizophrenic Development
by Alfred B. Heilbrun, Jr.

INDIVIDUAL DIFFERENCES IN CHILDREN
edited by Jack C. Westman

INDIVIDUAL DIFFERENCES IN CHILDREN

Edited by

JACK C. WESTMAN

A WILEY-INTERSCIENCE PUBLICATION

JOHN WILEY & SONS, New York · London · Sydney · Toronto

Library of Congress Cataloging in Publication Data:

Westman, Jack C.
  Individual differences in children.

  (Wiley series on personality processes)
  "A Wiley-Interscience publication."
  1. Individuality. 2. Child study. I. Title.
[DNLM: 1. Child behavior. 2. Child development.
WS 105 I39]

BF723.I56W47   155.4'18   72-10131
ISBN 0-471-93690-1

Printed in the United States of America

10   9   8   7   6   5   4   3   2   1

Contributors

Mourad Arganian, M.S.W.
Department of Psychiatry
University of Wisconsin
Madison, Wisconsin

Helen H. Baldwin, M.S.
Department of Psychiatry
University of Wisconsin
Madison, Wisconsin

Lorna Benjamin, Ph.D.
Associate Professor of Psychiatry
University of Wisconsin
Madison, Wisconsin

Fred Busch, Ph.D.
Assistant Professor of Clinical Psychology
University of Michigan Medical Center
Ann Arbor, Michigan

William B. Carey, M.D.
Private Practice of Pediatrics
Media, Pennsylvania

Stella Chess, M.D.
Associate Professor of Psychiatry
New York University Medical Center
New York, New York

Phyllis Click, M.S.
Director of Teacher Education
Center for Early Education
Los Angeles, California

David Elkind, Ph.D.
Professor of Psychology
University of Rochester
Rochester, New York

Sibylle K. Escalona, Ph.D.
Professor of Psychiatry
Albert Einstein College of Medicine
Yeshiva University
New York, New York

Grace S. Gregg, M.D.
Director, Developmental Clinic
Children's Hospital
Pittsburgh, Pennsylvania

Harry F. Harlow, Ph.D.
Director, Primate Laboratory and
    Research Center
University of Wisconsin
Madison, Wisconsin

Irving D. Harris, M.D.
Institute for Juvenile Research
Illinois State Psychiatric Institute
1601 West Taylor Street
Chicago, Illinois

Christoph M. Heinicke, Ph.D.
Director, Division of Research
Reiss-Davis Child Study Center
Los Angeles, California

v

Anneliese F. Korner, Ph.D.
Senior Scientist
Department of Psychiatry
Stanford University Medical Center
Stanford, California

Estelle Kramer, M.D.
Director of Children's Programs
Center for Early Education
Los Angeles, California

William McKinney, M.D.
Associate Professor of Psychiatry
University of Wisconsin
Madison, Wisconsin

Stephen J. Suomi, Ph.D.
Primate Laboratory & Research Center
University of Wisconsin
Madison, Wisconsin

J.M. Tanner, M.D., D.Sc. M.R.C.P., D.P.M.
Professor of Child Health and Growth
Institute of Child Health
University of London
London, England

Alexander Thomas, M.D.
Professor of Psychiatry
New York University School of Medicine
New York, New York

Jack C. Westman, M.D.
Professor of Psychiatry
University of Wisconsin
Madison, Wisconsin

Peter H. Wolff, M.D.
Director of Research
Judge Baker Guidance Center
Boston, Massachusetts

Series Preface

This series of books is addressed to behavioral scientists interested in the nature of human personality. Its scope should prove pertinent to personality theorists and researchers as well as to clinicians concerned with applying an understanding of personality processes to the amelioration of emotional difficulties in living. To this end, the series provides a scholarly integration of theoretical formulations, empirical data, and practical recommendations.

Six major aspects of studying and learning about human personality can be designated: personality theory, personality structure and dynamics, personality development, personality assessment, personality change, and personality adjustment. In exploring these aspects of personality, the books in the series discuss a number of distinct but related subject areas: the nature and implications of various theories of personality; personality characteristics that account for consistencies and variations in human behavior; the emergence of personality processes in children and adolescents; the use of interviewing and testing procedures to evaluate individual differences in personality; efforts to modify personality styles through psychotherapy, counseling, behavior therapy, and other methods of influence; and patterns of abnormal personality functioning that impair individual competence.

Irving B. Weiner

Case Western Reserve University
Cleveland, Ohio

Preface

For many children to be different has meant to be bad or sick. For them it is a revelation to discover that many human differences are maladaptive only because they are misunderstood. Actually, the ways in which children—and their parents—naturally differ contribute not only to the frustrations and problems but also to the joys of living.

This book was prepared for clinicians, educators, and students of child development who wish to sample the range of knowledge about the ways in which individual variants affect the lives of children. The theme and ideas are also pertinent to public planning for young children, particularly for those who differ from most.

Copyrighted materials have been used in this volume through the permission of several publishers. Chapter 4 is reprinted from Volume 41, No. 4, of the *American Journal of Orthopsychiatry*. Chapter 5 contains substantial material published by Brunner/Mazel, Inc., in their book *The Exceptional Infant*: Volume 1—*The Normal Infant*, Jerome Hellmuth, Editor, 1967. Chapter 7 is reprinted from the Fall, 1971, issue of Daedalus, *Journal of the American Academy of Arts and Sciences*, Boston, Massachusetts. In Chapter 10, excerpts appear from *Science and Psychoanalysis*, Volume VIII, Jules Masserman, Editor, 1965, with the permission of Grune and Stratton, Inc.

I wish to thank those who participated in the University of Wisconsin Conference on the Origins of Individuality for their encouragement in assembling this volume. My special appreciation goes to Helen Baldwin for her editorial assistance and to Grace Ballam for her painstaking preparation of the manuscript.

Jack C. Westman

Madison, Wisconsin
October 1972

Contents

Introduction   1

PART I FOUNDATIONS

Introduction   5

1 Foundations for the Study of Individual Children   9
   Jack. C. Westman and Helen H. Baldwin

2 Some Structural Determinants of Early Infant Behavior   27
   Peter H. Wolff

3 Sex Differences in Early Development   45
   Mourad Arganian

PART II DEVELOPMENTAL PERSPECTIVES

Introduction   65

4 Individual Differences at Birth: Implications for Early Experience
   and Later Development   69
   Anneliese F. Korner

5 Temperament in the Normal Infant   83
   Stella Chess and Alexander Thomas

6   Cognitive Structure in Latency Behavior   105

David Elkind

7   Sequence, Tempo and Individual Variation in Adolescent Growth   119
    and Development

J. M. Tanner

PART III   SITUATIONAL PERSPECTIVES

Introduction   141

8   The Differential Impact of Environmental Conditions as a Function   145
    of Different Reaction Patterns in Infancy

Sibylle K. Escalona

9   Parent-Child Relations, Adaptation to Nursery School and the   159
    Child's Task Orientation: A Contrast in the Development of
    Two Girls

Christoph M. Heinicke, Fred Busch, Phyllis Click, and Estelle Kramer

10 Differences in Cognitive Style and Birth Order   199

Irving D. Harris

PART IV   RESEARCH MODELS

Introduction   211

11 A Biological Model for Understanding the Behavior of Individuals   215

Lorna Smith Benjamin

12 A Methodology for the Intensive Observation of the   243
    Preschool Child

Christoph M. Heinicke, Fred Busch, Phyllis Click, and Estelle Kramer

13   Methods and Models in Primate Personality Research   265
      William T. McKinney, Jr., Stephen Suomi, and Harry Harlow

PART V   CLINICAL APPLICATIONS

Introduction   289

14   Measurement of Infant Temperament in Pediatric Practice   293
      William B. Carey

15   Clinical Experience with Efforts to Define Individual Differences 307
      in Temperament
      Grace S. Gregg

16   Significance of the Individual Difference Approach   323
      Jack C. Westman

Epilogue   335

Author Index   337

Subject Index   343

INDIVIDUAL DIFFERENCES IN CHILDREN

Introduction

Everyone knows that people are born with differing talents—the gifted musician, artist, and scientist stand as proof of the range of endowment. But how about the more subtle qualities that distinguish each of us from all others? What are the determinants of differences in mind and personality? Actually, very little is known about the origins of individuality. As a means of calling attention to this lack, this book samples current theoretical, research, and clinical interests in individual psychological differences in children.

The lack of knowledge about individuality is especially clear to the child psychiatrist in his work with children who are misunderstood by—and tribulations to—bewildered families, schools, and communities. Although our society seems to prize individualism, a strong undercurrent of expecting uniformity persistently surfaces in the tendency to label children who differ from most as abnormal or sick. This pervasive expectation that children should be similar collides with biological reality, which determines each person as unique whether by his fingerprint or his behavior. Intuitively aware of these individual variations, the clinician stands as an advocate of the collective and individual uniqueness of children, but he lacks proper language for describing individual qualities and the tools for measuring and evaluating them.

The tides of research in differential psychology and child development have ebbed and flowed, at times stressing individual differences in intellectual capacity and perception, but generally retreating from elusive variations in temperament and personality. Much progress has been made in distinguishing characteristics of children according to age and developmental stage, but little has been done to effectively distinguish variants within developmental stages. As a result, we can identify predictable differences between children of varying ages, but we founder in distinguishing random differences in children of the same age.

Until recently, the nature-nurture controversy sidetracked child development research on etiological questions of innate versus learned influences. The otherwise fruitful preoccupation with groups of people after World War II also

1

diverted attention from the individual person. A conceptual breakthrough, however, followed the insights that Piaget gained from studying children and that Lorenz gained from studying animals, regarding the alteration of brain structures by experience and learning. The critical issue no longer is determining whether a piece of mental activity or behavior is a product of nature or nurture but rather how the interplay between the two is reflected in the function of brain structures. Since the external environment is only significant for a person to the extent that it is perceived and processed by his central nervous system through its receptors and effectors, all mental and behavioral activities take place in and through the equipment of his body. We can now describe, therefore, individual differences in the structure and function of children's biological equipment without artificial separation of "innate" and "experiential" determinants.

The contents of the book illustrate trends in the theoretical, research, and clinical understanding of individual children. The first chapter traces the vascillating evolution of the concept of individual differences in the fields of child development, differential psychology, educational psychology, children's medicine, and psychoanalysis. The important influence of social climate upon interest in individuality is highlighted, laying a foundation for the current work reported in subsequent chapters.

In Chapter 2, Peter Wolff draws upon his broad background and detailed knowledge of the most thorough studies carried out on human individual differences: those related to the newborn and infant. He shows that the study of nonvariable, structurally determined individual differences is facilitated in this developmental stage by the feasibility of detailed experimental observations on infant subjects.

The most fundamental difference between individuals is their biological sex. In Chapter 3, Mourad Arganian reviews the literature on sex differences in early infancy prior to the significant influence of interpersonal and cultural factors.

A critical question is how individual differences at birth affect personality development. Chapter 4, by Anneliese Korner, highlights prominent differences in the newborn and relates them to behavior in later life.

Chapter 5 is devoted to an exposition by Stella Chess and Alexander Thomas of a scheme for describing and tracing differences in the temperaments of young children. She identifies clusters of behavioral characteristics that reflect basic individual temperamental qualities with practical clinical applications. Her focus on the young child offers guidance to parents in understanding characteristics of their children that can lead to strained relationships.

Next, in Chapter 6, David Elkind brings Piaget's insights to the understanding of children during their latency years, highlighting the cognitive styles that color a child's view of himself and the world. His original concepts of "assumptive reality" and "cognitive conceit" are relevant to parents, educators, and clinicians.

Although body size and physique are important influences upon personality characteristics during prior years, they critically affect the early adolescent, the focus of Chapter 7. J. M. Tanner reviews growth and development during this period with particular emphasis on the impact of differences in rate and sequence upon individual personality.

Sibylle Escalona, a pioneer in the systematic study of personality, describes in Chapter 8 her conceptualization of individual differences and her methods for observing and recording differential responses in infants to similar environmental inputs. Her procedures for observing and describing children vividly illustrate the shift of research from laboratory testing settings to naturally occurring life situations.

Christoph Heinecke and colleagues typify in Chapter 9 the current state of psychoanalytic developmental research through drawing dynamic inferences from behavioral observations and calling attention to the importance of the maternal relationships in shaping the contrasting developments of two young girls' personalities.

In Chapter 10, Irving Harris introduces a fresh slant on the influence of sibling birth order upon thinking and cognitive style, renewing and clarifying the recurrent, long-standing interest in family constellation position as a significant determinant of personality development.

Chapter 11 shifts to a research model focus as Lorna Benjamin describes her periodic chart of behavior as a method for identifying and measuring attitudes and behaviors of children in their natural social relationships, permitting comparison of children in order to clarify similarities and differences. She fruitfully blends psychodynamic insights into a rigorous research instrument.

In Chapter 12, Christoph Heinecke provides further information about his research model and methodology by showing how reasonable inferences can be linked to observations of children in naturally occurring situations.

William McKinney, Stephen Suomi, and Harry Harlow draw attention in Chapter 13 to the human implications emerging from work with rhesus monkeys, which are particularly well suited for research on individual differences because of their susceptibility to experimental manipulation. They describe individual differences in the responses of monkeys to standardized environmental conditions designed to create a model for the study of depression.

In Chapter 14, William Carey, a pediatrician, reports his experience in developing a clinically useful instrument for describing infant temperament profiles, by practical application of the work of the New York Longitudinal Study.

In Chapter 15, Grace Gregg deepens the transition from theory and research regarding individual differences to clinical application by reporting her experience in using scales for measuring individual differences in the study of clinical syndromes.

The concluding chapter draws inferences from the material incorporated in this book, highlighting those aspects which hold promise for further study and application.

Part I

FOUNDATIONS

"No two individuals of the same race are quite alike. We may compare millions of faces, and each will be distinct."

CHARLES DARWIN

INTRODUCTION

The subject of individual differences in children is both vast and diverse. Within its compass lie both highly specific questions regarding particular behavior patterns and wide-ranging metaphysical questions about the meaning of individuality. The first chapter of this volume serves to delimit the area for the reader and reduce it to a conceptually manageable size, not only by describing some of the traditional questions about individual differences in children but also by tracing the lines of research activities devoted to them.

In Chapter 2, Peter Wolff focuses on what it is to be human and emphasizes biological aspects of children's diversity, keynoting the remainder of the book. He points out that all individual members of a species predictably unfold universal similarities in accordance with a genetically determined master plan. He then speaks of fundamental differences between species based upon "wired in" structures. An unappreciated, yet obvious, consequence of these different structures is that each species experiences a different kind of world.

As human beings we live within a relatively limited segment of the physical world because our experience of "nature" is determined by our own equipment. For example, because we have a simple eye, we see our surroundings in a totally different manner than does an organism with a compound eye. Because our metabolic system operates at a characteristic rate, we move in a time dimension that is totally different from that of a starfish or a humming bird. A beginning point, therefore, in considering differences between organisms is through cross-species comparisons. It is the composite of similarities within a species, however, that determines its membership, since many common characteristics overlap between species. An illustration of a cross-species behavioral phenomenon is the protective reaction shown in mother dogs toward their young puppies. Their intolerance of intrusion on the physical space of their puppies touches a resonant chord with human mothers who experience a similar tendency in themselves toward their own infants.

The relative ease of determining differences between species has long been obvious; however, the question of establishing valid differences between individuals within a species is more complex and immediately raises the question of "differences in respect to what?" Comparisons of rhesus monkeys and humans are relatively straightforward because one can talk about differences between species. In contrast, the comparison of one human being with another presents the question of what differences may be distinguished from a background of overriding intraspecies similarities. No one argues with the fact that human beings vary one from another, but pinpointing exactly how they vary poses staggering conceptual and methodological problems.

Dr. Wolff calls attention to a useful model for identifying predispositions to individual variation in humans. Extending the idea of "wired in" constraints which determine the ontogenetic unfolding of a species, individual members within a species also can be seen as operating with differing equipment determined by constraints peculiar to each. Although undoubtedly an oversimplified comparison, the structures intrinsically present before significant environmental impact can be seen as analogous to the monitoring code of a computer before it is specifically programmed. The capacities of the computer and the nature of its operation are determined by its structure. This capacity filters and shapes the information that passes through it. The computer's monitoring code cannot function independently without a program. The computer is set to go in predetermined directions depending upon what is put into it. In a comparable way, there is something that distinguishes each human embryo from all others, guaranteeing that if it is in contact with appropriate environmental input, it will develop into a unique human being.

Dr. Wolff's approach contrasts with a descriptive scheme such as John Bowlby's notion of four basic attachment behaviors: crying, smiling, clinging, and following. Dr. Wolff would avoid a fixed classification such as this, maintaining that the situation is more complicated and fluid. For example, for him eye-to-eye contact is an additional extremely important method of communication and, therefore, an ingredient of attachment behavior. Although not present at birth, eye contact emerges as a function of early maturation of the visual apparatus. On the other hand, he feels more comfortable with an epigenetic theoretical system, such as Piaget's, in which interactions with the environment at one level of development give rise to new structures within the central nervous system. In this scheme the crucial factor is not the environment nor the organism, nor even the interface between them, but the interplay of the three. When Piaget describes a series of circular reactions, it is simply because they have been observed without the implication that nothing more is involved. In Dr. Wolff's eyes Piaget's biological theory of psychological development, which does not permit separation of structure from function but always looks upon the two as working together, is a valid prototype for a synthetic approach to human development.

The next chapter probes more deeply the most basic intraspecies variation alluded to by Dr. Wolff: differences between two individuals of opposite sexes. Although at first blush sex differences seem to explain much, a closer look reveals that, after dispelling mythologies of sex role stereotyping, intriguing, complicated questions arise about the true repercussions of a random encounter between an impartial ovum and either an X or Y chromosome-bearing sperm.

In Chapter 3, Mourad Arganian offers a selective review of the literature of biological, cross-cultural, behavioral, and interpersonal studies on sex differences prior to the age of three. He acknowledges the validity of the viewpoint that minimizes structural determinants and stresses learning of gender identity. However, the impact of the research evidence he has assembled leads him to favor the viewpoint that recognizes definite prefunctional structures established by genetic sex from which the experiential fabric of gender identity is woven.

In a general sense, clear sex differences in physical health and development indicate the male's vulnerability to illness and death and the female's more accelerated rate of maturation. Of special interest is the confirmation through cross-cultural studies of nearly universal gender differences in behavior, social role, emotional expression, and cognitive style. There is no human society that does not distinguish maleness and femaleness. Some cultures with subsistence economies stress and exaggerate these differences. The Western world, however, is witnessing progressive blurring of sex differences because of the decreasing economic justification for emphasizing gender role differences.

In another vein, primate behavioral research has progressed to the point where direct comparisons can be made between the play behavior and parent-child relationships of monkeys and humans. The result is that both male young monkeys and children show higher activity levels and more intrusiveness than their female counterparts. Of further interest is the parallel finding that both monkey and human mothers more consistently interact with female than male young, fostering more independent and aggressive behavioral styles in males. During the early months of life, however, human mothers attend more to their male than female infants, presumably because boys' behavior more strongly attracts and holds their mothers' attention. In a general species sense, the greater immaturity of the male baby appears to elicit more maternal caretaking.

Although the evidence suggests qualitative, structurally determined sex differences, as is true with other personal qualities, the most prominent determinants of a particular boy or girl's body, personality, and behavior are quantitive variations on dimensions that apply to both sexes. Simply stated, sex-determined personality and behavioral differences do exist and at times override all other factors; in daily living, however, they are subtle and ordinarily unseen.

CHAPTER 1

Foundations for the Study of Individual Children

Jack C. Westman

Helen H. Baldwin

On most counts human beings are more alike than different, yet in small, but crucial, ways each person differs from others sufficiently to permit recognition of *his* portrait and *his* personality. The resulting behavioral and temperamental diversities among people create both rewards and problems for society. Present times dramatically force attention to the dilemma of conveniently mass-processing people and simultaneously coping with their individual life situations. With gigantic advances both achieved and planned for the generalized "common man," it is remarkable that scant information is available about the basic characteristics and determinants of his specific individual forms.

Early awareness of fundamental differences in men with similar abilities is illustrated by the discovery of English astronomers two centuries ago that differences in the measurement of the movement of stars could result from genuine discrepancies in observers' visual motor reaction times. A prior long and bitter controversy was resolved by this appreciation of individual differences and the transformation of what had been "observer error" into "observer variability" (Tyler, 1956). In an entirely different vein, Renee Spitz (1945) called attention in the 1940s to the profound deleterious impact of maternal deprivation on infants, noting at the same time that many children did not show the damaging effects seen in the infants that attracted his attention. Countless other experiences confront us with the fact that individual persons respond very differently to comparable stimuli, whether the stimulus is a simple visual perception or a complicated life situation.

More recently, a rapidly expanding mass of information has accumulated about unique individual patterns of response, activity, cognition, maturation, and emotion. Most of the work has been carried out in the fields of: (1) *child development*, which laid the necessary groundwork for the study of individuality through establishing the common characteristics of persons at particular stages in their growth and development; (2) *differential psychology,* which attracted considerable attention through describing ranges of differences in particular mental qualities, most significantly intelligence in the form of genius and creativity; (3) *educational psychology,* which grew out of the need to educate exceptional children with differing educational capacities; (4) *children's medicine,* including pediatrics and child psychiatry with their interests in normal and troubled children; and (5) *psychoanalysis,* which intrinsically advocates the understanding of individuals. Intertwined with both developmental and differential psychology, interest in individual differences began with a focus on individual qualities and characteristics during a particular maturational period, but the powerful motives for continuing study arise from the practical needs of the educational and clinical management of children.

Having identified the major sources of present knowledge, this chapter will consider the past and present intellectual climates influencing their courses. Our aim is to provide a bird's-eye view of the foundations for studying the individual child, pointing out some of the solid blocks, connecting mortar, and unfilled gaps. In subsequent chapters of the book some of the foremost current students of individual children will offer samplings of their work.

THE REDISCOVERY OF INDIVIDUAL DIFFERENCES IN CHILDREN

During the last fifty years the study of individual differences in children has undergone a cyclic course that could erroneously be attributed to fads. Scanning the quantity of literature cited in *Psychological Abstracts* shows waves of popularity in the subject with a peak of enthusiasm in the 1920s, waning interest in the late 1930s, a gap in the 1940s, a strongly negative trend in the 1950s, followed by gradual revival and renewed concern with the topic in the 1960s. These trends, based on the numbers of papers and books devoted annually to "individual differences," reflect the extent to which authors (and indexers) viewed and labeled their investigations as directed toward individuals rather than groups. It conceals altogether the content and causes of the cyclic interest. Our attempt to probe the nature of these cycles led to a fascinating search through the intellectual currents of modern child psychology.

Published material on individual differences has been influenced by world events—the demands of a society recovering from one world war, undergoing a depression, then a second cataclysmic but also unifying war, the tensions of cold war rivalry, and the results of self-discovery among many groups within society. Before we leave to historians the intriguing topic of the interplay of societal needs and the course of scientific research, let us very quickly note some of the more obvious ways in which world events and concerns influenced the study of individual differences in children.

Our attention was drawn first to the 1920s. At this time the European world assessed a war in which thousands of young men died in the fields of France, many of them brilliant and able future leaders and creators. In reaction to both heroism and tragic loss, the exceptional person was exalted in literature, art, and science; living styles and genius were celebrated; and individuality, eminence, and eccentricity were admired. In this era we found the roots of the cult of the individual. Not surprisingly, the research of the period reflects this realization—here were the attempts to identify and differentiate among individuals' intellectual abilities and to describe or come to understand a single human. Indeed, toward the end of that decade, Alfred Adler's style of psychiatry, "individual psychology," attained prominence (Adler, 1962).

While the subsequent economic depression of the 1930s did not markedly alter the interests of those investigating children's behavior and personality, the impact of World War II was immediate and devastating. The primarily German interest in individual psychology, the English investigations of differences in intelligence, the instructional experimentation in French and Italian schools, and the beginnings of the study of individual differences in infants and preschool children in America: all stopped abruptly as manpower and resources were drawn into a war whose demands were pressing, goals clear, and effects consolidating. While most study ceased, large-scale intelligence and ability testing, supported by military screening needs, received a tremendous impetus. The aftermath of access to large samples of research subjects, federal funding, and team efforts, new to psychology, lingered in the postwar period.

After World War II, Europe, preoccupied with rebuilding, was less prominent in the psychological literature; America dominated the scene. The wartime demand that individual characteristics and needs be subordinated to group purposes seems to have affected strongly the popular and professional attitudes toward differences among children. During the late 1940s, ways to achieve adjustment to group living were emphasized, and techniques intended to minimize individual differences were evident. Greatly increased understanding of environmental effects, whether parental or societal, on children's development enhanced the dream of democratic equality.

These trends continued in the 1950s, a period when individual differences were often ignored, denied and ascribed to faulty upbringing or inadequate control of variables. In contrast, perhaps because the ever larger test populations revealed group differences, or because the special needs of ethnic, occupational, and economic groups were increasingly voiced, the lack of homogeneity in the national population also was becoming increasingly apparent. Great prosperity intensified, rather than reduced, awareness of economic differences. Foreign wars became divisive rather than unifying.

All of these developments revealed that sizeable, unhomogenized chunks were submerged in a society of apparently bland, conforming Americans. No longer did the view of America as a melting pot prevail, with its implication of a smooth uniform mix. Certainly psychologists played an important role in the self-discovery by ethnic and economic groups and in their pressures for recognition. As evidence, one need only recall that the milestone Supreme Court case in 1954, Brown versus the Board of Education, rested on the findings of psychologists that separate educations could not be equal. Not only did child psychologists influence aspects of the course of national policy, but they were invited to assist in the implementation of national policy.

The technological jousting of the "cold war" also demanded identifying and training bright young minds in scientific and mathematical skills. When Sputnik went up, psychologists were brought into the national search for creative, scientific minds. One sees tension between two efforts—one, the identification and amelioration of environmental and cultural factors oppressing minorities in the society, and the other, the identification of an exceptional group and intensification of that intellectual difference. Through the evaluation and increasing sophistication of these studies of the causes and nature of group differences, gradually and reluctantly, the factors of innate, individual differences came again to be admitted, talked about, and studied. By the late 1960s, one could state that individual differences in children had been rediscovered. Against this historical backdrop, we will now array the major streams of research on individual differences.

THE FORERUNNERS OF INDIVIDUAL DIFFERENCE RESEARCH

Important scientific studies often arise from the naive observations, associations, and causal relationships each of us make during our own early years of life. As young children we notice obvious physical differences among our peers, and later both intellectual and behavioral differences become apparent.   As preadolescents we notice the associations between physical appearance and behavior and give them causal significance. Folklore and folk literature reflect such views. In a similar vein, research psychologists first suspected connections between body form and personality.

Whether temperament and physique are in fact related has been a recurrent question in thinking about individual differences. Kretschmer (1925) brought this question to the association of body types with schizoid and manic-depressive mental disturbances. Sheldon's (1946) more elaborate typology, based upon three measurable components of body form, endomorphy, mesomorphy, and ectomorphy, and three discernable temperamental components, visceratonia, somatotonia, and cerebrotonia, set up ways for determining the relative proportions of each in a given individual and for testing their associations. Sheldon's report of a relatively high proportion of mesomorphic body types among delinquents started a wave of studies on younger persons. These tended to support a relationship between mesomorphy and a cluster of assertive, energetic, active behavior traits, and also between extreme ectomorphy and restrained behavior, submissiveness, and under-confidence. Nevertheless, such constitutional theories generally were held in disfavor until recently, in part because environmental expectations are related to body type and create or reinforce behavioral traits and in part because no theoretical framework for the observed relations existed.

In 1962, however, Walker's study of physique and behavior in preschool children appeared, showing that at an age when cultural impact and expectations are minimal, many of Sheldon's generalizations held (Walker, 1962). Mesomorphic boys were characteristically energetic, assertive, sociable, and not anxious; in contrast, ectomorphic boys tended to be self-assertive, aloof, and emotionally restrained. This evidence, at least, suggests that temperamental qualities seen in nursery-school mesomorphs and ectomorphs were similar to those found in earlier studies of adult mesomorphs and ectomorphs.

The issue of physique and temperament brought out several questions pertinent to our concern with the origins of individual differences. While hereditarians and environmentalists have each chosen to interpret such relations through their own biases, an alternate explanation lies in the possibility that certain temperamental qualities have close ties to organic functions—such as energy reserves and sensitivity thresholds which are obvious candidates for physiological qualities with temperamental effects. If a child has a high physical energy level coupled with relative perceptual insensitivity, his environment is perceived as relatively nonpunishing of adventurous, aggressive behavior; his environment may exert little constraint on his drives. On the other hand, a child with a low physical energy level limits the quantity of his environmental experience; however, great perceptual sensitivity may intensify environmental impact, reinforcing withdrawal from certain experiences and approach toward others, further limiting his range of experience. Unquestionably the manner in which others evaluate physique and behavior, and their expectations of both, also have a contributing effect. We suspect that questions regarding these relationships are not dead, but will be revived in more sophisticated form. Studies of the relationship between psychological correlates and physiological responses mediated by the autonomic nervous system in children, as carried out by Wenger (1941), and the extension of these to include correlation with body type, offer an interesting possibility of intermediate steps through which physique may influence behavior. More recent studies of biochemical and metabolic constitution also offer contributions to the nature of temperament (Williams, 1953).

The subsequent search for the origins of individual differences followed several paths, some rewarding, others virtual dead ends. The power of Mendelian genetics led some to attribute most, if not all, adult traits to hereditary factors.

Psychoanalytic, anthropological, and sociological findings supported those who took a totally environmental route. The controversy between those who espoused "nature" and those wedded to "nurture" raged with heat, words, and futility. Between these extremes other workers ploughed more fruitful fields. Attempts to determine the relative contributions of intrinsic and extrinsic factors led some to the studies of behavior of identical twins and others to look at newborn children. Today the old controversy seems almost absurd; thoughtful students find extrinsic-intrinsic, nature-nurture, and heredity-environment correlates to be interlocking and interactive dyads.

CHILD DEVELOPMENT STUDIES

Individuality in the behavior of preschool children was an early interest in this country. Gesell and his group at the Yale Clinic of Child Development wrote extensively about individual differences apparent in motor and verbal behavior, activity level, expressiveness, and perceptual sensitivity of individual nursery-school children. From observations and recordings, portraits describing individual patterns in play and life style were developed (Gesell, 1941).

Gesell's primary interest, norms of maturational development, did not deter him from maintaining an awareness of different, as well as similar, patterns of development. Indeed he supplied one of the first normative standards against which these differences could be measured. In 1929 he noted that "the experimental investigation of emotional behavior and personality in young children has been meager" (Gesell, 1929). Passing years and increasing research were to change that. Although the primary emphasis was to be on cognitive development, the revelations of ego psychology, and environmental factors, individual differences in young children were not ignored.

The early attempts to push back still farther the record of individual variation were documented in the 1920s and 1930s by Irwin's (1930) studies of perception in neonates and by a number of longitudinal studies of children (Gesell, 1937; Neilon, 1948; Stone, 1959). In 1927, speaking of nursery-age children, Gesell (1927) stated "the fact of great individual differences, even at these ages, and the problem of when such differences clearly assert themselves, is pushed still farther toward birth and early infancy." Later, he asserted with certainty that "close clinical and normative studies (of infants) reveal a wealth of variation which is comparable to that of later years" (Gesell, 1929). At that time there seemed to be little doubt that the differences observed were, in large part, genetic in origin. Shirley (1933) prefaced her impressive study with the statement, "obviously, infant behavior is of particular importance in any genetic view of life," and commented later, "training and conditioning [are] subservient to maturation and inborn trends."

While these early reports were of considerable significance, both in terms of paradigms for future studies and as an expression of current views, they suffered from lack of general recognition. In retrospect, one wonders whether there wasn't some naiveté in the approach, with excitement and enthusiasm about the diversity of the subjects, but little clarity about the purposes or controls of studies. Frequently the results were detailed portraits of children, unrelated to each other or to any developmental scheme or hypothesis. Studies in which a difference was measured by variance among individuals in a small group rather than against a stable standard, or those in which observations of persistent characteristics were not effectively linked to a theory of development, tended to become collections of miscellany that were more perceptive than instructive (see Damarin, 1968, and Swan, 1938, for comments). One outstanding exception was the research of Escalona, which by its theoretical basis, detailed observation, and timing, stands almost alone during the dry decades of the 1940s and 1950s. Her work (1959, 1965, 1969) and a changing intellectual climate stimulated a return to the subject of individual differences in infants. The establishment of the National Institute of Neurological Diseases and Blindness made research funds available, and in the 1960s a wealth of reports about neonate behavior and differences in behavior patterns and psychophysiological responses among neonates and young infants appeared (see Brackbill, 1967; Brackbill, 1967; and Bronson, 1966 for reviews). These and many other more recent studies resulted from the acceptance of the early appearance of individual differences and the appearance of technical developments enabling measurement of perceptual and behavioral characteristics.

Child development, a remarkably productive field since 1920, began in *media res*, and may have found, now, its first true frontier with the newborn. Its last challenge, the adolescent, still beckons, for our knowledge of school age and beyond is quite incomplete. Apart from efforts to delineate general or special factors in intellectual ability, motor skills, and aptitudes—for the purposes of educational classification and predicting academic success—neither the nature of the differences in older children nor their patterns of integrated individuality have attracted sufficient research. This relative indifference no doubt reflected the fact that too little was known about normative development in patterns of cognition, temperament, personality, and affect to justify research into individuality, and because the older subjects themselves are difficult ones, undergoing rapid change, and highly affected by peer relationships.

CONTRIBUTIONS OF DIFFERENTIAL PSYCHOLOGY

Although there has been strong evidence for physiological and temperamental differences in the youngest infants, the link between these factors and obvious variations among older children has been elusive—popular early, then ignored, and now once again attracting interest. During the 1940s, 1950s, and 1960s, the disagreement lay not in the acceptance or rejection of infant differences, but in differing opinions about their importance in determining later personality, ability, and behavior. The powerful effects of environmental and behavioral conditioning, so apparent to clinicians and research investigators, tended to overwhelm and obscure individual characteristics; the success of behavior modification techniques encouraged many to view undesirable traits as mutable, whether inherent or not; while the pervasive generalizations of psychoanalytical developmental psychology were construed to mean that all children, indeed, did mature in much the same manner. Furthermore, when detected, the apparent innate difference of infants were not always persistent, nor did they always permit reliable predictions about future behavior.

Differential psychology of children, bypassed by the mainstream of developmental and life experience (familial and extrafamilial) studies, tended toward cataloging and enumerating details of behavior. Unfortunately, the measurement of variance in a large population for a large number of personality traits does not assure the importance of the variations observed, as attested by many detailed reports (Hull, 1927; Hundleby, 1968). However, coherent approaches such as Eysenck's (1968) pragmatic conceptions of definable and predictable personality variables hold promise. The isolation of separable, measurable characteristics and the determination of the range of their variance is an important tool, which may be better utilized in the future.

Some outstanding present examples, models which attest to the possibility of analyzing behavior, merit at least brief mention. Escalona's studies of behavioral characteristics of individual infants were tied to psychoanalytic conceptions and psychologically measurable phases of development; they did not ignore environmental influences, but noted that experienced environment differs from externally observable environment, and that inherent responsivity contributes to the interplay of formative factors (Escalona, 1969). Her insights made prognosis possible and successful (Escalona, 1959). Terman's (1930) early study of gifted children also shows the interaction of cultural and genetic factors in determining productivity. Fries and Woolf (1953) rooted their study of congenital activity patterns and response to environment within a biological and psychological framework, following the earlier findings of Irwin (1930).

While these studies have been criticized for various methodological reasons, we applaud them for seeking differences which become significant later and for directing attention to the extraordinarily complex elements that interact with each other, changing over time, yet retaining an identity in that assimilative entity, an individual, recognizable child.

EDUCATIONAL PSYCHOLOGY

School teachers, faced daily by individual differences in the children in their classrooms, have never lost sight of the reality and importance of individuality. Not surprisingly, they are less concerned about causes than they are about the effects of individual differences on learning ability and adaptability to educational goals and procedures. Regardless of the causes of variability, teachers of even the youngest, nursery-age children must deal with these differences. For them, John's mathematical skill, Joan's musical ability, and Peter's slowness in reading are not hidden in the statistical norms and ranges.

The educational literature from 1925 to 1970 pursues two major themes—ways to identify differences in ability and aptitude and ways to adjust teaching methods (and more recently, goals) to these individual differences. Intelligence tests, notably those developed by Binet, Simon, and Spearman, and studies of the nature and structure of intelligence by Thurstone and Burt, were brought quickly into classrooms in this country, in England, and on the Continent (Anastasia, 1965; Jenkins, 1961; Freeman, 1934; Pinter, 1925). The means to measure intelligence suggested the possibility of grouping children by intellectual ability or mental age, rather than chronological age. Uniform "lockstep" procedures in the schools were criticized, and numerous suggestions were made for adapting instructional programs to the ability differences within an age group. Many papers appeared describing experiences with various "individualized" programs of instruction. Reflecting these proposals, "homogeneous grouping" and "grade skipping" based on intelligence tests were common features in American schools by the late 1930s and 1940s.*

The widespread early application of intelligence testing of school-age children spurred research into the effect of training and practice on individual differences. Many articles appeared reviewing and interpreting research attempting to determine whether training and education were means of decreasing or augmenting individual differences. Some found convergence and others divergence, the contradictions being due to the difficulty of controlling the effective amount of practice or training and differences caused by the type of task (Perl, 1933). Discouraging to egalitarian educators was the most usual finding—that on more difficult or more intellectual tasks (as opposed to motor) all improved, but the more able made greater gains more rapidly than those initially less able. The flurry of interest in the subject subsided rapidly after the mid 1930s.

The literature of the 1940s indicates disillusionment with the efficacy of

*These trends are evident in abstracts of the educational literature in *Psychological Abstracts,* 1925-1945.

ability groupings. Groups selected on the basis of general intellectual ability were still diverse in many ways; for example, the slow-to-read child might be facile in arithmetic, the child with limited manual dexterity and high IQ might have great difficulty writing, and so on. Increasingly sophisticated instruments for measuring intelligence revealed that many factors contribute to intelligence, confirming the view that individual differences are too complex to be dealt with by the simple division of classes into those for "bright" and those for "slow" children. Individualization of teaching methods on a subject-by-subject basis became a more common topic in the literature, as did pleas for consideration of individual patterns and profiles of abilities.

The paucity of educational reports on individual differences through the post-World War II era, and the nature of those that did appear, suggest that concern with other goals determined the thinking of educators. Through this period, as psychologists and psychoanalysts learned more of the effects of environment on personality and uncovered more of the course of development in children, the efforts of teachers and the teachers of teachers were directed toward improving the school environment to meet the normal developmental trends of children. The possibility of adjusting the child to the school through behavior modification, conditioning, and environmental manipulation was a popular, widespread, and attractive goal. The importance of social and emotional development came to the fore, as educators came to understand that academic learning could not be separated from the "whole child" and his experience. While critics complained that life adjustment, equal for all, rather than academic achievement, had become the goal of the schools, and that individual differences were ignored, we must also recognize that the schools, through greater understanding of children in general, greatly improved their practices and milieu. And most certainly classroom teachers could never lose sight of the differences among the children with whom they worked.

In the mid 1950s countervalent national needs impinged on the school, altering the trend of the previous decade. Disadvantaged economic and ethnic groups, discovering their historic educational neglect, demanded improved, special treatment. It was apparent that the "whole child" who was being taught or treated was viewed as Anglosaxon, suburban, middle class, and middle IQ; increasing numbers of real children were not, nor could they ever be, any of these. If life adjustment were interpreted as adjustment to and acceptance of life in suboptimal, disadvantaged conditions, these groups wanted none of it.

At about the same time, when technological rivalry became the pattern of the "cold war," schools emphasized the search for exceptionally bright, able children in order to enrich their education and presumably, enhance their value to society. A trend toward recognizing, accepting, and valuing inequality was beginning (Thomas, 1965), and adjusting school programs to various group differences became a major concern in education. In school counseling the importance of individual variations, also, has gained recognition (Rothney, 1972).

CHILDREN'S MEDICINE

Certainly, one of the most obvious differences among children is that many are inpaired in some manner. Although individual differences are often regarded as "normal" variations, the borderland between randomly occurring "normal" variants and defect-induced "abnormal" differences is an important gray zone. It is often difficult to decide whether a characteristic is *impairing* or *coloring* function.

Defective gene material, disadvantageous environment, developmental or birth traumata, or a combination of these, give rise to many constitutional abnormalities. Any of the human organ systems is susceptible to defect or injury, and the variation in kind and degree of resultant debility is enormous. Some of these, resulting from less than ideal maternal or prenatal conditions, are detectable on an epidemiological basis, challenging us to generally improve prenatal conditions (Montague, 1962: Pasamanick, 1961). Some are reversible or correctible, stimulating research on early detection and therapy. Most are accomplished facts which present challenges for therapeutic repair and habilitation. Certain of them affect primarily perceptual functions (e.g. developmental dyslexia); others limit cognitive development (e.g. the heterogeneous class of minimal brain dysfunction); and still others impair primarily communicative or motor output (e.g. asphasia and cerebral palsy).

This field and its literature are so enormous that it would be neither possible nor fruitful to explore here the diverse range of developmental abnormalities or the diagnostic and therapeutic techniques useful for each. The range of qualitative and quantative abnormalities is so great that most generalizations are useless, beyond stating that most abnormalities are negative in impact, limiting abilities in some areas, rather than adding positive functions or elements to individuality. Nevertheless, even when the effect of a disability is massive, one can profitably call attention to unaffected systems and behaviors, recognizing that unique individuality is maintained in these areas, and perhaps even more than usual, must be fostered. It is often more tempting to generalize about the brain-injured or deaf child by emphasizing common features about the disability than to keep in mind the uniqueness of the remainder of the child's behavior and interests.

Some recent research trends are concerned with detecting the effects and causes of minimal birth or developmental trauma, a field where effects are subtle, often late in appearance, confounded by subsequent environmental management, and difficult to detect except through the most widespread epidemiological and longitudinal research. Inborn biochemical errors of metabolism are actively being sought, a research field offering hope of preventing impairment through the replacement of defective genetic material. These efforts are now bringing to light biochemical variations which are less pervasive in their effects than well-known syndromes, such as phenylketonuria. Development cytogenetics continues to reveal and unravel chromosomal aberrations that lead to extensive subsequent abnormalities. The behavioral and cognitive effects of nutritional inadequacy are at last receiving research attention, an exciting field where cultural anthropology, sociology, biochemistry, and child psychology meet. For those who are curious about the related medical frontiers, the journal *Developmental Medicine and Child Neurology* is an especially useful source, providing book reviews and an index to the current literature in addition to its own articles. To further illustrate the extent of biomedical interest in individual differences, Tecce (1971) reported electroencephalographic correlates of variations in personality.

The ground-breaking work in a clinical setting of Thomas, Chess, and others, (Rutter, 1964; Thomas, 1963) embraces a receptivity to both innate (typologic) and environmental (reactive) theories of the development of individual differences. This underlying philosophy, distinguishing neither nature nor nurture, but assuming that both affect each other in the external and internal milieu, gives a great power to their studies, which employ large samples and carefully controlled interview techniques and the co-twin control method. Their aim is to identify critical features of a child's reactive patterns in early infancy; this information coupled with an equally thorough knowledge of the child's familial and extrafamilial environment has already shown therapeutic, preventative, and predictive value. In a further step Haar (1964) developed a rating scale that could be used by nurses to identify individual differences in newborns.

PSYCHOANALYSIS

The essence of psychoanalysis as a theoretical system and therapeutic method emphasizes the individual and his unique life history and personality structure. Although the developmental constants and the shared organizing fantasies of children have been stressed in the psychoanalytic psychosexual stages of development and in commonly encountered therapeutic issues, the individuality of each person has been implicitly recognized as a product of his particular constitution and life experience.

Freud (1950) explicitly referred to individual differences in endowment in drive strength and specific ego functions. He also faced the perplexing question of why certain individuals developed neuroses and others did not. Beyond the obvious explanation of varying life experiences, some constituting trauma and warping personality and others not, he proposed that differences in the pressures exerted by drives and innate vulnerabilities of personality structure predisposed to neurosis. Hartmann (1950) expanded upon Freud's work, linking individual differences in the primary ego apparatuses to later choice of defense and by implication to choice of neurosis. Lustman (1956) later demonstrated differential sensitivity of the erogenous zones of the body among neonates and discussed its impact upon psychosexual development through predisposing arrests in developmental progress. Fries and Woolf (1953) were among the first investigators to capture variations in ego endowment through their description of "congenital activity types." Escalona (1962) has worked within the framework of psychoanalytic theory. Much subsequent attention has been devoted to the study of variations in autonomic reactivity in newborns in the hope of detecting physiological antecedents to clinical illnesses, particularly the psychosomatic disorders (Richmond, 1962). Korner's (1967) work illustrates further efforts to define individual differences at birth.

The careful, systematic research of child psychoanalysis at the Hampstead Child-Therapy Clinic under the leadership of Anna Freud (1965) represents a basic refinement of the body of child development knowledge through a linear concept of personality developmental lines. Although drawn from a clinical context, the Hampstead group offers promising leads for the description and assessment of personality over time. The language of ego psychology permits a sophisticated analysis of the components of a child's personality, and, therefore, a means of describing dimensions upon which individual differences can be measured.

PROSPECTS

This brief review suggests that an intellectual and social climate exists now in which to build, on the foundations of child development with tools from differential psychology, an understanding of individuality applicable to educational and clinical fields. Subsequent chapters illustrate the kind of work currently renewing the study of the individual child. But before proceeding to them, some of their possible rewards deserve mention.

The accumulating evidence shows that the existence of individual differences from earliest infancy on is undeniable, and that these differences have their origins both in constitutional factors in the individual and peculiar features of the environmental experience he encounters. The crucial importance of social attitudes toward individual differences also emerges.

On the positive side, the stance of the current era appears to be: "vive la difference." We seem prepared to go beyond admitting the existence of human differences to actively desiring to value, nurture, and protect them from abrading influences. Just as the devoted mother perceives and is responsive to the special characteristics of each of her children, treating them differentially, so the optimal school program aims at enhancing, not minimizing, the differences among its students. Home and school settings that recognize and support the development of unique behavioral and mental styles promote human well-being at several levels.

Foremost, the individual child can be valued and encouraged in his own attainments and interests, not merely as he measures up to group or family goals. For education the challenges are great, as perceptivity, creativity, and individual attention demand much from overworked teachers. Nevertheless, redefining success in terms of enhancement of each child's own abilities and interests means that a teacher's personal rewards for successful teaching can come more from the child and less from the students' scores on normative tests.

Second, the onerous and impossible demands on parents and teachers to bend the twig to produce a tree of particular incline are removed with extraordinary relief to well-meaning parents, who often seem anguished either by their unavailing efforts to train a child to conform to a particular scheme, or by their sense of guilt for difficult behavior.

Third, the rewards promise to be great for society. A society undergoing rapid change, one in which survival is an issue, upheaval a way of life, and the future roles and functions of its members unpredictable, can best safeguard its continuance by promoting the greatest possible diversity among its population.

On the negative side, the ongoing tug-of-war between individual rights and conformity to the requirements of social living reflects society's present inability to distinguish *acceptance* of individuality from *license* to express individuality. Our social thinking tends toward an either-or generalization of permission for total self-expression or requirement for total conformity. Perhaps one explanation for this rather primitive, alternating attitude of extremes is that, in fact, the social sciences have not yet themselves defined the basic ingredients of individuality. Underlying society's reticence to accept individuality lurks a fear that individual recognition may not have social utility and that individual expression can be unacceptable and destructive to society's regulating functions. More knowledge about what individual differences actually *are* would provide a basis for evaluating which individual qualities have social utility and which are also socially acceptable. More precise definitions of individual qualities would permit a more sophisticated evaluation and acceptance of them by society.

Who knows what the indispensable person of the twenty-first century will be like? Clearly, no one does. The best assurance that he will be there when needed is to increase the range of acceptable life styles; we are almost certain to fail if we define the goal now and attempt to mold our children to it. While we struggle with the immediate problem of survival of our species, we cannot limit our future by adjustment programs to a life that ultimately may not be possible or desirable.

REFERENCES

Adler, A. (1963). *The problem child*. New York: Capricorn.

Anastasi, A. (1965). *Individual differences*. New York: John Wiley & Sons, Inc.

Brackbill, Y. (1967). *Infancy and early childhood*. New York: The Free Press.

Brackbill, Y. and Thompson, G.C. (1967). *Behavior in infancy and early childhood*. New York: The Free Press.

Bronson, W. C. (1966). Central orientation: A study of behavior organization from childhood to adolescence. *Child Development*, **37**, 125-155.

Damarin, F. L. and Cattell, R. B. (1968). Personality factors in early childhood and their relation to intelligence. *Society for Research in Child Development Monograph*, **33**, 1-95.

Escalona, S. K. and Heider, C. M. (1959). *Prediction and outcome*. New York: Basic Books.

Escalona, S. K. (1962). Individual differences and the problem of state. *Journal of the Academy of Child Psychiatry*, **1**, 11-37.

Escalona, S. K. (1965). Some determinants of individual differences. *Transactions of the New York Academy of Sciences*, **27**, 802-816.

Escalona, S. K. (1969). *The roots of the individual*. London: Tavistock Publications.

Eysenck, H. J. and Eysenck, S. B. G. (1968). *Personality, structure and measurement*. London: Routledge and Kegan.

Freeman, F. S. (1934). *Individual differences: The nature and causes of variation in intelligence and special abilities*. New York: Holt.

Freud, A. (1965). *Normality and pathology in childhood: Assessments of development*. New York: International Universities Press.

Freud, S. (1950). Analysis terminable and interminable. *Collected papers*, **5**, 316-357. London: Hogarth Press.

Fries, M. E. and Woolf, P. J. (1953). Some hypotheses on the role of the congenital activity type in personality development. *The Psychoanalytic Study of the Child*, **8**, 48-62. New York: International Universities Press.

Gesell, A. and Lord, E. E. (1927). A psychological comparison of nursery school children from homes of low and high economic status. *Pediatrics Seminar*, **34**, 339-356.

Gesell, A. (1929). The individual in infancy. In *Foundations of experimental psychology*. Worcester, Mass.: Clark University Press.

Gesell, A. and Ames, L. B. (1937). Early evidence of individuality in the human infant. *Journal of Genetic Psychology*, **47**, 339-361.

Gesell, A. and Amatruda, C. S. (1941). *Developmental diagnosis*. New York: Hoeber.

Haar, E., et al. (1964). Personality differentiation of neonates: A nurse scale method. *Journal of the American Academy of Child Psychiatry*, **3**, 330-342.

Hartmann, H. I. (1950). Comments on the psychoanalytic theory of the ego. *The Psychoanalytic Study of the Child*, **5**, 74-96, New York: International Universities Press.

Hull, C. L. (1927). Variability in amount of different traits possessed by the individual. *Journal of Educational Psychology*, **18**, 97-106.

Hundleby, J. D. and Cahell, R. B. (1968). Personality structure in the middle school and the prediction of school achievement and adjustment. *Society for Research in Child Development Monographs*, **33**, 1-61.

Irwin, O. C. (1930). The amount and nature of activity of newborn infants under constant stimulating conditions during the first ten days of life. *Genetic Psychology Monographs*, **8**, 1-92.

Jenkins, J. J. and Paterson, D. G. (Eds.) (1961). *Studies in individual differences*. New York: Appleton-Century Crofts.

Korner, A. F. and Grobstein, R. I. (1967). Individual differences at birth. *Journal of the American Academy of Child Psychiatry*, **6**, 676-690.

Kretschmer, E. (1925). *Physique and character*. New York: Harcourt Brace.

Lustman, D. L. (1956). Rudiments of the ego. *The Psychoanalytic Study of the Child*, **11**, 89-98, New York: International Universities Press.

Montague, A. (1972). *Prenatal influences*. Springfield, Ill.: Charles C. Thomas.

Neilon, P. (1948). Shirley's babies after fifteen years: A personality study. *Journal of Genetic Psychology*, **73**, 195-196.

Pasamanick, B. and Knobloch, H. (1961). Epidemiological studies on the complications of pregnancy and the birth process. In *Prevention of mental disorders in children*. Caplan, G. (Ed.). New York: Basic Books.

Perl, R. E. (1933). The effect of practice upon individual differences. *Archives of Psychology*, **159**, 5-54.

Pinter, R. (1929). The individual in school: General ability. In *Foundations of experimental psychology*. Murchison, C. (Ed.). Worcester, Mass.: Clark University Press.

Richmond, J. B., et al. (1962). Observations on differences in autonomic function between and within individuals during infancy. *Journal of the Academy of Child Psychiatry*, **1**, 33-91.

Rothney, J. W. M. (1972). *Adaptive counseling in schools*. Englewood Cliffs, New Jersey: Prentice Hall.

Rutter, M., Birch, H. G., Thomas, A., and Chess, S. (1964). Temperamental characteristics in infancy and later development of behavioral disorders. *British Journal of Psychiatry*, **110**, 651-661.

Sheldon, W. H. and Stevens, S. S. (1946). *The varieties of temperament*. New York: Harper and Row.

Shirley, M. M. (1933). *The first two years: A study of twenty-five babies*. Minneapolis, Minn.: University of Minnesota Press, 3 vols.

Spitz, R. A. (1945). Hospitalism: An inquiry into the genesis of psychiatric conditions in early childhood. *The Psychoanalytic Study of the Child*, **1**, 53-74. New York: International Universities Press.

Stone, A. A. and Onqùe, G. C. (1959). *Longitudinal studies of child personality*. Cambridge, Mass.: Harvard University Press.

Swan, C. (1938). Individual differences in the facial expressive behavior of preschool children: A study by the time-sampling method. *Genetic Psychology Monographs*, **20**, 557-650.

Tecce, J. J. (1971). Contingent negative variation and individual differences. *Archives of General Psychiatry*, **24**, 1-16.

Terman, L. M., Burks, B., and Jensen, D. Y. (1930). *Genetic studies of genius: The promise of youth, Volume III*. Stanford, California: Stanford University Press.

Thomas, A., et al. (1963). *Behavioral individuality in early childhood*. New York City: New York University Press.

Thomas, R. M. and Thomas, S. M. (1965), *Individual differences in the classroom*. New York: McKay Books.

Tyler, L. E. (1956). *The psychology of human differences*. New York: Appleton-Century Crofts.

Walker, R. N. (1962). Body build and behavior in young children: I. Body build and nursery school teachers' ratings. *Society for Research in Child Development Monographs*.

Wenger, M. A. (1941). The measurement of individual differences in autonomic balance. *Psychosomatic Medicine*, **3**, 427-434.

Williams, R. J. (1953). *Free and unequal: The biological basis*. Austin: University of Texas Press.

CHAPTER 2

Some Structural Determinants of Early Infant Behavior

Peter H. Wolff *

INTRODUCTION

This chapter deals with the period of early infancy. It might seem appropriate to begin with an inventory of all the behavior patterns that can be observed in young infants, and catalog what is known about their individual variations. However, the repertory of motor patterns, sensory capacities, and states in the newborn infant has been reviewed several times in the recent past, so that the effort need not be duplicated here (see for example, Peiper, 1963; Escalona, 1968; Prechtl and Lenard, 1968). Moreover, since the range of possible variations in newborn behavior is almost infinite, a listing of the possibilities by itself would not resolve the formal problems that concern us in this volume. Contrary to other chapters in this book, this one begins with a consideration of some ways in which normal infants are the same rather than different, hoping in this way to identify the species-specific constants that set the stage for individual variation. Although this approach stresses group similarity, it requires the implicit or explicit analysis of differences, since we cannot identify behavior patterns common to one biologically distinct group without making appropriate comparisons with other groups or species.

SPECIES-SPECIFIC CHARACTERISTICS OF HUMAN INFANTS

For all their differences in anatomy, immunology, neurological organization, intellectual potential, and position of social privilege, human beings are far more

*Work for this presentation was completed while the author was supported by a Career Development Grant of the U.S.P.H.S., Grant No. MK 3461, a research grant of the U.S.P.H.S., No. MH 6034, and the Children's Hospital Medical Center Mental Retardation and Human Development Research Program (HD 03-0773).

alike as a group than different from each other when we compare them to other animals. This banal fact and its corollary of irreducible species differences are often accepted in principle but overlooked in practice when psychology investigates individual differences exclusively in terms of their social determinants, or focuses single-mindedly on the ways in which the environment shapes behavior.

Phylogenetic discontinuities between human and nonhuman species are not evident for every morphological or functional aspect of adaptation. Nor should limited evidence lead us to conclude that man is totally isolated by his behavior from other species, merely because his is the only species that is also the only member of its family. Evolutionary discontinuities in behavior become most apparent when we consider intellectual development, the elaboration of culture, and the acquisition of language. Thus it is not the infant's behavior at birth but his developmental "potential" that differentiates man most clearly from other mammals.

The acquisition of natural languages from diverse language environments, a disposition to create symbol and myth, and the elaboration of social and technological cultures have been identified as the critical species-specific endpoints of human development (Washburn and Avis, 1958; Huxley, 1960; Waddinton, 1962; Lenneberg, 1967). Although the antecedents for these uniquely human achievements cannot be identified in the behavior of the neonate, all normal human infants and no other animals will eventually acquire them.

How, then, are we to identify the structural ground-plan which set the stage for individuality at birth? Searching in the naive organism for diminutive isomorphs of adult behavior is obviously a hopeless task, when there is nothing in the infant's surface behavior to suggest how it will acquire language, abstract thought, or historical awareness. Moreover, the species attributes do not emerge in a vacuum. They are developmental acquisitions emerging from the interaction between a competent organism and the intellectual environment created by other members of the species. At first glance, it might therefore seem like an impossible task to identify behavior patterns in the neonatal period which could in any way clarify for us the universals in human development, unless we undertook a functional analysis of developmental transformations at the same time (Werner, 1939; Piaget, 1950).

In the following remarks I nevertheless focus on the intrinsic organization of human behavior, without considering its ontogenetic changes in any detail. To do so, I will attempt to define the infant's prefunctional competence without, on one hand, retreating to an untestable preformism, or, on the other hand, becoming immersed in empiricist explanations that ultimately reject species differences and biologically determined intraspecies variations. This will require a consideration of the *forms* of prefunctional structures as reflected in the behavior of the organism at birth, as well as a consideration of the unlearned *"transformation rules"* which make it possible for structures to change with experience. The scope of the task is enormous and the relevant evidence very limited. Therefore, I cannot hope to do more than outline the nature of the problem and suggest some of the empirical approaches that are no longer entirely out of our reach.

The structural specifications of a naive nervous system that could satisfy the conditions outlined here might be compared to the "electronic logic" of a time-sharing computer before it is specifically programmed by its peripheral terminals. The unlearned transformation rules might then be compared to the ways in which the computer is instructed to interact with its terminals for information processing. Since most computer analogies, however, do not inform us about the actual constitution of the nervous system, which differs qualitatively from any computer that has yet been built (Von Neuman, 1958), it will be more fruitful to consider the evidence at hand and to extend our developmental investigations from a base of concrete information.

Motor Development

Experiments in neuroembryology summarized by Weiss (1955, 1965, 1969), Sperry (1950, 1958), Szentagothai (1961), and others converge on the conclusion that the motor behavior of lower vertebrates is rigidly organized before birth according to a prefunctional blueprint, and that this blueprint can be modified by experience only to a limited extent. In one of many classic experiments, Weiss, for example, transplanted and reversed the limb of the amphibian embryo so that the foot faced in the wrong direction. He permitted the tranplanted limb to reestablish motor connections with the central nervous system and then observed the functions of the reversed limb. If sensory feedback (learning) were essential for the development of motor control, one should expect the animal to adjust the movements of the reversed limb in accordance with experience and "reinforcement." Although the reversed limb functioned normally when considered as an isolated unit, it never made the appropriate compensations but continued to move backwards when the other limbs and body moved forward. In a similar experiment Anokhin (1941) excised all four limb buds from the amphibian embryo. After the amputated animal matured, Anokhin grafted full-sized limbs from a mature donor onto the *dorsal* surface of the experimental animal at the level of the cervical and lumbar cord segments so that the limbs would be of no use to the animal. Once the donor limbs had established neural connections with the motor neurons of the host spinal cord, they began to move in a normal quadripedal gait even though the movements were of no functional value (Anokhin, 1941, as cited in Weiss, 1965). From such evidence we can infer that in lower vertebrates the neural patterns for coordinated locomotion, including the integration between motor neuron pools of the cervical and lumbar segments, are intrinsic to the central nervous system and require no sensory feedback for proper function.

Because the mammalian fetus is isolated in the mother's uterus, we cannot determine the extent to which its basic movement patterns are rigidly fixed in prefunctional structures. The available evidence suggests that adult forms of mammalian motor activity are far less determined at birth and more easily modified by experience (Windle, 1950; Weiss, 1955). A greater plasticity of motor patterns at birth does not mean, however, that the adult forms of mammalian motor activity are in any sense less specific to the species.

Detailed observations on abortuses by Hooker (1952) and Humphrey (1969) have provided partial evidence that the basic elements of motor action of human fetuses (e.g. flexion and extension of the head, all reflexes, synergistic grasping movements, withdrawal movements of the limbs, etc.) are well represented in the naive nervous system. The orderly appearance of motor reflexes at well-defined intervals after conception suggests that the sequence of motor acquisition also belongs to the species-specific organization of human behavior (Minkowski, 1938). The possibilities for multiple combinations among the basic motor units present at birth are so extensive that the acquisition of skills might on casual inspection appear to be controlled almost exclusively by the environment. Yet, motor development does not begin as an amorphous mass of random twitches which is shaped progressively by accidental variations in the environment until it achieves those differentiated forms which are more or less specific to the human adult. Some a priori structures determine how any species, including man, starts postnatal development; and some prefunctional schedule of transformations determines how the more complex motor actions are elaborated through practice and experience. Although the repertory of motor patterns available to the infant at birth has been carefully cataloged (Peiper, 1963), we know very little about the finer details of the intrinsic coordination and synergism that might reveal to us the rules of transformation by which reflex activity is changed to voluntary action. Some congenital motor patterns will drop out as the infant acquires new modes of behavior. Others will remain essentially unchanged throughout life although the locus of their control may shift (Wolff, 1972a, in press). The congenital motor patterns of greatest interest for the study of psychological development undergo such radical transformations that the original components can usually not be recognized in the mature forms without a detailed functional analysis (Werner, 1939; Piaget, 1936, 1937). Piaget has documented how some of the sensorimotor patterns present at birth may constitute the earliest functional basis for intellectual adaptation. His intent was not to provide an exhaustive classification of such prefunctional patterns, but to analyze how selected "reflex circulary actions" are changed through experience and "equilibration" to make intellectual adaptation possible. Investigations that focus on the infant's competence at birth indicate that the naive infant is far more proficient than was suggested even by Piaget's analysis, and that many of the skills and "practical concepts" which were once thought to be acquired through interaction with the postnatal environment, are in fact given in prefunctional structures and guided by unlearned rules of learning.

Sensory Development

Among lower vertebrate species a similar degree of prefunctional organization characterizes perceptual competence in the naive organism. When the frog's eye is severed from its nerve, rotated through 180 degrees and allowed to reestablish central connections, for example, visual function can be entirely restored. After the rotated eye sees again, however, the frog lunges to the right whenever a fly appears on his left, and no amount of training can correct the maladaptive behavior (Sperry, 1958). The capacity of the lower vertebrate nervous system to reestablish a point-to-point correspondence with elements of the sensory organ from which it was severed and the resistance of these connections to retraining suggests that experience (seeing and looking) probably does not contribute to the original topography of neural connections which determine how the naive organism orients visually in space, detects and locates movement, and perceives forms (Sperry, 1950, 1958; Lettvin et al., 1959).

Like the motor rearrangement experiments, the neuroembryological and surgical experiments on sensory organs have of necessity been limited to lower-vertebrate species. Refined neurophysiological experiments on mammals have, however, provided evidence of a similarly precise blueprint of prefunctional connection between the retina and the central nervous system, for example, in the newborn kitten. The perception of movement, the orientation of body in space, and perhaps a primitive ability for the discrimination of forms appears to be guaranteed prior to function by connecting the receptor elements of the retina, the lateral geniculate body, and the primary visual cortex. The neuroanatomical arrangement of cells in the retina and central visual system as columns and rows and of row interconnections among such structures, as well as their connections to peripheral neural structures, is by no means random, and appears to be intimately associated with the way in which the visual system functions prior to experience (Kuffler, 1953; Hubel and Wiesel, 1962; Rock, 1971). Such a priori structures determine at least in part how the naive organism "recognizes" form, shape, and the direction of movement; but they imply no isomorphic correspondence between the geometric properties of the stimulus and the topography of cortical cells activated by the stimulus. In other words, the primary optic cortex does not "light up" as a triangle when the eye is presented with a triangular stimulus. On the contrary, visual information is reorganized repeatedly and extensively first at the retina, then at the level of the lateral geniculate body before it ever reaches the visual cortex. It is precisely this systematic rearrangement of sensory information by the naive visual systems that argues persuasively for the existence of prefunctional "transformation rules," as well as for the interdependence of neuroanatomic structure and early function. Such an interdependence has been demonstrated in detail for the mammalian visual system, but is probably of equal importance for hearing, touch, proprioception, and so on (von Bekesey, 1960; Wall, 1959). The transformation rules will vary with the system and species in question. They are not learned, yet they determine how the animal will learn and how learning will alter the existing structures. Modern technology enables us to identify such transformation rules not only by computer simulation, but also in isolated cases in the infant animal. Therefore it provides a window into the functional logic of the mammalian nervous system.

At present, similar transformation rules cannot be determined with equal precision in the human nervous system and we must be content with experimental observations that do not depend on single-cell recordings. Newborn infants spend more time looking at complex than at simple figures; they look more frequently and for longer periods at certain shapes and angles than at others (Fantz, 1965; Kessen, 1967). Visual preference studies provide no critical evidence for a prefunctional basis of pattern recognition since they probably depend on subcortical mechanisms responding to particular properties of an optical stimulus without telling us what the infant sees. Nevertheless, such studies provide a primitive outline of how the naive infant "sees" and how he learns to look. Bower's observations go one step further in defining the prefunctional organization of visual perception by suggesting that the structural prerequisites for size constancy and the intersensory transfer of visual and tactile information are probably present at birth and provide the infant with a primitive "foreknowledge" of object permanence long before experience has taught him that visible objects can also be touched (Bower, 1966, 1971).

Apparently, the young infant can also analyze sound qualities and distinguish selected features of human speech (Eisenberg, 1967; Eimas et al., 1971). Such evidence suggests that human auditory perception like vision does not begin as a neutral network of equipotential connections, and that some a priori structures determine how the newborn infant hears and how he learns to listen.

Temporal Organization

The evidence summarized so far pertains mostly to structures that determine the organization of behavior in *space*. Equally refined structures determine the initial organization of behavior in *time*. Instances of this were implied when I discussed the prefunctional organization of motor action and perception in space. For any concrete instance, the spatial and temporal dimensions of behavior can, in fact, not be isolated entirely; yet the distinction proves useful for purposes of this discussion (Lashley, 1951).

The intrinsic temporal organization of behavior falls into at least two major populations of periodicities which may be distinguished not only in terms of their distinct time bases but also in terms of the mechanisms that are presumed to regulate their cyclical repetition. "Macro-rhythms" pertain to the regulation of physiological and behavioral cycles recurring at intervals of hours, days, and months. These periodicites tend to be regulated by "hard" or temperature-insensitive clocks and are observed in activity cycles, temperature variations, sleep-waking patterns, chlorophyl production, and the like (Cloudsley-Thompson, 1961; Bunning, 1964; Solberger, 1965). "Ultradian" or "microrhythms" pertain to the rhythmical repetition of events in seconds and fractions of seconds. Because these periodicites tend to vary directly with changes of body temperature, it has been concluded that they are determined by "soft" or metabolic clocks (Pittendrigh, 1957; Solberger, 1965; Halberg et al., 1964).

Because of their direct associations with central nervous system function, only microrhythms will be of primary concern here. Rhythmicity appears to be an intrinsic property of all nervous tissue. It becomes most apparent when the nervous system is totally isolated from sensory input (Adrian and Matthews, 1934; Von Holst, 1949; Wall, 1959; Solberger, 1965). Among invertebrates, nerve cells with no apparent function beyond emitting pulses at regular intervals have been isolated (Whitrow, 1963). "Spontaneous" neural pulses generated by populations of cells firing in synchrony are thought to be the underlying motors for many rhythmical movements of vertebrate species, including those essential for locomotion, flight, and swimming (Von Holst, 1937, 1939; Weiss, 1969, 1965; Hebb, 1949; Walter, 1959). Wiener (1946) proposed that the human alpha frequency serves as a "gating" device which limits the transmission of nerve impulses to specified time epochs, and thereby makes possible the recruitment of potentials as well as the orderly interaction between excitatory and inhibitory pulses on the cell surface. Evidence assembled by Lenneberg indicates that frequencies of the electroencephalogram outside the alpha range exercise a similar gating function for the temporal organization of speech production and speech perception (Lenneberg, 1967). Komisaruk has demonstrated a direct association between the theta activity of the rat limbic system and rhythmical sniffing movements (1970). Lindsley, in turn, has presented evidence which suggests that brain waves in the alpha range set upper limits on the rate of voluntary motor tapping. Whether any of the spontaneous neural rhythms identified so far will prove to be the "basic clocks" controlling the temporal organization of human behavior, or whether they merely represent vectors resulting from the interaction of two or more basic clocks acting in synchrony, is not known at present and not essential to our discussion. Some prefunctional clocks must be assumed to regulate the sequential organization of primitive behavior if we are to account for the acquisition of such complex sequences as playing a musical instrument, speech, and linguistic syntax (Lashley, 1951; Whitrow, 1963). The earliest clocks cannot be acquired by experience since even the simplest environmental sequences that would make up such clocks could not be ordered properly in time without some intrinsic timing device. We know next to nothing about the "transformation rules" by which the fixed frequencies of spontaneous neural rhythms are altered in ontogenesis to become the determining devices which regulate the complex and flexible sequences characteristic of all differentiated human activities. Modern neurophysiological technology makes it possible, however, to study such rules both in animals and man and to analyze their transformation in development.

Social Adaptation

Social cooperation among lower vertebrates is to a large extent regulated by fixed sign stimuli which will develop even in the animals who are raised in total isolation (Lorenz, 1943; Tinbergen, 1953; Marler and Hamilton, 1966). Variations in experience can, however, modify the finer details of certain signalling systems (Marler and Tamura, 1964); and in many cases some social interaction is essential for transforming the primitive signal into an effective communication (Tinbergen, 1953; Sauer, 1954; Thorpe, 1961). Only among mammals with highly developed intelligence do facial expressions become prominent means for social interchange (Marler, 1964). The unlearned smiling response, which makes such an important contribution to the formation of a social bond between mother and infant, is probably unique to the human species (Ambrose, 1960; Bowlby, 1969; see, however, Darwin, 1873, for instances of smiling in other species). The early development of smiling has been described in considerable detail; yet its prefunctional organization remains a matter of controversy (Wolff, 1963). Even less is known about the origins of other nonverbal social signals such as frowning, laughter, and babbling, and eye-to-eye contact, some of which are unique to human infants, others being more widely distributed among primates. The qualitative difference between man and other mammals is not that intrinsic facial gestures contribute to the regulation of social interaction; but how the form-function relationship of facial (and other) gestures changes in ontogenesis. Humans can learn to smile maliciously, through their tears, or while they are furious; they can shed crocodile tears and cry to elicit sympathy. In other words, humans can communicate feelings that contradict their inner psychological state (Wolff, 1969). While ritualization and appeasement behavior may be considered as phylogenetic counterparts to such changes of function in social communication, the relation between a ritualized behavior and its state is more or less fixed within the life-span of the individual

(Hinde, 1966). The capacity for dissociating social signals from their corresponding states appears to be a human characteristic that makes their social interaction more flexible and far less predictable.

Earlier ethological studies were concerned primarily with the form and function of relatively fixed signalling systems in diadic social units that were analyzed in relative isolation from each other. The premature importation of concepts derived from such studies into human psychology, and their subsequent translation into causal propositions about the early social development of children engendered a justified skepticism about the contributions that animal studies could make to the understanding of human social interaction. The study of social behavior among extended groups of primates also stimulated a renewed interest in the biological basis of *human* social interaction (DeVore, 1965; Lawick-Goodall, 1967; Altman, 1967). The comparative study of primates revealed, for example, that aspects of social interaction once regarded as uniquely human are, in fact, well represented among other primates (Schaller, 1963; Goodall, 1964). Furthermore, the specific structures of social interaction were found to vary significantly even across closely related species (Kaufman and Rosenblum, 1969a, 1969b). Thus, the investigation of species-specific dimensions in social behavior could no longer be restricted to the analysis of fixed action patterns and their unlearned perceptual "releasers," but had to include also those variations in "programs of development" that determine how extended groups interact while they develop as social systems, and those species-specific attributes which determine the range of ecologies that any species can tolerate by virtue of its nutritional requirements, defensive capacities, and mating habits (Washburn and DeVore, 1961). The comparative study of primate social behavior thus provided ample reason for reconsidering the biological basis of human social interactions which were once attributed exclusively to arbitrary cultural variations. The significant biological constraints to be considered in the development of human social development must include not only the prefunctional signalling systems that can be identified by direct observation, but also the range of variations in social adaptation and group structure that characterize different cultures. Recent anthropological studies reflect such a shift in emphasis by turning from an exclusive preoccupation with cultural differences, for example, in child-rearing practices, to an analysis of the universals in human social interaction and their possible genetic determinants (Freedman, 1965; Eibl-Eibesfelt, 1965, 1968; Ekman et al., 1969).

INTRASPECIES DIFFERENCES

A discussion of biological determinants in early human behavior, therefore, must consider the *intraspecies* variations that contribute to development, as well as the species differences that were partially discussed above. The genetic analysis of human behavior was, until recently, limited to the study of family pedigrees, twin comparisons, and the biometric analysis of large populations. From such studies it was possible to collate a long list of isolated phenotypic traits, such as personal rhythm, critical flicker-fusion threshold, and susceptibility to optical illusion, and to infer the genetic contribution to some forms of mental retardation and mental illness as well as to differential abilities of intellectual adaptation (Fuller and Thompson, 1960; Gottesman, 1968). Until now, however, the specific genetic mechanisms which regulate variations in human behavior have not been clarified with any satisfactory degree of precision. When the genetic basis for isolated "inborn errors of metabolism" was identified it was possible to delineate the behavioral disturbances associated with single gene defects (Anderson et al., 1968). To date, however, behavioral disturbances associated with metabolic disorders have proven to be so nonspecific that no detailed analysis of interaction between genetic factors and behavior was possible. Lejeune provided another approach for the study of genetic variations in human behavior when he demonstrated the specific chromosomal defect of children with Down's Syndrome (Lejeune et al., 1959). Again, major autosomal chromosome defects tend to have such devastating effects on central nervous system function that only the most general conclusions for behavior genetics can be inferred from such studies at present. In time, however, a systematic investigation of the relations between inborn errors of metabolism or major chromosome variations and behavior could advance our knowledge of behavior genetics significantly.

A normal chromosome variation that makes human life infinitely more interesting is the celebrated difference between the sexes. Contemporary personality psychology has emphasized the effects of social-cultural variations on sexual dimorphism in behavior. The possibility that sex differences that are not directly or indirectly associated with mating behavior might also have a biological basis, has not been entertained as seriously as it should (see, for example, Maccoby, 1965, for a recent review).

While the observation of young infants in the nursery leaves one with the strong prejudice that girls and boys differ significantly in their behavior at birth, empirical evidence to support this prejudice is not persuasive. The greater resistance of newborn females to various stresses including perinatal anoxia, noninfectious diseases, infections, and the like has been well documented (Hamburg and Lund, 1966). A greater skin sensitivity in girls has been reported by Bell and Costello (1964) and Wolff (1969) but Rosenblith has found that this difference depends on a "chubbiness index" rather than on the infant's sex (Rosenblith and DeLucia, 1965). Sex differences in congenital activity level have been reported, but their genetic basis remains unproven. Sex differences in color sensitivity are present at birth and apparently remain stable throughout life (Peiper, 1963).

Among older children sex differences in intellectual performance and cognitive style have been investigated in considerable detail, but any potential biological contributions are generally so intertwined with cultural attitudes that their significance has for the most part been accepted in principle and ignored in practice.

Not even a hardened environmentalist, however, will entirely dismiss the influence of specific biological factors on sexual dimorphism in behavior. Experimental animal studies indicate, for example, that sex steroids can radically alter courtship behavior and mating of sexually mature animals (Beach, 1965). Sex steroids can also have *irreversible* effects on the mating behavior of animals exposed to an abnormal endocrine environment before birth. Male offspring of rats to whom large doses of estrogen are given during pregnancy will engage in typically female sexual behavior when they reach maturity although the experimental endocrine treatment is stopped at birth. Similarly, female offspring of rats treated with large doses of testosterone during pregnancy will engage in typically male sexual behavior and reject the male partner during estrus even though they are biologically fertile. There is at present no corresponding experimental evidence to indicate that sex steroids influence the prefunctional organization of nonsexual aspects in behavior, but a lack of evidence on this point is partly due to the fact that behavioral sex differences that are not related to mating, courtship, and similar events have rarely been studied in animals.

Female rhesus monkeys artificially androgenized early in infancy will behave in a "masculine" way during early childhood and adolescence (Young et al., 1965). Money and Ehrhardt (1968) have described the behavior of a series of girls with congenital adrenal hyperplasia who, although adequately treated shortly after birth, differed significantly from normal girls on specific behavioral items like choice of clothing, motor activity, and "tomboyishness." Girls with ovarian dysgenesis (Turner's Syndrome) have greater difficulties on tasks of spatial organization than might be expected from their general intellectual attainment. Broverman and his associates have investigated the influence of circulating sex steroids on specific cognitive functions in normal young adults. Using a series of overlearned repetitive tasks for measuring the "automatization cognitive style" the authors found that high androgen-producing males tend to be consistently better "automatizers" than low androgen-producing males. In contrast, females with high levels of circulating androgens do significantly poorer on the automatization tasks than low androgen-producing females (Broverman et al., 1961). Although levels of circulating sex steroids are correlated with performance on differential cognitive abilities, the association is complex and varies systematically between the sexes. Not only the amount of a particular biological substance, but also its interaction with the sex of the individual will determine how circulating steroids influence cognitive style.

Race Differences

The classification of human beings into mating populations or races is far more difficult than their classification by sex. The subdivision of human beings into races or mating populations by phenotypic traits such as bone or tooth structure, hair formations, skin color, and the like is meaningful only when it is achieved by statistical techniques. Since individual variations within "homogeneous" mating populations are often as great as differences across mating populations, assertions regarding immutable race differences are almost certain to be erroneous. Yet it would be absurd to deny that the incidence of the epicanthic fold is significantly higher among Mongoloid than Caucasoid peoples, or to deny that the skin color of Caucasoids is generally paler than that of Negroids. In principle, it should also be equally absurd to deny the *possibility* that specific behavioral traits may be distributed unequally across mating populations, even though the evidence on this point is very limited. The investigation of behavioral differences across races is therefore a legitimate enterprise, which in selected instances may provide answers that cannot be obtained in any other way.

Informed knowledge concerning psychobiological differences across mating groups is almost nonexistent at present (for exceptions, see Freedman, 1965, 1968; Wolff, 1972). Methodological difficulties alone cannot account for our ignorance. The tendency to equate *difference* with *inequality* and to attribute value statements to the observation of differences has probably considerably inhibited systematic efforts in this direction. The behavioral analysis of racial differences provides a unique opportunity for exploring how biological variations determine cultural differences, and may free us from the traditional one-sided view that culture alone can account for geographic variations in personality structure and adaptation. That such differences should exist seems likely; and that their analysis would increase our understanding of behavior genetic variations in normal populations seems probable.

CONCLUSIONS

In the preceding remarks I have speculated on some specific biological factors that contribute to the organization of human behavior, emphasizing "prefunctional structures" common to the species as well as intra-species variations. My aim was to outline some domains in the psychobiology of early human development that can now or in the near future be explored empirically. The investigations to be reported in subsequent chapters will be concerned primarily with development proper. My departure from the main thesis was based on the assumption that the study of ontogenesis must be complemented by an investigation of the biological constraints within which experience determines individual differences.

Whether we study individual variations or features of behavior common to a species, sex, or mating group—whether we investigate the biological or the social determinants of behavior—should be a matter of theoretical preference. Neither approach is inherently better; neither is ethically more sound. Unfortunately, the choice of strategies has taken on irrational overtones having nothing to do with the study of development. A zealous insistence on preformism has been perverted to serve as an apology for the status quo. According to this doctrine there are said to be stupid and intelligent people, rich and poor, sensitive individuals and dullards, and thinkers and workers. Little can be done to alter the situation, and the disadvantaged must be content with their lot. The doctrine has been exploited to keep women in subservient positions and to justify genocidal wars between black and white, slant-eyed and round-eyed, pale-face and red-skin—each group making grandiose claims for its superiority on the basis of trivial phenotypic differences. It is not surprising that thoughtful investigators would turn from the study of intrinsic human differences and undertake studies based on the contrary view that the naive organism is more or less equipotential at birth. In its extreme expression, radical environmentalism has contributed as much confusion to our understanding of development as preformism, by insisting on man's unlimited capacity to shape his behavior by controlling the environment (Skinner, 1971). Less extreme versions of this view, which do not deny the importance of intrinsic behavioral structures in theory but only in practice, are likely to disregard intrinsic behavioral differences between species, races, and sexes.

The social and political consequences that might one day follow from a doctrine of "radical environmentalism" are as pernicious as those which have resulted from a doctrine of preformism in the past. *If* it were possible to mold the neutral infant into anything the society chose, the decency of the technician programming the curriculum and his views of the good life would ultimately determine whether or not the infant grew up to be a decent individual (provided, of course, that decency were still a quality to be considered). The behavior shaper, himself programmed to become a behaviorist, would assume final responsibility for the range of individual differences that could be tolerated by the society, and human development would become a capricious adventure directed by government agencies and their scientific advisors. Our greatest safeguard against the unacceptable consequences of such systematic environmental controls over development is, of course, the essential failure of behaviorism to influence exactly those dimensions of psychobiological adaptation which were here identified as prefunctional structures and species—specific programs of development.

Distinct as the preformist and environmentalist doctrines appear on the surface, they are very much alike in their potential threat to an open society—the one by appealing to divine right and genetic law, the other by appealing to the self-evident wisdom of psychological technicians. The biological foundations of human behavior and development serve, in a sense, as fundamental guarantees that mutual understanding and cooperation among human beings is at least possible, even if not very probable. By their inherent diversity and ability to resist mischievous environmental manipulation, they also safeguard us against the excesses of behavioral technology and thereby help to preserve human freedom and dignity in an age of "scientific psychology."

REFERENCES

Adrian, E. D., and Matthews, B. C. H. (1934). The interpretation of potential waves in the cortex. *J. Physiol., 81,* 440-471.

Altman, S. A. (1967). *Social communication among primates.* Chicago: University of Chicago Press.

Ambrose, J. A. (1960). The smiling and related responses in early human infancy: an experimental and theoretical study of their course and significance. Ph.D. thesis, University of London.

Anderson, E. V., Siegel, F. S., Tellgen, A., and Fitch, R. O. Manual dexterity in phenylketonuric children. *Perceptual and Motor Skills, 26:*827-834.

Anokhin, P. (1941). Motor function of transplanted extremities after secondary regeneration. *Bull. Exp. Biol. Med. II:* 16-18 (Russian). Cited by P. Weiss in *Neurosciences Research Program Bulletin, 3,* 5-35.

Beach, F. A. (1965). Retrospect and prospect. In *Sex and behavior.* F. A. Beach (Ed.) New York: Wiley. Pp. 535-569.

Bekesy, G. V. (1960). *Experiments in hearing.* New York: McGraw-Hill.

Bell, R., and Costello, N. (1964). Three tests of sex differences in tactile sensitivity in the newborn. *Biol. Neonat.,7,* 335-347.

Bock, R. D., and Vandenberg, S. G. (1968). Components of heritable variation in mental test scores. In *Progress in human behavior genetics.* Vandenberg, S. G. (Ed.). Baltimore: Johns Hopkins University Press.

Bower, T. G. R. (1966). The visual world of infants. *Sci. Amer.* **215,** 80-92.

Bower, T. G. R. (1971). The object in the world of the infant. *Sci. Amer.* **225:**30-47.

Bowlby, J. (1969) *Attachment.* New York: Basic Books.

Broverman, D. M., Broverman, I. K., Vogel, W., Palmer, R. D., and Klaiber, E. I. (1964). The automatization cognitive style and physical development. *Child Development,* **35,** 1343-1359.

Bunning, E. (1964). *The physiological clock.* New York: Academic Press.

Cloudsley-Thompson, J. L. (1961). *Rhythmic activity in animal physiology and behavior.* New York: Academic Press.

Darwin, C. R. (1872). *Expression of the emotions in man and animals.* London, Murray.

DeVore, I. (Ed.) (1965). *Primate behavior: field studies of monkeys and apes.*

New York: Holt, Rinehart and Winston.

Eibl-Eibesfeldt, I. (1967). *Grundriss der vergleichenden Verhaltungsforschung.* Munchen: Piper.

Eibl-Eibesfeldt, I. (1968). Zur Ethologie des menschlichen Grussverhaltens. I Beobachtungen an Balinesen, Papuas, und Samoanern nebst vergleichenden Bemerkungen. *Z. Tierpsychol.* **25**, 727-779.

Eimas, P. D., Siqueland, E. R., Jusezyk, P., and Vigorito, J. (1971). Speech perception in infants. *Science,* **171**, 303-306.

Ekman, P., Sorenson, E. R., and Friesen, W. V. (1969). Pan-cultural elements in facial displays of emotion. *Science* **164**, 86-88.

Eisenberg, R. E. J. (1967). Auditory behavior in the human neonate: Methodological problems and the logical design of research procedures. *J. Audit. Res.* **5**, 159.

Fantz, R. L. (1965). Visual perception from birth as shown by pattern selectivity. *Ann. N.Y. Acad. Sci.* **118**, 793-814.

Freedman, D. G. (1965). An ethological approach to the genetical study of human behavior. In *Methods and goals in human behavior genetics.* S. G. Vandenberg (Ed.). New York: Academic Press. Pp. 141-161.

Freedman, D. G. (1968). Hereditary control of early social behavior. In *Determinants of Infant Behavior*—III, B. Foss (Ed.). London, Methuen.

Fuller, J. L., and Thompson, W. R. (1960). *Behavior genetics.* New York: Wiley.

Goodall, J. (1964). Tool-using and aimed throwing in a community of free-living chimpanzees. *Nature* **201**, 1264-1266.

Gottesman, I. I. (1968). A sampler of human behavior genetics. In *Evolutionary biology,* Vol. II. T. Dobzhansky, M. K. Hecht, and W. L. Steere (Eds.). New York: Appleton-Century Crofts, Pp. 276-313.

Halberg, F., Panofsky, H., Stein, M., and Adkins, G. (1964). Computer techniques in the study of biologic rhythms. *Ann. N.Y. Acad. Sci.* **15**, 695-720.

Hamburg, D. A., and Lunde, D. T. (1966). Sex hormones in the development of sex differences in human behavior. *The development of sex differences.* In E. Maccoby (Ed.). Stanford, California: Stanford University Press. Pp. 1-24.

Hebb, D. O. (1949). *The organization of behavior.* New York: Wiley.

Hinde, R. A. (1966). *Animal behavior: A synthesis of ethology and comparative psychology.* New York: McGraw-Hill.

Holst, E. V. (1937). Vom Wesen der Ordnung im Zentral Nerven System, *Naturwiss.* **25**, 625-641.

Holst, E. V. (1939). Die relative koordination. *Ergeb. Physiol.* **42**, 228.

Hooker, D. (1952). *Prenatal origin of behavior.* Lawrence, Kansas: University of Kansas Press.

Hubel, D. H., and Wiesel, T. M. (1962). Receptive fields binocular interaction and functional architecture in the cat's visual cortex. *J. Physiol.,* **160**, 106-154.

Humphrey, T. (1969). The prenatal development of mouth opening and mouth closure reflexes. *Ped. Dig.* 11, 28-39.

Huxley, J. (1960). The evolutionary vision. In *Issues in evolution.* S. Tax (Ed.). Chicago: University of Chicago Press. Pp. 249-261.

Kaufman, I. C. and Rosenblum, L. A. (1969a). Effects of separation from mother on the emotional behavior of infant monkeys. *Ann. N.Y. Acad. Sci.* 159, 681-695.

Kaufman, I. C., and Rosenblum, L. A. (1969b). The waning of the mother-infant bond in two species of macaque. In *Determinants of infant behavior IV.* B. Foss (Ed.). London: Methuen. Pp. 41-59.

Kessen, W. (1967) Sucking and looking: two organized congenital patterns of behavior in the human newborn. In *Early behavior: comparative and developmental approaches.* H. W. Stevenson, E. H. Hess, and H. L. Rheingold (Eds.). New York: Wiley and Sons. Pp. 147-179.

Komisaruk, B. R. (1970). Synchrony between limbic system theta activity and rhythmical behavior in rats. *J. Com. and Phys. Psychol.* 70, 482-492, No. 3.

Kuffler, S. W. (1953). Discharge patterns and functional organization of the mammalian retina. *J. Neurophysiol.,* 16, 37-68.

Lashley, K. W. (1951). The problem of serial order in behavior. In *The neuropsychology of Lashley.* F. A. Beach, D. O. Hebb, C. T. Morgan, and H. W. Nissen (Eds.). New York: McGraw-Hill.

Lawick-Goodall, J. V. (1967). *My friends the wild chimpanzees.* Washington: National Geographic Society.

Lejeune, J., Gautier, M., and Turpin, R. (1959). Etudes des chromosomes somatique de neuf enfants mongoliens. *C. R. Acad. Sci.* (Paris) 248, 1721.

Lenneberg, E. L. (1967). *The biological foundations of language.* New York: Wiley.

Lettvin, J. Y., Maturana, H. R., McCullough, W. S., and Pitts, W. H.(1959). What the frog's eye tells the frog's brain. *I. R. E. Proc.* 47, 1940-1951.

Lorenz, K. (1943). Die angeborenen Formen moeglicher Erfahrung. *Ztsch. Tierpsychol.,* 5, 235-409.

Maccoby, E. (1966). Sex differences in intellectual functioning. In *The development of sex differences.* E. Maccoby (Ed.). Stanford, California: Stanford University Press. Pp. 25-55.

Marler, P. (1964). Developments in the study of animal communication. In *Darwin's biological work.* R. Bell (Ed.). New York: Wiley, Pp. 150-206.

Marler, P., and Hamilton, W. J. III (1966). *Mechanisms of Animal Behavior.* New York: Wiley.

Marler, P., and Tamura, M. (1964). Culturally transmitted patterns of vocal behavior in sparrows. *Science* 146, 1483-1486.

Minkowski, M. (1938). L'elaboration du systeme nerveux. In *Encyclopedie francaise,* t. 8, *La vie mentale.*

Money, J., and Ehrhardt, A. (1968). Prenatal hormone exposure: Possible effects on behavior in man. In *Endocrinology and human behavior.* R. P. Michael (Ed.). London: Oxford University Press. Pp. 32-48.

Neuman, J. von (1958). *The computer and the brain.* New Haven: Yale University Press.

Peiper, A. (1963). *Cerebral function in infancy and childhood.* New York, Consultants Bureau.

Piaget, J. (1950). *Introduction a l'epistemologie genetique.* Tome I-III. Paris: Presses Universitaires.

Piaget, J. (1952). *The origins of intelligence in the child.* New York: International University Press.

Piaget, J. (1954). *The construction of reality in the child.* New York: Basic Books.

Pittendrigh, C. S. and Bruce, V. G. (1957). An oscillator model for biological clocks. In *Rhythmic and synthetic processes in growth.* Dorothea Rudnick (Ed.). Princeton: Princeton University.

Prechtl, H. F. R., and Lenard, H. G. (1968). Verhaltensphysiologie des Neugeborenen. In *Fortschritte der Paedologie, Vol. II.* F. Linneweh (Ed.). Berlin: Springler. Pp. 88-102.

Rosenblith, J. F., and DeLucia, L. A. (1965). Tactile sensitivity and muscular strength in the neonate. *Biol. Neonat.* **3**, 133.

Sauer, F. (1954). Die Entwickelung der Lautausserung vom Ei ab schalldicht gehaltener Dorngrassmucken (Sylvia C. Communis latham) im Vergleich mit spater isolierten und mit wild lebenben Artgenossen. *Z. Tierpsychol.* **11**, 341-441.

Schaller, G. B. (1963). *The mountain gorilla.* Chicago: University of Chicago Press.

Skinner, B. G. (1971). *Beyond freedom and dignity.* New York: Knopf.

Sollberger, A. (1965). *Biological rhythm research.* Amsterdam: Elsevier.

Sperry, R. W. (1950). Mechanisms of neural maturation. In *Handbook of experimental psychology.* Stevens, S. S. (Ed.). New York: Wiley, Pp. 236-280.

Sperry, R. W. (1958). Physiological plasticity and brain circuit theory. In *Biological and biochemical basis of behavior.* H. F. Harlow and G. F. Woolsey (Eds.). Madison: University of Wisconsin Press. Pp. 401, 424.

Szentagothai, J. (1961). Specificity and plasticity of neural structures and functions. In *Brain and behavior I.* M. A. Brazier (Ed.). Washington: American Institute of Biological Sciences. Pp. 49-66.

Thorpe, W. H. Bird Song (1961). *The biology of vocal communication and expression in birds.* Cambridge: The University Press.

Tinbergen, N. (1953). *Social behavior in animals.* London: Methuen.

Waddinton, C. H. (1962). *The nature of life.* New York: Atheneum.

Wall, P. D. (1959). Repetitive discharge of neurons. *J. Neurophysiol.* **22**, 305-320.

Walter, G. Intrinsic rhythms of the brain. In *Handbook of physiology, sec. I: neurophysiology,* Vol. 1. J. Field (Ed.). Washington, D. C.: American Physiological Society. Pp. 279-298.

Washburn, S. L., and Avis, V. (1958). Evolution of human behavior. In *Behavior and evolution.* Anne Roe and G. G. Simpson (Eds.). New Haven: Yale University Press.

Washburn, S. L. and DeVore, I. (1961). Social behavior of baboons and early man. In *The social life of early man.* S. L. Washburn (Ed.). Chicago: Aldine. Pp. 91-105.

Weiss, P. A. (1969). *Principles of development.* Riverside, N.J.: Hafner. 2nd ed.

Weiss, P. A. (1955). Nervous system: neurogenesis. In *Analysis of development.* B. H. Willier, P. A. Weiss, T. V. Hamburger (Eds.) Philadelphia: Sanders. Pp. 346-401.

Weiss, P. A. (1965). Specificity in the neurosciences: A report of an NRP work session. *Neurosciences Research Program Bulletin.* **3**, 5-35.

Werner, H. (1957). *The comparative psychology of mental development.* New York: International Universities Press. 3rd. ed.

Whitrow, G. S. (1961). *The natural philosophy of time.* New York: Harper.

Wiener, N. (1946). *Cybernetics.* Cambridge, Mass.: M.I.T. Press.

Windle, W. F. (1950). Reflexes of mammalian embryos and fetuses. In *Genetic neurology.* P. Weiss (Ed.). Chicago: University of Chicago Press. Pp. 214-222.

Wolff, P. H. (1963). The early development of smiling. In *Determinants of infant behavior II.* B. Foss (Ed.). London: Methuen, Pp. 113-134.

Wolff, P. H. (1969). The natural history of crying and other vocalizations in early infancy. In *Determinants of infant behavior IV.* B. Foss (Ed.). London: Methuen. Pp. 81-109.

Wolff, P. H. (1972). Ethnic differences in alcohol sensitivity. *Science,* **175**, 449-450.

Young, N. C., Goy, R. W., and Phoenix, C. H. (1965). In *Sex research, new developments.* J. Money (Ed.). New York: Holt, Rinehart, and Winston.

CHAPTER 3

Sex Differences in Early Development

Mourad Arganian

INTRODUCTION

The most salient and irreducible human differences are those which separate male from female. A naive visitor to any foreign country can more readily discern differences in gender than in any other variable, including socioeconomic status, age, or race. This appears to be reasonable in light of the fact that gender is not simply a quantitative variable. Genetically, one is either male or female. Gender thus appears to be the exception to Anastasi's (1958) view that each human characteristic is distributed along a continuum and that differences among people are quantitative.

Some readers at this point may feel that the above is so obvious as to be banal since sex-typed traits and behaviors that comprise one's gender *are* quantitative. This fact has tended to obscure the basic qualitative differences that do exist between the sexes, particularly in the light of the growing recognition that many culturally supported stereotypes of masculinity and femininity are without scientific basis. In this chapter, the author will examine the research evidence available on the early development of biological and behavioral sex differences. In an attempt to explicate the underlying developmental processes, we will examine the positive findings of sex differences in the first three years of life, when the role of biological variables and their interaction with exogenous influences can be more clearly seen than in later life.

There are two polar positions on the origins and development of sex differences in humans. The first maintains that the human organism is psychosexually neutral at birth and is an extremely plastic entity in its developing responses to the exigencies of life. Although there necessarily are some biological constraints on this plasticity, the content of experience and socialization practices can shape a given organism in any direction. More simply stated, the view holds that there are no absolute or inherent masculine or feminine behavioral characteristics and that males and females can be equally socialized to become aggressive, dependent or passive, etc. Money and the Hampsons (1961) exemplify this view in their report of a series in which all but 2 of 25 hemaphroditic individuals who were reared in the assigned sex which was contrary to the subsequent appearance of their external genitalia did establish gender identities consistent with their assigned sex. As adults they appeared to be well-adjusted individuals. Money (1961) set one qualification, however, which is that reassignment of sex must occur prior to the age of 3 in order for the individual to experience a favorable psychological outcome. Another example of this position is Mischel (1966, 1970), who explicitly argues that sex-typing is a result of social-learning (imitative learning and differential rewarding and punishing of sex-typed behaviors). This point of view gains support from research which demonstrates, at least experimentally, that the human infant is more malleable and more susceptible to learning than heretofore thought possible (McV. Hunt, 1971). The latter research typically demonstrates the efficacy of some form of stimulus enrichment provided to a group of infants.

The alternate position adheres to a view of the infant as an inherent psychosexual entity, either male or female, who will in the aggregate be more like others of the same sex than the opposite sex within various trait or behavioral dimensions. This hypothesis states that males and females differ significantly in both physical and, as a consequence, in psychological attributes. This position, as argued by Diamond (1965) is not an antilearning position and does not deny the important influence of experience, both idiosyncratic and culturally determined. While Hampson and Hampson (1961) assume sexual neutrality at birth, Diamond regards sexual behavior as influenced by a composite of prenatal and postnatal factors superimposed on a definite inherent sexuality.

The latter position raises many questions, for which there are only partial answers at the present time. This paper will address itself to several of the most important. If the human neonate is not psychosexually neutral at birth, but in fact has sex-linked potentialities and limits, then should not men and women be universally different along sex-linked mental or behavorial trait dimensions, regardless of cultural context? If the malleability of socialization practices can reduce or even obliterate the traces of early sex differences, then is the understanding or contribution of early sex differences meaningless to developmental theory? Or have we simply come full circle to this question: what are the relative contributions of nature and nurture? When sex-linked differential socialization practices exist, do these practices reflect or exploit biological differences? Finally, and most important, how do biological and organismic influences interact with socialization experience to produce masculinity and femininity in the young child?

In the remainder of this chapter, the contents of sex differences will be selectively reviewed, followed by this author's interpretation of the development of sex differences. At the conclusion, individual differences will be reexamined in light of the data presented here.

BIOLOGICAL STUDIES

From gametogenesis through conception and from birth to death, there is solid evidence for biological differences between the sexes. In contrast with asexual parthenogenesis, sexual reproduction markedly facilitates evolution because it mixes the genetic pools of individuals providing variability upon which natural selection operates. Sexual reproduction itself was made possible by the evolution of specific sex-determining chromosomes. The female has two large X chromosomes (genotype XX): the male has only one X chromosome and one male-determining Y chromosome which is smaller than the X (genotype XY). When an egg is fertilized by a sperm carrying an X chromosome (a gynosperm), a female results. When fertilized by a sperm carrying a Y chromosome (an androsperm), the egg results in a male. The evolutionary functional and genetic basis for distinct genders (sexual dimorphism) is further described by Freedman et al. (1967).

The presence of the lighter and more motile androsperm in the male appears to have pervasive consequences for development. Its size and/or its apparently greater abundance very likely contribute to the larger ratio of males conceived, the estimates varying from 120-170 males per 100 females (Rhodes, 1965; Shettles, 1961; Rorvik and Shettles, 1970; Szilard, 1960). The 20-70 percent difference at conception reduces to a ratio of 105:100 male to female live births, as a result of the higher incidence of abortions, miscarriages, and stillbirths for males (Baumgartner et al., 1950; Childs, 1963; Rhodes, 1965). Furthermore, during the first year of life one-third more males than females die in the United States *(Vital Statistics of the U. S., 1967, 1969)*. In fact, more males than females die at every age from conception through middle age.

Singer et al. (1968) carried out a study of physical, psychological, and neurological development from birth through the fourth year of life. They found significant sex differences favoring female subjects during the neonatal period and in subsequent performance on all scales. In their sample of 15,000 infants, significantly more males had low Apgar scores (Apgar, 1953) indicating biological vulnerability at birth. Of 187 abnormalities detected during neonatal life, 72 percent occurred predominantly among males, 25 percent among females, and only 3 percent among both sexes. Furthermore, controlling for birth weight did not alter sex differences in performance during the first year of life. Singer et al. (1968) suggest that the greater incidence of abnormal performance of males result: (a) directly from genetic difference, (b) from obstetric problems which have a genetic cause, (c) from neonatal distress of primary or secondary genetic origin, and (d) from destructive maternal attitudes arising out of a stressing perinatal experience.

Thus, the greater vulnerability to exogenous influence and the greater incidence of biological defectiveness in males from conception to early childhood is well established. The matter, however, does not rest here. Most sex-linked nonfectious diseases such as hemophilia, hyperthyroidism, and color vision defects affect males either exclusively or more often than females (Hamburg and Lunde, 1968; McClearn, 1970). Garai and Scheinfeld (1968) observed that throughout life, all major diseases including heart diseases, cancer, cirrhosis of the liver, influenza, and pneumonia cause more deaths and serious injuries to males than to females, who are affected more severely than men only by diabetes, strokes, and cerebral hemorrhages. Further, Scheinfeld (1955) points out that in the modern world, which has reduced the environmental hazards and death rates and created more equalized conditions for both sexes, the pattern of greater male susceptibility to most diseases and defects has become more pronounced than in former times. This leads him to the conclusion that, under similar conditions, females are better adapted than men to cope with most human afflictions (Garai and Scheinfeld, 1968).

A host of studies (Bell, 1960; Bell and Costello, 1964; Gullickson and Crowell, 1964; Lipsitt and Levy, 1959; Rosenblith and De Lucia, 1963; Weller and Bell, 1965) show that female neonates are more sensitive to tactile stimulation and pain. The Singer (1968) data suggest that the differences in sensitivity could be accounted for by either the greater neurological maturity in female neonates or a higher frequency of neonatal abnormality for any group of male infants as opposed to female infants. The point here is that major organismic differences between male and female infants cloud the meaning of findings of differences for any behavioral variable.

As reported by many studies of schoolage children, significantly more males than females develop learning, language, and behavior disorders (Bentzen, 1963; Macfarlane, Allen and Honzik, 1954; Peterson et al., 1959; Anthony, 1970). While there are a number of experiential, motivational, and educational factors contributing to these school-based problems, they do correspond to other data on the biological vulnerability of the male.

From birth onward, males are taller, heavier, progressively stronger and have a greater vital capacity than females (Anastasi, 1958; Asmussen and Heeboll-Nielsen, 1956). In addition, a larger proportion of the body mass of males is composed of muscle tissue. The interaction of these factors results in higher activity levels, restlessness, and superior performance in those activities requiring great vigor and/or strength even in infancy. Hetherington (1970) stated that such data as these suggest, "a genetically determined predisposition for assertiveness in males." Other data presented in this chapter drawn from comparative psychology, anthropology, and observation of infants strongly suggest a correlation between morphology and aggressive behavior.

Regarding differences in maturational rates between the sexes, Garai and Scheinfeld (1968) note that at birth, the most significant sex difference is the developmental leap which is taken by the girl baby. Although she is, on the average, one-half to one centimeter smaller in size and 300 grams lighter in weight than the newborn boy, she is actually a much better developed organism. Maturation-study surveys show that the female neonate is approximately one month to six weeks ahead of the male neonate in developmental rate. The gap in maturation widens in scope with the progressive increase in age, with women reaching terminal physical maturation at approximately 21 years and men at 24 years (Scheinfeld, 1965).

The more accelerated maturation of the female child is confirmed by the findings of Singer et al. (1968). Accordingly, Singer and her associates recommend that performance tests be standardized by sex, rather than by chronological age alone, in order to control for maturational differences between boys and girls at a given age. Thus, a different test would be administered to members of each sex. Michael Lewis (1969) urges infant researchers to analyze their data for sex differences and to avoid pooling their data across all subjects, as is frequently the case. Still others have reacted to the differential maturation of boys and girls with the belief that sex-segregated education would be more efficient. In one experiment (Lyles, 1966), boys in sex-segregated classes performed better on a number of variables over a six-year period than did boys in a coeducational class.

One final piece of evidence for a genetic factor in sexual behavior is the corroborating results of two separate studies of homosexuality. Psychological theories on the development of homosexuality have emphasized early life experience, particularly related to the parent-child relationship. In a striking study, Kallman (1952a, 1952b) found 100% concordance for homosexuality in 40 pairs of monozygotic twins (that is, both members of a twin pair were homosexual) while for 45 pairs of dyzgotic twins, the frequency of homosexuality was similar to that in the general population. In support of Kallman's work, Schlegel (1962) found 95% concordance for homosexuality in monozygotic twins as compared with 5% concordance among dyzgotic twins.

Some findings relative to hormonal influence on behavioral sex differences will be briefly touched on here. There is a vast amount of research on the complex interaction of hormone secretion, genetic programming, and sexual and nonsexual behavior in infrahumans, which has been discussed by Hamburg and Lunde (1968), Hamburg (1970), Levine (1970), and Gadpaille (1972). It has been demonstrated in lower mammalian species that fetal and neonatal life are critical periods when the secretion or nonsecretion of testosterone results first in sexual differentiation and then masculinized or feminized brain structure and function. These differential CNS structures, in turn, interact with genetic programming to produce distinctly different gender behaviors. However suggestive such data is for human dimorphism, conclusive evidence for the influence of sex hormones on human behavior is not yet available.

CROSS-CULTURAL STUDIES

D'Andrade (1966) has written a comprehensive review of anthropological data pertaining to sex differences. He found nearly universal gender differences in behavioral, social, emotional, and cognitive variables, each of which derives from differences in primary and secondary sex characteristics found in every society studied and the subsistence activities which sustained each society. D'Andrade saw the importance of genetically programmed gender differences and of cultural institutions in shaping specific roles which in turn feed back and affect the process of natural selection of those physical and temperamental traits that are required and valued in carrying out social role functions.

According to D'Andrade, the division of labor by sex in most societies is a result of "generalization from activities directly related to physical sex differences to activities only indirectly related to these differences; that is, from behaviors which are differentially reinforced as a result of physical differences to behaviors which are anticipatory or similar to such directly conditioned activities." He also found that every society institutionalizes maleness or femaleness as a status, which affects the developing psychological identities of individuals.

D'Andrade provides an interesting example from Mead (1949) of the interaction of somatotype with culture: "In Bali, where males do little heavy lifting work, preferring instead light, steady many-handed labor, both males and females have slender somatotypes. However, Balinese men who work as dock coolies under European supervision develop the heavy musculature more typical of males."

John Whiting (1970) cites findings from his cross-cultural study of child-rearing practices and personality development. He and his coinvestigators found across six diverse cultures that boys were more aggressive and wandered farther from home than girls. Moreover, the differences were greater at an earlier age than later, thus suggesting that the early divergence in aggression is biologically determined.

Barry, Bacon, and Child (1957) examined 200 ethnographic studies which contained socialization data and judged whether there were sex differences in training for the following five traits: achievement, self-reliance, responsibility, nurturance, and obedience. Their findings were that most cultures socialize girls for nurturance and responsibility while boys are most often trained for achievement and self-reliance. The majority of cultures were nondirectional for obedience training, although one-third of the societies expected girls to obey more than boys.

In another analysis of their data, they found, as did D'Andrade, that the quantity and quality of socialization for sex differences was very much affected by the subsistence activities and the economic structure of a given society. In economically underdeveloped countries, the nature of subsistence is more closely tied to differences in secondary sex characteristics, thus exploiting and reinforcing sex differences. In technologically developed countries, where the economy is less dependent on gross morphological differences in strength, speed, or endurance, sex-role socialization and typing is less divergent.

Barry et al. (1957) believe that the isolated nuclear family, which represents the typical family organization in highly industrialized societies, mediates the decrease in gender-differential socialization because of the role flexibility and interchangeability demanded when mother and father are the sole responsible adults. They note that some persons believe, advocate, and perhaps prophesy that, in Western nations, the gap in sex-role socialization may ultimately be narrowed to the point of extinguishing sex differences. However, they assert that the difference in biological substrate for sex-typed behaviors will render total extinction of differences unlikely. They further argue that severe minimization of sex differences would likely be dysfunctional for identity formation. One might also cite Desmond Morris' (1967) discussion of the evolution and importance of sex differences in morphology, physiology, and behavior for pair-bonding, which is a universal human phenomenon and which promotes the tie between male and female subsequent to mating and parturition.

BEHAVIORAL AND INTERPERSONAL STUDIES

By now it is obvious that the play of children is an important source of information for students of development. Play, after nutrition and nurturance, is an essential ingredient for the development and exercise of cognitive structures (Piaget, 1951), of interpersonal skills, of mechanisms for managing and expressing emotion and for experimentation with and elaboration of roles (Erikson, 1950).

The observation of children at play has yielded a body of data that sheds some light on the acquisition of gender identity and the interaction of genetic and cultural mandates. Both human and infrahuman illustrations of these observations will now be mentioned.

Harlow and his associates at the University of Wisconsin Primate Laboratory and Research Center see play behavior as a rich source of psychological information as well as a necessary ingredient in the social development of rhesus monkeys.

> ". . .we have found that of all monkey behaviors, play is probably the most informative. Merely noting the manner in which a monkey plays in a social situation can tell us the approximate age, sex, social position on the dominance scale, and rearing history of the animal, as well as permit us to make a fair prediction of a young monkey's future social capability and status, adequacy as a mother or father, and likelihood of developing abnormal behavior patterns. Systematic study of play behavior in monkeys has permitted the identification of variables that determine how, where, and with whom a specific monkey will play. More importantly, such research has promoted an understanding of the general function of play in social development, the process by which a helpless infant gradually becomes a competent, contributing member of monkey society. This function has implications for an understanding of human play (Suomi and Harlow, 1971).

Harlow has charted the normative gender differences in immature monkeys. He presents a summary of his research findings in this area:

> Beginning very early in life young male monkeys differ from young female monkeys in their behaviors. These differences are first and foremost evident in play. Males play more actively, physically, and aggressively than females. Few females get caught in rough-and-tumble play, and in approach-avoidance exchanges they are chased more than they pursue. A female infant rarely initiates a play bout with a male. Male monkeys, however, try to play with anybody and anything.

> As infants grow older and play becomes more sophisticated, sex differences become more obvious. By six months of age males are far more active and enthusiastic in their over-all play behavior than females. Furthermore, sexual posturing and positioning become more sex-appropriate. Initially, both males and females mount and thrust, which are adult male sexual behaviors, and both exhibit the adult female sexual "present" with equal frequency and proficiency. By seven months, however, female mounts are infrequent and are directed almost exclusively toward other females. Males may present toward other males, but seldom toward females. In addition, female monkeys groom their peers considerably more than do males. These differences emerge regardless of whether male or female adults are present. The differences persist in modified form through adulthood. We strongly believe that they are biologically determined (Suomi and Harlow, 1971).

Jane Van Lawick-Goodall (1971) similarly reported on chimpanzees in the wild. She found that male infants tend to indulge in more rough-and-tumble play than do females, and they practice aggressive display patterns more often during their games, such as dragging branches and swaggering about. Also, male infants usually start to threaten and attack others at an earlier age than do females.

Benjamin (1971) has challenged the notion that male monkeys are genetically programmed for dominant behaviors vis-a-vis females. She believes that the greater size and strength of the male rather than inborn disposition is a better explanation of male dominance and female deference. This is undoubtedly a valid explanation for the *maintenance* of male dominance in mature rhesus monkeys and perhaps is a significant factor in the affairs of adult humans. However, in a recent study by Harlow and Suomi (1971), male monkeys who had been individually isolated for the first six months of life exhibited virtually all of the normative sex differences, reported above, following rehabilitation. This suggests that male behaviors in monkeys are expressions of genetic arrangements.

Differential socialization practices on the part of monkey mothers also appear to affect male-female differences. Mitchell (1968) has reported a series of studies which related the behavior of rhesus monkey mothers to the sex of their infants. He found that, contrary to what one might assume, monkey mothers do not provide equal dosages of protection and punishment to both male and female offspring. In the first three months of life, the mothers restrained their female infants more often. During the second three months, mothers of females exhibited more nonspecific contact, more embraces, more clasps, and fewer withdrawals than did mothers of males, and they groomed their female young more often than they did males. Toward their male young, they presented (sexually) significantly more often and they significantly increased rejection and threat behavior as compared with females.

Here we have evidence of rhesus monkey mothers shaping greater independence in their male infants by withdrawing from them, providing less physical contact and protection. Two other bits of data are important here. First:

> Despite the relatively low level of positive physical contact between male infants and their mothers, the physical interaction that did occur was quite intense. Mothers of males were more frequently involved in bouts of social play with their infants, and this play involved vigorous bouncing and wrestling. Although these interactions were not observed frequently, even between males and their mothers, they were almost never seen between females and their mothers (Mitchell, 1968).

Second: "The only two infants aggressed by their mothers were males" (Mitchell, 1968).

Here we have evidence of rhesus monkey mothers directly raising their male infants to be more aggressive and encouraging "masculinity" through occasional vigorous roughhousing and eliciting heterosexual feelings through presenting their buttocks. In contrast we see the mothers of females shaping greater restraint of impulses and dependence while modeling a nurturant maternal role.

Mitchell concludes his series with succinctness:

> One can best characterize the mothers of males as 'punishers,' mothers of females as 'protectors,' male infants as 'doers,' and female infants as 'watchers.' The mother plays a role in prompting the greater independence and activity that is typical of males (Mitchell and Brandt, 1970).

Before considering the play of humans, one might ask whether gender-differential play behavior depends on and is subsequent to that point in development when boys are aware of being boys and girls are conscious of their gender. That is, do sex differences in play occur prior to the development of cognitive awareness of gender? The cognitive-developmental theory of Kohlberg (1966, 1969) argues that a child does not conform to sex-role socialization practices solely for the purpose of obtaining rewards but rather that once the boy has stably categorized himself as male, he then values those objects and acts consistent with his gender identity.

At what age does self-categorization according to gender occur? By age three most children can correctly label themselves according to gender (Rabban, 1950) but they cannot yet label others accurately, nor do they know whether they will grow up to become mothers or fathers. By age four, children can discriminate the gender of others by perceiving superficial physical attributes such as hair length or clothing style. It is not until age six to seven that children can "conserve" gender identity across contexts, that is, recognize that gender identity is fixed for life regardless of changes in age or changes in superficialities such as hair or clothing.

Lehman and Witty (1927) in their landmark monograph on the psychology of play, while cautioning against generalization, noted that boys engaged more frequently than girls in active, vigorous play and games; in play and games involving muscular dexterity and skill; in games involving competition, and in organized play and games. Girls engaged more often in "sedentary activities involving restricted range of action." They found the largest sex difference in play at ages 8 to 10, while differences in play activities decreased with further increase in age.

Would one expect to find sex differences in play at age three, which is the period when gender identity has been shown to be unstable? Fagot and Patterson (1969) set out to answer this question and found in two nursery schools with equal numbers of girls and boys that play behaviors of the two sexes were distinct and stable over an entire school year.

What is especially enticing about this study is the light it sheds on the processes involved in gender-role acquisition and maintenance. Fagot and Patterson discovered that the female teachers reinforced with boys and girls but primarily for engaging in "feminine" behaviors, or those play activities preferred by a majority of girls. However, boys reinforced each other for "masculine" behaviors, thus establishing the importance of the peer groups as a socializing agent for sex-role acquisition and maintenance. It seems surprising that the presumably powerful female teachers who dispensed reinforcement only for feminine behaviors and who put masculine behaviors on extinction schedules for an entire school year, should have been so unsuccessful in altering the masculine play behavior of the boys. It suggests that for boys, the same-sexed parents or other adult males may have more power in shaping behavior or that, beyond infancy, the peer group may be equally or more powerful than adults in teaching and maintaining gender-consistent values and behaviors.

Almost as an aside, the Fagot and Patterson research is valuable in demonstrating the importance of peer-mediated learning at an early age whether for sex or nonsex typed behaviors. American developmental psychologists have largely overvalued the classical parent-to-child socialization model for their explanation of most child learning, and have not appreciated major peer influences prior to adolescence. Harlow has recognized the importance of peer learning in rhesus monkeys and Bronfenbrenner (1970) has contrasted American with Soviet education by demonstrating the latter's efficacious use of peers from the earliest age to inculcate values and to shape and maintain behaviors in accord with official beliefs. The important point here is that a complete understanding of the development of sex differences will not be possible without a further understanding of peers and siblings in addition to parent and nonparent adult models.

Is it possible that year-old infants differ in play behavior according to gender? Goldberg and Lewis (1969) observed 32 boys and 32 girls, each 13 months old, with their mothers in a standardized free-play situation. At 13 months there were strong sex differences in response to the mother. After the daughters were removed from the mother's lap in the play room (which initiated the 15-minute observation period), they (female infants) returned to the mother more frequently and in less time, spent more time touching the mother, vocalized more to mother, spent more time looking at mother and spent more time in the floor space closest to the mothers than boys. All of these differences were significant.

The second area of interest at 13 months was toy preference measured by the mean time playing with a variety of specific toys placed in the playroom. Four significant sex differences were found in this experiment relative to toy choice, style of play, overall activity level, and vigor of play level. There were no sex differences in overall toy preferences but girls played with blocks, pegboard, and with the dog and cat (the only toys with faces) more than did the boys. Boys spent more time playing with the nontoys (doorknob, covered outlets, lights, etc.) Observations of girls' play showed that girls chose toys which involved more fine than gross muscle coordination, while the reverse was true for boys. Boys were more active than girls, who tended to sit and play with combinations of toys. Boys also played and used their toys more vigorously.

Following the free play, the mothers were instructed to place their infants behind a wood-and-mesh barrier which divided the room in half and which separated the infants from their mothers. The girls responded by crying and motioning for help significantly while standing at the middle of the barrier more than the boys, and boys spent more time at the ends of the barrier attempting to get around it.

Previously, it was shown that monkey mothers treat their offspring differently according to the sex of the infants. It also appears that human male infants, at 13 months, play and behave differently in the presence of their mothers than females. An important question then, is whether or not human mothers respond to and treat their male and female infants differently in early infancy.

Moss (1967) studied 30 first-born children and their mothers in the naturalistic setting of their homes. He made direct observations of the mother-infant behaviors at three weeks and at three months for the entire sample.

Moss found that the frequency of maternal behaviors was significantly related to sex. At three weeks and three months of life, the mothers were considerably more involved with their male infants, especially holding them, attending to them, stressing their musculature, stimulating, arousing, and looking at them. Each of these variables approached statistical significance at three weeks but decreased by three months, at which point they were no longer significant but still higher for males. Females were significantly higher on only one maternal variable—the mothers imitated them more at three months.

When Moss observed and charted the infant variables, these data on maternal behavior were found to be logically related. Male infants were significantly more fussy, irritable, supine, visually fixated on mothers and, most importantly, awake more than female infants. Females slept significantly more than males and when they were awake, engaged in more social behavior such as smiling or vocalizing.

Thus the boys by their greater irritability combined with greater wakefulness stimulated higher frequencies of nearly every kind of maternal response. By three months, however, the mothers become less responsive to male infants and more responsive to females than previously. Moss speculates that the mothers gradually learn that their male infants persist in their behavior despite maternal response, and the fussiness and crying are no longer interpreted as distress signals. The presence of social behaviors in female infants serve as reinforcements for maternal responsiveness, which increase. Goldberg and Lewis (1969) found that at six months, mothers of girls touched their infants more than mothers of boys. In summary, male babies are more difficult and demanding while females are more rewarding, with the net result that mothers respond quite differently to their boy and girl babies.

The Moss study is consistent with Singer's data on the greater incidence of neonatal abnormality in males and the greater maturity in female neonates. Whether due to greater neurological maturity or other factors, the female infants seem to be buffered against the hardships of experience early in life. They thus gave the impression of being easier to please, and males conversely were more difficult to soothe.

Appropriate sex typing for boys subsequent to infancy seems to depend on both the availability of fathers, especially those perceived by their sons as warm, nurturant, and rewarding (Mussen and Rutherford, 1963) and participation in a same-sexed peer group (Fagot and Patterson, 1969; Patterson, Littman and Bricker, 1967). The father-absence literature, in general, corroborates those findings that the presence of a father, particularly during the first five years of life, facilitates gender identification (Hetherington, 1966, 1970; Stolz, 1954). Furthermore, one particular father-absence study (Stolz, 1954) with a well-matched control group, found that early father absence had serious detrimental effects on first-born sons in many areas of development and impaired their ability to relate to peers. Very important here is the finding that those boys had poorer peer relationships and fewer group-membership skills than the boys in the control group. Thus, boys who have fathers with whom they can identify, appear to be likely to attain skills for peer-group participation which also consolidates male identification. Conversely, sons of absent fathers seem to lack the requisite social skills for peer-group participation, which they sorely need, since they lack the critical adult model.

Family composition and the sensitivity of mothers have a bearing on the development of boys with absent fathers. Maternal encouragement of masculinity increased sex role preference for father-absent boys (Biller, 1969). Sutton-Smith, Rosenberg and Landy (1968) using American College Entrance Examination scores as the dependent measure, found that father-absent boys with male siblings performed better than those boys without brothers. It seems likely that the family constellation plays a part in sex typing for all children. Interestingly, Biller found that maternal encouragement did not affect the masculinity of sons whose fathers were present, which reinforces the findings that fathers are the significant shapers of role models for masculinity.

Feshbach (1970) summarized all known studies of aggression that controlled for sex, including 21 that had preschool-age subjects. In each of the latter series, boys exceeded girls in physical aggression, quarrelling, negative behavior, and overall aggression. In six studies there was no differentiation for verbal aggression. Preschool girls exceeded boys in only one study and in only one variable, which was verbal aggression in a doll-play situation.

Given extremely different socialization practices by adults and peers for aggressive behavior, what is not known is the degree of overlap in the capacity for aggression in males and females. However, if males and females were trained alike for aggression, it seems likely that the greater body size and muscle-to-fat ratio of males would result in greater aggressive potential or performance.

SUMMARY

To say that the development of sex differences is a product of genetic, constitutional, physiological, social, and cultural influences at once explains all developmental phenomena and yet explains nothing specifically. The data presented in this chapter do suggest, however, some of the mechanisms involved in the production of masculinity and femininity. The mere presence or absence of the Y chromosome at conception appears to account for much of the variance between sexes for such variables as mortality rate, rates of neurological and physical maturation, size, strength, muscle-to-fat ratio, susceptibility to disease, activity level, and neonatal abnormalities. The outcome of the chance union of an ovum and either an X-bearing or a Y-bearing sperm cell is a major source of variance of subsequent differences in physique, behavior, experience, social role, and social status between individuals of both sexes within a given society.

Conception thus initiates for a given organism in a specific society a developmental trajectory, the contours of which are, on the whole, unlike those of opposite-sexed members. However, knowledge of an individual's gender allows only limited prediction for the development of that individual because there is variance for any trait between members of the same sex and there is an overlapping of traits between the sexes.

Singer's data, supported by previous reports, demonstrate that in the aggregate newborn males are less well-developed neurologically than females. This difference in biological baseline subsequently affects differences in socialization practice as shown by Moss. As was discussed, mothers are initially more involved with male infants but subsequently learn to regard the fussiness and fretfulness as typical male behavior at the same time that they learn to respond to the earlier smiling and vocalization of the female infant.

The latter data are in accord with work that focuses on the offspring stimulus effects on caretaker behaviors in mammals (Harper, 1971) and in humans (Bell, 1971). Thomas, Chess, and Birch (1968) have also shown that the wide variance of temperamental dispositions in infants precipitate a new socialization model in which parental behavior is conceptualized as the effect as well as the cause of child behaviors. These data collectively demonstrate that socialization practice is not independent of the biological nature of the organism.

The Singer, Moss, and Goldberg and Lewis studies suggest a progression of decreasing involvement of mothers with male infants and increasing involvement of mothers with their female babies, as a result of differing organismic states and rates of maturation of the two sexes. By thirteen months, the sex differences in play behavior and in dependence on mothers are remarkably in evidence and in the direction found in later childhood and adulthood. The parallel of human infant data with the Harlow and Mitchell data on rhesus monkeys is intriguing, especially Mitchell's belief that the rejection of male monkeys by their mothers is elicited by the greater activity level of the male.

There is one longitudinal study which concerned itself with the stability of behaviors and traits, including gender role traits, from infancy to adulthood. Kagan and Moss (1962) found that the presence of traits consistent with sex role, as socially defined, endured and were stable from childhood to adulthood. As Anastasi (1958) points out, however, if a group of boys should have a higher mean than a group of girls for a variable, such as aggression, there may nevertheless be variability such that some individual girls may be more aggressive than most boys. Suomi (1972) adds that rhesus monkeys also demonstrate considerable individual differences, even though groups of males differ from groups of females in their central tendencies.

In conclusion, the development of masculinity or femininity is a complex process in which there is an interaction and an interdependence of biological and experiential factors. The earliest years of childhood do appear to be critical for sex-role typing. Those processes which illuminate and account for sex differences also help to clarify the development of individual differences. The biological baselines for males and females differ, but at the same time there is considerable variance across all neonatal variables. Mothers respond differently to their infants according to gender, and this differential response is elicited by the temperamental nature of the infant, the mother's subjective perception and interpretation of her culture's expectation, and finally her idiosyncratic life experiences with significant persons of the same sex.

REFERENCES

Anastasi, A. (1958). *Differential psychology*. New York: Macmillan.

Anthony, E. J. (1970). Behavior Disorders. In *Carmichael's Manual of Child Psychology*, Mussen, P. H. (Ed.). New York: John Wiley and Sons.

Apgar, V. A. (1953). A proposal for a new method of evaluation of the newborn infant. *Current Researches in Anesthesia and Analgesia, 32,* 260-267.

Asmussen, E. and Heeboll-Nielsen, K. (1956). Physical performance and growth in children, influence of sex, age and intelligence. *Journal of Applied Psychology, 40,* 371-380.

Barry, H., Bacon, M., and Child, I. L. (1957). A cross-cultural survey of some sex differences in socialization. *Journal of Abnormal and Social Psychology, 55,* 327-332.

Baumgartner, L., Pessin, V., Wegmen, M., and Parker, S. (1950). Weight in relation to fetal and newborn mortality; influence of sex and color. *Pediatrics, 6,* 329-342.

Bell, R. Q. (1960). Relations between behavior manifestations in the human neonate. *Child Development,* **31**, 463-477.

Bell, R. Q. (1971). Stimulus control of parent or caretaker behavior by offspring. *Developmental Psychology,* **4**, 63-72.

Bell, R. Q. and Costello, N. S. (1964). Three tests for sex differences in tactile sensitivity in the newborn. *Biologia Neonatorum,* **7**, 335-347.

Benjamin, L. S. (1971). Anatomy is destiny--Reflections by the editor. *Forum, Wisconsin Psychiatric Institute,* No. 2, 27-30.

Bentzen, F. (1963). Sex ratios in learning and behavior disorders. *American Journal of Orthopsychiatry,* **33**, 92-98.

Biller, H. (1969). Father absence, maternal encouragement, and sex role development in kindergarten-age boys. *Child Development,* **40**, 539-546.

Bronfenbrenner, U. (1970). *Two worlds of childhood.* New York: Russell Sage Foundation.

Childs, B. (1963). Genetic origin of some sex differences among human beings. *Pediatrics,* **35**, 798-872.

D'Andrade, R. G. (1966). Sex differences and cultural institutions. In *The development of sex differences,* E. E. Maccoby (Ed.). Stanford, Calif.: Stanford University Press. Pp. 173-204.

Diamond, M. (1965). A critical evaluation of the ontogeny of human behavior. *Quarterly Review of Biology,* **40**, 147-175.

Erikson, E. (1950). *Childhood and society.* New York: Norton.

Fagot, B. I. and Patterson, G. R. (1969). An in vivo analysis of reinforcing contingencies for sex-role behaviors in the preschool child. *Developmental Psychology,* **1**, 563-568.

Feshbach, S. (1970). Aggression. In *Carmichael's manual of child psychology,* P. H. Mussen (Ed.). New York: Wiley. Pp. 159-260.

Freedman, D. G., Loring, C. B., and Martin, R. M. (1967). Emotional behavior and personality development. In *Infancy and early childhood,* Y. Brackbill (Ed.). New York: Free Press. Pp. 427-502.

Gadpaille, W. J. (1972). Research into the physiology of maleness and femaleness. *Archives of General Psychiatry,* **26**, 193-206.

Garai, J. E. and Scheinfeld, A. (1968). Sex differences in mental and behavioral traits. *Genetic Psychology Monographs,* **77**, 169-299.

Goldberg, S. and Lewis, M. (1969). Play behavior in the year old infant: Early sex differences. *Child development,* **40**, 21-32.

Gullickson, G. R. and Crowell, D. H. (1964). Neonatal habituation to electrotactual stimulation. *Journal of Experimental Child Psychology,* **1**, 388-396.

Hamburg, D. A. (1970). Hormone influences on adaptive behavior. In *Behavioral sciences and mental health: an anthology of program reports,* E. A. Rubinstein and G. V. Coelho (Eds.). Chevy Chase, Maryland: U.S.

Department of Health, Education, and Welfare, National Institute of Mental Health, Pp. 192-223.

Hamburg, D. A. and Lunde, D. T. (1966). Sex hormones and the development of sex differences in behavior. In *The development of sex differences,* E. E. Maccoby (Ed.). Stanford: Stanford University Press. Pp. 1-24.

Hampson, J. L. and Hampson, J. G. (1961). The ontogenesis of sexual behavior in man. In *Sex and internal secretions,* C. W. Young (Ed.). Baltimore: Williams and Wilkins. Pp. 1401-1432.

Harlow, H. F. and Suomi, S. J. (1971). Social recovery by isolation-reared monkeys. *Proceedings of the National Academy of Science, USA,* **68,** 1534-1538.

Harper, L. (1971). The young as a source of stimuli controlling caretaker behavior. *Developmental Psychology,* **4,** 73-88.

Hetherington, M. (1966). Effects of paternal absence on sex-typed behaviors in negro and white preadolescent males. *Journal of Personality and Social Psychology,* **4,** 87-91.

Hetherington, M. (1970). Sex typing, dependency, and aggression. In *Perspectives in child psychology,* T. D. Spencer and N. Koss (Eds.). New York: McGraw-Hill. Pp. 193-231.

Hunt, J. McV. (1971). Parent and child center: Their basis in the behavioral and educational sciences. *American Journal of Orthopsychiatry,* **41,** 13-38.

Kagen, J. and Moss, H. A. (1962). *Birth to maturity: A study in psychological development.* New York: Wiley.

Kallman, F. J. (1952a). Comparative twin study of the genetic aspects of male homosexuality. *Journal of Nervous and Mental Diseases,* **115,** 283-298.

Kallman, E. J. (1952b). Twin and sibship study of overt male homosexuality. *American Journal of Human Genetics,* **4,** 136-146.

Kohlberg, L. (1966). A cognitive-developmental analysis. In *The development of sex differences,* E. E. Maccoby (Ed.). Stanford: Stanford University Press. Pp. 82-173.

Kohlberg, L. (1969). Stage and sequence: the cognitive-developmental approach to socialization. In *Handbook of socialization theory and research,* D. A. Goslin (Ed.). Chicago: Rand-McNally. Pp. 347-480.

Lehman, H. C. and Witty, P. A. (1927). *The psychology of play activities.* New York: Barnes and Noble.

Levine, S. (1970). Hormones in the development of behavior. In *Behavioral sciences and mental health: an anthology of program reports,* E. A. Rubinstein and G. V. Coelho (Eds.). Chevy Chase, Maryland: U. S. Department of Health, Education, and Welfare, National Institute of Mental Health. Pp. 224-244.

Lewis, M. (1969). Infant's responses to facial stimuli during the first year of life. *Developmental Psychology,* **2,** 75-86.

Lipsett, L. P. and Levy, N. (1959). Electrotactual threshold in the neonate. *Child Development,* **30,** 547-554.

Lyles, T. B. (1966). Grouping by sex. *National Elementary School Principal,* **46,** 38-41.

McClearn, G. E. (1970). Genetic influence on behavior and development. In *Carmichael's manual of child psychology,* P. H. Mussen (Ed.). New York: Wiley. Pp. 39-76.

MacFarlane, J. A., Allen, L., and Honzik, M. P. (1954). A developmental study of the behavior problems of normal children between 21 months and 14 years. *University of California Publications in Child Development,* No. 2.

Mead, M. (1949). *Male and female.* New York: William Morrow.

Mischel, W. (1966). A social-learning view of sex differences in behavior. In *The development of sex differences,* E. Maccoby (Ed.). Stanford, California: Stanford University Press. Pp. 56-81.

Mischel, W. (1970). Sex typing and socialization. In *Carmichael's manual of child psychology,* P. H. Mussen (Ed.). New York: Wiley. Pp. 3-72.

Mitchell, G. (1968). Attachment differences in male and female infant monkeys. *Child Development,* **39,** 611-620.

Mitchell, G. and Brandt, E. M. (1970). Behavioral differences related to experience of mother and sex of infant in the rhesus monkey. *Developmental Psychology,* **3,** 149.

Money, J. (1961). Sex hormones and other variables in human eroticism. In *Sex and internal secretions,* Vol. II, W. C. Young (Ed.). Baltimore: Williams and Wilkins. Pp. 1383-1400.

Morris, D. (1967). *The naked ape.* New York: McGraw-Hill.

Moss, H. A. (1967). Sex, age, and state as determinants of mother-infant interaction. *Merrill-Palmer Quarterly,* **13,** 19-36.

Mussen, P. and Rutherford, E. (1963). Parent-child relations and parental personality in relation to young children's sex-role preferences. *Child Development,* **34,** 589-607.

Patterson, G. R., Littmon, R. A, and Bricker, W. (1967). Assertive behavior in children: A step toward a theory of aggression. *Monographs of the Society for Research in Child Development,* **32,** No. 5.

Peterson, D. R., Becker, W. C., Hellmer, L. A., Shoemaker, D. J., and Quay, H. C. (1959). Parental attitudes and child adjustment. *Child Development,* **30,** 119-130.

Piaget, J. (1951). *Play, dreams, and imitation in childhood.* New York: Norton.

Rabban, M. (1950). Sex-role identification in young children in two diverse social groups. *Genetic Psychology Monographs,* **42,** 81-158.

Rhodes, P. (1965). Sex of the fetus in ante partum hemorrhage. *Lancet,* **2,** 718-719.

Rorvik, D. M. and Shettles, L. B. (1970). You can choose your baby's sex. *Look,* **34,** 78-98.

Rosenblith, J. F. and De Lucia, L. A. (1963). Tactile sensitivity and muscular strength in neonate. *Biologia Neonatorium,* **5,** 266-282.

Scheinfeld, A. (1965). *Your heredity and environment.* Philadelphia: Lippincott.

Schlegel, W. S. (1962). Die konstitutionsbiologischen grundlagen der homosexualitat. *Zeitscheift fur Menschliches Vererberung: Konstitutionslehre,* **36,** 341-364.

Shettles, L. B. (1961). Conception and birth sex ratios. *Obstetrics and Gynecology,* **18,** 123-127.

Singer, J. E., Westphal, M., and Niswander, K. R. (1968). Sex differences in the incidence of neonatal abnormalities and abnormal performance in early childhood. *Child Development,* **39,** 103-112.

Stolz, L. M. et al. (1954). *Father relations of war-born children.* Stanford, California: Stanford University Press.

Suomi, S. J. (1972). Personal communication.

Suomi, S. J. and Harlow, H. F. (1971). Monkeys at play. *Natural History,* **80,** 72-76.

Sutton-Smith, B., Rosenberg, B. G., and Landy, F. (1968). Father-absence effects in families of different sibling compositions. *Child Development,* **39,** 1213-1221.

Szilard, L. (1960). Dependence of the sex ratio at birth on the age of the father. *Nature,* **86,** 67-79.

Thomas, A., Chess, S., and Birch, H. G. (1968). *Temperament and behavior disorders in children.* New York: New York University Press.

Van Lawick-Goodall, J. (1971). *In the shadow of man.* Boston: Houghton Mifflin.

Vital Statistics of the U. S., 1967, (1969). U. S. Department of Health, Education, and Welfare, Public Health Service, Washington, D.C.

Weller, G. M. and Bell, R. Q. (1965). Basal skin conductance and neonatal state. *Child Development,* **36,** 647-657.

Whiting, J. (1970). An anthropological investigation of child-rearing practices and adult personality. In *Behavioral sciences and mental health*: an *anthology of program reports*, Rubinstein, E. A. and Coelho, G. V. (Eds.). Chevy Chase, Maryland: Department of Health, Education, and Welfare, National Institute of Mental Health. Pp. 320-343.

Part II

DEVELOPMENTAL PERSPECTIVES

"Each individual ego is endowed from the beginning with its own peculiar dispositions and tendencies."

—SIGMUND FREUD

INTRODUCTION

In contrast with the preceding section, which discusses the fact that most of our knowledge about individual differences pertains to early infancy, the following chapters, devoted to succeeding stages of development, dwindle in specifics about individual variance. The intent of this section is to sample current interest in defining individuality in older children, but, also, to call attention to the still pressing need for establishing commonalities, particularly during the school years and adolescence.

In Chapter 4, Anneliese Korner draws from her own research and the work of others to illustrate that the newborn baby is not the passive, receptive organism he is commonly believed to be and that he plays a critical role in shaping the mother-child relationship. For example, infants initiate interaction far more than has been recognized. Furthermore, variations in how readily they are soothed and how long they remain comforted have considerable impact on their mothers' feelings of competence as caretakers.

Dr. Korner proposes the intriguing idea that early predispositions toward dealing with overstimulation influence later ego functions, defenses, and cognitive styles. She postulates that one basic regulatory principle is to diminish and make manageable incoming stimuli, with heavy reliance upon absorbing, reflecting, and analyzing stimuli and inhibiting motor discharge. Later outgrowths of this regulatory principle could be obsessive-compulsive mechanisms and the defenses of isolation, intellectualization, and rationalization. Such a child later also might show caution toward or avoidance of novel stimuli and strong excitation.

In contrast, a second basic regulatory principle favors the management of strong stimulation through motor or affective discharge with much less sensory exploration. Children with this orientation could later show hypermotility, impulsivity, and action as characteristic behaviors in response to novel and strong stimulation.

The implications for child rearing of the evidence assembled by Dr. Korner are clear. In working with parents it is important not only to stress their influence on their children's development but also to help them to see, hear, tune into, and trust their own intuitions in dealing differentially with what their children present as unique individuals.

In Chapter 5, Stella Chess outlines her group's approach to early life and provides specific illustrations of their work. She emphasizes the advantages in parent counseling of separating primary family disturbances from those arising from parental misunderstanding of the range of variability in infant behavior. Her group's nine categories of temperamental qualities offer an understandable and specific means of describing a child's temperament. Both clinicians and parents recognize the validity of the simply described clusters of temperamental styles that lead children to be viewed by adults as "difficult," "easy" or "slow-to-warm-up."

Dr. Chess thinks of individuality as being expressed through changing, evolving patterns, emphasizing the mother-child interaction. One of the most striking outcomes of the work of her group is their belief that maladaptation may come first, later being followed by anxiety, an idea which contradicts a psychodynamic view that maladaptive behavior always results from anxiety. As she sees it, maladaptation can produce anxiety. For example, a young child who is absorbed in her own creations to the extent that she does not listen to her teacher or find gratification in routine play activities has difficulty adapting to her nursery-school environment. When she discovers that other children do not choose to play with her and that she cannot compete in the school setting, she experiences rejection and resulting anxiety. Her problem is then compounded if she loses interest in nursery school. In other words, anxiety can result from an early discrepancy between individual inclinations and social expectations.

Dr. Chess illustrates the relative unimportance of distinguishing between nature and nurture by synthesizing both endowment and experience in her classification of children. She does not take a position on the question of whether temperament is intrinsically or experientially determined. Even though a temperamental quality can be observed earlier in life rather than later, she does not necessarily view it as more intrinsic and less experiential in origin. Many characteristics depend upon maturation and do not appear until later in life, such as, for example, the capacity to voluntarily control the expression of emotion.

In Chapter 6, David Elkind adds to our understanding of the developmental tasks of middle childhood through reviewing Piaget's concepts of latency age thinking and describing several original cognitive landmarks common to children of this age. He highlights the need for further elucidation of the commonalities of this age in order to establish dimensions upon which individual variation can be measured. Although earlier developmental stages have reasonably well-described milestones, norms have yet to be established for latency-age children and adolescents. He identifies as a latency-age developmental phenomena the tendency to make assumptions about reality on the basis of limited information and in the face of contradictory evidence. He coins the notion of "assumptive realities" as outgrowths of the egocentricism that color the child's newly acquired ability to reason. A typical "assumptive reality" is "cognitive conceit," a child's persistent belief that he knows more than adults. Dr. Elkind notes that differences in the rate of maturation during the latency age can be responsible for individual variations. An example of individual differences in rates of conceptual development can be seen in an argument between two 10-year old children in which each accused the other of being a cheater. One accused the other of cheating whenever he didn't like the way things were going. The other accused the first youngster of being a cheater too, but on the basis of the misapplication of rules. In this instance, the second child was at a later cognitive stage of applying the abstract concept of fairness to facts, and the first was construing fairness in earlier concrete, egocentric terms.

In Chapter 7, J. M. Tanner calls attention to the particular importance of individual variations in growth and development to adolescents. Already immersed in the rapid and erratic changes within his own body, the teenager also is confronted with the psychological impact of the relationship of his personal experience to that of his peers. Differences between the sexes are particularly prominent during the adolescent years, girls typically leading boys in maturation by a two-year margin. However, the great variability within the sexes is illustrated by the fact that the normal physical growth of two 14-year old boys leads one boy to appear as a 12-year old and the other as a 17-year old. The psychological, athletic, educational, and social impact of these individual variations are profound.

Dr. Tanner emphasizes the special importance of distinguishing between chronological age and developmental age during the adolescent years, although he notes that children tend to be consistently advanced or retarded during their whole growth period, particularly after the age of three. He finds skeletal age to be the most generally useful measurement of an individual's developmental level; however, he sees little justification for the concept of "organismic age" in which almost wholly disparate measures of developmental maturity are lumped together.

Dr. Tanner concludes with a discussion of the general human trend toward larger physical size and earlier maturation. He also points out secular variations in development, such as a year earlier onset of menarche for American than for Danish girls. These biological ingredients of adolescence play a vital role in shaping the unique identity of each adolescent.

CHAPTER 4

Individual Differences at Birth: Implications for Early Experience and Later Development *

Anneliese F. Korner

In recent years, a growing number of investigators have become interested in infant research. This research has taken three different directions with markedly different goals. One group of investigators has focused on the effect of early sensory stimulation on the infant's cognitive development, another on the impact of the mother-child relationship and still another on the role of individual differences in the unfolding of later development. By far the greatest concern of clinicians has been the importance of the earliest mother-infant relationship on the infant's development. Since the infant in this diad is frequently viewed as the passive recipient of maternal care, the focus most often has been on the mother, her attitudes, conscious or unconscious, her ministrations and child care practices, and her acceptance of the maternal role. What the infant brings to the mother-infant relationship, what *he* represents right from the very start, is frequently overlooked. (For a discussion of the historical reasons for this onesided view, see Korner, 1965.)

Much of the impetus to study individual differences among infants and what these may contribute from the start to the reciprocal exchange between mother and child, came from the field of psychoanalysis. For example, Freud (1937) emphatically stated his conviction that "each individual ego is endowed from the beginning with its own peculiar dispositions and tendencies." Hartmann (1958) pointed out that variations in the primary ego apparatuses may influence the choice of later defenses. It was mostly after the appearance of a series of psychoanalytic articles that stressed the importance of predispositions in the

* Reprinted by permission from *American Journal of Orthopsychiatry*, **41**, 608-619, July, 1971. The author's research was supported by U.S. Public Health Service Grants HD 00825 and HD 03591 from the National Institute of Child Health and Human Development.

development of the neuroses that reports of systematic observations of innate differences among young infants began to appear in the literature. (Birns, 1965; Escalona et al., 1952; Fries and Woolf, 1953; Thomas et al., 1963.)

My own interest in the field of individual differences originated from clinical work with adults and children in which I was struck over and over again by the enduring style of an individual's reaction patterns and by the logical cohesion of his adaptive efforts. In taking developmental histories, one can see impressive evidence not only of the impact of historical events and experiential factors, such as the effect of traumatic experiences, pathological parent-child interactions and identifications with parental models, but also of the consistency of a person's life style. Also striking is the logic and cohesion of a person's ways of *resisting* change and of making new adaptations *after* change.

I thus began my neonatal studies with the working hypothesis that, if one wants to understand the earliest phases of development, one must assess not only the mother's mothering but also the infant's characteristics and what these represent as a stimulus to his caretaker. As the work progressed, the following subsidiary hypotheses become useful in conceptualizing the factors involved in individual development:

1. Individual differences at birth, when they *do* contain the rudiments of later characteristics, may affect development in either short-range or long-range terms. The differences that may have long-range effects, and that in all likelihood originate from differences in neurophysiological make-up, may, in conjunction with reinforcing experiential conditions, favor the later adoption of certain modes of impulse management and the choice of later defenses and cognitive and characterological attributes. These are the differences that probably are most contributory to the persistence in the *style* with which each developmental task is approached and mastered. By contrast, other types of innate differences, while probably also exerting a powerful, though indirect, influence on later development, may be observable in their original form only for a brief period of time in that they become absorbed and transformed in the ever-changing *content* of the developmental sequences. Part of Piaget's (1936) developmental theories may help conceptualize this process. Piaget postulated that there exist inborn schemata that are related, though not identical, to their precursors. With this conceptualization one can readily see both the continuity and the diversity of the developmental process in that specific behavior patterns, observable shortly after birth, will exert an influence on subsequent developmental acquisitions but may change radically in their form of expression.

2. Innate differences will not only influence the unfolding of many later functions but will also affect the manner in which different infants will subjectively experience and perceive the world and universal childhood events (Benjamin, 1961).

3. Individual differences among infants *should* evoke differences in mother-

ing, if mutuality is to develop between mother and child. Such differences may thus be instrumental in shaping the child's environment.

Added to this is, of course, *what the mother as a person in her own right* brings to this situation, her attitudes, conscious and unconscious, her child rearing philosophy, her aspirations, her cognitive style and mode of impulse management, not to speak of what the father adds in all these dimensions. Added also are the effects of sheer circumstance, such as being born a boy or a girl, first born or one of many siblings, black or white or of a given socioeconomic or ethnic origin. This profusion of interacting variables, both internal and external, highlights how truly difficult it is to make any kind of longitudinal predictions.

METHODOLOGICAL CONSIDERATIONS

If, neverthless, one wishes to tackle the problem of assessing innate differences among infants and their influence on short-range or long-range development, one has to take a number of methodological precautions to obtain reliable results. For example, in our neonatal studies, which included both naturalistic observations and a wide variety of experimental procedures, we attempted to assess the differences among babies before differential maternal handling could have materially affected the infants' responses. Thus, the assessments were made when the infants were between two and four days old. This decision was based on the rationale that with an uneventful, normal delivery, the infant will have largely recovered from the birth process, and if given routine nursery care, his experience up to that point will have been fairly uniform. To forestall finding "individual differences" among newborns that are merely a reflection of prenatal or postnatal complications, precautions have to be taken to exclude all infants whose behavior might be affected by such complications. We thus developed stringent selection criteria to include for study only healthy, full-term neonates of average weight, delivered vaginally, spontaneously or through low forceps, whose Apgar ratings were eight or above one minute after delivery, and whose physical examinations reflected no abnormalities during the entire lying-in period. Excluded were infants who showed any signs of fetal or postnatal anoxia, whose mothers had excessively long or short labors or large doses of sedative drugs, or whose parents had a history of any kind of metabolic or neurological disease. Since we and others have found differences in arousal levels of first born infants and infants born to multiparae, and of breast and bottle-fed infants, and since the sexes differ, at least in their spontaneous discharge behaviors during sleep (Korner, 1969), precautions also have to be taken to consider these groups separately, and if compared, matched in numbers.

It should be stressed that when reference is made to individual differences, more is meant than merely the variations of behavior among infants that invariably occur by chance whenever any trait is measured. To obtain reliable individual differences in any behavior, infants have to differ significantly from each other in statistical terms and, on repeated testing, they have to hold their ranks reasonably well relative to the sample. It should also be stressed that it is easy to find individual differences that are totally meaningless if the conditions of observations vary from infant to infant. While it is not possible to present here the many details of the methods used in each of our studies, I shall present in broad outline how we attempted to insure that the infants were observed under identical external conditions and how we tried to control for variations of internal state. All the infants were observed at the same time of day; illumination and temperature were kept constant. In our experimental studies, the sensory stimuli provided were standard in duration and intensity. Since sensory thresholds vary greatly not only with each state the baby happens to be in, but also with hunger and satiation, we controlled for the time elapsed since the last feeding and the infant's state with each type of stimulation (Korner, 1972). Were one not to control for these factors one would surely observe differences among the infants that are purely the function of their state and not of their individuality. To determine the infants' states, we used Wolff's (1966) behavioral criteria with very minor variations to classify the states of regular sleep, REM or paradoxical sleep, irregular sleep, drowse, alert inactivity, waking activity and crying. At the beginning of each study and periodically throughout, we checked observer reliability. Agreements between two observers have ranged from 86 percent to 100 percent depending on the behavior categories observed.

In one of our studies (Korner and Grobstein, 1967), we used film to record the infants' behavior. In fact, we have taken 1000 feet of film on each of thirty-two babies and we have thus accumulated a bank of behavioral data on the neonate that can be used by us and other investigators for any number of investigative purposes. Rather than using movies as is commonly done to illustrate certain points, we used film to record periodic and unselected time samples of the infant's behavior. A timer attached to the camera automatically turned the camera on and off, thus taking behavior samples that were identical in length and in the interval since the last feeding for each child. These time samples provide a permanent and objective record of a multitude of neonatal behaviors which permit both a qualitative and quantitative comparison among the babies in any variable we choose to study.

FINDINGS

In presenting evidence regarding individual differences among young infants, I shall draw not only upon my own research with newborns, but also upon the findings of other investigators. In dealing with my own research findings, I shall pool our observations from three separate studies (Korner and Grobstein, 1966, 1967; Korner and Thoman, 1970) and discuss them topically. I hope to show not only how much infants differ from each other from the start, but also to elucidate, whenever possible, how these differences may affect short-range or long-range developmental acquisitions, how they *must* affect the infant's early experience, and how they *should* evoke differences in mothering. At the very least I hope our observations will convey that the newborn is neither the unorganized nor the passive receptive organism he is commonly believed to be.

How truly unpassive the infant is was very nicely shown by Moss and Robson (1968) in a study of fifty-four mother-infant pairs. In a six-hour home visit of infants one month old, these authors recorded, among other things, the frequency with which either the baby or the mother started an interaction sequence. In roughly four out of five instances, it was the infant who initiated the exchange. Since newborns cry much more than one-month-old infants, this ratio must be even higher during the neonatal period. In my own study, in which I monitored the infants' states continuously over four half-hour periods at predetermined times during two feeding cycles, I found that infants differ significantly from each other both in the frequency and the duration of spontaneous crying (with an analysis of variance, $p < .01$ and $< .05$, respectively). It follows that infants will vary markedly from each other in how much they initiate interaction with their mothers and, as a consequence, how much caretaking they will elicit.

Not only do babies vary in irritability, but they also differ significantly in how readily they are soothed and how long they remain comforted ($p < .01$). These differences must have considerable impact on the mother and her feelings of competence as a caretaker. This should be particularly true if she is inexperienced. Also of interest, incidentally, were the kinds of interventions that proved most soothing to neonates. Contrary to folklore and much of the early stimulation literature, it was *not* body contact that produced the most striking effects. We recently completed an experimental study (Korner and Thoman, 1970) in which we explored the relative efficacy of body contact and of vestibular stimulation, with and without the upright position, both in soothing babies and producing visual alertness in them. These types of stimulation were given singly and in combination and within the context of common maternal ministrations. In summary, the results showed the vestibular stimulation, the experience of being picked up and moved, had a far greater effect both in soothing the infant and in rendering him alert than did body contact. The findings imply that, at least during the neonatal period, the vestibular stimulation that is part and parcel of almost every caretaking activity may be a far more potent form of stimulation than touch and body contact. Yet, with the prevailing emphasis on the importance of body contact, this hidden form of stimulation is often overlooked.

Returning to individual differences among babies and the effects these differences may have on early experience, we have noted marked variations in the degree to which newborns make postural adjustments or mold to the person holding them. The lack of this quality has often been associated with severe pathology and while this may be true for extreme cases, it is amazing how much normal infants vary in how cuddly they are. Again, it should be pointed out how much this must affect the mother's feelings of relatedness, particularly if her own needs for this kind of closeness happen to be strong. While it is difficult to quantify the degree to which an infant molds to the body, it has been my impression that the restless, highly aroused and active babies are the ones who are the least cuddly. This impression dovetails with the findings of a longitudinal study that highlighted the far-reaching developmental permutations of this simple ·trait. Schaffer and Emerson (1964) closely followed thirty-seven mother-infant pairs over the first eighteen months of life. On the basis of the infants' behavior in a variety of commonly occurring contact situations, the authors classified nine subjects as "non-cuddlers," nineteen subjects as "cuddlers," and the remaining nine infants as an intermediate group. "Non-cuddlers" were so classified if, throughout the eigthteen months, the infants responded negatively to cuddling, even when they were tired, frightened or ill. Infants were classified as "cuddlers" if they consistently enjoyed, accepted and actively sought physical contact in all forms. "Non-cuddlers" were found to be more active, more restless and quite intolerant of physical restraint. Their motor development was significantly accelerated as compared with the "cuddlers" and probably as a consequence of this, their developmental quotients were significantly higher. The "cuddlers," on the other hand, were generally more placid, needed significantly more sleep and formed specific attachments to others earlier and with much greater intensity. They also tended more frequently to acquire transitional objects and to engage in autoerotic activities.

In examining their data on the mother-infant interaction, the authors were unable to demonstrate consistent differences among the mothers of "cuddlers" and "non-cuddlers" in handling their infants. From this and other data analyses, the authors concluded that the need for and resistance against close physical contact is not primarily a reactive or social phenomenon but an expression of a general aspect of the infant's personality to be observed above all in the level of his activity drive. They also concluded that deprivation of physical contact may affect some infants more than others, and that it may be primarily the "cuddlers" who require contact comfort for satisfactory developmental progress.

Returning to our own studies, we found from our film analyses that infants differed significantly from each other in how much they engaged in spontaneous oral activity, such as sucking and mouthing, and in the degree to which they sought, persisted and succeeded in self-comforting as expressed in such behaviors as fingersucking and hand-mouth contact. [With an analysis of variance p was < .01 with respect to each of these behaviors (Korner, 1972.)] We thus found marked quantitative differences in the manifestations of oral drive and the capacity to deal with this drive. Obviously, these differences should affect early experience both by way of differences in the kind of homeostatic adjustment the infant will make in the earliest weeks of life, and in the degree to which the infant will require his mother to be a mediating, tension-reducing agent. These variations in the strength of the oral drive and the capacity for self-comforting may also influence the intensity with which weaning is experienced, quite apart from what the mother's handling of this situation may contribute to this experience.

So far then, I have presented evidence that babies differ significantly from each other in how much they cry, how soothable they are and how capable they are of self-comforting behavior. Differences in these dimensions should help set the stage for many aspects of the infant's early weeks of life, both in terms of his experience of pleasure and of pain and the memory traces these may leave, and in terms of what is required for optimal mothering. These variations in early behavior suggest that there may exist, from the very start, differences in the degree to which infants avail themselves of others for purposes of seeking comfort. This, in addition to the mother's contribution and reactions, may differentially influence the intensity and depth of the infant's first attachment. I believe that, while these differences exert a subtle though profound influence on later development, these are the types of differences that become part of larger schemata so that they are not necessarily recognizable in their original form at a later time. More specifically, it is probably these types of differences that are contributory to vague feelings of helplessness, omnipotence, dependence, separateness or oneness with the mother and which, in combination with maternal differences, will feed into the kinds of object relations the child will develop.

Next, I will present evidence of individual differences at birth, the derivatives of which are perhaps more directly traceable in later functioning than the ones described so far. I am referring to qualitative and quantitative differences in the capacity to take in and synthesize sensory stimuli. Optimally, these functions should be reciprocal in strength. When they are widely discrepant, this may constitute a major source of vulnerability.

First, I will present some evidence regarding the neonate's sensory capacities and the variations observed in sensory thresholds. Recent experimental work in many different laboratories has shown that the neonate is a good deal more capable of seeing and hearing than had formerly been assumed. Fantz (1963), for example, demonstrated that infants less than forty-eight hours old show consistent preferences for certain visual stimuli. Interestingly enough it is the picture of a human face they look at significantly longer than at any other patterns. Neonates respond even to soft tones with changes in behavior, in heart rate and respiration. Furthermore, newborns can be made to follow visually a moving object and the source of a sound (Wolff, 1966). In our studies, we took measures of the frequencies and durations of spontaneous visual alertness, levels of alertness in response to maternal types of ministrations, frequency of visual pursuit of a moving object and frequencies of response to a buzzer and to the sound of the camera. We found that infants differ from each other in most of these to a highly significant degree. When, in one of the studies, we inter-correlated the visual measures with each other and with the auditory measures, the correlations were sufficiently high so that one could designate the infants as having high, moderate or low thresholds within the visual modality as well as across the visual and auditory modality (Korner, 1970) (see also Birns, 1965).

Differences among infants in sensory sensitivity obviously have major implications for how they will experience the world around them, how much stimulation they require, and how much stimulation they can take. Benjamin (1961), for example, suggested that infants with low sensory thresholds are very prone to develop colic during the third and fourth postnatal week, when all babies go through a maturational spurt in their sensory capacities but when they have not as yet developed an adequate stimulus barrier. Very sensitive babies tend to become overwhelmed with over-stimulation unless a mothering person acts as a shield and tension-reducing agent. Benjamin postulated that the outcome of this "crisis" may even have important implications for the predisposition to anxiety.

Contrasting to this are the infants who have high sensory thresholds to all sensory stimuli. These are the infants who, for optimal development, require a great deal of stimulation. Two of our studies (Korner and Grobstein, 1966; Korner and Thoman, 1970) shed light on one of the best ways a mother can provide stimulation for her infant in the first weeks of life. Paradoxically, it is by soothing the infant. When a crying baby is picked up and put to the shoulder he not only usually stops crying, but he almost invariably will become bright-eyed and he will scan all over his visual surroundings. Quite apart from whatever effect this soothing experience may have on the infant's *affective* development, this type of comforting will inadvertently provide him with a great deal of visual stimulation. Considering only the opportunities for visual experiences, it will be the infants with high sensory thresholds who will need the experience of being picked up more than infants who are more capable of providing visual experiences for themselves. This also suggests that infants with high sensory thresholds will show the effects of maternal neglect more acutely than infants who, unaided, are more receptive to environmental stimuli.

Judging from the literature, the balance between sensory threshold levels and the individual's integrative functions may exert a major influence both on pathological and normal development. In pathological development (e.g., childhood psychosis, autism) it has as yet not been possible to identify whether excessively low sensory thresholds, a defect in the integrative functions, or a combination of both are contributory factors. That an imbalance of these functions is involved in these major pathologies is strongly suggested by the work of Mednick (1966) with high risk children for schizophrenia, by Ornitz and Ritvo's (1968) work on perceptual inconstancy in infantile autism and by Bergman and Escalona's (1949) retrospective study, which linked unusual sensory sensitivity in early childhood to later psychosis. Within the sphere of more normal development, it likewise seems plausible that it is the balance between sensory threshold levels and the integrative functions that may be critically contributory to *how* development will proceed. It is in this balance that we may some day find the predispositional core that will influence the choice of later cognitive control and defense structures and preferred and enduring ways of impulse and affect management.

In searching the literature for personal characteristics that persist through development, one finds in different guises and from workers of different persuasions, consistent evidence that the most enduring characteristics of an individual derive from his capacity to take in and to synthesize sensory stimuli. For example, Honzik (1964), in discussing the results of the Berkeley Guidance Study, concluded that the tendency that was most persistent throughout childhood and adolescence was the propensity to be primarily "reactive-expressive" or "retractive-inhibitive." Thomas et al. (1963), in longitudinal work with infants aged three months to two years, found strong persistence in the children's tendency to seek out new stimuli or to withdraw from new situations. Kagan (1967), also through longitudinal work, found a consistent and enduring cognitive style that made some children respond quickly and impulsively to any problem situations and made others respond consistently with reflectiveness and caution. Pavlov (1927), in his work with dogs, described temperamental differences in his animals which, when extreme, required totally different handling for conditioning to be effective. Pavlov believed that these dogs had different types of nervous systems. He described one extreme as reacting quickly to every stimulus, vivacious, exuberant, and when meeting new people, becoming demonstrative to the point of annoyance. It was possible to condition this kind of dog only by continuously varying stimulation. The other extreme was a dog who responded to every new and unfamiliar stimulus by cowering to the floor or by inhibiting his movements. This kind of dog was extremely slow in getting used to new surroundings, but, once familiar, he became an excellent subject for conditioning.

Meili-Dworetzki (1959), who studied in great detail the contrasting development of two brothers from birth through the ninth year of life, found that
throughout this span, the hyperkinetic child Hans responded to every stimulus
with global action. He had weak boundaries between seeing and moving. He was
attracted to strong and to new stimuli and he experienced pleasure with
surprises. Fatigue augmented his restlessness. Fantasy was put in the service of
wish fulfillment. He perceived the world as a source of total pleasure or total
disappointment. By contrast, Max, a moderately active child, showed strong
boundaries between seeing and moving. Seeing an object inhibited his motility.
Instead of moving or acting, he looked attentively and, as he grew older, he
became very persistent in attempting to cope through cognitive mastery. Novel
stimuli evoked avoidance, motor inhibition, and rejection. He disliked surprises.
Fatigue diminished his restlessness. Fantasy was put in the service of mastering
insecurity on the one hand and reality on the other. Life was perceived and
experienced as a difficult task. Escalona (1963), found very similar behavioral
characteristics in the two most and the two least active infants from her Topeka
sample. She described the active babies as engaging mostly in forceful, total
body activation. Fatigue increased restlessness and evoked loud screaming and
often continuous crying. The inactive babies, by contrast, very rarely moved
forcefully, relied mostly on gentle, coordinated small body movements and on
looking instead of acting. Fatigue often decreased activation, usually led to
whimpering, sometimes crying, but never to loud screaming. Escalona's
description not only highlighted the differences in reaction patterns of these
children, but also the differences in stimulus requirements for bringing out their
optimal functioning.

These, and other examples in the literature, suggest that the individuals
described represent clear-cut and extreme examples of differing ways of dealing
with excitation. Such differences in the responsiveness, regulation and synthesis
of strong external and internal stimuli are, in all likelihood, an expression of
differences in neurophysiological makeup. From the evidence in the literature, I
would postulate that there are two basic regulatory principles for dealing with
overstimulation, each of which, if excessively relied upon, favors the adoption of
broad categories of ego characteristics, ego defenses and cognitive styles. One of
these will serve to sift, to diminish, or to make manageable incoming stimuli.
Focusing, sharpening (Gardner et al., 1959), a field independent (Witkin, 1965)
and an analytic and reflective approach (Kagan, 1967) come to mind as cognitive
control principles; obsessive-compulsive mechanisms, isolation, intellectualization, and rationalization as defense mechanisms; and caution or avoidance of
novel stimuli or strong excitation as general ego characteristics. The other
regulatory principle, if strongly relied upon, would favor the management of
strong stimulation through motor or affective discharge, through hypermotility,

impulsivity, action rather than reflection, externalization, field-dependence, and/or displacement behavior. Novelty, change and strong excitation would be experienced as ego-syntonic. The choice or heavy reliance on any one type of coping strategy or defense mechanism *within* these two broad categories of reaction are very likely rooted within an experiential and/or maturational matrix. Maturationally, certain defenses may be adopted with the emergence of certain age-specific modes of thought or as a consequence of issues generated by the psychosexual stages. Experientially, this choice may be influenced by the kind or the intensity of the conflict to be defended against, or may be mediated through identification with, or internalization of parental modes of defense.

Obviously, it would be of great interest to identify in the neonate manifestations of the preponderance of either of the two postulated regulatory principles of dealing with overstimulation. In one of our studies, we have made a small beginning in identifying the associations of organismic tendencies in the neonate that resemble the behavioral clusters noted in Meili-Dworetzki's (1959) and Escalona's (1963) children. We found statistically significant correlations between the infants' tendency toward motor inhibition and the frequency of visual behavior on the one hand and the reliance on small motions on the other. Infants prone toward motor discharge, by contrast, were much less visually exploratory and tended to rely heavily on diffuse motor activity. We are currently getting equipped to test the hypotheses generated by this earlier study with a larger group of babies and through longer observations. We thus will monitor automatically the infants' activity on a 24-hour basis during their entire hospital stay with apparatus that will yield a differential count of large and of small motions. We will also assess the predominance of the infants' tendency to respond to sensory stimulation through motor abreaction or through motor inhibition. This will be done with the help of an instrumental bottle that records changes in rate and amplitude of nonnutritive sucking and that can be used to test the infant's reaction to a wide variety of sensory stimuli, including the strong and stressful ones that usually attend routine medical procedures in the newborn nursery.

CONCLUSION

The observations presented here have implications both for child rearing and for longitudinal research. The finding that infants differ significantly from each other right from the very start suggests that there is more than one way of providing good child care; that, in fact, the only way to do so is to respond flexibly to the individual requirements of each and every child. It is regrettable that the trend of our times is exactly in the opposite direction. In clinical practice, for example, individual assessment and diagnosis have become devalued skills. The prevailing emphasis is on the fervent advocacy of one treatment method or another, rather than on the importance of a case-specific *choice* of treatment. Certain child care practices and certain forms of early stimulation are considered universally beneficial regardless of a given child's particular needs. We are thus forever looking for *the* method to raise children, to educate, to cure. One aspect of this trend is to see the mother and the care and stimulation she provides as almost solely responsible for the normality and deviation of her child's development. While this stance feeds into the illusion that with the "correct methods" and the "right attitudes" we are in control of our children's destiny, it also produces a lot of guilt. This, in turn, undercuts parental effectiveness in dealing flexibly with each child's strengths and vulnerabilities. The practical implications of our findings are quite clear: In working with parents, it is important that we stress not only their crucial influence on their children's development but also that we free them to see, to hear, to tune in and to trust their own intuition in dealing differentially with what their children present as *separate* individuals.

The findings presented here also suggest that certain individual characteristics in the newborn will affect shortrange adaptations, and others may color much of later development. For longitudinal follow-up of the latter, it would be strategic to follow mostly those infants who show a given tendency with unusual clarity, consistency, and strength. This is based on the assumption that the combination of "an average expectable environment" (Hartman, 1958) with, "an average expectable child," will mostly reflect the successful amalgamation between the child's original tendencies and his environmental influences. This is apt to be less true of infants who are strongly endowed in one direction or another, since the persistence of a trait, or the derivative of a trait, may largely depend on its original strength. In line with this reasoning, it would be strategic to explore the range of responses in a given variable, or a group of variables, in a large sample of neonates, and then to follow longitudinally the extreme or the most clear-cut cases.

REFERENCES

Benjamin, J. (1961). The innate and the experiential in development. In *Lectures on experimental psychiatry,* H. Brosin (Ed.). Pittsburgh: University of Pittsburgh.

Bergman, P. and Escalona, S. (1949). Unusual sensitivities in very young children. In *The psychoanalytic study of the child,* Vol. 3/4, P. Greenacre et al. (Eds.). New York: International Universities Press.

Birns, B. (1965). Individual differences in human neonates' responses to stimulation. *Child Developm.* **36**, 249-256.

Escalona, S. (1963). Patterns of infantile experience and the developmental process. In *The psychoanalytic study of the child.* Vol. 18, R. Eissler et al. (Eds.). New York: International Universities Press.

Escalona, S. et al. (1952). Early phases of personality development: a non-normative study of infant behavior. Monograph of the Society for Research in Child Development 17 (Serial No. 54, No. 1).

Fantz, R. (1963). Pattern vision in newborn infants. *Science* **140**, 296-297.

Freud, S. (1937). Analysis terminable and interminable. In *Collected papers,* Vol. 5, London: Hogarth Press. 1950.

Fries, M. and Woolf, P. (1953). Some hypotheses on the role of the congenital activity type in personality development. In *The psychoanalytic study of the child,* Vol. 8, R. Eissler et al. (Eds.). New York: International Universities Press.

Gardner, R. et al. (1959). Cognitive controls. A study of individual consistencies in cognitive behavior. *Psychological Issues* 1(4), Monograph 4.

Hartman, H. (1958). Ego psychology and the problem of adaptation. New York: International Universities Press.

Honzik, M. (1964). Personality consistency and change: some comments on papers by Bayley, Macfarlane, Moss and Kagan, and Murphy. *Vita Humana* **7**, 139-142.

Kagan, J. (1967). Biological aspects of inhibition systems. *Amer. J. Dis. Children* **114**, 507-512.

Korner, A. (1965). Mother-child interaction: one- or two-way street? *Social Work* **10**, 47-51.

Korner, A. (1969). Neonatal startles, smiles, erections, and reflex sucks as related to state, sex, and individuality. *Child Developm.* **40**, 1039-1053.

Korner, A. (1970). Visual alertness in neonates: individual differences and their correlates. *Perceptual and Motor Skills* **31**, 499-509.

Korner, A. (1972). State as variable, as obstacle and as mediator of stimulation in infant research. *Merrill-Palmer Quart.* **18**, 2, 77-94.

Korner, A. and Kraemer, H. (1972). Individual differences of spontaneous oral behavior in neonates. *Third symposium on oral sensation and perception: The mouth of the infant,* J. Bosma (Ed.). Springfield, Ill.: Charles C. Thomas. 335-346.

Korner, A. and Grobstein, R. (1966). Visual alertness as related to soothing in neonates: implications for maternal stimulation and early deprivation. *Child Developm.* **37**, 867-876.

Korner, A. and Grobstein, R. (1967). Individual differences at birth: implications for mother-infant relationship and later development. *J. Amer. Acad. Child Psychiat.* **6**, 676-690.

Korner, A. and Thoman, E. (1970). Visual alertness in neonates as evoked by maternal care. *J. Exper. Child Psychol.* **10**, 67-78.

Mednick, S. (1966). A longitudinal study of children with a high risk for schizophrenia. *Ment. Hyg.* **50**, 522-535.

Meli-Dworetzki, G. (1959). *Lust und Angst. Regulative Momente in der Persönlichkeitsentwicklung zweier Brüder. Beiträge zur Genetischen Charakterologie,* No. 3. Bern: Hans Huber.

Moss, H. and Robson, K. (1968). The role of protest behavior in the development of the mother-infant attachment. Paper presented at a symposium on attachment behaviors in humans and animals. *76th Annual Convention of the American Psychological Association,* San Francisco.

Ornitz, E. and Ritvo, E. (1968). Perceptual inconstancy in early infantile autism. *Arch. Gen. Psychiat.* **18**, 76-98.

Pavlov, I. (1927). Conditioned reflexes. New York: Dover Publications. P. 1960.

Piaget, J. (1936). *The origins of intelligence in children.* New York: International Universities Press. 1952.

Schaffer, H. and Emerson, P. (1964). Patterns of response to physical contact in early human development. *J. Child Psychol. Psychiat.* **5**, 1-13.

Thomas, A., et al. (1963). *Behavioral individuality in early childhood.* New York: New York Universities Press.

Witkin, H. (1965). Psychological differentiation and forms of pathology. *J. Abnorm. Psychol.* **70**, 317-336.

Wolff, P. (1966). The causes, controls, and organization of behavior in the neonate. *Psychological Issues* **5**, Monograph 17.

CHAPTER 5

Temperament in the Normal Infant

Stella Chess and

Alexander Thomas

Some 25 years ago the authors found that clinical features of both adult and child behavioral pathology could not be satisfactorily explained by the psychodynamic formulations we had learned. The expected consequences of pathological parental handling failed to materialize in many children. Nor did the degree or kind of behavior disorder found in other children appear predictable from parental behavior. Such clinical experience raised troubling doubts about the prevailing theory of the child-parent relationship. These doubts were not put to rest by the argument that, in the first situation, there must have been unidentified stabilizing individuals in the child's life accounting for the healthy development. Conversely, we could not accept the reasoning that when child psychopathology was unexpectedly high, parental pathology must have been greater than appeared on the surface and that its subtlety of expression heightened its noxious effects.

As mounting evidence increased our doubts, we concluded that something important must be missing from the standard accounts of child-parent interaction. We suspected that the missing ingredient was some aspect of the individuals' styles of reactivity, and we had some ideas about how this was demonstrated in both child and adult patients. But it was clear that much definition, observation, and conceptualization was required to convert a clinical hunch into a clinical tool. We decided to make the question of behavioral individuality a major aspect of our professional work.

At the time we began this work in the early 1950s there were few systematic studies of a child's pattern of individuality and its contribution to his psychological development (Witmer and Kotinsky, 1952). In the preceding decades, environmental approaches to the study of behavioral development had predominated. These studies had identified many aspects of parental attitude and practice, sib and family relationships, social values, and cultural norms that may affect a child's normal or deviant behavioral development. But the studies omitted an important factor—the child as he himself was.

In 1937, Freud asserted that "each individual ego is endowed from the beginning with its own peculiar disposition and tendencies." Also in the 1930s, two pioneer workers in the field of child development, Gesell (1947) and Shirley (1931, 1933), reported significant individual differences in the behavioral characteristics of infants. However, these beginnings were followed by only scattered studies that were insufficient to provide the basis for systematic and comprehensive understanding of behavioral individuality for psychological development (Thomas et al., 1960). The neglect of this area of investigation was in part due to the general disrepute of previously influential views which had explained complex personality structures and elaborate psychopathological syndromes in terms of heredity and physical constitution. It was the authors' repeated personal experience in the 1950s, when they and their co-workers suggested that young children may have individual organismic differences in behavior important for development, to find most of their colleagues reproaching them for returning to an outdated and discredited constitutionalist view. Nevertheless, the fact remained that a purely environmentalist approach did not adequately explain the great variability in the responses of children to similar child-care practices. Nor did it explain the absence of a one-to-one relationship between parental functioning and the presence of psychological abnormality in the child.

Traditional constitutionalist views had, of course, erred in discounting environmental influences. Was it not possible that environmentalist views might also be erring in ignoring significant organismic characteristics of the child? Did not the fact demand an alternative approach in which psychological development was viewed as the result of interactions between the child having specific characteristics of individuality and significant features of his environment? Such an approach was being considered in the 1950s by a number of workers (Alpert et al., 1956; Fries and Woolf, 1953; Murphy et al., 1962; Ritvo and Solnit, 1958), and led to studies which considered limited aspects of behavioral differences or explored them within a specific theoretical framework. Correlations were sought by other investigators between neurological functioning and behavioral styles. Thus, it was postulated (Walter, 1953) that patterns of electroencephalographic activity might be correlated with various types of personality. Similarly, Mirsky (1953) and Williams (1956) looked for indications of biochemical individuality that might offer clues to initial sources of individuality in children.

Still other investigators who approached the question of innate differences within a psychoanalytic framework sought their answers in such terms as the child's intensity and mode of expression of presumed drive states (Murphy,

1957), while others (Escalona et al., 1952; Fries and Woolf, 1953) concentrated on certain explicit characteristics of the child, such as his feeding and sleep patterns, his responses to sensory stimulation or his congenital activity type.

Most of these studies, however, were based upon a limited number of children or focused on at most a few aspects of individuality. In addition, these selective observations did not include a systematic longitudinal study of the child's behavior over time and, therefore, provided an inadequate basis for determining the relationship of the specific characteristics to the development and later functioning of the child.

For the child's individuality seriously to be incorporated into the body of developmental theory and psychiatric practice, more substantial information on the nature of individual differences was required. It was clear that the pertinent initial characteristics of individuality in infancy had to be identified, their continuities and discontinuities studied over time, and their relevance to various features of the child's psychological development determined. Such an analysis required a long-term longitudinal study in which data on the behavioral characteristics of a substantial sample of children could be gathered and analyzed from early infancy onward. The New York Longitudinal Study was initiated in 1956 and has been pursued since that time in order to provide such substance.

As a first practical step to insure not only pertinence but also both parsimony and sufficiency in data collection, we selected 15 normal children ranging in age from 5 to 15. From their parents we obtained retrospective behavioral histories and details of current functioning. The children's behavior while taking a standardized intelligence test was recorded. Since all these children had been known to the investigators throughout childhood, it was possible to add the longitudinal impressions relating to them to the information concerning the deviant children seen in psychiatric practice over a period of years. From scrutiny of this combined material we were alerted to certain aspects of individual reactivity which appear to show continuity, to bear some relationship to their functioning, and to have had important influences on the environment. The individual reactive qualities of the children acted as moderators and selectors of those aspects of their overall surroundings which were effective stimuli. Even the actual events and experiences in the children's lives were, in part, determined by the parent's anticipation of their infants' reactions.

At first, we obtained behavior records on 20 infants starting within the first week of life. With experience, we decided to schedule the initial interview at age 2-3 months with succeeding interviews at three-month intervals. The data were then subjected to independent inductive analysis by Dr. Herbert Birch. Dr. Birch continued as one of the three major investigators of the New York Longitudinal Study, involving himself together with the authors in conceptualizations, strategies of investigation, and analysis.

It became evident that the aspect of initial difference most likely to have pertinence for later development was behavioral style or temperament. Our longitudinal study therefore concentrated on this issue. The term temperament, as it is used here, refers to the behavioral style of a child and contains no inferences as to etiology, whether genetic, somatologic, endocrinal, or environmental. It is a phenomenologic term used to describe the characteristic tempo, energy expenditure, focus, mood, and rhythmicity that typify the behaviors of an individual child independently of their content. Temperament refers only to the *how*, not the *why*, of behavior and implies neither immutability nor permanence.

Through inductive content analyses of the infant behavior protocols it was possible to characterize the individual behavior style of each child in the study in terms of nine categories of reactivity. These qualities, which were defined when the child was only two to three months of age, can also be identified at all subsequent age periods in infancy and childhood. The nine categories of reactivity in which temperamental attributes are subsumed are:

1. *Activity level:* the motor component present in a given child's functioning and the diurnal proportion of active and inactive periods. Protocol data on the child's motility when he is being bathed, fed, dressed, and handled, as well as information concerning his sleep-wake cycle and his reaching, crawling, walking, and play patterns are used in scoring this functional category.

2. *Rhythmicity (biological regularity):* the predictability and rhythmicity and/or the unpredictability and arrhythmicity in time of any function. This is analyzed in relation to the child's sleep-wake cycle, his hunger or feeding patterns, and his elimination schedule.

3. *Approach-withdrawal (positive-negative initial responses):* the nature of the child's initial response to a new or altered stimulus, be it a new food, a new toy, or a new person.

4. *Adaptability:* the nature of a child's responses to new or altered situations with respect to the ease with which they are modified in a desired direction, irrespective of the initial response.

5. *Intensity of reaction:* the energy level or vigor of a child's response, independent of its direction (either a negative or a positive response can be mild or intense). Responses to stimuli, to preelimination tension, to hunger, to repletion, to new foods, to attempts at control, to restraint, to dressing, and to diapering, all provide scorable items for this category.

6. *Threshold of responsiveness:* the intensity level of stimulation that is necessary to evoke a discernible response, without regard to the specific form that the response may take or the sensory modality affected. The behaviors used are responses to (a) sensory stimuli, (b) environmental objects, and (c) social contacts.

7. *Quality of mood:* the amount of pleased, joyful, and friendly versus the amount of displeased, crying, and unfriendly behavior is determined; i.e., does the child show more smiling and laughing or more fussing and crying behavior?

8. *Distractibility:* the ease with which a child can be diverted from an ongoing activity by extraneous peripheral stimuli.

9. *Attention span and persistence:* these two categories are related. Attention span is the length of time a particular activity is pursued by the child. Persistence refers to the continuation of an activity by the child in the face of obstacles to the maintenance of the activity direction.

Infant behavior records were obtained by scheduled interview of the parents of the 136 children in the study population every three months for the first year and every six months thereafter to obtain information on the details of the child's behavior in daily activities. Questions were designed to elicit noninterpretative descriptions of the child's actions, the stimuli evoking the described behaviors, and the full sequence of child-environment interaction to the conclusion of each such descriptive sequence. A sample of children was observed at home by two independent observers as a check on the accuracy of parental description.

In addition to gathering the infant records, we conducted parent interviews every six months until age five, and yearly thereafter, gaining anterospective information on the nature of the child's own individual characteristics of functioning as well as on parental attitudes and child care practices, and on special environmental events and the child's reaction to them.

Also, there have been standard test-play interviews at ages three and six, teacher interviews and direct observation of the child at home, in school, and during psychological testing. Whenever indicated, we have carried out special perceptual, psychological, and neurological testing. In each case of behavioral disturbance, we have done a systematic psychiatric evaluation and periodic clinical follow-up examination.

The data have been analyzed by both quantitative and qualitative methods. The composition of the sample and the techniques of data collection and data analysis have been described in detail in a number of previous publications (Birch et al., 1964; Chess et al., 1959; Chess et al., 1962; Chess et al., 1963; Chess et al., 1966; Chess, in press; Raph, 1965; Robbins, 1963; Terestman, 1964; Thomas et al., 1961; Thomas et al., 1963).

In the first two years of life there has been consistency in temperamental identification that satisfies statistical criteria. In the succeeding years one sees in some children the modification of temperamental scores as interaction with the environment progresses. These qualitatively described clusters of characteristics have been quantitatively confirmed by a factor analysis over the first five years of life in which significant clustering of the categories adaptability, approach-withdrawal, mood, and intensity was obtained in each year. Comparison of the scores of one year agrees closely with the year before and after but in some there is a drift making for changes, for example, between the scores of two and five.

CLUSTERS OF TEMPERAMENTAL STYLES

As a whole, the children have shown consistency over time in their characteristics of reactivity. While it was found that individual temperamental attributes were important, the greater impact was seen when one examined the clusters. Both in qualitative inspection of the data and also in factor analysis by computer techniques, it appeared that certain combinations often occurred together. As we followed the children and began to deal both with normal problems of everyday living and also with behavior disorders, these clusters were clearly of importance in understanding the interactions themselves and in supplying keys to effective intervention. There were three such groupings which came up so frequently that it seemed sensible to call them by everyday terms. They were, therefore, dubbed *the easy child, the difficult child*, and *the slow-to-warm-up child.*

In general, the largest single group of children can be characterized as exhibiting regularity of biological function, positive (approach) responses to new stimuli, easy adaptability to change, a preponderance of positive mood, and reactions of mild to moderate intensity. A child with such a constellation has been designated "the easy child." This child develops regular sleep and feeding schedules easily, takes to most new foods at once, smiles at strangers, adapts quickly to a new school, accepts most frustrations with a minimum of fuss, and learns new rules quickly. Parents, pediatricians, and teachers usually respond to him positively and not infrequently assume that his smooth development owes much to their expert handling. An occasional parent will worry that his child is so adaptable that he is "too easy going" or a "pushover."

The opposite temperamental type is also present, but in smaller numbers. Such a child shows irregularity in biological function, predominantly negative (withdrawal) responses to new stimuli, slow adaptability to change, frequent negative mood, and responses of high intensity. He is aptly designated "the difficult child." This child is not easy to feed, to put to sleep, to bathe, or to dress. New places, new activities, and strange faces may produce initial responses of loud protest or crying. Frustration often results in a tantrum. However, when these children finally adapt they often function easily, consistently, and even ebulliently. In the infant years it is the difficult child who has the most day-to-day potential for apparent malfunctions; certainly his behavior is more likely than that of the easy baby to reinforce self-doubts in the new mother and father. While the final adaptations of these youngsters may be excellent, the environmental handling is crucial in determining whether they are enabled to move, episode by episode, toward adaptive as opposed to maladaptive interactions.

Yet another temperamental type delineated by qualitative analysis combines negative responses of mild intensity to new stimuli with slow adaptability after repeated contact. An infant with these characteristics differs from a difficult child in that he withdraws from anything new quietly rather than loudly. In addition, he usually does not exhibit the intense reactions, frequent negative mood, and irregularity of biological function of the difficult infant. The infant's mildly expressed withdrawal from the new will occur with his first encounter with a food, a bath, or a stranger. When first given a new food, he will turn away quietly and let it dribble out of his mouth; when first put in the tub, he will lie quietly and fuss mildly; when introduced to a stranger, he will cling to his mother. Such a child will gradually come to show positive involvement and interest in new situations, if he is allowed to reexperience them frequently and without pressure.

This characteristic sequence of responses suggests "slow to warm up" as an apt if inelegant appellation for these children. Such quiet withdrawal does not have the same potential for evoking self-doubt in parents; nor is it as likely to potentiate a parental posture of "I'll show who is the boss around here." However, it can be quite a puzzle to decide when to shield the child from an experience and when it is appropriate to provide exposures so that the youngster can have his opportunity to become familiar and at ease. Equally important can be questions as to optimum pace of exposure.

There is no indication that the temperamental characteristics of these children—whether difficult, easy, or slow to warm up—are caused by the parents. However, the difficult child makes extra demands for handling that not infrequently stimulate reactions of resentment, guilt, or even helplessness in the parent. Other parents do not feel guilty or put upon by such a child's behavior and not uncommonly learn to enjoy the vigor, lustiness, and even "stubbornness" of a difficult child. The slow-to-warm-up child can make parents feel very much needed. But very shy behavior is sometimes interpreted to or by the parents as insecurity, with the finger of standard psychodynamic interpretation pointing directly at the mother as the culprit.

Our study of the pertinence of these temperamental characteristics has focused on each child's responses to child-care practices and to special environmental events such as the birth of a sibling, on his adaptation to school, and in greatest detail, on the factors involved in the origin and evolution of behavior problems. In each area, the outcome for any individual child was determined not by parental functioning and/or other environmental influences alone, nor by temperamental characteristics alone, but by the nature of the temperament-environment interactional process. In each instance, the influence of the parent could be understood only by a simultaneous consideration of the child's temperament, and the influence of temperament only by a simultaneous consideration of environmental factors. Each of these topics will be discussed.

Child-care practices have been an area of intense concern to professionals who are concerned with personality development. Direct analogies are often made between optimum physical care of infants as an aid in producing healthy bodies and optimum emotional care of infants as a creator of healthy personalities.

Despite numerous investigations, however, no one-to-one correlation has been found between specific parental child-care attitudes and practices and the course of a child's development (Bruch, 1954; Chess et al., 1959; Klatskin et al., 1956; Orlansky, 1949; Stevenson, 1957). Different children respond differently to the same parental approaches to feeding, sleeping, toilet training, or general discipline. Data from our longitudinal study indicate that differences in temperamental characteristics played a significant role in interaction with parental practices and other environmental influences in determining the course of the child's reactions to specific child-care practices, thus explaining the lack of one-to-one correlations in the above studies. This overall finding can be illustrated by some examples from our anterospective longitudinal records.

The parents of two infants in the group used a self-demand approach to feedings. The signal for prompt feeding was the child's cry, interpreted as a sign of hunger, when he awoke. None of the parents attempted to modify their child's spontaneous sleep-wake cycle. One child rapidly developed a four-hour feeding schedule, slept through the night by the time he was six weeks of age, and by six months had developed a routine of regular short-morning and long-afternoon naps. All of this was accomplished without any deliberate effort by his parents to structure his feeding and sleeping schedules. This baby had a regular biological clock. Self-demand feeding permitted the biological rhythmicity to demonstrate itself. He was a show case for self-demand feeding. However, this child could have been an equally fine proof of the excellence of scheduled feedings. He would have settled into the imposed four-hour schedule without difficulty, and the two daily naps that occurred spontaneously could just as easily have been imposed.

The second child, handled in a similar manner, woke and cried at irregular intervals varying from one to five hours. He was fed each time he awoke and his intake at each feeding varied greatly. By the time he was one year of age, his sleep cycle was still irregular and unpredictable as to frequency and duration. He might awaken several times a night or sleep through the night, take a daytime nap or refuse one.

The parents conscientiously attempted to follow the pediatrically advocated "demand feeding" approach, awaiting the promised arrival of spontaneous regularity and predictability. Since biological irregularity was characteristic of this baby, only an imposed regularity could have given the predictability seen in the first infant. From the point of view of healthy versus unhealthy physical or emotional development, neither behavior is superior. However, from the point of view of parental convenience and possible irritability with the child after several nights of broken sleep, the regular child is more desirable. In addition, broken sleep is often interpreted to parents as evidence of insecurity. A vicious cycle can easily be established: child's sleep irregular—parents awakened during night— parent irritability—child's reaction by showing apprehension regarding parental annoyance either through more frequent awakening or greater fussing when waking—parental guilt and greater solicitude leading to reinforcement of night awakening and/or greater parental annoyance—and round and round.

A third child, like the first, was highly regular and developed a predictable sleep pattern. At three months of age, however, he developed an upper respiratory infection which caused him to awaken crying several times a night for four nights. Each time he woke up he was comforted, given medication, and put back to sleep. After his recovery, his pattern of awakening at night and crying continued with the same timing as when he had been ill. The determining influence here was this infant's very high adaptability. He adapted to changes quickly and persisted in any new habituation until another environmental change stimulated another alteration in functioning. In fact, after the parents were reassured that the awakening represented only habituation, not need, the child was allowed to cry it out, and he very quickly resumed his previous pattern of sleeping through the night.

Another aspect of child-care practices in which temperamental individuality can demonstrate itself is weaning. The shift from breast or bottle to drinking from a receptacle is an occurrence of every culture and every century. The timing and the manner of weaning have varied from harsh to very permissive. In some cultures and epochs, weaning has, in fact, included general rejection of the child, whereas in other cultures the overall nurturing continues as before. Our study children were weaned in an era when 18 months was declared the proper starting age but continuing on the bottle until age two or three years was not frowned upon. Early weaning, that is before 18 months, was widely considered unwise and coercive.

Two examples involved the outcome of similar parental approaches to the weaning of 18-month-old children. Both sets of parents initiated weaning gradually. The first child quickly began to push away the bottle and reach for the cup. Although the parents had expected and planned that cup training would take much longer, within one week the youngster was completely weaned. The second child, on the other hand, when offered milk in a cup, pushed it away violently, arched his back and screamed until he was given his familiar bottle. This scene was repeated daily until the parents gave up and decided to wait six months because the child "wasn't ready." The same sequence was repeated when weaning was attempted at ages two and two-and-a-half years. Finally at three years, the parents persisted in their efforts. After a week, the child took tentative sips from the cup, and within several weeks he, too, was completely and contentedly weaned.

Again in this instance, temperamental characteristics played their part in determining the outcome of a child-care practice. The first child was highly adaptable and displayed positive approach responses to almost all new experiences and situations. The second child was very slowly adaptable and displayed predominantly negative withdrawal responses to new stimuli. Thus, the response of each child to weaning was typical of the differences in their reactions to almost all new situations.

In contrast, the mother of another "difficult child" had become used to the phenomenon of violent rejection of the new. In presenting her 18-month infant with the cup for the first time, she correctly and calmly expected him to flail his arms, shriek, and kick. For two weeks she continued to offer the cup at each feeding, then produced the bottle at his refusal. Finally he began to take sips from the cup, then gradually learned to drain it competently, and finally the bottle was no longer prepared for him. A month later he shrieked in protest as he shoved away the bottle offered on the sly by his compassionate grandmother. Once this slowly adaptive baby had become accustomed to the cup as his standard receptacle for milk, the bottle became the unfamiliar intruding stimulus to which he gave the full flavor of his intense negative response.

Similar examples could be cited with regard to other aspects of child-care practices, such as toilet training and discipline. It appeared throughout that differences in other temperamental characteristics, especially persistence, activity level, intensity, and quality of mood, as well as in the categories illustrated above, were relevant and influential in determining a child's reaction to overall training procedures. Thus, while the parental attitudes definitely do play a role in influencing the child's development, the child's individual temperament will significantly affect the direction of this influence.

The regular baby with low or moderate activity level is likely to respond quickly to toilet training unless he is slow to adapt and must first be given an opportunity to become accustomed to a potty chair itself. For the irregular baby it is not possible to be certain that the attempt at training will coincide with a spontaneous impulse to evacuate, hence sitting still time becomes longer. If this irregular baby is also highly active, he will protest against sitting still. If he is also a slow adapter, the likelihood is that the training will not take place speedily. It is in the latter situation that parents most need guidance in child care practices—with strategy based on knowledge of those features of the baby's temperamental individuality pertinent to the particular child care practice. Parents, of course, will handle the situation quite differently depending upon their own personalities; some may become locked in battle, some may defer the effort, some may start a very gradual plan to familiarize the child with the potty chair. Parents differ in their subjective reaction. Some feel the issue is of no great moment, others act as if their basic self-esteem depends on successful accomplishment; still others believe that the child's future personality will be determined by the way in which toilet training has proceeded.

The child's individual temperament also significantly affects general personality development. For example, two children whose mothers were pressuring and domineering in their approaches developed strong negativistic trends. However, a third child became acquiescent and even submissive to his mother's demands. The difference in great part lay in the temperamental differences between the children. The first two had negative, intense, and nonadaptive qualities whereas the third child was positive, mild, and adaptive.

TEMPERAMENT AND RESPONSE TO LIFE EVENTS

By the time the children were three years of age it was possible to examine their behavior in response to certain environmental events that are generally considered as important influences on child adaptation and personality. Specifically, the birth of a younger sibling and the return of a mother to work occurred in enough cases to permit us to observe variability of response to these events.

In the first 18 families in which a younger sibling was born during the study, we investigated the character and intensity of the older child's reaction. Over half of the 18 children showed disturbances at this event. The two main types of disturbance noted were: (1) reversion to more infantile patterns of functioning in socialization, sleeping, feeding, and toileting, and (2) aggressive behavior toward the new baby. In six cases the reactions were mild and transient, in one moderate and in three prolonged and severe. Three children showed no discernible disturbance in functioning and five actually showed an improvement in their social responses. Thus, children reacted with various degrees of positive and negative behavior to a new sibling.

Both environmental factors and the characteristics of primary reactivity in the individual child appear to contribute to variability of response to new children. The entry of a younger sibling into the family group necessarily affects the amount of time and attention given to the child by the mother and by other members of the household. Where this change in circumstances leads to disturbance in the child, the mother is objectively unable to modify the situation appreciably as she can for weaning or toilet training. It is of interest, therefore, that the intensity and duration of negative responses were greater in those who were themselves first children than in those who already had older siblings. For the only child, the entry of a new baby into the family group seemed to constitute a much greater environmental change. Age at the time of new births also influenced reactions. There was less disturbance in those children who were under 18 months of age when the new sibling was born. A third influential factor was the degree of prior paternal involvement. In several children whose fathers had been especially active in caring for them and whose fathers continued to do so even after the arrival of the new baby, the turning of the mother's attention to the younger sibling was not an especially disturbing event. In one family where both parents were very much involved with the first child, there was no reaction when the mother took care of the new baby, but the child, a boy in his third year, developed stuttering as soon as the father began to handle the baby. As soon as the father stopped this and devoted himself again to the older child, the stuttering stopped.

On the organismic side, qualitative analysis of the data has shown a definite relationship between the temperament of the child and the type of response to the birth of a sibling. Those children who from early infancy on showed mild, positive, regular responses with quick adaptability to new stimuli, such as the bath, change in sleep schedule, and the introduction of new foods, manifested a similar pattern with the new baby. In this group, disturbances were minimal or nonexistent. On the other hand, those children characterized by intense, negative, and irregular responses with slow adaptibility tended to show greater and more prolonged disturbances after the birth of a sibling.

We were also able to explore the effect on a child of mother's return to work. Six of the mothers returned to full-time professional work when the child was two to three months old. There was intense, prolonged disturbance in one child and none observable in the other five. The child who was upset had intense, irregular, negative and nonadaptive responses as the overall temperamental pattern. The other five, who were checked in the fourth year of life, showed no significant disturbance in functioning. The temperamental patterns of these children were of the regular, mild, positive, and adaptive type.

Adaptation to school showed a distinct relatedness to temperamental individuality among the study children. In the nursery age there was the usual wide diversity of the children's approach to this new situation, ranging from immediate enthusiastic interaction to intense withdrawal and clinging to mother. Those children who had been slow to adapt in their prior interactions carried this characteristic into nursery school. For those whose mood expression was mild, the solution was uncomplicated. Their participation in school increased with familiarity. The difficult child required greater tolerance, and during the stormy familiarization phase, there were pleas by nurseries that such children be given psychotherapy to eliminate anger and aggression. These difficult children adapted to nursery in accordance with their prior patterns of reaction to almost all new situations: food, people, and schedules. The degree to which a highly active child was identified as a problem appeared to depend on the amount of space provided for the child and whether he combined negative and intense qualities with his high activity.

Moving beyond infancy to the early grades of school, temperament also bore a relationship to successes and failures in learning. A striking example is provided by a child of very superior intelligence who had been placed by her first-grade teacher in an experimental accelerated program. The new teacher informed the child's mother in the second month of school that some error appeared to have been made, for the child was quite incapable of doing the work and never volunteered. This was a familiar picture. This youngster's typical early reaction in each new situation was to be a quiet observer. The teacher reluctantly yielded to the request that the child be retained in the class. Reassessment in the second half of the year showed not only that the child was grasping the work capably, but also that she was being selected by the teacher to help other children because of her patience and ability to explain things clearly. All temperamental qualities have an influence on school work, either enhancing or hindering. The effect of such qualities as distractibility and attention span is not difficult to predict. In all cases, it is not the temperament alone that determines the outcome, but the interaction between temperament and environment.

The reciprocal nature of child-parent interaction showed up with particular clarity when we examined the twins in our study. What has been noteworthy is the manner in which the child's temperamental characteristics have influenced the mother's attitudes. Where the child's qualities have made his care easy, the mother has often more quickly developed positive attitudes than in those cases where the child's temperament has made his care more difficult and time-consuming. This was especially highlighted in two families where twins showed definite differences in temperament from early infancy on. In each family, the mother started with the same attitude toward the two infants but progressively developed increasingly dissimilar responses to them as they grew older, in large part because of their temperamental differences. In three other families in which twins have similar qualities, this differentiation of the mother's attitude has not been evident.

TEMPERAMENT AND BEHAVIOR DISORDERS

The original impetus for the New York Longitudinal Study arose from a belief that both the development of well-functioning children and the psychodynamics of behavior disorder were insufficiently accounted for by current theories. As our study children moved from infancy into the demands of the preschool and school-age culture, behavior problems did emerge.

By 1966, 10 years after the beginning of the longitudinal study, 42 children had developed behavior problems of varying types, duration, and degrees of severity. This sample is of great interest since it may be argued that although other longitudinal studies (Kagan and Moss, 1962; Kris, 1957; MacFarlane et al., 1962; Murphy et al., 1962) have contributed to the understanding of the development of behavioral disturbances, the present study has fulfilled the criteria for a systematic analysis of the pathogenesis of behavior problems in childhood. These criteria include: (1) a body of anterospectively gathered longitudinal data that does not rely on retrospective parental report of a child's earlier development [this stricture is of great importance in the light of a number of studies revealing substantial inaccuracies and systematic distortions in such retrospective reports (Chess et al., 1966; Robbins, 1963; Wenar, 1963)]; (2) a total sample large enough to permit generalization of the findings; and (3) systematic clinical psychiatric evaluation of the children with behavior problems.

Detailed culling and analysis of the anterospective longitudinal data in each of the 42 cases clearly revealed the fundamental importance of the temperament-environment interactional process in the genesis of behavior problems. In several cases, special factors such as brain damage or physical abnormality also operated in interaction with temperament and environment to produce behavior problems. No single temperamental characteristic or combination of characteristics necessarily produced a behavior problem or made the child immune to one. Behavior problems, as well as the absence of behavior problems, were found among children with very different characteristics. However, in each case in which a behavior disturbance did develop, it was possible to define the etiological factors in the genesis and course of the problem in terms of the child's significant characteristics (temperament and other additional components such as brain damage or physical handicaps) and his specific interactive process with influential features of the environment (parental functioning and extra-familial circumstances, such as peer group and school). It should be emphasized that behavioral normality as well as disturbance depends upon this interaction between the child with his given temperament and characteristics and significant features of his developmental environment.

The findings also indicate that the environmental demands and expectations that are most stressful for a child bear a relationship to his temperamental characteristics. The parental or other environmental approaches that intensify such stressful demands to the point of symptom formation may be different for children of different temperaments. What may be pathogenic for one child may not be so for another. This interplay of factors at the core of a child's behavior problem can be distilled into three fundamental issues: (1) The child's individual temperamental pattern; (2) the environmental demands which are most stressful for children with this type of behavior style; and (3) the parental and/or environmental approaches that intensify such stressful demands to the point of symptom formation in the child.

The data have shown that several normal patterns of child temperament, while nonpathological in themselves, make a child vulnerable to destructive interaction with the environment and to the development of behavior problems. Recognition of this fact is crucial because correct identification of these temperamental patterns and appropriate handling of the child will minimize or even eliminate the development of behavior disorders.

An example of such a pattern is the highly active child whose activity is within physiologically normal limits and is not caused by any intrinsic pathology. Such a youngster encounters more restrictions, prohibitions, and expressions of disapproval than does a motorically quiet child who is less likely to expose himself to dangers or to annoy people around him. In an environment that does not provide for such a child's needs, normal behavior often becomes equivalent to misbehavior, and the youngster frequently develops patterns of ignoring prohibitions, of teasing, or of oppositional and negative interpersonal relationships.

The child who adapts slowly to new situations is also vulnerable to an unhealthy interaction with his environment. This youngster initially reacts to new situations and new demands by nonparticipation, be this quiet or noisy. He needs opportunities for multiple exposures to the new situation so that he may become familiar with it and ultimately form a constructive adaptive adjustment. If his parents remove him from new situations too quickly because of his initial discomfort, he may lose the opportunity to adapt and hence be prevented from developing a repertoire of familiar situations. When he eventually moves into more active child relationships, he may be under the double handicap of being a slow adapter and having had fewer experiences than his peers. Thus, he may become an actual outsider, and a vicious cycle of withdrawal, rejection, and unhappiness or of apprehensive and aggressive tantrum behavior may become the dominant pattern.

Stress may also develop for the slow-to-warm-up child when his parents or teachers insist on an immediate positive involvement with the new, something which is difficult or impossible for such a youngster. If the adult recognizes that the child's slow adaptation to a new experience reflects his normal temperamental style, one may expect patient encouragement. However, if the child's slow adaptability is interpreted as timidity or lack of interest and he is pressured into a fast warm-up, his normal withdrawal tendency may be intensified. And, if this increased holding back in turn stimulates increased impatience and pressure on the part of the parent or teacher, an unhealthy child-environment interactive process will be set in motion.

Difficult children, who in general show a significantly higher percentage of behavior problems (Rutter et al., 1964), typically exhibit disturbed reactions if the demands of socialization, particularly demands for altering spontaneous responses and patterns to conform to the rules of living of the family or the peer group, are presented inconsistently, impatiently, or punitively. In such cases, it becomes stressful or even impossible for the child to effect appropriate behavior changes. Negativism is a frequent outcome of such handling.

The easy child usually adapts to the demands of socialization with little or no stress. However, his very ease of adaptability may be the basis for the development of behavior problems, specifically when there is a severe dissonance between the expectations and demands of the intra- and extrafamilial environments. The child first adapts easily to the standards and behavioral expectations of his parents. But, when he moves into functional situations where expectations conflict with those he has learned at home and if environmental conditions impede a secondary adaptation, stress and malfunctioning will develop.

Such dissonance between intra- and extrafamilial demands may, of course, produce stress and disturbance in many types of children; but in our longitudinal study this pathogenic factor has been most apparent in easy children.

For the persistent child, stress is most likely to develop not with his initial contact with a situation, but rather when arbitrary or forcible attempts are made to remove him from an ongoing activity in which he is absorbed. In these instances, tension and frustration will develop in the persistent child and may reach explosive proportions.

Other temperamental type-specific sources of stress can be identified. These include unrealistic scheduling demands for a biologically irregular child and insistence on long uninterrupted concentration on a task for a highly distractible child.

It is of interest that in the three cases of brain damage in the study, the extent of behavioral dysfunction could not be understood solely in terms of the neurological findings, intellectual capacity, and parental functioning. However, a consideration of factors of temperament in interaction with these other influences made it possible to define more comprehensively the differences in course of behavioral development in each of these three children (Birch et al., 1964).

Clearly, this analysis of the ontogenesis of behavior problems in young children has not used prevailing concepts of anxiety, intrapsychic conflict, and psychodynamic defenses. Anxiety has not been found to be operative in the basic pathogenic process of maladaptive temperament-environment interactions. Rather it appears secondarily, in many cases, as one aspect of the child's response to the unfavorable and sometimes even threatening consequences of the initial maladaptive process. Psychodynamic defense mechanisms of an ideational character, such as denial, projection, or rationalization have also been notably absent in young children at an age where action and direct behavioral expression dominate the processes of psychological functioning. Such defense mechanisms do become evident at an older age when ideation, abstraction, and symbolic representation become increasingly prominent in the child's psychological organization. As to presumed intrapsychic conflict, the ability to account for the development of behavior problems in young children without invoking this or similar hypothetical constructs leads one to question the necessity of such formulations.

Other investigators have also been concerned with the contribution that the child's own characteristics make to normal and disturbed development. In a psychiatric study of children with poor school achievement, Ross (1966) suggests that the combination of high distractibility, short attention span, and low persistence in interaction with an over-permissive or disorganized environment may lead to a specific type of behavioral disturbance which he calls "the unorganized child." He also suggests that specific manifestations of this syndrome will depend upon whether the above temperamental qualities are combined with high or low activity level and intense or mild mood responses. It may very well be that further studies from those centers now utilizing the classification of temperament established by the New York Longitudinal Study will identify other significant clusters or new categories beyond those already delineated. Korner (1964) had postulated a number of behavioral variables in the neonate derived from her work and the work of other investigators, especially Wolff. As she herself points out, the task of demonstrating the pertinence of these factors for the child's psychological development still remains. The same issue of pertinence is involved in evaluating the interesting findings of individuality in autonomic reactivity of the neonate reported by a number of investigators (Bridger and Resier, 1959; Lipton et al., 1960).

The findings in our behavior problem cases suggest that we need to restructure traditional approaches to the diagnostic process in clinical child psychiatry (Chess, 1967). An infant with irregular sleep cycles who cries loudly at night may be responding to a hostile, rejecting mother, but he also may be expressing the typical behavioral characteristics of the difficult child. A child who stands at the periphery of a play group may be anxious and insecure, but he may also be expressing his normal slow-to-warm-up temperamental pattern. A mother's guilt and anxiety may be the result of a deep-seated neurosis, but it may also be the result of her problems and confusion in handling an infant with the temperamental constellation of a very difficult child.

In each of these examples, the appropriate therapeutic regime will depend upon which interpretation is the correct one. Awareness of the concept of behavioral style will help the psychiatrist avoid the error of assuming that all behavioral phenomena necessarily have a primarily psychodynamic basis. An accurate diagnostic judgment requires that data on the child's temperamental characteristics be gathered with the same care and regard for detail that are considered essential in the evaluation of parental attitudes and practices, family relationships, and sociocultural influences. By so doing and by carefully distinguishing between those undesirable characteristics which are largely psychodynamic in origin and therefore capable of basic change, and those attributes such as irregularity and withdrawal responses which are inherent temperamental qualities not readily subject to change, it becomes possible to advise parents as to the optimal approach to a child. Although the basic pattern may not be changed in the latter instance, the parents of such a child can be guided to understand their offspring so that their functioning is aimed at minimizing the undesirable behavior by channeling it as much as possible in a constructive direction.

For example, if the parents of a child who tends to retreat initially from new experiences with an intense expression of negative mood can be made aware that this behavior is not a result of motivated negativism, underlying insecurity, or psychodynamically initiated hostility, they themselves can better maintain objectivity and consistency in their handling of the reaction. If they anticipate that the child will have a tantrum in each new situation but realize that it will eventually wear itself out and be replaced by tentative positive overtures, they can learn to wait out each storm patiently and without complicating it by their own subjective reactions. On the other hand, if they react each time with anger and attempt to pressure the child into premature contact or try to persuade him to express a positive mood from the beginning, they may precipitate a defensive negativism and hostility which will create actual anticipatory insecurity for the child each time he approaches a new experience. With patient, consistent handling, however, such a child eventually can learn that his initial disturbance in the face of new experiences will pass with time, and he will then be able to explore the situation with ease and even with pleasure.

CONCLUSIONS

In the past few years the literature on child development and psychiatry has shown an increasing awareness of the significance of individual differences of an organismic character. This no doubt reflects the beginning of a widespread recognition that a child's development cannot be adequately understood by unilateral consideration of parental influences (Beiser, 1964) and that consideration of the influence of the child's individuality is also required. Despite this increasing agreement that children, indeed, are initially different, certain current formulations continue to avoid the implications of this fact. Typical of such formulations is the following statement, "It would seem fairly obvious . . . that infants come into the world with different constitutional dispositions and that parents need to take these differences into account. More fundamental, however, is the question of why many parents cannot intuitively understand their children's differences. Above and beyond that is the fact that some people will not be good parents to any child, regardless of his constitutional disposition" (Finch, 1966).

First, if contemporary work on temperamental individuality merely indicated that infants had "different constitutional dispositions" it would indeed not be new but represent a restatement of a prejudice held by many thinkers since antiquity. What is new is not the knowledge that children differ but knowledge of how they differ and how these differences in temperamental organization are continually expressed as a significant determinative factor in psychological growth. What is new, then, is that temperament has its own dynamics which contribute to developmental interactions.

Furthermore, there is no good reason for assuming in advance that the characteristics of temperamental individuality are less fundamental and parents' ability to understand them intuitively or otherwise "more fundamental." The establishment of such an a priori hierarchy is indicative of a failure to consider seriously the changes in older conceptualizations that new knowledge demands. What is needed is not the absorption of new ideas by old ones but a recognition of the independent contributions to the interactive process that are made by parent and by child. Only such serious consideration of individuality can, in the long run, lead to a sound rather than a presumptive basis for the assignment of relative fundamental value.

Finally, the phrase "some people will not be good parents to any child, regardless of his constitutional disposition," though an obvious half-truth, is explicit in its one-sidedness. To have contemporary meaning, it must be supplemented by the understanding that some children have characteristics which make it extremely difficult or, in some cases, virtually impossible for parents, no matter how "good," to function in such a way as to guarantee an easy, smooth developmental course.

The new data on the role of temperamental individuality in development cannot be of profit to psychiatry with this type of acceptance. What is needed is their full incorporation into the body of concepts, diagnostic procedures, and therapeutic activities as a co-equal with other dynamic aspects of developmental influences.

REFERENCES

Alpert, A., Neubauer, P. B., and Weil, A. P. (1956). Unusual variations in drive endowment. *Psychoan. Study of the Child*, 2, 125.

Beiser, H. R. (1964). Discrepancies in the symptomatology of parents and children. *Journal of the American Academy of Child Psychiatry*, 3, 457.

Birch, H. G., Thomas, A., and Chess, S. (1964). Behavioral development in brain damaged children. *Archives of General Psychiatry*, 1, 6.

Bridger, W. and Resier, M. (1959). Psychophysiologic studies of the neonate. *Psychosom. Med.*, 21, 265.

Bruch, H. (1954). Parent education or the illusion of omnipotence. *Amer. J. Orthopsychiatry*, 24, 723-732.

Chess, S., Thomas, A., and Birch, H. G. (1967). Behavior problems revisited: findings of an anterospective study. *Journal of the American Academy of Child Psychiatry*, 6, 321-331.

Chess, S., Thomas, A., and Birch, H. G. (1959). Characteristics of the individual child's behavioral responses to the environment. *Am. J. Orthopsy.*, **29**, 791.

Chess, S., Thomas, A., and Birch, H. G. (1966). Distortions in developmental reporting made by parents of behaviorally disturbed children. *J. Am. Acad. of Child Psychiat.*, **5**, 226-234.

Chess, S., Thomas, A., Rutter, M., and Birch, H. G. (1963). Interaction of temperament and environment in the production of behavior disturbances in children. *Am. J. Psychiat.* **20**, 142.

Chess, S., Hertzig, M., Birch, H. G., and Thomas, A. (1962). Methodology of a study of adaptive functions of the preschool child. *J. Am. Acad. Child Psychiat.* **1**, 236.

Chess, S., Thomas, A., and Birch, H. G. (1968). *Temperament and behavior disorders.* New York: Brunner and Mazel.

Escalona, S. and Letch, M., et al. (1952). Early phases of personality development. *Monograph Soc. Res. Child Development,* **17**, Number 1.

Finch, S. (1966). Book review of *your child is a person. American J. Psych.* **122**, 955.

Fries, M. E. and Woolf, P. J. (1953). Some hypotheses on the role of the congenital activity type in personality development. *Psychoan. Study of the Child,* **8**, 48.

Freud, S. (1950). *Collected papers.* London: The Hogarth Press Ltd., Vol. II. P. 226.

Gesell, A. and Ames, L. B. (1947). Early evidences of individuality in the human infant. *J. Genetic Psychol.* **47**, 339.

Kagan, J. and Moss, H. A. (1962). *Birth to maturity.* New York: Wiley.

Klatskin, E. H., Jackson, E. B., and Wilkin, L. C. (1956). The influence of degree of flexibility in maternal child care practices on early child behavior. *Am. J. Orthopsychiat.* **26**, 79-93.

Korner, A. F. (1964). Some hypotheses regarding the significance of individual differences in birth for later development. *Psychoan. Study of the Child,* **19**, 58.

Kris, M. (1957). The use of prediction in a longitudinal study. *Psychoanal. Study of the Child,* **12**, 175.

Lipton, E. I., Steinschneider, A., and Richmond, J. B. (1960). Autonomic function in the neonate. *Psychosom. Med.* **22**, 57.

MacFarlane, J. W., Allen, L., and Honzik, M. P., (1962). *A developmental study of the behavior problems of normal children between 24 months and 14 years.* Berkeley: University of California Press.

Mirsky, I. A. (1953). Psychoanalysis and the biological sciences. In *20 years of psychoanalysis,* F. Alexander and H. Ross (Eds.). New York: Norton. Pp. 155-176.

Murphy, L. B., et al. (1962). *The widening world of childhood.* New York: Basic Books.

Murphy, L.B. (1957). Psychoanalysis and child behavior. *Bulletin of the Menninger Clinic* **21**, 177.

Orlansky, H. (1949). Infant care and personality. *Psychol. Bull.* **46**, 1.

Raph, J. (1965). Social functioning in young children. Presented at the Annual Meeting of the *Am. Ortho. Assn.,* New York City.

Ritvo, S. and Solnit, A. J. (1958). Influences of early mother-child interaction on identification processes. *Psychoan. Study of the Child,* **13**, 64.

Robbins, L. D. (1963). The accuracy of parental recall of aspects of child development and of child rearing practices. *J. Abnorm. Soc. Psychol.,* **66**, 261.

Ross, D. C. (1966). Poor school achievement: A psychiatric study and classification. *Clinical Ped.* **5**, 109.

Rutter, M., Birch, H. G., Thomas, A., and Chess, S. (1964). Temperamental characteristics in infancy and the later development of behavior disorders. *Brit. J. Psychiat.* **110**, 651.

Shirley, M. M. (1931 and 1933). *The first two years: A study of 25 babies.* Minneapolis: University of Minnesota Press.

Stevenson, I. (1957). Is the human personality more plastic in infancy and childhood? *Am. J. Psychiat.* **144**, 152.

Terestman, N. (1964). Consistency and change in mood quality and intensity studied as aspects of temperament in preschool children. Ph.D. thesis, New York School of Social Work, Columbia University.

Thomas, A., Birch, H. G., Chess, S., Hertzig, M. E., and Korn, S. (1963). *Behavioral individuality in early childhood.* New York: New York University Press.

Thomas, A., Birch, H. G., Chess, S., and Robbins, L. (1961). Individuality in responses of children to similar environmental situations. *Am. J. of Psych.,* **117**, 798.

Thomas, A., Chess, S., Birch, H. G., and Hertzig, M. (1960). A longitudinal study of primary reaction patterns in children. *Compreh. Psych.,* **1**, 103.

Walter, W. Gray (1953). Electroencephalographic development of children. In *Discussion on child development,* Vol. 1, J. M. Tanner and B. Inhelder (Eds.). New York: International Universities Press. Pp. 132-160.

Wenar, C. (1963). The reliability of developmental histories. *Psychosom. Med.* **25**, 505.

Williams, R. V. (1956). *Biochemical individuality.* New York: Wiley.

Witmer, H. L., and Kotinsky, R. (Eds.) (1952). Personality in the making. In *Fact finding report of Mid-Century White House Conference on Children and Youth.* New York: Harper and Brothers. P. 35.

CHAPTER 6

Cognitive Structure in Latency Behavior

David Elkind

One of Jean Piaget's most important contributions to psychology is his description of the development of cognitive structures in children. Like the mental apparatuses described by Freud, the cognitive structures detailed by Piaget provide us with powerful tools for the analysis of behavior and experience at all levels of development. Elsewhere (Elkind, 1967) I have tried to show how consideration of the cognitive structures of adolescence (the formal operations) amplifies and complements the dynamic interpretation of adolescent phenomena. In this chapter, I will attempt to do the same for the cognitive structures (the concrete operations) which dominate thought and action during the age span which dynamic psychology defines as the latency period (roughly the years from 7 to 11). By further definition of the commonly shared characteristics of this developmental stage perhaps we can establish a framework for assaying individual variations.

Before proceeding, however, some preliminary remarks about cognitive growth in general are in order. At each stage of mental development described by Piaget (1950) we can detect two related phenomena. On the one hand, we can observe the many intellectual accomplishments that derive from the new mental system that has just been attained. On the other hand, we can also observe the many new intellectual quandaries produced by this same mental system. That is, mental growth proceeds in a dialectic fashion such that the new mental structures which appear at a particular age level serve to resolve the intellectual dilemmas encountered at the previous stage but at the same time serve to create new dilemmas that will only be overcome at the next developmental level.

This general developmental principle holds true for the cognitive structures dominant during the latency period. The concrete operations which usually emerge at about the age of six or seven make possible truly remarkable intellectual attainments. At the same time, however, these operations also give rise to new forms of egocentric (undifferentiated) behavior characteristic of this period. In discussing the role of cognitive structures in latency behavior, therefore, I want to deal first with the consequences attributable to the new mental attainments of the period and then with those consequences attributable to concrete operational egocentrism. More attention will be paid to the egocentrism of this period than to the positive accomplishments which are generally more well known.

LATENCY BEHAVIOR ATTRIBUTABLE TO CONCRETE OPERATIONS

The age of six to seven years has long been regarded as the "age of reason" and Piaget's (1950) work on children's thinking has shown that this label was well chosen. It is only at about elementary-school age that children manifest the ability to move from premise to conclusion in their arguments, to nest smaller class concepts within larger class concepts and to perform elementary arithmetical operations such as addition and subtraction. Moreover, as a consequence of concrete operations, children gradually come to appreciate, among other things, clock, calendar, and historical time, Euclidian, geographical, and celestial space, and the distinction between physical and psychological causality.

For our purposes, however, the latency-age child's attainments in the field of interpersonal communication and relations are of primary importance. Among these attainments, three are of particular note. First, the child at this stage can take another person's point of view and engage in true communication, with give and take about a particular subject. Second, the child at this level is capable of comparing what he hears and sees with what he knows and is, therefore, able to make judgments regarding truth and falsehood and regarding reality and appearance. Third, the latency-age child is now able not only to reason from premise to conclusion but also from general to particular instance so that he can now operate according to rules.

The ability to understand another person's point of view and to engage in true communication makes possible the child's assimilation within the peer culture. Assimilation within this peer culture is facilitated by the existence of a large body of language and lore (which has been abundantly described by such writers as Opie and Opie, 1959, and others) which provides the child with modes of peer interaction such as jokes, jeers, taunts, superstition, quasi beliefs, ritual, and so on. Adults, in effect, never teach children how to relate to peers and since these modes of interaction are not innate they must be acquired. The language and lore of childhood fulfills this function. Much of this language and lore is in the form of simple couplets such as

"Roses are red
Violets are blue
Onions smell
And so do you"

which resemble the syllogism and provide the child with material upon which to practice his budding reasoning abilities.

Coupled with this assimilation to the peer culture is a new estrangement from forms of fantasy material which is attributable to the child's ability to compare what he knows with what he hears and sees. Among other things, his new understanding of the difference between the real and the apparent brings about the deduction that there is no Santa Claus and no such thing as fairies, giants, and the like. The latency-age child may still enjoy such fictions but he makes it known that he is well aware that they are not real and are merely make believe.

Finally, the child's new ability to behave according to rules makes it possible for him to engage in organized play and to profit from formal instruction. With respect to play behavior, the child of elementary-school age gets interested in every game from tic-tac-toe to chess. While initially he may have trouble learning and following the rules, the significant accomplishment of the period is his new recognition that the game must be played according to certain regulations. The ability to profit from formal instruction rests upon the same accomplishment. All formal education involves the transmission of rules whether these are the rules of phonics, grammar, or arithmetic. Concrete operational thought is a necessary prerequisite to formal education because it makes possible the comprehension of rules upon which all formal education is based.

These are but a few of the many new attainments of the concrete operational period. Perhaps these examples will nonetheless suffice to illustrate the extent to which the system of concrete operations brings the latency-age child closer to the intellectual level of adolescents and adults. Let us turn now to the more negative consequences of concrete operation and consider the unique form of egocentrism generated by these operations and some of its consequences.

LATENCY BEHAVIOR ATTRIBUTABLE TO EGOCENTRISM

In the most general sense, egocentrism refers to a lack of differentiation in some sphere of subject-object interaction. In the case of the latency-age child this lack of differentiation derives directly from his new-found ability—thanks to concrete operations—to reason from assumptions and hypotheses. In the course of such reasoning the child often fails to distinguish between his hypotheses and assumptions on the one hand and empirical evidence on the other. It is this lack of differentiation between assumption and fact that constitutes the egocentrism of the concrete operational period.

This form of egocentrism has been clearly demonstrated in several research studies. An English investigator, Peel (1960), read children and adolescents a paragraph about Stonehenge which described the structures in general terms and without identifying their function. The subjects were then asked whether the stones were arranged as a fort or as a religious shrine. Replies of children (age nine years) were fairly uniform in nature. They chose one bit of information and made their judgment on that basis. When they were given additional, contradictory data, they rationalized the facts to fit their original hypothesis. Adolescents, in contrast, behaved quite differently. In the first place, they made their initial judgments on the basis of many different facts rather than upon a single datum. Secondly, when they were given additional information that contradicted their hypotheses they were quite willing to adopt a different hypothesis consistent with all the data available.

Similar findings were reported by Weir (1964), who used a quite different approach. In his studies Weir used a simple probability learning task. Subjects, ranging in age from 4 to 17 years, were confronted with a box containing three knobs and a payoff chute. The knobs were programmed so that one of them would pay off (in candy or tokens) 66% of the time, another was programmed to pay off 33% of the time, and a third knob paid off 0% of the time. The task was to find the maximal payoff strategy in the system and the maximizing solution was simply to keep pushing the knob that paid off 66% of the time.

Results showed that preoperational children maximized early (when it comes to candy young children learn quickly!). Adolescents had somewhat more trouble. They invented a wide range of hypotheses regarding the patterns and sequences of knob pressing to attain maximization. After trying and rejecting these hypotheses they eventually discovered that one knob was more likely to pay off than others and finally reverted to pressing the 66% knob all of the time. Latency-age children (7-10 years), however, had considerable difficulty with the problem. They often adopted a "win stick" and "lose shift" strategy in which they persisted despite all the evidence that this was not a maximizing procedure. These children were likely to blame the machine rather than their strategy for their difficulty.

The failure to distinguish between hypotheses and reality means in effect that the child often treats hypotheses as if they were facts and facts as if they were hypotheses. That is to say, ordinarily we test hypotheses against evidence, and if the evidence contradicts the hypotheses we reject it and try another. Children, in contrast, often reject or reinterpret facts to fit the hypotheses. As a consequence such youngsters often operate according to what might be called *assumptive realities*, assumptions about reality that children make on the basis of limited information and which they will not alter in the face of new and contradictory evidence. Although assumptive realities have something in common with delusions, in the sense that both involve a failure to distinguish between thought and reality, assumptive realities derive, at least originally, from new cognitive abilities and lack the systematization and narcissism of true delusions. Moreover the assumptive behavior engaged in by children is often entered into in the spirit of "fun" or "play" which suggests that at some level of consciousness the child is aware that he is operating according to a convenient fiction.

Perhaps the most pervasive assumptive reality of latency has its origins in the child's ability to detect flaws in reasoning and errors in supposed statements of fact. Concrete operations insure that the child will discover that his parents are not after all omniscient. This discovery was sensitively described by Edmund Gosse (1909, pp. 33-34):

> My mother always deferred to my father and in his absence spoke of him to me as if he were all wise. I confused him in some sense with God; at all events I believed that my father knew everything and saw everything. One morning in my sixth year, my mother and I were alone in the morning room, when my father came in and announced some fact to us. I was standing on the rug, gazing at him, and when he made this statement, I remember turning quickly, in embarrass-ment and looking into the fire. The shock to me was as that of a thunderbolt for what my father said *was not true.* . . . . Here was the appalling discovery, never suspected before, that my father was not as God and did not know everything. The shock was not caused by any suspicion that he was not telling the truth, as it appeared to him, but by the awful proof that he was not, as I had supposed, omniscient.

This discovery, which is inevitably made by all children, is the basis for two complementary assumptive realities that pervade the latency period. One of these is that adults are, to put it gently, not very bright. Again Gosse (p. 36) insightfully records the formation of this cognition:

> The theory that my father was omniscient or infallible was now dead and buried. He probably knew very little; in this case he had not known a fact of such importance that if you did not know that, it could hardly matter what you knew.

The complementary assumptive reality, also suggested by this passage, derives from the child's discovery that he, in some instances at least, knows more than the parents. In effect, the child assumes, as Gosse suggests, that if the adult is wrong in one thing then he must be wrong in nearly everything. Moreover, he also assumes that he himself, since he is right in one thing, must be correct in most things. This assumption is abetted by the fact that the child is often unaware of the origin of his knowledge and believes that he comes by it himself (Piaget, 1929). We might call this complex of assumptive realities involving the conception of the adult as none too bright and the child as clever, *cognitive conceit.* *

Although cognitive conceit is not a very overt psychic formation in children, it is an underlying orientation which is easily brought to the fore and helps to account, in part at least, for many different facets of latency behavior. Let us look now at some latency phenomena from the standpoint of cognitive conceit.

Consider first the Peter Pan fantasy (the wish to remain a child) that derives from the antipathy many latency-age children feel towards the prospect of growing up. To be sure, children are ambivalent and still want many of the prerogatives of older children and grownups. Yet, since adults are not very bright and are easily outwitted, as Peter Pan showed in his use of the alarm clock to best Captain Hook, the latency-age child has real qualms about growing up. That is to say, the latency-age child may suspect that he will become stupid as he matures and be reluctant to give up his cognitive conceit. His perception of adults as hairy and smelly does not increase his enthusiasm in this regard. While I would not want to deny the dynamic reasons for the child's wish to remain a child, the cognitive factors may well be an equally potent factor in the Peter Pan fantasy.

In addition to the Peter Pan fantasy, children's literature abounds in evidence of the cognitive conceit of children. Whether it is *Emile and the Detectives* or *Tom Sawyer* or *A High Wind in Jamaica* or *Alice in Wonderland*, in each story adults are outwitted and made to look like fools by children. Indeed I would not be surprised if young people regard Winnie the Pooh (that bear of little brain) as the essence of adult bumbling while they themselves identify with the superbly cool and clever, Christopher Robin. (Captain Kangaroo, by the way, is always outwitted by the bunny just as Tom is always outwitted by Jerry in the cartoons.) Children enjoy such fiction at least in part because it reinforces their cognitive conceit with respect to adults.

The well-known foundling fantasy (Lehrman, 1927) could be interpreted as still another manifestation of cognitive conceit. In its most usual form, the foundling fantasy involves the belief that one has been adopted and that one's real parents are in fact wealthy and of royal descent. Clearly this fantasy derives from a sensed discrepancy on the part of the child in the comparison between his parents and himself. The area in which this sensed discrepancy is most likely to occur (as the quotation from Gosse suggests) is in the realm of mental ability and knowledge. Again I do not want to deny the dynamic significance of the

---

*Some children, however, who continually meet failure and never give up their belief in the omniscience of parents develop a different assumptive reality "cognitive ineptitude," a sense of being duller than adults and other children.

foundling fantasy but only wish to insist upon taking into account its, at least partial, cognitive origin.

A similar case could be made for children's jokes which have been so ably described by Wolfenstein (1954). A typical joke of this age period is of the following variety: A mother loses her child named "Heine". She asks a policeman, "Have you seen my Heine?" to which the policeman replies "No, but I sure would like to!" Another variant might be as follows: A woman owns a dog named "Free Show." While the woman is taking a bath, the dog gets out of the house. The woman discovers this and runs out of the house naked shouting "Free Show—Free Show."

One would, I think, be hard put to deny the hostile and sexual aspects of these stories. Note, however, that the joke also depends upon the gullibility and stupidity of the adult, namely, that the mother in the first story would not know the meaning of "Heine" or that the woman in the second story would be stupid enough to run out into the street naked shouting "Free Show." Such jokes recapture the situation in which the parent is discovered not to be omniscient and in which the child knows more than the parent. Accordingly, such jokes also derive some of their impact from the reinforcement they provide for the child's cognitive conceit.

Still other evidence for the pervasiveness of cognitive conceit in children comes from the parodies of adult manners and morals which are an integral component of child language and lore. Children make fun of much that adults regard as serious and even sacred. For example,

> Jesus lover of my soul
> Lead me to the sugar bowl
> If the sugar bowl is empty
> Lead me to my mother's pantry

Even before the formal abdication of the Duke of Windsor, English children were singing

> Hark the Herald angels sing
> Mrs. Simpson's swiped our King

Several years ago, our six-year old came home chanting

> Jingle bells, jingle bells
> Wallace smells and Humphrey ran away
> Oh what fun it is to run
> In a Nixon Cheverolet

Such parodies reflect, among other things, the child's amused attitude at the sorts of things grown-up people regard as serious and important.

Similarly, a good deal of juvenile sophistry also reflects cognitive conceit. The strategy is to hoist the adult on his own petard. A case in point is the eight-year-old boy who came to the dinner table with his hands dripping wet. When his mother asked why he had not wiped his hands he replied, "But you told me not to wipe my dirty hands on the clean towels." Children delight in such sophistries both because they reaffirm cognitive conceit and because they provide good practice material for their new reasoning abilities. While juvenile sophistry is clearly a passive-aggressive maneuver, its dependence upon cognitive structure and the satisfaction it provides for cognitive needs should not be ignored.

A more far-reaching consequence of cognitive conceit can be observed in children's moral behavior. While it is true that by the age of six to seven years children have internalized rules and know what is right and wrong, they nonetheless continue throughout most of latency to take what does not belong to them and to deviate from the truth. A possible reason for this discrepancy between what the child knows and what he does is that he perceives the rules as coming from adults. While the child has respect for adult authority (the power to punish) he has little respect for adult intelligence. He thus sees no reason, other than fear of punishment, to obey rules adults have laid down. Accordingly, convinced as he is of his own intellectual superiority, the child takes the rules as a challenge to his own cleverness and attempts to break them without getting caught. For the child, breaking rules is not primarily a moral matter but much more a matter of proving his cleverness by outwitting adults.

With regard to moral behavior, then, we might speak of an *external conscience* operative during the elementary-school years. It is external in the sense that the child views the rules and the reasons for obeying them as residing outside rather than within himself. Jiminey Cricket, for example, is Pinocchio's external conscience and Pinocchio's cavalier relationship to Jiminey nicely reflects the child's attitudes towards a conscience imposed by adults. It is only toward the end of childhood and the onset of adolescence, when young people formulate their own rules, that these rules begin to internally regulate behavior. The asceticism, the physical regimes of adolescents, as well as their rigidly maintained group mores demonstrate how binding are those rules which the young person formulates himself or accepts on the basis of personal commitment. At adolescence, then, a true conscience begins to be formed whereas during childhood conscience is still external to the child's personal values and beliefs.

As a final example, I would like to show how cognitive conceit operates in one major form of latency behavior, namely, children's games. Concrete operations make it possible for children to play games with rules, a type of play not known in preschool children. When latency-age children play games with rules they play with one aim in mind—to win. This is particularly true when they are playing a child's game with an adult, but it is also true, to a lesser extent, when children play among themselves.

Now the desire to win could be said to derive, in part at any rate, from cognitive conceit—the child's belief in his own cleverness and his need to prove it. Obviously competitiveness has other dynamics as well, but the need to win can also reflect a desire to reassert the child's conception of himself as superior in knowledge and in ability. This is obvious in the way the children often boast when they win. The assumptive reality aspect of cognitive conceit becomes manifest when the child loses. In this event, the child will often overtly or covertly find reasons why he lost and why he will win in the future. Often the reasons are at best gratuitous and ad hoc but serve nonetheless to maintain the assumption of intellectual superiority.

An assumptive reality related to cognitive conceit is the belief that adults are benevolent and well intentioned. The child usually has some evidence to support this assumption but he also tends to deny or distort evidence to the contrary. The assumptive reality of the "good parent" may also help to account for the difficulty one finds in getting disturbed (as well as normal) children to say anything negative about their parents in a therapeutic situation. This is true even when it is clear, from other information, that the child has plenty to be unhappy about.

Here is a clinical example provided by Woltmann (1964, p. 360) in which the attempts to maintain the assumptive reality of parental "goodness" are exaggerated:

One eight year old boy showed a great deal of preoccupation with the figure of what he called "a good man." First he referred to a piece of clay as a house and said that a good man lived in the house selling vegetables then he changed the story and said that the house was full of candy and that all the candy belonged to a man inside the house. Finally, he made a clay face of a man which he covered completely with bits of clay. He said, "The man is good because his whole face is covered with candy." The boy came from a broken home which the father had deserted. His preoccupation with the good man obviously was an attempt to create an ideal image of the father figure and the wish to have the father come back. It also turned out that this boy, who could not accept the harsh reality of the irresponsible father, had to convince himself over and over again that there was such a thing as a good father.

Clearly there is, among other things, denial operating here, but denial might be defined as the tendency to cling to a hypothesis or assumption which is contradicted by the facts and to reinterpret the data to fit the hypothesis.

The child's conviction of the benevolence of parents and adults provides a healthy balance to cognitive conceit. A conviction regarding adult good intentions tempers and mellows the child's eagerness to outwit the adult and to make him appear foolish. If it were not for this assumptive reality with regard to adults, the latency child would be much more difficult to live with than is usually the case.

Assumptive realities can also be more temporary and arise in particular situations. This frequently occurs when the child does something he knows to be wrong. Although the child may be aware that he has committed a wrong he may also make some assumption about his behavior that excuses or exonerates his act so that he feels genuinely innocent. When he denies the action on the basis of this assumptive reality he is more than likely to infuriate the adult. Many toe-to-toe shouting matches between parent and child follow upon the child's denial of guilt and the parent's adamant demand that the child confess his misdeed. At such times the parent fails to appreciate that for the child an assumptive reality is the *truth*.

It might be noted in passing that some rigidities that workers like Wertheimer (1959) have noted in the thinking of school children may result from assumptive realities. In math, for example, children often learn a rule and assume that this applies to all figures or problems. At least some intellectual difficulties encountered by latency-age children may, in part, be explained by this tendency to take a rule or conviction as a self-evident reality which must be applied to all and sundry situations. It might be, for example, that some so-called "learning blocks" are exaggerations of a "normal" cognitive formation that has become exaggerated and exacerbated because of emotional problems.

The assumptive realities which derive from the egocentrism of the latency-age child also help to account for the unique character of play, fantasy, and imagination during this period. Although children have given up the fairy-tale type fantasy and are geared to finding out about the real world, they often approach this reality in an assumptive way. Davidson and Fay (1964, p. 402) nicely illustrate how assumptive realities emerge in the play of latency-age children and the tenacity with which these children cling to assumptions about reality despite the arguments and evidence offered by adults to dissuade them:

> Many of the interests of seven to eleven year old children, although strongly tied to reality can be seen to be deeply rooted in fantasy. For instance, Paul, eight, would periodically spend days digging in the yard to find buried treasure—"jewels" and "olden day things." He dug up several pieces of china which he carefully washed and tried to fit together, convinced that they were fragments of ancient pottery and probably of great value.

Whether young people are digging for treasure, building a fort, or planning a money-making project, they often persist despite the cautions and evidences to the contrary given by adults. Cognitive conceit is but one of the assumptive realities operative in such situations.

It should be said, too, that the egocentrism of this period probably also plays a part in the latency-aged child's love of mystery, adventure, and magic.

Assumptive realities presuppose a particular view of the world in which facts can be made to do your bidding and hence have something flexible and uncertain but controllable about them. Children like stories of mystery, adventure, and magic because these stories also presuppose a world in which new and unexpected events repeatedly occur but are always susceptible to mastery. The success of the Nancy Drew as well as the "Hardy Boys" series is ample testimony that girls as well as boys perceive the world in this way.

Before closing it is perhaps well to make clear that although the child believes in and acts upon cognitive conceit and assumptive realities, he also operates at a more concrete practical level of reality. Just as primitive man prayed for rain but also irrigated his fields, so children believe in their intellectual superiority while frequently behaving as if adults were wiser and more knowledgeable. Stated differently, at the practical level, the child often accepts the adult's greater knowledge and ability while he continues to deny it in the plane of cognition. The same holds true for assumptive realities. At the practical level, for example, a child may know that his father is mean and that he had better keep out of his way, while on the cognitive plane he maintains the assumption of parental benevolence.

It is only in adolescence, with the advent of formal operations, that these two planes of action and thought are brought into coordination. With formal operations, the young person can conceptualize his own thought and discover the arbitrariness of his hypothesis. He discovers, too, the rules for testing hypotheses against facts and hence is now able to deal with facts and hypotheses in an experimental fashion. This leads to the recognition that many of his hypotheses are wrong and gives him a new respect for facts. He then begins to be self-critical so that cognitive conceit is given up as is the tendency to operate according to assumptive realities.

CONCLUSIONS

In concluding this general discussion of cognitive structure and latency behavior, I would like to stress two general points. The first concerns the permanence of the mental formations attributable to concrete operations and the second has to do with the relation of the interpretations made here to those offered by dynamic psychology and psychiatry.

As in the case of most developmental phenomena, formations that appear at one level of development do not disappear at the following stages and may manifest themselves at each succeeding stage in the life cycle. This appears to hold true for the assumptive realities in general, and for the cognitive conceit and external conscience in particular, that emerge during the concrete operational period.

Evidence of adult behavior governed by assumptive realities in general is easy to come by. Indeed, the old saying, "love is blind" captures very well the fact that under some circumstances an individual may adopt an hypothesis and cling to it regardless of factual evidence to the contrary. Similarly, the romantic image of love and marriage held by so many young women in our society, despite all of the everyday evidence which gainsays this image, is a good example of how even young adults can believe in and behave according to assumptive realities.

With regard to cognitive conceit, we are all familiar with the young scholar who attacks a major figure, such as Freud or Piaget, on some minor point and then proceeds to dismiss the whole body of the master's work. At the same time, having found the real or imagined error, the young scholar is convinced of his own intellectual superiority. This is cognitive conceit at the adult level repeated with a parent-like figure. Behavior regulated by external conscience is also easy to discern among adults. Men away from home at a convention will sometimes do things which they would never do at home. In a different or a foreign setting, the instrumentalities of the external conscience (neighbors, employers, friends, marital partners) are absent and, as is true for children, one of the satisfactions of misbehavior in this context is the thought of having outwitted the inhibiting external forces. This is often expressed as "If the folks back home could only see me now."

The second point I want to make has to do with the status of the mental formations and the interpretations offered above. In order not to be misunderstood, I have tried throughout the discussion to indicate that I believe the cognitive structure interpretation of latency behavior is a necessary complement to and *not* a substitute for dynamic interpretations. In their use of multiple models both Freud and Piaget have made it very clear that at this stage in our understanding we need many different models to give a comprehensive account of human thought and action. Hopefully, and this is the spirit in which the above discussion has been offered, interpretations of the same phenomena from the standpoint of many different models will prepare the way for a truly comprehensive psychological theory that is at once cognitive and dynamic.

REFERENCES

Davidson, Audrey and Fay, Judith (1964). Fantasy in middle childhood. In *Child psychotherapy*, Mary R. Haworth (Ed.). New York: Basic Books. Pp. 401-406.

Elkind, D. (1967). Egocentrism in adolescence. Child Development, **38**, 1025-1034.

Gosse, E. (1909). *Father and son: A study of two temperaments*. London: Heinemann.

Inhelder, B., and Piaget, J. (1958). *The growth of logical thinking from childhood to adolescence*. New York: Basic Books.

Lehrman, P. R. (1927). The fantasy of not belonging to one's family. *Archives of Neurology and Psychiatry*, **18**, 1015-1023.

Opie, Iona, and Opie, P. (1959). *The lore and language of school children*. London: Oxford University Press.

Peel, E. A. (1960). *The pupil's thinking*. London: Oldhourne.

Piaget, J. (1929). *The child's conception of the world*. New York: Humanities.

Piaget, J. (1950). *The psychology of intelligence*. London: Routledge and Kegan Paul, Ltd.

Weir, M. W. (1964). Development changes in problem solving strategies. *Psychological Review*, **71**, 473-590.

Wertheimer, M. (1959). *Productive thinking*. New York: Harper (2nd ed.).

Wolfenstein, Martha (1954). *Children's humor*. Glencoe, Illinois: The Free Press.

Woltmann, A. G. (1964). Mud and clay, their functions as developmental aids and as media of projection. In *Child psychotherapy*, Mary R. Haworth (Ed.). New York: Basic Books. Pp. 349-363.

CHAPTER 7

Sequence, Tempo, and Individual Variation in Adolescent Growth and Development*

J. M. Tanner

For the majority of young persons, the years from twelve to sixteen are the most eventful ones of their lives so far as their growth and development is concerned. Admittedly during fetal life and the first year or two after birth developments occurred still faster, and a sympathetic environment was probably even more crucial, but the subject himself was not the fascinated, charmed, or horrified spectator that watches the developments, or lack of developments, of adolescence. Growth is a very regular and highly regulated process, and from birth onward the growth rate of most bodily tissues decreases steadily, the fall being swift at first and slower from about three years. Body shape changes gradually since the rate of growth of some parts, such as the arms and legs, is greater than the rate of growth of others, such as the trunk. But the change is a steady one, a smoothly continuous development rather than any passage through a series of separate stages.

Then at puberty, a very considerable alteration in growth rate occurs. There is a swift increase in body size, a change in the shape and body composition, and a rapid development of the gonads, the reproductive organs, and the characters signaling sexual maturity. Some of these changes are common to both sexes, but most are sex-specific. Boys have a great increase in muscle size and strength, together with a series of physiological changes, making them more capable than girls of doing heavy physical work and running faster and longer. The changes specifically adapt the male to his primitive primate role of dominating, fighting, and foraging. Such adolescent changes occur generally in primates, but are more marked in some species than in others. Male, female, and prepubescent gibbons are hard to distinguish when they are together, let alone apart. No such problem

*Reprinted by permission of *Daedalus*, Journal of the American Academy of Arts and Sciences, Boston, Mass., Fall 1971, *Twelve to Sixteen: Early Adolescence*.

arises with gorillas or rhesus monkeys. Man lies at about the middle of the primate range, both in adolescent size increase and degree of sexual differentiation.

The adolescent changes are brought about by hormones, either secreted for the first time, or secreted in much higher amounts than previously. Each hormone acts on a set of targets or receptors, but these are often not concentrated in a single organ, nor in a single type of tissue. Testosterone, for example, acts on receptors in the cells of the penis, the skin of the face, the cartilages of the shoulder joints, and certain parts of the brain. Whether all these cells respond by virtue of having the same enzyme system, or whether different enzymes are involved at different sites is not yet clear. The systems have developed through natural selection, producing a functional response of obvious biological usefulness in societies of hunter gatherers, but of less certain benefit in the culture of invoice clerk and shop assistant. Evolutionary adaptations of bodily structure usually carry with them an increased proclivity for using those structures in behavior, and there is no reason to suppose this principle suddenly stops short at twentieth-century man. There is no need to take sides in the current debate on the origins of aggression to realize that a major task of any culture is the channeling of this less specifically sexual adolescent energy into creative and playful activity.

The adolescent changes have not altered in the last fifteen years, or the last fifty, or probably the last five thousand. Girls still develop two years earlier than boys; some boys still have completed their whole bodily adolescent development before other boys of the same chronological age have begun theirs. These are perhaps the two major biological facts to be borne in mind when thinking of the adolescent's view of himself in relation to his society. The sequence of the biological events remains the same. But there has been one considerable change; the events occur now at an earlier age than formerly. Forty years ago the average British girl had her first menstrual period (menarche) at about her fifteenth birthday; nowadays it is shortly before her thirteenth. Fifty years ago in Britain social class differences played a considerable part in causing the variation of age of menarche in the population, the less well-off growing up more slowly. Nowadays, age at menarche is almost the same in different classes and most of the variation is due to genetical factors.

In this essay, I shall discuss (1) the growth of the body at adolescence and its changes in size, shape, and tissue composition, (2) sex dimorphism and the development of the reproductive system, (3) the concept of developmental age and the interaction of physical and behavioral advancement, (4) the interaction of genetic and environmental influences on the age of occurrence of puberty and the secular trend toward earlier maturation.

GROWTH OF THE BODY DURING ADOLESCENCE

The extent of the adolescent spurt in height is shown in Figure 1. For a year or more the velocity of growth approximately doubles; a boy is likely to be growing again at the rate he last experienced about age two. The peak velocity of height (PHV, a point much used in growth studies) averages about 10.5 centimeters a year (cm/yr) in boys and 9.0 cm/yr in girls (with a standard deviation of about 1.0 cm/yr) but this is the "instantaneous" peak given by a smooth curve drawn through the observations. The velocity over the whole year encompassing the six months before and after the peak is naturally somewhat less. During this year a boy usually grows between 7 and 12 cm and a girl between 6 and 11 cm. Children who have their peak early reach a somewhat higher peak than those who have it late.

The average age at which the peak is reached depends on the nature and circumstances of the group studied more, probably, than does the height of the peak. In moderately well-off British or North American children at present the peak occurs on average at about 14.0 years in boys and 12.0 years in girls. The standard deviations are about 0.9 years in each instance. Though the absolute average ages differ from series to series the two-year sex difference is invariant.

The adolescent spurt is at least partly under different hormonal control from growth in the period before. Probably as a consequence of this the amount of height added during the spurt is to a considerable degree independent of the amount attained prior to it. Most children who have grown steadily up, say, the 30th centile line on a height chart till adolescence end up at the 30th centile as adults, it is true; but a number end as high as the 50th or as low as the 10th, and a very few at the 55th or 5th. The correlation between adult height and height just before the spurt starts is about 0.8. This leaves some 30 per cent of the variability in adult height as due to differences in the magnitude of the adolescent spurt. So some adolescents get a nasty and unavoidable shock; though probably the effects of early and late maturing (see below) almost totally confuse the issue of final height during the years we are considering.

Practically all skeletal and muscular dimensions take part in the spurt, though not to an equal degree. Most of the spurt in height is due to acceleration of trunk length rather than length of legs. There is a fairly regular order in which the dimensions accelerate; leg length as a rule reaches its peak first, followed by the body breadths, with shoulder width last. Thus a boy stops growing out of his trousers (at least in length) a year before he stops growing out of his jackets. The earliest structures to reach their adult status are the head, hands, and feet. At adolescence, children, particularly girls, sometimes complain of having large hands and feet. They can be reassured that by the time they are fully grown

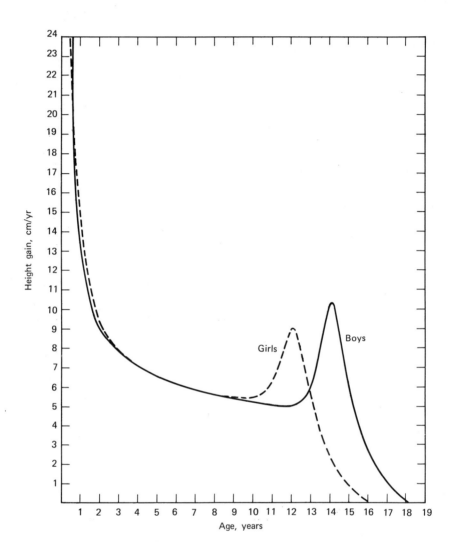

Figure 1. Typical individual velocity curves for supine length or height in boys and girls. These curves represent the velocity of the typical boy and girl at any given instant. [From J. M. Tanner, R. H. Whitehouse, and M. Takaishi, "Standards from Birth to Maturity for Height, Weight Height Velocity and Weight Velocity; British Children, 1965," *Archives of the Diseases of Childhood*, 41 (1966), 455-471.]

122

their hands and feet will be a little smaller in proportion to their arms and legs, and considerably smaller in proportion to their trunk.

The spurt in muscle, both of limbs and heart, coincides with the spurt in skeletal growth, for both are caused by the same hormones. Boys' muscle widths reach a peak velocity of growth considerably greater than those reached by girls. But since girls have their spurt earlier, there is actually a period, from about twelve and a half to thirteen and a half, when girls on the average have larger muscles than boys of the same age.

Simultaneously with the spurt in muscle there is a loss of fat in boys, particularly on the limbs. Girls have a velocity curve of fat identical in shape to that of boys; that is to say, their fat accumulation (going on in both sexes from about age six) decelerates. But the decrease in velocity in girls is not sufficiently great to carry the average velocity below zero, that is to give an absolute loss. Most girls have to content themselves with a temporary go-slow in fat accumulation. As the adolescent growth spurt draws to an end, fat tends to accumulate again in both sexes.

The marked increase in muscle size in boys at adolescence leads to an increase in strength, illustrated in Figure 2. Before adolescence, boys and girls are similar in strength for a given body size and shape; after, boys are much stronger, probably due to developing more force per gram of muscle as well as absolutely larger muscles. They also develop larger hearts and lungs relative to their size, a higher systolic blood pressure, a lower resting heart rate, a greater capacity for carrying oxygen in the blood, and a greater power for neutralizing the chemical products of muscular exercise such as lactic acid (Tanner, 1962). In short, the male becomes at adolescence more adapted for the tasks of hunting, fighting, and manipulating all sorts of heavy objects, as is necessary in some forms of food-gathering.

The increase in hemoglobin, associated with a parallel increase in the number of red blood cells, is illustrated in Figure 3 (Young, 1963). The hemoglobin concentration is plotted in relation to the development of secondary sex characters instead of chronological age, to obviate the spread due to early and late maturing (see below). Girls lack the rise in red cells and hemoglobin, which is brought about by the action of testosterone.

It is as a direct result of these anatomical and physiological changes that athletic ability increases so much in boys at adolescence. The popular notion of a boy "outgrowing his strength" at this time has little scientific support. It is true that the peak velocity of strength is reached a year or so later than that of height, so that a short period may exist when the adolescent, having completed his skeletal and probably also muscular growth, still does not have the strength of a young adult of the same body size and shape. But this is a temporary phase; considered absolutely, power, athletic skill, and physical endurance all increase progressively and rapidly throughout adolescence. It is certainly not true that

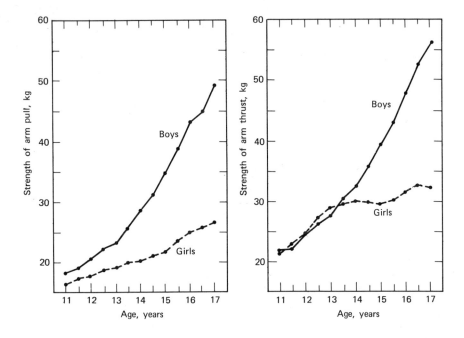

Figure 2. Strength of arm pull and arm thrust from age eleven to seventeen. Mixed longitudinal data, sixty-five to ninety-five boys and sixty-six to ninety-three girls in each age group. [From J. M. Tanner, *Growth at Adolescence*, 2d ed. (Oxford: Blackwell Scientific Publications, 1962); data from H. E. Jones, *Motor Performance and Growth* (Berkeley: University of California Press, 1949).]

the changes accompanying adolescence enfeeble, even temporarily. If the adolescent becomes weak and easily exhausted it is for psychological reasons and not physiological ones.

SEX DIMORPHISM AND THE DEVELOPMENT OF THE REPRODUCTIVE SYSTEM

The adolescent spurt in skeletal and muscular dimensions is closely related to the rapid development of the reproductive system which takes place at this time. The course of this development is outlined diagrammatically in Figure 4. The solid areas marked "breast" in the girls and "penis" and "testis" in the boys represent the period of accelerated growth of these organs and the horizontal

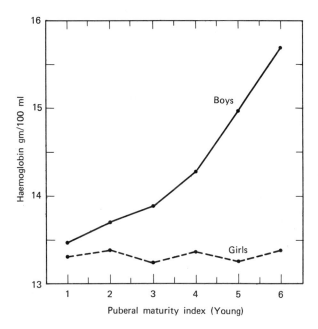

Figure 3. Blood hemoglobin level in girls and boys according to stage of puberty; cross-sectional data. [From H. B. Young, "Ageing and Adolescence," *Developmental Medicine and Child Neurology,* 5 (1963), 451-460, cited in J. M. Tanner, "Growth and Endocrinology of the Adolescent," in L. Gardner, ed., *Endocrine and Genetic Diseases of Childhood* (Philadelphia and London: Saunders, 1969).]

lines and the rating numbers marked "pubic hair" stand for its advent and development (Tanner, 1962). The sequences and timings given represent in each case average values for British boys and girls; the North American average is within two or three months of this. To give an idea of the individual departures from the average, figures for the range of age at which the various events begin and end are inserted under the first and last point of the bars. The acceleration of penis growth, for example, begins on the average at about age twelve and a half, but sometimes as early as ten and a half and sometimes as late as fourteen and a half. The completion of penis development usually occurs at about age fourteen and a half but in some boys is at twelve and a half and in others at sixteen and a half. There are a few boys, it will be noticed, who do not begin their spurts in height or penis development until the earliest maturers have entirely completed theirs. At age thirteen, fourteen, and fifteen there is an enormous variability among any group of boys, who range all the way from

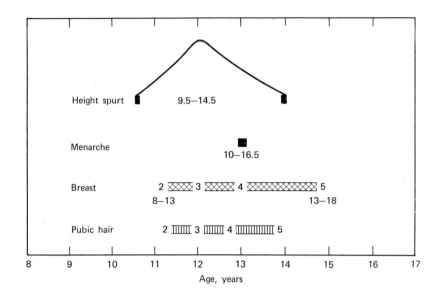

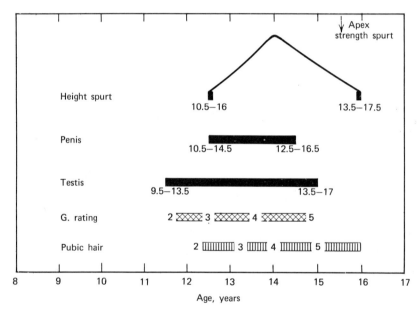

Figure 4. Diagram of sequence of events at adolescence in boys and girls. The average boy and girl are represented. The range of ages within which each event charted may begin and end is given by the figures placed directly below its start and finish. [From W. A. Marshall and J. M. Tanner, "Variations in the Pattern of Pubertal Changes in Boys," *Archives of the Diseases of Childhood,* 45 (1970), 13.]

practically complete maturity to absolute preadolescence. The same is true of girls aged eleven, twelve, and thirteen.

In Figure 5 three boys are illustrated, all aged exactly 14.75 years and three girls all aged exactly 12.75. All are entirely normal and healthy, yet the first boy could be mistaken easily for a twelve-year-old and the third for a young man of seventeen or eighteen. Manifestly it is ridiculous to consider all three boys or all three girls as equally grown up either physically, or, since much behavior at this age is conditioned by physical status, in their social relations. The statement that a boy is fourteen is in most contexts hopelessly vague; all depends, morphologically, physiologically, and to a considerable extent sociologically too, on whether he is preadolescent, midadolescent, or postadolescent.

The psychological and social importance of this difference in the tempo of development, as it has been called, is very great, particularly in boys. Boys who are advanced in development are likely to dominate their contemporaries in athletic achievement and sexual interest alike. Conversely the late developer is the one who all too often loses out in the rough and tumble of the adolescent world; and he may begin to wonder whether he will ever develop his body properly or be as well endowed sexually as those others he has seen developing around him. A very important part of the educationist's and the doctor's task at this time is to provide information about growth and its variability to preadolescents and adolescents and to give sympathetic support and reassurance to those who need it.

The *sequence* of events, though not exactly the same for each boy or girl, is much less variable than the age at which the events occur. The first sign of puberty in the boy is usually an acceleration of the growth of the testes and scrotum with reddening and wrinkling of the scrotal skin. Slight growth of pubic hair may begin about the same time, but is usually a trifle later. The spurts in height and penis growth begin on average about a year after the first testicular acceleration. Concomitantly with the growth of the penis, and under the same stimulus, the seminal vesicles and the prostate and bulbo-urethral glands enlarge and develop. The time of the first ejaculation of seminal fluid is to some extent culturally as well as biologically determined, but as a rule is during adolescence, and about a year after the beginning of accelerated penis growth.

Axillary hair appears on the average some two years after the beginning of pubic hair growth—that is, when pubic hair is reaching stage 4. However, there is enough variability and dissociation in these events that a very few children's axillary hair actually appears first. In boys, facial hair begins to grow at about the time the axillary hair appears. There is a definite order in which the hairs of moustache and beard appear; first at the corners of the upper lip, then over all the upper lip, then at the upper part of the cheeks in the mid-line below the lower lip, and finally along the sides and lower border of the chin. The remainder of the body hair appears from about the time of first axillary hair

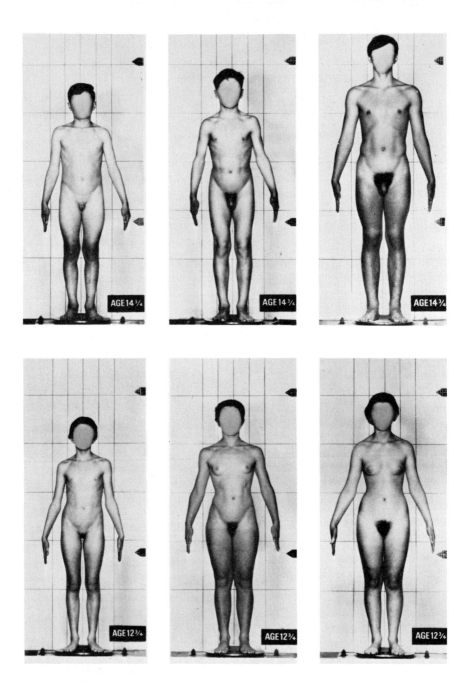

Figure 5. Differing degrees of pubertal development at the same chronological age. Upper row, three boys all aged 14.75 years. Lower row, three girls all aged 12.75 years. (From Tanner, "Growth and Endocrinology of the Adolescent.")

development until a considerable time after puberty. The ultimate amount of body hair an individual develops seems to depend largely on heredity, though whether because of the kinds and amounts of hormones secreted or because of the reactivity of the end-organs is not known.

Breaking of the voice occurs relatively late in adolescence; it is often a gradual process and so not suitable as a criterion of puberty. The change in pitch accompanies enlargement of the larynx and lengthening of the vocal cords, caused by the action of testosterone on the laryngeal cartilages. During the period of breaking, the pitch is variable, and the true adult pitch associated with full growth of the larynx may not be established until late adolescence. In addition to change in pitch, there is also a change in quality or timbre which distinguishes the voice (more particularly the vowel sounds) of both male and female adults from that of children. This is dependent on the enlargement of the resonating spaces above the larynx, due to the rapid growth of the mouth, nose, and maxilla which occurs during adolescence.

In the skin the sebaceous and apocrine sweat glands, particularly of the axillae and genital and anal regions, develop rapidly during puberty and give rise to a characteristic odor; the changes occur in both sexes but are more marked in the male. Enlargement of the pores at the root of the nose and the appearance of comedones and acne, though liable to occur in either sex, are considerably commoner in adolescent boys than girls, since the underlying skin changes are the result of androgenic activity. A roughening of the skin, particularly over the outer aspects of the thighs and upper arms, may be seen in both sexes during adolescence, but again is commoner in boys than girls.

During adolescence the male breast undergoes changes, some temporary and some permanent. The diameter of the areola, which is equal in both sexes before puberty, increases considerably, though less than it does in girls. Representative figures are 12.5 millimeters before puberty, 21.5 millimeters in mature men, and 35.5 millimeters in mature women. In some boys (between a fifth and a third of most groups studied) there is a distinct enlargement of the breast (sometimes unilaterally) about midway through adolescence. This usually regresses again after about one year.

In girls the appearance of the "breast bud" is as a rule the first sign of puberty, though the appearance of pubic hair precedes it in about one in three. The uterus and vagina develop simultaneously with the breast. The labia and clitoris also enlarge. Menarche, the first menstrual period, is a late event in the sequence. It occurs almost invariably after the peak of the height spurt has been passed. Though it marks a definitive and probably mature stage of uterine development, it does not usually signify the attainment of full reproductive function. The early cycles may be more irregular than later ones and are in some girls, but by no means all, accompanied by dysmenorrhea. They are often anovulatory, that is unaccompanied by the shedding of an egg. Thus there is frequently a period of adolescent sterility lasting a year to eighteen months after menarche; but it cannot be relied on in the individual case. Similar considerations may apply to the male, but there is no reliable information about this. On the average, girls grow about 6 cm more after menarche, though gains of up to twice this amount may occur. The gain is practically independent of whether menarche occurs early or late.

NORMAL VARIATIONS IN PUBERTAL DEVELOPMENT

The diagram of Figure 4 must not be allowed to obscure the fact that children vary a great deal both in the rapidity with which they pass through the various stages of puberty and in the closeness with which the various events are linked together. At one extreme one may find a perfectly healthy girl who has not yet menstruated though she has reached adult breast and pubic hair ratings and is already two years past her peak height velocity; at the other a girl who has passed all the stages of puberty within the space of two years. Details of the limits of what may be considered normal can be found in the articles of Marshall and Tanner (Marshall, 1969).

In girls the interval from the first sign of puberty to complete maturity varies from one and a half to six years. From the moment when the breast bud first appears to menarche averages two and a half years but may be as little as six months or as much as five and a half years. The rapidity with which a child passes through puberty seems to be independent of whether puberty is occurring early or late. There is some independence between breast and pubic hair developments, as one might expect on endocrinological grounds. A few girls reach pubic hair stage 3 (see Figure 4) before any breast development starts; conversely breast stage 3 may be reached before any pubic hair appears. At breast stage 5, however, pubic hair is always present in girls. Menarche usually occurs in breast stage 4 and pubic hair stage 4, but in about 10 per cent of girls occurs in stage 5 for both, and occasionally may occur in stage 2 or even 1 of pubic hair. Menarche invariably occurs after peak height velocity is passed, so the tall girl can be reassured about future growth if her periods have begun.

In boys a similar variability occurs. The genitalia may take any time between two and five years to pass from G2 to G5, and some boys complete the whole process while others have still not gone from G2 to G3. Pubic hair growth in the absence of genital development is very unusual in normal boys, but in a small percentage of boys the genitalia develop as far as stage 4 before the pubic hair starts to grow.

The height spurt occurs relatively later in boys than in girls. Thus there is a difference between the average boy and girl of two years in age of peak height velocity, but of only one year in the first appearance of pubic hair. The PHV occurs in very few boys before genital stage 4, whereas 75 per cent of girls reach PHV before breast stage 4. Indeed in some girls the acceleration in height is the first sign of puberty; this is never so in boys. A small boy whose genitalia are just beginning to develop can be unequivocally reassured that an acceleration in height is soon to take place, but a girl in the corresponding situation may already have had her height spurt.

The basis of some children having loose and some tight linkages between pubertal events is not known. Probably the linkage reflects the degree of integration of various processes in the hypothalamus and the pituitary gland, for breast growth is controlled by one group of hormones, pubic hair growth by another, and the height spurt probably by a third. In rare pathological instances the events may become widely divorced.

THE DEVELOPMENT OF SEX DIMORPHISM

The differential effects on the growth of bone, muscle, and fat at puberty increase considerably the difference in body composition between the sexes. Boys have a greater increase not only in the length of bones but in the thickness of cortex, and girls have a smaller loss of fat. The most striking dimorphism, however, are the man's greater stature and breadth of shoulders and the woman's wider hips. These are produced chiefly by the changes and timing of puberty but it is important to remember that sex dimorphisms do not arise only at that time. Many appear much earlier. Some, like the external genital difference itself, develop during fetal life. Others develop continuously throughout the whole growth period by a sustained differential growth rate. An example of this is the greater relative length and breadth of the forearm in the male when compared with whole arm length or whole body length.

Part of the sex difference in pelvic shape antedates puberty. Girls at birth already have a wider pelvic outlet. Thus the adaptation for child bearing is present from a very early age. The changes at puberty are concerned more with widening the pelvic inlet and broadening the much more noticeable hips. It seems likely that these changes are more important in attracting the male's attention than in dealing with its ultimate product.

These sex-differentiated morphological characters arising at puberty—to which we can add the corresponding physiological and perhaps psychological ones as well—are secondary sex characters in the straightforward sense that they are caused by sex hormone or sex-differential hormone secretion and serve reproductive activity. The penis is directly concerned in copulation, the mammary gland in lactation. The wide shoulders and muscular power of the male, together with the canine teeth and brow ridges in man's an-cestors, developed probably for driving away other males and insuring peace, an adaptation which soon becomes social.

A number of traits persist, perhaps through another mechanism known to the ethologists as ritualization. In the course of evolution a morphological character or a piece of behavior may lose its original function and, becoming further elaborated, complicated, or simplified, may serve as a sign stimulus to other members of the same species, releasing behavior that is in some ways advantageous to the spread or survival of the species. It requires little insight into human erotics to suppose that the shoulders, the hips and buttocks, and the breasts (at least in a number of widespread cultures) serve as releasers of mating behavior. The pubic hair (about whose function the textbooks have always preserved a cautious silence) probably survives as a ritualized stimulus for sexual activity, developed by simplification from the hair remaining in the inguinal and axillary regions for the infant to cling to when still transported, as in present apes and monkeys, under the mother's body. Similar considerations may apply to axillary hair, which is associated with special apocrine glands which themselves only develop at puberty and are related histologically to scent glands in other mammals. The beard, on the other hand, may still be more frightening to other males than enticing to females. At least ritual use in past communities suggests this is the case; but perhaps there are two sorts of beards.

THE INITIATION OF PUBERTY

The manner in which puberty is initiated has a general importance for the clarification of developmental mechanisms. Certain children develop all the changes of puberty, up to and including spermatogenesis and ovulation, at a very early age, either as the result of a brain lesion or as an isolated developmental, sometimes genetic defect. The youngest mother on record was such a case, and gave birth to a full-term healthy infant by Caesarian section at the age of five years, eight months. The existence of precocious puberty and the results of accidental ingestion by small children of male or female sex hormones indicate that breasts, uterus, and penis will respond to hormonal stimulation long before puberty. Evidently an increased end-organ sensitivity plays at most a minor part in pubertal events.

The signal to start the sequence of events is given by the brain, not the pituitary. Just as the brain holds the information on sex, so it holds information on maturity. The pituitary of a newborn rat successfully grafted in place of an adult pituitary begins at once to function in an adult fashion, and does not have to wait till its normal age of maturation has been reached. It is the hypothalamus, not the pituitary, which has to mature before puberty begins.

Maturation, however, does not come out of the blue and at least in rats a little more is known about this mechanism. In these animals small amounts of sex hormones circulate from the time of birth and these appear to inhibit the prepubertal hypothalamus from producing gonadotrophin releasers. At puberty it is supposed that the hypothalamic cells become less sensitive to sex hormone. The small amount of sex hormones circulating then fails to inhibit the hypothalamus and gonadotrophins are released; these stimulate the production of testosterone by the testis or estrogen by the ovary. The level of the sex hormone rises until the same feedback circuit is reestablished, but now at a higher level of gonadotrophins and sex hormones. The sex hormones are now high enough to stimulate the growth of secondary sex characters and support mating behavior.

DEVELOPMENTAL AGE AND THE INTERACTION OF PHYSICAL AND BEHAVIORAL ADVANCEMENT

Children vary greatly in their tempo of growth. The effects are most dramatically seen at adolescence, as illustrated in Figure 5, but they are present at all ages from birth and even before. Girls, for example, do not suddenly become two years ahead of boys at adolescence; on the contrary they are born with slightly more mature skeletons and nervous systems, and gradually increase their developmental lead (in absolute terms) throughout childhood.

Clearly, the concept of *developmental* age, as opposed to *chronological* age, is a very important one. To measure developmental age we need some way of determining the percentage of the child's growth process which has been attained at any time. In retrospective research studies, the per cent of final adult height may be very effectively used; but in the clinic we need something that is immediate in its application. The difficulty about using height, for example, is that different children end up at different heights, so that a tall-for-his-age twelve-year-old may either be a tall adult in the making with average maturational tempo, or an average adult in the making with an accelerated tempo. Precisely the same applies to the child who scores above average on most tests of mental ability.

To measure developmental age we need something which ends up the same for everyone and is applicable throughout the whole period of growth. Many physiological measures meet these criteria, in whole or in part. They range from the number of erupted teeth to the percentage of water in muscle cells. The various developmental "age" scales do not necessarily coincide, and each has its particular use. By far the most generally useful, however, is skeletal maturity or *bone* age. A less important one is dental maturity.

Skeletal maturity is usually measured by taking a radiograph of the hand and wrist (using the same radiation exposure that a child inevitably gets, and to more sensitive areas, by spending a week on vacation in the mountains). The appearances of the developing bones can be rated and formed into a scale; the scale is applicable to boys and girls of all genetic backgrounds, though girls on the average reach any given score at a younger age than boys, and blacks on the average, at least in the first few years after birth, reach a given score younger than do whites. Other areas of the body may be used if required. Skeletal maturity is closely related to the age at which adolescence occurs, that is to maturity measured by secondary sex character development. Thus the range of *chronological* age within which menarche may normally fall is about ten to sixteen and a half, but the corresponding range of *skeletal* age for menarche is only twelve to fourteen and a half. Evidently the physiological processes controlling progression of skeletal development are in most instances closely linked with those which initiate the events of adolescence. Furthermore children tend to be consistently advanced or retarded during their whole growth period, or at any rate after about age three.

Dental maturity partly shares in this general skeletal and bodily maturation. At all ages from six to thirteen children who are advanced skeletally have on the average more erupted teeth than those who are skeletally retarded. Likewise those who have an early adolescence on the average erupt their teeth early. Girls usually have more erupted teeth than boys. But this relationship is not a very close one, and quantitatively speaking, it is the relative independence of teeth and general skeletal development which should be emphasized. There is some general factor of bodily maturity creating a tendency for a child to be advanced or retarded as a whole: in his skeletal ossification, in the percentage attained of his eventual size, in his permanent dentition, doubtless in his physiological reactions, and possibly in the results of his tests of ability. But not too much should be made of this general factor; and especially it should be noted how very limited is the loading, so to speak, of brain growth in it. There is little justification in the facts of physical growth and development for the concept of "organismic age" in which almost wholly disparate measures of developmental maturity are lumped together.

PHYSICAL MATURATION, MENTAL ABILITY, AND EMOTIONAL DEVELOPMENT

Clearly the occurrence of tempo differences in human growth has profound implications for educational theory and practice. This would especially be so if advancement in physical growth were linked to any significant degree with advancement in intellectual ability and in emotional maturity.

There is good evidence that in the European and North American school systems children who are physically advanced toward maturity score on the average slightly higher in most tests of mental ability than children of the same age who are physically less mature. The difference is not great, but it is consistent and it occurs at all ages that have been studied—that is, back as far as six and a half years. Similarly the intelligence test score of postmenarcheal girls is higher than the score of premenarcheal girls of the same age (Tanner, 1966). Thus in age-linked examinations physically fast-maturing children have a significantly better chance than slow-maturing.

It is also true that physically large children score higher than small ones, at all ages from six onward. In a random sample of all Scottish eleven-year-old children, for example, comprising 6,440 pupils, the correlation between height and score in the Moray House group test was 0.25 ± 0.01 which leads to an average increase of one and a half points Terman-Merrill I.Q. per inch of stature. A similar correlation was found in London children. The effects can be very significant for individual children. In ten-year-old girls there was nine points difference in I.Q. between those whose height was above the 75th percentile and those whose height was below the 15th. This is two-thirds of the standard deviation of the test score.

It was usually thought that both the relationships between test score and height and between test score and early maturing would disappear in adulthood. If the correlations represented only the effects of co-advancement both of mental ability and physical growth this might be expected to happen. There is no difference in height between early and late maturing boys when both have finished growing. But it is now clear that, curiously, at least part of the height-I.Q. correlation persists in adults (Tanner, 1966). It is not clear in what proportion genetic and environmental factors are responsible for this.

There is little doubt that being an early or a late maturer may have repercussions on behavior, and that in some children these repercussions may be considerable. There is little enough solid information on the relation between emotional and physiological development, but what there is supports the common sense notion that emotional attitudes are clearly related to physiological events.

The boy's world is one where physical powers bring prestige as well as success, where the body is very much an instrument of the person. Boys who are advanced in development, not only at puberty, but before as well, are more likely than others to be leaders. Indeed, this is reinforced by the fact that muscular, powerful boys on the average mature earlier than others and have an early adolescent growth spurt. The athletically-built boy not only tends to dominate his fellows before puberty, but also by getting an early start he is in a good position to continue that domination. The unathletic, lanky boy, unable, perhaps, to hold his own in the preadolescent rough and tumble, gets still further pushed to the wall at adolescence, as he sees others shoot up while he remains nearly stationary in growth. Even boys several years younger now suddenly surpass him in size, athletic skill, and perhaps, too, in social graces. Figure 6 shows the height curves of two boys, the first an early-maturing muscular boy, the other a late-maturing lanky one. Though both boys are of average height at age eleven, and together again at average height at seventeen, the early maturer is four inches taller during the peak of adolescence.

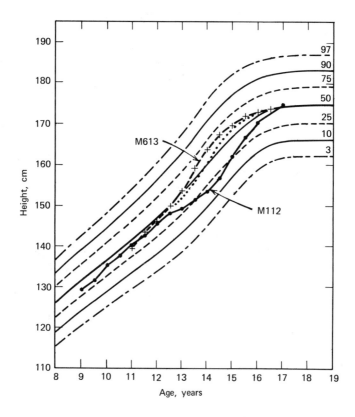

Figure 6. Height attained of two boys, one with an early and the other with a late adolescent spurt. Note how at age eleven and again at age seventeen the boys are the same height. [From J. M. Tanner, *Education and Physical Growth: Implications of the Study of Children's Growth for Educational Theory and Practice* (London: University of London Press, 1961).]

At a much deeper level the late developer at adolescence may sometimes have doubts about whether he will ever develop his body properly and whether he will be as well endowed sexually as those others he has seen developing around him. The lack of events of adolescence may act as a trigger to reverberate fears accumulated deep in the mind during the early years of life.

It may seem as though the early maturers have things all their own way. It is indeed true that most studies of the later personalities of children whose growth history is known do show early maturers as more stable, more sociable, less neurotic, and more successful in society, at least in the United States (Mussen, 1967). But early maturers have their difficulties also, particularly the girls in some societies. Though some glory in their new possessions, others are embarrassed by them. The early maturer, too, has a longer period of frustration of sex drive and of drive toward independence and the establishment of vocational orientation.

Little can be done to reduce the individual differences in children's tempo of growth, for they are biologically rooted and not significantly reducible by any social steps we may take. It, therefore, behooves all teachers, psychologists, and pediatricians to be fully aware of the facts and alert to the individual problems they raise.

TREND TOWARD LARGE SIZE AND EARLIER MATURATION

The rate of maturing and the age at onset of puberty are dependent, naturally, on a complex interaction of genetic and environmental factors. Where the environment is good, most of the variability in age at menarche in a population is due to genetic differences. In France in the 1950's the mean difference between identical twins was two months, while that between nonidentical twin sisters was eight months (Tisserand-Perrier, 1953). In many societies puberty occurs later in the poorly-off, and in most societies investigated children with many siblings grow less fast than children with few.

Recent investigations in Northeast England showed that social class differences are now only those associated with different sizes of family. The median age of menarche for only girls was 13.0 years, for girls with one sibling 13.2, two siblings 13.4, three siblings and over 13.7. For a given number of siblings the social class as indicated by father's occupation was unrelated to menarcheal age (Roberts, 1971). Environment is still clearly a factor in control of menarcheal age, but in England at least occupation is a less effective indication of poor housing, poor expenditure on food, and poor child care than is the number of children in the family.

During the last hundred years there has been a striking tendency for children to become progressively larger at all ages (Tanner, 1968). This is known as the "secular trend." The magnitude of the trend in Europe and America is such that it dwarfs the differences between socioeconomic classes.

The data from Europe and America agree well: from about 1900, or a little earlier, to the present, children in average economic circumstances have increased in height at age five to seven by about 1 to 2 cm each decade, and at ten to fourteen by 2 to 3 cm each decade. Preschool data show that the trend starts directly after birth and may, indeed, be relatively greater from age two to five than subsequently. The trend started, at least in Britain, a considerable time ago, because Roberts, a factory physician, writing in 1876 said that "a factory child of the present day at the age of nine years weighs as much as one of 10 years did in 1833 . . . each age has gained one year in forty years" (Tanner, 1962). The trend in Europe is still continuing at the time of writing but there is some evidence to show that in the United States the best-off sections of the population are now growing up at something approaching the fastest possible speed.

During the same period there has been an upward trend in adult height, but to a considerably lower degree. In earlier times final height was not reached till twenty-five years or later, whereas now it is reached in men at eighteen or nineteen. Data exist, however, which enable us to compare fully grown men at different periods. They lead to the conclusion that in Western Europe men increased in adult height little if at all from 1760 to 1830, about 0.3 cm per decade from 1830 to 1880, and about 0.6 cm per decade from 1880 to 1960. The trend is apparently still continuing in Europe, though not in the best-off section of American society.

Most of the trend toward greater size in children reflects a more rapid maturation; only a minor part reflects a greater ultimate size. The trend toward earlier maturing is best shown in the statistics on age at menarche. A selection of the best data is illustrated in Figure 7. The trend is between three and four months per decade since 1850 in average sections of Western European populations. Well-off persons show a trend of about half this magnitude, having never been so retarded in menarche as the worse-off (Tanner, 1966).

Most, though not all, of the differences between populations are probably due to nutritional factors, operating during the whole of the growth period, from conception onward. The well-nourished Western populations have median menarcheal ages of about 12.8 to 13.2 years; the latest recorded ages, by contrast, are 18 years in the Highlands of New Guinea, 17 years in Central Africa, and 15.5 years in poorly-off Bantu in the South African Transkei. Well-nourished Africans have a median age of 13.4 (Kampala upper classes) or less, comparable with Europeans. Asians at the same nutritional level as Europeans probably have an earlier menarche, the figure for well-off Chinese in Hong Kong being 12.5 years.

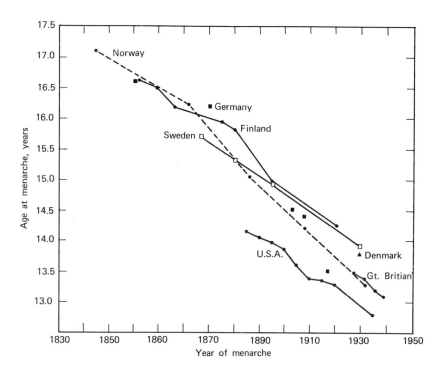

Figure 7. Secular trend in age at menarche, 1830-1960. (Sources of data and method of plotting detailed in Tanner, *Growth at Adolescence.)*

The causes of the secular trend are probably multiple. Certainly better nutrition is a major one, and perhaps in particular more protein and calories in early infancy. A lessening of disease may also have contributed. Hot climates used to be cited as a potent cause of early menarche, but it seems now that their effect, if any, is considerably less than that of nutrition. The annual mean world temperature rose from 1850 to about 1940 (when it began to fall again); the polar ice caps have been melting and the glaciers retreating, but on present evidence it seems unlikely that this general warming up has contributed significantly to the earlier menarche of girls.

Some authors have supposed that the increased psychosexual stimulation consequent on modern urban living has contributed, but there is no positive evidence for this. Girls in single-sex schools have menarche at exactly the same age as girls in coeducational schools, but whether this is a fair test of difference in psychosexual stimulation is hard to say.

REFERENCES

Tanner, J. M. (1962). *Growth at adolescence.* Oxford: Blackwell Scientific Publications. 2nd ed.

Young, H.B. (1963). Ageing and adolescence. *Developmental Medicine and Child Neurology,* **5**, 451-460.

Marshall, W. A. and Tanner, J. M. (1969 and 1970). Variations in the pattern of pubertal changes in girls. *Archives of the Diseases of Childhood,* **44**, 291, and Variations in the pattern of pubertal changes in boys. *Archives of the Diseases of Childhood,* **45**, 13.

Tanner, J. M. (1966). Galtonian eugenics and the study of growth. *The Eugenics Review,* **58**, 122-135.

Mussen, P. H. and Jones, M. C. (1957). "Self-concepting motivations and interpersonal attitudes of late- and early-maturing boys." *Child Development,* **28**, 243-256.

Tisserand-Perrier, M. (1953). Etude comparative de certains processus de croissance chez les jeuneaux. *Journal de génétique humaine,* **2**, 87-102.

Roberts, D. F., Rozner, L. M. and Swan, A. V. (1971). Age at menarche, physique and environment in industrial north-east England. *Acta Paediatrica Scandinavica,* **60**, 158-164.

Tanner, J. M. (1968). Earlier maturation in man. *Scientific American,* **218**, 21-27.

Part III

SITUATIONAL PERSPECTIVES

"Not only can innate differences in drive organization, in ego functions and in maturational rates determine different responses to objectively identical experiences, but they can also help to determine what experiences will be experienced and how they will be perceived."

JOHN BENJAMIN

INTRODUCTION

Sibylle Escalona has pioneered the study of infancy with the aim of establishing links with later behavior. In Chapter 8, she briefly reviews her experience, noting that generally most infant behaviors are not maintained over time. The exceptions to this are of importance, however, since those children who do show persistent behaviors have in common significant developmental deviations or outright maladjustment.

Dr. Escalona suggests that a more useful approach to prediction, rather than expecting later persistence of behavior, is to identify *predispositions*, such as high activity level, and correlate them with later *dispositions,* such as gross motor coordination.

Still not satisfied with dealing with fragments of behavior, Dr. Escalona takes into account the interaction between the organism and the environmental field by focusing her attention upon *patterns of experience.* She thereby looks for naturally occurring behavioral responses to specific environmental events, often the stimulation of a child by an adult—for example, an infant's pattern of gazing at his mother.

Dr. Escalona describes both her research methodology and techniques for practical application. For example, she suggests that day-care centers base their programs not on general convictions of what is good for babies nor for a shy child or an anxious one, but instead on an empirical determination of those conditions under which a given child, at a particular time, is able to show the behavior or have the experience that promotes his development.

A perplexing question faced by Dr. Escalona as she studies interactional patterns is, how close can one get to the actual experience of the child? A baby cannot describe what he is feeling. One can say that if a baby gazes at a person for a significant time and with a certain intensity, he is experiencing that input from the environment. One can also say that if a baby smiles at the sight of something or reaches to manipulate it, then he is experiencing whatever goes with the execution of these points of coordination. Dr. Escalona does not hesitate to say that when a baby cries desperately, he is feeling displeasure, and if he radiates joy and turns to a person and smiles, then something akin to pleasure is taking place. As soon as the child is able to smile when he is angry, however, things become much more complicated.

Actually it may never be possible to know what an infant is subjectively experiencing. There is a gap between what a child is subjectively feeling, on the one hand, and what is inferred from the juxtaposition of what he is doing in a given situation on the other. The behavioral sciences may never completely objectify the subjective experience of those who cannot report it.

Christoph Heinecke and his group illustrate in Chapter 9 the importance of studying the mother-child unit in context, calling attention to the further complexity of individuality as the infant advances into the childhood years. His work stands as a model for integrating behavior and psychodynamic insights. He uses detailed observations of children and their mothers in order to relate the task orientation of two contrasting children in nursery school to the character of their relationships with their mothers. He describes the step-by-step process whereby two three-year-olds adapt to nursery school and, particularly, to certain tasks encountered in the school's curriculum. Given the disappointment in the followup results of educational programs, often limited only to work with the child, one looks to the family environment for insuring permanent learning and developmental gains.

Dr. Heinecke presents directly observed vignettes of the behavior of each child and her mother and then provides his explanation of the meaning of these events. The reader is free to formulate his own interpretations and compare them with the writer's. Whether or not one agrees with his explanations, the vital role of parent-teacher relationships can be seen in determining the child's degree of participation in and engagement with the nursery-school program. Conversely, the support offered by the nursery-school staff and interaction with peers can be helpful in aiding a child to manage stress at home, such as that engendered by parental separation. This chapter further shows that definable differences in children's behavior can be observed in reasonably constant and comparable settings such as that provided in a nursery school.

In Chapter 10, Irving Harris highlights the importance of birth order and sibling constellation as influences upon attitudes and personality. Alfred Adler brought family structure into his formulations of individual psychology. Dr. Harris updates Adler's work by relating family position to cognitive style. Although generalizations about the specific effects of birth order on personality pose the hazard of oversimplification, Dr. Harris notes that two tendencies can be observed in the educational style of students. Certain students think abstractly with facility and have a high degree of involvement with reading and books. Other students tend to be oriented toward nonacademic activities, finding themselves most at home on the playground and in the neighborhood. He postulates that the academically facile have been adult-civilized and the action-oriented, peer-civilized. Dr. Harris then correlates these educational types with rank in sibling order. He postulates that the academically oriented are predominantly first-born children and the peer-oriented largely later children. The first born necessarily are raised under the direct influence of their parents, having only senior adult models. The later born have older siblings in addition to parental figures as socializing models and agents. His clinical experience leads him to conclude that these relationships are pivotal. The first-born children tend to be oriented toward deductive and synthetic thinking, facilitating their ability to connect parts with their whole. They are rewarded in our present academic system which prizes their attributes. The later born tend to be more inclined toward the management of immediate problems, more comfortable with inductive thinking from disconnected parts and more prone to self-expressiveness. They are less successful in academic pursuits but more successful in the practical world of achievement. Dr. Harris complements the preceding discussions of individuality by succinctly calling attention to an important experiential variable, one's order of birth.

CHAPTER 8

The Differential Impact of Environmental Conditions as a Function of Different Reaction Patterns in Infancy

Sibylle K. Escalona*

The term "individuality" has broad connotations. It evokes association to the uniqueness of each individual which, in turn, refers more to the quality of inner psychic life than to overt and specific behavioral manifestations. In my view, established methods and theories of behavioral science are ill equipped to deal with individuality in the broad meaning of that term. This chapter will be more mundane and will concern itself with individual differences in behavior and responsiveness. For present purposes, I will remain with the conventional usage of the term "individual differences," that is variability among subjects that have in common one or several antecedent determinants. In other words, that portion of the variance not accounted for by whatever lawful regularity is under study.

In most psychological studies individual differences are treated almost as error factors. For instance, children reared in old-fashioned institutions do not develop normally; however, some are severely retarded, others mildly so, and a few not at all. These exceptions tend to be ascribed to individual differences. However, in this book we attempt the opposite approach and ask ourselves what factors are at work to account for the fact that such differences are always found, even if samples are most carefully selected. We are, also, concerned with related questions: namely, do individual differences make a difference, and to what extent is it important for both theory and practice to include consideration of these phenomena?

Most research on the nature and origin of individual difference has concerned itself either with the stability of early characteristics (does an active neonate

*Work for this presentation was performed while the author was supported by U.S.P.H.S. research scientist grant, MH-16,723. The data derived in part from work supported by U.S.P.H.S. research grant HD-01155.

tend to be a highly active adolescent?) or with the correlation between infantile characteristics and individual differences at later ages (are active neonates likely to be very independent adolescents?). As we all know, results so far have been meager and sometimes contradictory. Certain infantile characteristics were reported as highly stable at least during the preschool ages (Thomas, et al., 1963). Yet longitudinal studies that included at least closely related variables (Kagan and Moss, 1962) found no remarkable consistencies. In the latter studies correlations between a variety of infancy variables and a host of individual difference measures in late childhood were also unimpressive. (The partial exception was a movement characteristic in infancy, called passivity, or by inverse definition, rapidity of movement, which did show a small but consistent relationship to some later behavioral characteristics.)

Another approach, with which I have some experience, is predictive. With Grace Heider I reported on research in which observation of infants and their families before the infants were eight months old led to predictions about individual characteristics during the late preschool ages. The subjects of this predictive study were examined by extensive clinical descriptive methods which included a battery of psychological tests and standard play interviews. These preschool evaluations were made by Lois Murphy and her associates at a time when these investigators had no access to the infancy data nor to the predictions. The comparison of "Predictions and Outcome" (Escalona and Heider, 1959) is no more than a highly exploratory study, yet some of the results are relevant to our topic.

It turned out that certain categories of prediction were surprisingly successful, and others not at all. We found, as others have, that by and large infant behavior characteristics are not maintained over time. Ratings of activity level, movement qualities, irritability, and the like tended to converge toward the mean, or else children shifted their position on the continuum. However, and this is potentially important, certain children did carry into the preschool years behavior attributes that had been noted when they were as young as 16 weeks. This minority of self-consistent children had one thing in common: all had shown significant developmental deviation or outright maladjustment. Whether their difficulties were due to repeated serious illness, surgery and hospitalization, or to the impact of grave conflict and unhappiness within the family made no difference. The first hypothesis for consideration is as follows: Many infant characteristics of motility, expressive behavior, response to sensory stimuli, and the like dissolve during the course of normal development, as schemas and adaptive patterns break up to permit new behavior integrations. In fact, developmental advance requires that earlier, less mature schemas break up so that new modes of functioning can take their place. It is when development and adaptation proceed stressfully and not entirely successfully that certain early patterns are more likely to remain intact and continue to be present in unaltered form at later ages.

When predictions were based on the predisposing influence of certain infancy characteristics upon subsequent developmental course, they fared much better. Such predictions are necessarily based upon a cohesive theory of development, as they establish links between qualitatively different aspects of behavior. For instance, we thought that high activity level in infancy should interfere with the delay and inhibition of movement impulse required for fine motor coordination, while at the same time it would enhance the frequency of gross-motor activation and facilitate development in that sphere. A total of 37 predictions specified for active infants that at preschool age the level of gross coordination would be substantially superior to ability in fine coordination. The reverse discrepancy between these functions was predicted for infants whose activity level had been low. Thirty-two or 86% of these predictions were borne out. It should be noted that no infant developed a discrepancy in a direction opposite to that anticipated; that is, there were no reversals.

The following predictions, equally based on theoretical assumptions, also were confirmed in the great majority of instances: High activity level was also thought to be an obstacle to the learning of verbal symbols, early abstraction, and early concept formation. Hence, we predicted that high activity level infants would, on intelligence tests administered at age 5, have higher scores on performance than on verbal items, while the opposite discrepancy among the test scores was predicted for infants whose activity level had been distinctly low. Of 10 such predictions 7 were confirmed, and no reversals occurred. Note that we made no attempt to predict the absolute level of performance in these areas. Whether a child proved precocious, average or slow, we merely predicted that each child would show a differential level of performance in different areas of functioning.

Another infancy characteristic of potential importance is perceptual sensitivity. Infants who respond to slight stimuli in the visual, auditory, tactile, and thermal modes, and who also discriminate small differences in the intensity of such stimuli, we have designated as highly sensitive. In the samples studied so far, infants who make overt response to slight stimuli are also infants easily overwhelmed and disorganized by stimuli of exceptional intensity, such as loud sounds or very bright light. For infants who are highly sensitive we predicted that as 4- and 5-year olds they would show exceptionally differentiated expressive behavior (i.e., that physiognomy, voice quality, posture, and gesture would be subtly variable and reflect feeling states with unusual clarity). We also thought that highly sensitive infants were predisposed to the early development of a rich imaginative life and intense fantasies. A rather low level of perceptual sensitivity in early infancy was taken to indicate a predisposition for relatively undifferentiated expressive behavior and for a realistic orientation with relatively little active fantasy life at the preschool age. Combining the results, 92 predictions based on these hypotheses were made of which 68 or 74% could be confirmed. This suggests that perceptual sensitivity does have an influence on expressive behavior and the development of imaginative faculties, just as activity level plays a role in the pattern of cognitive development. But I am more impressed with what can be learned from the predictive failures. For when the conspicuous absence of either expressiveness or imaginativeness was predicted, on the basis of low sensitivity in infancy, the very great majority conformed to expectation, while a few at preschool age did not differ enough from what is usually seen in children at this age to satisfy criteria. None of the low-sensitivity babies developed to an outstanding degree that attribute for which they were thought to lack the potential, just as none of the low-activity babies showed the pattern we thought to be linked with high activity. Yet among the *high*-sensitivity infants some failed to show the richly imaginative or highly expressive characteristics that had been anticipated, some showed these attributes to an average degree, and two actually reversed and became somewhat constricted, extraordinarily realistic children. By definition, a potential can be realized, modified, or suppressed, and information available to date suggests that high perceptual sensitivity may well prove to be an infant characteristic denoting a potential. So far, such infant characteristics as we have been able to link to specific aspects of later functioning may be characterized either as predispositions for certain patterns of development and adaptation later on, or else as potentials for excellence or unusually strong development in particular areas.

The question of how early predispositions may affect the child's response to environmental input is closely related to the broader topic of what determines whether potentials are realized or not, which, in turn, is a burning issue in biology in general. When the problem is put in such a very broad form it is probably insoluble, but I do have suggestions for more limited approaches that are relevant.

Time does not permit a statement of the developmental theory, incomplete as it is, that led to the substantive and methodological proposals I am about to make. But it is necessary to state a few underlying assumptions. In common with most psychologists, I assume that human development comes about in consequence of interaction between the organism and the conditions and events that constitute the environmental field. These interactions can be described as a continuous and overlapping series of behavioral events, *if* the term "behavior" is made to include affects, thoughts, ideation, and other forms of mentation. This series of behavioral events is what we mean by a child's experience. By this definition, experience is indivisible from the environmental input, yet by no means identical with it. A baby cannot have the experience of reaching for a toy if no toys are available—thus this particular event is wholly dependent on the fact that the environment contains the toy. But a baby may fail to have the experience of reaching for a toy even when they are amply provided, if he sucks his thumb instead, or if he is crying at the time. It requires the convergence of an infant both capable of and inclined to reach for objects, and the availability of suitable objects to create this single experience or behavioral event. The same applies to any and all aspects of experience, whether they involve a sense of failure or success, intimacy with the mother, or anything else that can happen to the human creature.

Therefore, and this is the second assumption I have to make, the study of the effect of environmental conditions or events upon development requires that one first determine the effect of environmental circumstance upon experience. It follows that the child's experience cannot be inferred from the objective properties of the environment. (A home full of toys does not mean that the child is necessarily experiencing rich object stimulation.) It is what the child does or does not do, how he behaves in the context of whatever the environment provides, that defines and describes his actual life experience.

Let me give two examples of how these assumptions can be applied to our problem. It is well established that hospitalization and the attendant separation from the mother have measurable effects upon the behavior and development of infants. In general, developmental progress is arrested, and a retrograde change to less mature behavior is not at all uncommon. It is equally well established that infants differ from one another in the severity of their response to hospitalization. In my terms, what these infants experience while in the hospital, the degree and kind of alteration in their life that occurs with the hospitalization, ought to be different for those who respond by severe regression and those whose development is impeded to a lesser degree. Among the many factors that are likely to play a role in accounting for the difference, one has to do with the organismic characteristic of activity level. From a comparison of very active with markedly inactive infants, living in their own homes and entirely normal in their development so far, I concluded that at these early ages active infants differ from inactive ones in the conditions that elicit their most complex and mature behavior integrations. Active babies often practiced their most advanced skills in response to the normal background animation provided in a family. That is, they reached for and manipulated objects, kicked, crawled, changed their positions, etc., while no one was talking to them, showing them toys, or touching them. Among inactive babies, on the other hand, the more complex learning activities occurred almost only when another person, usually the mother, provided social and bodily stimulation in direct and focused interaction with the baby. The frequency with which infants engage in the more complex behavior integrations that are in the process of being learned proved highly correlated to developmental status as measured by tests. For the active infants, there was no relationship between the frequency with which they were played with, and otherwise attended, and test results. For the inactive infants it was found that the more they were appropriately stimulated, the higher their test scores. For the ages between one and eight months I concluded that social and physical stimulation will have a differential impact, depending upon activity level (Escalona, 1967, 1968). Shaffer (1966) reasoned that if the hypothesis were correct, hospitalization should affect active infants less severely than inactive ones. On a sample of Glasgow babies of suitable age he ascertained that the developmental retardation, as measured by change in Developmental Quotients, was significantly greater for those infants who had independently been classified as inactive. The mean D.Q. and the range was much the same for each activity group, so that the severity of impact upon developmental progress differed as a function of activity level.

The detailed investigation of the specific effects of infant reaction patterns tends to get complicated, because interaction effects occur not only between predispositions and environmental factors, but among different organismic characteristics and a wide range of environmental inputs. For instance, the study of normal infants to which I have referred also showed that the direct contact with the mother could affect behavior in opposite directions. Very active infants, again up to eight months, reduce their activity in response to appropriate social stimulation, while inactive infants are roused to what are for them relatively high levels of activity. Yet in another way being played with and handled produced the same result for all, in that both groups of infants tended to achieve a medium level of behavioral arousal which I have called "optimal animation" and which is a close cousin to Peter Wolff's state of "alert wakefulness" in neonates. In this optimal state, which very active babies reach by calming down while inactive babies have to get there by becoming a little more excited than they were before, the reciprocal social interactions that we consider prime elements of development at these ages, are most likely to occur. I refer to mutual smiling, reciprocal vocalizing, the kind of peek-a-boo in which the baby actively participates, and the like. Not all infants in either group showed these reciprocal behavior adaptations during social and bodily contacts with their mothers. When they did not it was because the mother (or whoever was the social partner) did not provide the kind of playful stimulation to which the infant could respond. In the face of overly intense stimulation, such as being tossed about, tickled vigorously, exposed to sudden loud sound and the like, many active infants lose all focus upon the environment, as they thrash about and giggle helplessly. In response to the same kind of stimulus bombardment, many inactive infants become nearly motionless, avert their heads, may close their eyes, and sometimes flex into a little ball in their efforts to protect against overstimulation. Similarly, some mothers offer such slight and delicate attentions that the babies' behavior alters hardly at all. While regarding mother and perhaps smiling in response, the complexity of their behavior and the level of activity remains much the same as at other times. Yet what constitutes "too much" or "too little" stimulation to bring the baby to a state of optimal animation depends upon another organismic characteristic—perceptual sensitivity. In our sample, activity level and perceptual sensitivity were independent of one another, the distribution of highly sensitive, moderately sensitive, and relatively insensitive babies being the same in both activity groups. It turned out that the kind of mauling and overly intense attention I described was just exactly right for those sturdy, relatively unresponsive babies rated low in sensitivity. By the same token, the exceedingly gentle and low-keyed approach that made no difference to most babies served to calm active ones and to rouse inactive ones, *if* they happened to be highly sensitive.

In short, it is unrealistic to expect that a single infancy characteristic will lead to a particular kind of response to a specific environmental variable. Each infant organism has a whole series of separate reaction tendencies, and it is the combination of these organismic characteristics that determines the child's responsiveness to environmental influence.

So far this discussion has been limited to a few examples of how behavior tendencies in infancy, presumably biologically rooted, may affect the growing child's response to whatever life conditions he encounters. However, human beings not only arrive on the scene differently endowed and predisposed, but they acquire new reaction tendencies as they grow. It is convenient to refer to early observable organismic characteristics as *pre*dispositions, and to label those reaction tendencies that develop later as *dis*positions. It is my belief that most of the important individual differences in personality and functioning are acquired over time, and are only indirectly related to some of the primary predispositions. When it comes to the more complex individual variations in such things as basic attitude, cognitive style, the quality of interpersonal relationships, the organization and content of affective life, novelists are far ahead of psychologists in tracing the origin of these characteristics.

The key difficulty is practical rather than conceptual. How is one to obtain information about what a child's experience is and has been? And how does one choose the elements of experience to focus on, in view of the fact that it is probably the total configuration and the sequence of experience that matters, rather than isolated events? Our research group has made a small beginning which, in the present form, is applicable only to the first two years of life. Yet it points a way of studying individuation processes that are now feasible, with the aid of videotape and computers.

Our design is based on the recognition that despite the infinite variety of life experience, certain elements or components tend to be relatively stable. For instance, a child who is raised strictly and expected to conform to certain modes of conduct is likely to encounter prohibition, constraint, restraint, and disapproval more often than a child raised by indulgent parents. Whatever his mode of experiencing his milieu might be, the parents are not likely to change their basic style from one month to the next. By the same token, once a child has become timid, anxious, or especially interested in certain varieties of play, these dispositions will help to shape his responsiveness to whatever happens and therefore his experience, for weeks or months and sometimes longer. In other words experience is not a random aggregate, but has some stability over time. Such relative stability in the behavioral events that make up a child's daily life we refer to as *patterns of experience.*

Our current study is based on the assumption that differences in stable components of experience should account for a good many individual differences in abilities, behavioral style, and personality functioning.

As we have said, a determination of experience patterns requires a full account of what the child does in the course of his everyday life, which includes a full and specific account also of the environmental settings and the events taking place within his field of awareness. It is impossible to trail a child, even an infant, through every waking day. But if important aspects of experience have stability over time, judicious sampling ought to provide a fair approximation of these more enduring aspects of experience.

In our study, in which we attempt to obtain experience patterns for children from birth to two years of age, weekly visits are timed in such a way that every portion of the baby's waking day is covered every six weeks. In other words, we are there when he awakens in the morning; in successive weeks we cover every portion of his day—including evenings and weekends. Visits are also scheduled so as to reflect the settings and situations that are recurrent in his life. If he is taken daily to the park, an appropriate proportion of our observations are in the park. If he is left with relatives or sitters, we see to it that the observation time in those localities corresponds more or less to the proportion of his total time spent in these situations. The data we obtain differ from the observational data reported by others, not only by the fact that we relentlessly pursue our subjects for 104 successive weeks and into all the places where they regularly spend some time (except for nocturnal events in the bedroom).

The more important feature of the data is that what we record as *primary* data is not how the infant was spoken to or picked up, or any other separate account of the environmental events. We record the child's behavior, and the extent to which each behavior episode was related to environmental circumstance is made specific. Thus, in noting and counting the instances in which the baby gazed at something intently, we know how many times such visual regard was focused on the mother, an intimate adult (father or other permanent members of the household), a sibling, another person, an aspect of the inanimate environment, or a portion of his own body, such as his hand. A tiny and fragmented example of what we mean by a pattern of experience would be, for instance, that in comparing two four-month old babies, one of them regarded his own hands or something in the immediate physical environment far more than the other. For the first baby the percent of all instances of intent gazing directed at another human being might be 55, and for the other 80% of all gazes might be directed at a social partner. Provided such a discrepancy is maintained for at least six weeks we should call it a component of a stable experience pattern. Incidentally, the six-week interval is somewhat arbitrary and derives from the practical constraints of how much data one can get in a given time and still remain friends with the participating families. Our approach also implies that the quality of each encounter between the baby and an adult is judged not by the adult's intention, but by the child's behavioral response. Thus, if someone means to play with the baby but the baby starts to cry, we score this as being hurt or displeased by the other person. If mother scolds and the baby looks at her in pleased fascination, the records indicate a neutral pleasant social input; if, in dressing, the baby's mother holds him down and he resists, we would score this as having been restrained. But should the baby have made no effort toward movement, the same action of being held would not constitute restraint in his experience.

This is not the place to discuss either the methodological or the theoretical characteristics of a research program. For present purposes I need only mention that just about all observable environmental inputs (as I have just defined them) and behavior outputs are recorded, scored in accordance with an elaborate manual that saw many revisions before reliability could be established, and that these scores go directly on to IBM cards and into the computer. For our subjects I can tell you for the periods of observation how many times we saw them smile at mother, how often we saw them cry and when, what they did with objects, how often and how much they vocalized, how often their behavior altered in response to sounds or to sights and sounds combined, how often and for how long they sucked their thumbs or rocked or chewed at objects or pulled their hair, and a host of other things. From these data, patterns of experience are searched for and calculated by the computer, and to the extent that experience constellations show stability over time, we have obtained an empiric and quantitative measure of experience patterns. Quite independent of these experience measures, the babies were of course tested, rated, and examined periodically so that there is an array of individual difference measures. These include an assessment of the children at age two performed by guest evaluators who know nothing about either the children or about our hypotheses.

Use of this method has convinced us that the general principle of using behavior-in-context as a quantitative index of the content, structure, and range of the child's experience, lends itself to the study of individual differences in many areas. If we are seeking to explain why identical or similar external events, such as hospitalization, or conditions such as poverty, or a particular style of child rearing, have unequal and sometimes paradoxical effects upon different children, the study of the differential impact which environmental events have upon these children ought to provide us with more specific information about those reaction proclivities on the child's part (whether inborn or acquired) that make the difference.

The formal structure of a research design based upon this notion will differ somewhat from those currently most widely used. Given a focus on a single variable, be it brain damage, activity level, sensory defect, institutionalization, slum living, or attendance at a day-care center, the inquiry would be broken down into several phases. Ordinarily we know or can learn the direction of the general and more or less universal effect of an environmental variable. For instance, institutional rearing of the old-fashioned type tends to retard or distort development, as do degraded styles of life in ghettos. On the other hand, day-care centers are expected to provide appropriate stimulation and to enhance cognitive and social development, and so on. In the light of this background information, the first step in the research design I would propose is to study in detail *how* a sample of children subject to a particular environmental influence behave. For instance, knowing that well-conducted day-care centers tend to enhance cognitive development, the first step would be to observe a group of children in such a way as to specify stable components of each one's experience while at the center. This would tell us which experience patterns characterize those children who maximally benefited from the program, by contrast to the behavioral event structures found among children on whom the program had less beneficial impact. In a manner of speaking, we should then know what day-care meant for one child as contrasted to another, in behavioral and quantitative terms.

This information will take us forward in two separate ways. We shall know the events and behaviors in the day-care center that are associated with the end result of cognitive gains on the child's part, and we shall also know which of the established reaction tendencies of different children are associated with particular patterns of experience in a given setting.

The next step in the proposed design is predictive. From observations and/or measures made on a new sample before they enter the day-care center, those individual differences previously found relevant would be ascertained, and consequent differences in the experience patterns and cognitive gains of these children would be predicted. If successful, we should then have solved the problem of what determines individual differences with respect to the response to day-care attendance.

The problem of what has led to these individual differences in the first place is relegated, in my model, to a separate investigation. Instead of jumping from a hypothesized early determinant to the outcome, I suggest that we first focus on the nature and the immediate consequence of such differences in disposition and experience as we find. In other words, instead of relating early characteristics such as low activity level or having a certain kind of mother to such outcome variables as gains derived from day-care centers, I would establish lawful relationships in smaller steps, gradually work backwards to more remote antecedents, and make room in the research design for totally diverse developments and outcomes in response to experience during the intervening years.

All of this sounds abstract and somehow remote from the immediate concern of guiding social and educative practice in the light of individual difference factors. I would like to conclude with an example to illustrate that the focus on experience patterns can be applied even now to achieve more effectively whatever we set out to do in behalf of children. For the sake of convenience I shall stay with the day-care center, which is on my mind because I am involved with developing such centers for children under age three years.

We know from past research results that there are certain activities or experiences that tend to foster cognitive advance during the second year of life. These include (1) the frequent manipulation of a variety of objects differing in size, color, shape, texture, and functional properties, (2) frequent occasion to connect or combine verbal labels with sensorimotor categories of action and perception, (3) frequent and varied activation of the large muscle system, as in running, climbing, and the like, and (4) a diversity of social interactions with people some of whom, by virtue of their constant presence, become objects of affection and trust for the child. There are others, but for purposes of this example we shall assume that the presence of these four categories of experience is important for developmental progress at these ages.

Day-care programs serving toddlers are designed to provide these particular experiences, yet children differ in the frequency with which these varieties of behavior do in fact take place. The pattern-of-experience measures might show that some stick to stereotyped activity with only one type of toy, and thus fail to experience richly varied transactions with the physical properties and categories of the object world. It may show that some fail to attend and do not themselves apply the verbal designations constantly offered by the staff. Yet others may be so restless that sustained involvement in any activity is rare, etc., etc. An analysis of experience patterns does more than identify the children who do not avail themselves of the opportunities provided by the milieu. It specifies for each child the environmental circumstances under which he shows his greatest readiness to participate in learning experiences. It also defines the conditions under which stereotypy, passivity, restlessness, or disabling anxiety and discomfort tend to take over.

Long before future study shows how certain children respond to the stimulation provided in the center in ways that diminish their chance of profiting from what is offered, the experience-pattern analysis can be used to systematically modify what is provided by the center. In other words, the program could be individually tailored to what was learned about the reaction tendencies of each child. For instance, some toddlers cannot deal with toys at all if more than one or two are in their perceptual field—a heap of toys and lots of children and adults engaged in using them would be enough to put them out of action. Whatever the reason for this vulnerability, day-care staff can create the situation in which such children will engage in object play, by frequently providing a protected territory and uncluttered field, thereby altering the pattern of experience of these children in the direction of providing more of that which is desired. Or again, some toddlers will engage in sustained play almost only in situations where such activity is constantly supported by a playful and animated adult who contributes just enough to keep the baby going but constantly supports the child's action impulses. Less well recognized is the syndrome of the 13- to about 18-month old who shows complex play only when undiverted by simultaneous social stimulation. Social events for such babies are so absorbing or exciting that they suppress focused attention to inanimate things. Some of the most highly recommended teaching exercises will fail in their purpose with such a child. The list of individual difference variables is nearly endless. It can have to do with noise levels, with color preferences, with position habits, with the quality of social approach made to them, and so forth.

Good child-care workers note such dispositions, especially if they are extreme, and adapt to them. But even our limited experience shows that systematic analysis of experience patterns uncovers obstacles and aids to the actualization of particular behavioral engagements that astute impressionistic observation overlooks. In addition, deliberate design of at least small portions of each waking day's experience particularized for the child in terms of his needs is vastly different from occasional accommodations by a busy caretaker or teacher. Such a program is based neither on general convictions of what is good for babies nor upon convictions of what is good for a shy child or an anxious one. It is based on systematic empirical determination of those conditions under which a given child, at a particular time, is able to show the behavior or have the experience that we know to promote learning.

In short summary, I have suggested that individual differences in very early infancy can be regarded as predispositions toward certain modes of functioning, or as indices of the presence or absence of a potential for specific later characteristics. Some research results were cited to support the hypothesis that such predispositions play a role in shaping the infant's responsiveness and adaptation throughout the first half-year and perhaps beyond, but that individuation and the most centrally important kinds of individual difference come about as the infant and child acquire differential, relatively stable reaction tendencies and patterns of functioning to which I have referred as dispositions. In my view, neither predispositions nor dispositions remain stable attributes of the personality for all time, although certain individual characteristics may be maintained if subsequent experience supports and strengthens them. For some organismic characteristics we suggested specific links to functions and behavior characteristics that emerge during the preschool years. It was implied that the import of particular predispositions can best be discovered and tested within the framework of developmental theory, rather than by large-scale correlational analyses covering wide age spans.

To come to grips with the investigation of individual differences it seems necessary to focus on smaller segments of developmental time and on process studies. Differences in the day-by-day experiences of children were asserted to have relative stability, and I proposed that such stable differences in experience foreshadow and reflect individual differences in behavior, performance, or response to specific environmental input at later times. A technique for the empirical and quantitative assessment of experience patterns was briefly mentioned. Finally, I tried to condense into a single illustration the thesis that the study of experience patterns lends itself to several purposes. It can identify significant dimensions of individual difference; it can uncover the antecedents or determinants of individual difference; and it can be an aid to clinical, educative, or preventive action in behalf of children when each child dealt with is responded to in ways adapted to his particular dispositions.

REFERENCES

Escalona, S. K. and Heider, G. M. (1959). *Predictions and outcome: a study of child development.* New York: Basic Books, Inc.

Escalona, S. K. (1965). Some determinants of individual differences in early ego development. *Transactions of the New York Academy of Sciences,* **27,** 802-817.

Escalona, S. K. (1968). *The roots of individuality: normal patterns of development in infancy.* Chicago: Aldine Press.

Kagan, I. and Moss, H. (1962). *Birth to maturity: A study in psychological development.* New York: Wiley.

Shaffer, H. R. (1966). Activity level as a constitutional determinant of infantile reaction to deprivation. *Child Development,* **37,** 595-602.

Thomas, A., Birch, H. G., Chess, S., Hertzig, M. E., and Korn, S. (1963). *Behavioral individuality in early childhood.* New York: New York University Press.

CHAPTER 9

Parent-Child Relations, Adaptation to Nursery School, and the Child's Task Orientation: A Contrast in the Development of Two Girls

Christoph M. Heinicke,
Fred Busch,
Phyllis Click, and
Estelle Kramer

A great interest has recently developed in delineating the conditions which allow the young child to learn to the optimal extent. The observations to be reported here focus on those individual differences in his development and his environment that are related to the task orientation of the three-year-old child, namely, his ability to engage in, produce in, persist in, and enjoy nursery-school tasks.

Some evidence already exists linking parent-child relationships, adaptation to nursery school, and the child's task orientation (Kagan and Moss, 1962; Baumrind, 1967; Heinicke, 1968). In our pilot study the parent-child profiles rated after six weeks of nursery school differed greatly but could also be divided into two groups: (1) those where the mother-to-child affection and acceptance was adequate, her availability defined, new relationships encouraged, limits set, and pressure exerted for independent achievement, and (2) those where these conditions were not met. The children from the first as opposed to the second group of families showed a more adequate task orientation at the age of four. This tends to replicate the association between parent-child variables and "competence" in nursery-school children as reported by Baumrind (1967).

Equally important, other research has shown that variations in task orientation during the nursery-school years are clearly related to performance on intelligence and achievement tests in the period following nursery school. (Kagan and Moss, 1962; Heinicke, 1968; Attwell, Orpet, and Meyers, 1967). However, review of the total literature linking parental influence and cognitive development in early childhood reveals a very contradictory picture (Freeberg and

Payne, 1967). Some investigators working in the early learning field have, for all practical purposes, ignored the realm of family influences. Given the disappointment in the followup results of some current educational efforts (Operation Headstart, for example), others, including ourselves, have once more looked to the family environment as a potential source for insuring permanent learning gains.

It is the assumption of the research to be reported here that methodological refinements in both the observations of the child and his family will elucidate the nature of their mutual influence. Thus, we evaluate a particular piece of the child's behavior, such as his engagement in a task, in the context of his other behavior in order to understand what he is experiencing and if it is similar to the engagement of other children. Further evaluation of this behavior, as well as the actual impact on its development of nursery school and family events, is made possible by daily process observations. Chapter 12 of this book sets forth the strategy and implementation of the methodology used in this study.

This chapter gives illustrative evidence from the contrasting development of two girls, Paula and Jean, in relation to the hypotheses that have guided our work. The most general of these are: (1) that variations in the child's task orientation at age four are anticipated by variations in his initial adaptation to nursery school, and (2) that variations in this adaptation can be linked to variations in the nature of his existing and ongoing family relationships as well as to the new relationships that he is able to form with teachers and peers.

Like others (A. Freud, 1965; Mahler, 1963), we stress that certain profiles of existing and ongoing family-child relationships encourage the child to separate psychologically as well as physically from the family and to form new relationships in nursery school. We also stress that the teachers and peers are important not only because they provide new relationship opportunities, but because they may be critical in filling relationship needs which the family has not been able to meet. We thus see both the quality of the existing and ongoing family relationships and the type of new relationship opportunities as central to determining whether the child can progressively resolve conflicts related to the past and present, or whether maladaptive solutions to conflicts are prominent, and thus, among other things, impair the child's task orientation.

We recognize that the child's complex development before and after age three is influenced by many factors other than his family relationships, and, indeed, has influenced the nature of the family's response. For purposes of intervention we are nevertheless very interested in the continuing influence of the child's family relationships on his adaptation and how this adaptation links to his future task orientation.

The choice of the age three-to-seven interval needs further explanation. In the first place, available longitudinal studies indicate both that nursery-school adaptation is predictive of later academic achievement, and yet that the child's development is still subject to considerable influence (Attwell, Orpet, and Meyers, 1967; Cohen, 1963; Kagan and Moss, 1962; and Westman, 1967). In planning efforts to prevent later academic difficulty, it seemed appropriate to choose an age where serious developmental difficulties are not likely to be reversed if left unattended but where intervention nevertheless has a chance of making a considerable impact.

Second, this interval was chosen because the likelihood of some of the children seeking treatment during the time of study was considerable. It was felt that the combination of observational and child analytic data on certain children would be invaluable.

Observations in the pilot study from which the following material is derived were made on a total of 10 three-year olds and their intact middle-class families, entering a private nursery school in a large metropolitan area. The remainder of this chapter focuses specifically on Paula and Jean, two three-year olds who entered nursery school at the same time. The presentation is structured to describe the step-by-step development from shortly before entrance into nursery school until departure for kindergarten two years later. This includes the nature of the child's general adaptation to nursery school, the nature of her relationship to teachers and peers, the additional information on the parent-child relationship during the course of the study, and the behavior seen in special task and assessment situations at the end of the first and second year of nursery school.

To facilitate the reader's view of the changes occurring in each child, the intensive observations of about the first three months have been organized around a series of periods of development. The method of abstracting these periods is described in Chapter 12. The same method of period analysis is also employed, but less rigorously so, for the observations of the remainder of the first year of nursery school.

Consistent with the way in which the observations were made, they have been separated from the inferences made in relation to specific pieces or several pieces of data. The observations will be given in full paragraph while the interpretations will be placed in indented paragraphs below each observation. Further, to organize these inferences, an interpretative summary of the child's overall adaptation is given at the end of each account.

I. DESCRIPTION OF PAULA'S DEVELOPMENT IN NURSERY SCHOOL

A. Background and Parent-Child Relationships

Paula is a blonde-haired, petite, and very pretty little girl who entered nursery school when she was three years and three months old. She has an older brother seven years of age, and comes from an economically comfortable family.

In the initial home visit the mother made clear that she was very favorably inclined to the school, on the basis of her son's "wonderful experience." She was warm and yet reticent to pursue matters of feeling. An awareness of possible stress for her and her daughter around the separation involved in entrance into nursery school yielded quickly to a slightly stoical attitude. However, the mother stated that she and her husband were very ready to help Paula with any difficulties that she might encounter. Both of them felt that they had not had this kind of help from their parents and were eager to provide this for their children.

During the interview, Paula came running in from the other room. She had been playing with the teacher. She requested some potato chips, and after she got them, curled up in mother's lap. She was vigorously sucking her thumb. The mother accepted this completely and contributed further to it by rocking her a very little bit.

> This need to return to a familiar lap and the pleasure in rocking seemed Paula's way of meeting the anticipated demands of entering nursery school.

Summarizing such information as was available on the family relationships at the end of the first six weeks, the following tentative profile emerges. The mother impressed all observers during the first six weeks as a well-functioning woman who could organize her household and effectively, though not harshly, limit her daughter. She obviously allowed her daughter's messy play, but would then complain in her quiet way. Her reticence indeed left more than the usual number of questions unanswered. Thus, she had obviously had some difficulty with her son but little was revealed here. It was clear that Paula was afraid of her brother's intrusions, particularly the aggressive ones.

While the mother made clear when she was and was not available, the absolute amount of affection that Paula needed was not quite gratified by her. What little was known about the father stressed by contrast that he was giving and affectionate.

> That the mother's acceptance and clarity of availability should be complemented by the father's open affection was thought to be of importance in facilitating Paula's development.

B. Paula's Initial Adaptation to Nursery School

1. Paula makes a confident but tentative entrance with her mother and asks how far she can go with the activities in the school. September 19th through 26th. Days 1-6.

Paula moved into the nursery school classroom tentatively, with her finger between her teeth. Although she was initially cautious, she soon seemed quite confident to be there, did not cling to her mother, and her facial expressions relaxed. Carefully, she fed or cleaned various dolls. At times she would go over to her mother to receive very quiet and warm affection, and then move away from her again in order to resume her play in the doll corner. Throughout this first period there was, however, little noticeable contact with the teacher or student teachers.

It would seem that engagement in the activities of the school was initially dependent on the affectionate reassurance from a physically present mother. The longing, associated anxiety and the disruption of her engagement became even more pronounced as the mother actually began leaving.

During the next two days the mother was often gone for short periods of time. In contrast to the first day, Paula was now very often near tears. Most important, even when the mother was there she was often involved reading a newspaper or doing some sewing. Yet she was still very much available and very loving when Paula could get her attention. The mother would reach out to Paula on a verbal level but the physical contact was minimal. When the mother was momentarily gone, Paula characteristically just sat still, or as on the second day of her entrance into nursery school, moved rapidly from one activity to another. The sucking of her thumb became more prominent as did her hunger for juice and crackers. Somewhat in contrast to this behavior was her obvious wish to please the grownups by insisting on putting on her own shoes and socks.

We would interpret both this premature move toward dressing herself and the maternal play with dolls as indications of a defensive identification with maternal roles and expectations. She pleases a mother whose departure she fears. She provides the mothering which she longs for. She controls her impulses, especially messing ones. Figuratively speaking, she holds on to a mother who is gradually disappearing.

On the fourth day Paula initially made her greatest move toward engagement in the nursery school. In a rather messy kind of soap bubble group activity, she at first became extremely cheerful and almost manic, but then suddenly as she noticed that her dress was getting wetter and wetter, became concerned. She turned to her mother, who had been sitting near her all this time, but the mother turned her over to a teacher to have her changed. Despite this experience Paula did not give up the water but played with it again in the more controlled setting of feeding and cleaning the dolls.

These and similar observations suggest that Paula's cautious approach into the nursery was, among other things, related to her anxiety that she might go too far and be judged a dirty little girl. The maternal play with the dolls reestablishes control, but through the cleaning also allows continued use of water. Since the teachers as opposed to the mother are involved, a new type of mastery is attained.

On the same day Paula also, for the first time, initiated feminine dress-up peer play by putting on high-heeled shoes, bracelets, and so on, and went out of her way to read a book to Bob, who was delighted. This was in sharp contrast to the observation that during the home visit, Paula simply would not do anything with the teacher until Michael, the older brother, was removed.

2. Paula misses her mother and turns to her thumb and the student teacher's lap for comfort. September 27th through October 5th. Days 7-13.

This was the period in which the mother began leaving her daughter and Paula actively turned to the teachers. From Day 9 on, the mother no longer stayed at all. Generally speaking, this was a period in which Paula looked extremely sad. She did not cry very frequently, but looked down and put her thumb in her mouth as the mother left. It remained there for much of her stay in the nursery during these days. Mother, on the other hand, would depart from the nursery in a very matter-of-fact manner. However, occasionally she asked why Paula should resist her departure, but would not discuss the problem further.

Increasingly, Paula was observed not only sucking her thumb, but also turning to the lap of one of the teachers. For a while it seemed that almost any lap would do. Or she would stand next to a teacher, holding her leg, as she had done with her mother. As time progressed, the student teacher, Sarah, became the favorite person from whom Paula sought bodily comfort.

It would seem that Paula could show, but was unable actively to express her great longing for mother. One might infer an identification with a mother who expects control of emotions. Even when mother's desperation briefly broke through, it was moved away from quickly.

Illustrating much of the above and representing both a point of extensive regression and a turning point, are the events of the 12th Day: "When Paula arrived that morning her thumb was in her mouth and her eyes were down. Her mother was watching this scene. She seemed taller and in some sense more distant than she really is. Showing for once a little desperation, she turned to one of the observers and said, 'I just don't understand why she does this: Why does she react to my leaving by putting her thumb in her mouth, by not saying anything or not even crying, when she actually is happy to come to school?' As they were talking and Paula was still looking down, she did then allow the teacher to swing her on the swings for a short time, and mother could leave. When the teacher had to tend to another child, however, Paula again put her thumb in her mouth and showed no involvement. The impression of depression was enhanced by a running nose and staff now considered sending her home."

At this point, teacher Molly's quiet and gentle encouragement to return to the maternal play with dolls cheered Paula. Following this, she was again ready for a long and more robust swing from Sarah. The aggressive approach of the boys temporarily disrupted this recovery, but lunchtime enhanced her cheer and activity again. After lunch, though, during a period when some mothers were already arriving, Paula again became extremely sad and was then found crying quietly in the bathroom. It is of interest that Molly could again stop her, comfort her, and ultimately move her once again into the play of the doll corner.

One can see how at this crisis point, even at moments of intense longing, Paula's trend to regressive behavior and disinvolvement could be modified by the teacher's intervention. Specific activities such as doll play, swinging, and feeding lead to affectual change and engagement in activities. The type of play and bodily comfort which satisfied Paula and allowed her to move forward is reminiscent of the quiet affection from mother, and formed a pattern which was seen throughout her adaptation to nursery school. However, the stability of her coping mechanisms, at this point, was still quite tenuous.

3. Special affection from the student teachers allows Paula some engagement in activities and peer relationships. October 6th through 20th. Days 14-24.

This is the period when Paula's longing for her parents was still very evident, but when she also increasingly developed relationships in the nursery school and became involved in various activities. The longing and sadness continued to be most evident at the beginning of the day and also emerged toward the end as the mothers would come to pick up their children. The longing was never very specific. She neither actively mentioned her mother or father, nor cried for them during this time. Being held in Sarah's lap or being given a long swing continued to brighten her up and allow her engagement in the nursery school. On the other hand, the student teacher, Molly, could interest her in the play in the doll corner, and this again would definitely brighten her up as it had already done in the previous period of development.

With the other children Paula was more able now to defend her own property against attack, and was in general less bothered by aggressive approaches. By Day

16 there was evidence that she was developing clearcut relationships to certain children, specifically two girls, Ethel and Joan. In play-acting with Ethel she was often the mother. Quite a different relationship could be seen with Joan. With Joan she would dance and sing to the music, often even to the point of silly exuberance. Also, sand play and other forms of messing were increasingly incorporated into whatever the game happened to be.

> Significant in this seemed to be Paula's increasing relationship to other children. Where before she had been mother to the dolls, now another girl was treated as the baby. Furthermore, one could see in her play the ability to be free of excessive adult expectations.

Of various games one very important one consisted of both running away and running toward the teacher's arms. This was done with the head teacher and Sarah at the very beginning of this period, and was not observed again.

> We think that the appearance of this turning the passively experienced separation into an active game, is both in the service of making a further transition toward involvement with the people and the activities of the nursery school, and in another sense is a sign of that very transition.

Emerging at about this time was Paula's increasing assertiveness. At home she stood up to her brother for the first time. In school she had no trouble telling other children what to do and now became a peer leader.

4. Special affection from the student teachers allows growing engagement: Paula develops a more intense relationship to the head teacher and becomes a peer leader. October 21st through November 14th. Days 25-41.

In most important respects, this period was not strikingly different from the preceding one. There were, however, some changes that warrant the separation of these days from the previous ones. Most important was the change in the relation to the head teacher. If previously the evidence had suggested that, while important, this relationship was not an obvious one, now Paula could allow more interaction with, and encouragement from, the head teacher. Perhaps most important, while swinging on the swings on Day 41, Paula sang a song to the teacher expressing, "I belong to you, I love you."

> This seemed indicative of Paula's total commitment to relationships in the school. Our inference is that the important changes which soon occurred after this were reflected in and in part made possible by this greater trust and involvement with the head teacher.

With the other children, while signs of leadership in organizing the play in the doll corner had developed previously, the elaborateness of a game which she now initiated again pointed to new qualities. Details of the observations on the morning of Day 26, the second day of this period, are as follows: "While Paula was cleaning the floor with a mop, Robert emerged from the next room as a monster. In response to him and with her mop still in hand, Paula quickly organized all the children into a game which eventually incorporated Robert, the monster. They all had to sit on chairs first, and then like an enlightened despot she made all of them march around the jungle gym, only to have them come back again. Next she let them chase each other while Robert was the frightening monster, and then she began playfully attacking the other children and making a tremendously ferocious face while doing all this."

> A number of factors seemed to be emergent in this activity. As so often was the case with Paula, a particular form of turning the passively experienced separation into an active experience occurred, this time by directing the comings and goings of a whole group of children. Also, one can see an attempt of resolution of her problems vis-a-vis aggression through a variety of methods. First of all, she incorporates aggression into a game of her choosing which she controls and where others are directed to be aggressive. Secondly, an identification with a benevolent aggressive figure is established. Finally, aggressive attacks are acted upon by her in a benign fashion within the context of play.

However, Paula still broke down in very severe tears when the two most aggressive and strongest boys in the group attacked her. As will be seen in the next period, she was ultimately even able to handle this.

5. *Paula's need for special affection from the student teacher lessens and her engagement in the nursery school is further enhanced.* November 15th through December 7th. Days 42-56.

In this period Paula took another important step towards increasing involvement in the activities of the nursery school. The pattern of reluctantly letting go of the parents to standing silently and looking around, sucking her thumb, and finally receiving a big swing from one of the student teachers could still be seen, but was greatly telescoped in time or hardly occurred at all. If in the first weeks of entrance into nursery school the longing for the parents was quite evident; it had been replaced in the fourth period by various indications of longing for Sarah, the teacher, or even her friend Joan. In this period even those indirect indications of separation anxiety were absent. However, it was still noted that if Paula moved too quickly into the nursery and was rather happy in the beginning, there was a tendency to go back to more regressive types of behavior later in the morning. By contrast, if she had shown this earlier in the day, it was much less likely to appear later on. Thus on Day 49, after two hours of assertive free play involving both the other children and various materials, Paula was once more heavily planted on Sarah's lap, sucking her thumb, and looking somewhat miserable. When her favorite songs were sung, she could take part very well. Otherwise, however, she was a silent partner to this group activity.

6. Paula's engagement in peer relationships and various activities including somewhat academic tasks is complete and at moments of stress she can comfort herself. December 8th through December 15th. Days 57-62.

During this period Paula's engagement in the activities of the nursery school were not only initiated rather immediately, but were sustained throughout the whole day. She had learned now to swing herself, and pleasure in singing and riding a tricycle was in evidence. She was also observed to extensively draw with a pencil for the first time.

> In the above description one can see Paula's growing independence in the nursery. There is no longer any evidence of direct or displaced longings for the parents. In contrast to the regressive thumb-sucking and dependence on Sarah, she can now swing herself. Also striking is the involvement and persistence in pre-academic tasks. It would seem that the tenuous coping methods of the previous periods have become stabilized, and allowed growth and interest in ego-oriented activities.

As before, Paula made extensive use of the doll corner to play certain games with her friends—Joan, Ethel, and now also Gloria. Primarily with Gloria she engaged in sand-and-mud play which still afforded much pleasure, but now involved such things as making cookies.

> As a further sign of growth one can see previous behavior that induced anxiety (i.e., messing) being enjoyed, and used in goal-directed activities.

With Joan, her obvious favorite at this time, she once more dealt with a number of important themes in her games. On Day 57, she and Joan sat in two chairs and pretended they were flying to San Francisco. They made it clear that the whole thing was a highly pleasurable event.

> One could certainly infer that they were identifying here with their parents and at the same time again turning the passively experienced

separation into an active one. So here again was an outstanding example of this defense that seemed to mark a new period of development. In contrast to the earlier games of simply running into the arms of the teacher, the structure of this game was highly complicated.

Similarly, if on previous occasions she had been frightened of the boys and had also quite often injured herself, both of these trends were no longer seen during this period but were incorporated into various games. On Day 62, Sarah tried to read the children a book but soon had to give up when they wanted to start running around. Suddenly they had hurt themselves. They had scratches on their arms which could hardly be seen, but the girls insisted on Band-Aids. They were obviously playing with and excited by the idea of being injured. This was developed further in a play with Arthur, a boy who had not at this point been as aggressive as some of the other children, but who could defend himself very well. Without much invitation he suddenly volunteered to become a gargantuan monster and acted well how such a monster would come at them. They in turn would get frightened and excited and become very girlish. He then would retreat into one of the big packing boxes in the yard and lie there waiting for them. Now they would come up, sneak around the box, only to be frightened again and then to run away in an excited fashion.

> Here again, Paula's ability to work on a conflictual area in a manner that is growth-producing seems evident. That this kind of game did help Paula to deal with one aggressive child in particular, Kurt, seems suggested by the fact that for the first time now, despite his rather strong attacks, she withstood them, did not cry, and yelled at him in a vigorous and defiant manner. We would infer, of course, that this was not simply a product of a particular game with its defensive implications, but rather a part of Paula's total development over the various periods which allowed for beginning mastery to take place.

C. Paula's Development from the Fifth to the Tenth Month of Nursery School

In the five months following the Christmas vacation Paula continued her progressive development. This was particularly evidenced in relation to her peers and in her response to the reading of books and the various art tasks set out by the teacher. At the same time she showed signs of regression in relation to certain events, the most important of these being the separation of her parents. Tensions had no doubt existed in the marriage previous to this time, but there had not been and were not to be any obvious signs of this tension. Moreover, the mother's decision to seek a separation came fairly suddenly.

Initially more important was the long Christmas holiday and the problems of reentry into nursery school that this posed. Paula returned during January 3rd to 17th to a type of entrance spelling reluctance. Observations made on January 12th were typical. She came in with a big frown on her face, wandered around for a few minutes, then wanted a push on the swings from the main teacher, and soon was swinging herself. Her very gay expression once more returned. Furthermore, following this she quickly assumed an active leadership role in the doll corner which the other children accepted. Moreover, her previous achievements in singing, dancing and tricycle riding were very much in evidence at this time.

> Paula's reluctant reentry into the nursery seems to be indicative, once again, of difficulty in leaving the home. However, the adaptive moves that occurred in the first three months are repeated in abbreviated form leading to a rapid readjustment. Important, also, is the fact that Paula's functioning in various skill areas was maintained during the absence from the nursery.

From January 19th through February 10th Paula's progress continued. In addition, her outstanding ability to answer questions during book time first became evident. Contrary to the first three weeks, both the nature of Paula's entrance at the beginning of the day and her general adaptation varied from immediate and joyful engagement to a sudden burst of tears and unhappiness. For example, on January 26th she suddenly burst into desperate tears and sucked her thumb because the main teacher would not let her have a certain purse. A lovely cuddle in the teacher's lap restored her quickly, and she was soon participating in activities. Both her anger at being controlled by the main teacher and her increasing seeking of affection from this teacher in general, characterized this period.

> It would seem likely that the increase in affectual disruptions, as well as the intense positive and negative affect now shown with the main teacher, had to do with the impact of the marital tensions. Even during this difficult time, though, Paula's striving towards growth is shown as a new skill becomes evident.

Although her reactions during the period from teacher Sarah's move to an adjoining classroom just before February 16th, to the parents' actual separation just after March 2nd, are not strikingly different from those of the previous period, some differences are noteworthy. One might well expect that the departure of a teacher who had played a crucial role in Paula's adjustment to school would accentuate her longing. Thus, on February 16th Paula initially spent some time looking searchingly at teacher Sarah in the other yard. She then got on the swing and asked Joan, her best friend, to swing her. But Joan was too rough and so in a whiny, low-pitched tone, Paula called for the head teacher. After receiving some sympathetic help and a swing, Paula could leave the swing and again become involved with Joan in the doll corner. Unlike previous times, Paula did occasionally interrupt the play to go whining to the head teacher, saying that she was cold. Increasingly during this time one could hear: "Esther (head teacher), I want you." In Paula's and Joan's play a theme emerged where they would yell at a boy of separated parents: "Get out! Get out!"

> Fascinating in the above is Paula's continued use of special activities and existing relationships to help with the impact of the two separation experiences. While longing for Sarah, Paula engages her best friend and the head teacher in a favorite activity formerly shared with Sarah. It is inferred, also, that in the play with Joan she is attempting to deal with the impact of the home situation.

Following the father's move to another residence, Paula's sadness on the next day was again overwhelming and now had a quality of depression that had not been seen before. A period on the swings and sucking her thumb did help her, and by midmorning she was giving the greatest number of correct responses during book time. As in February, throughout March she fluctuated between independent and competent functioning on the one hand, and sudden tears, turning to the swing, and seeking comfort from the head teacher on the other hand. Her behavior on March 16th was typical of this time. After initial exuberance she suddenly had to look at Sarah in the next yard. While standing there she somehow fell. There were no noticeable injuries, but Paula cried bitterly. A hug from the head teacher helped to restore her but the downcast look and thumb in the mouth persisted. She asked the teacher for a swing, was soon swinging herself, and after another sudden bout of crying again became exuberant. She and Joan now shifted to jumping off the boxes. For the first time Paula suddenly pleaded that the teacher catch her, "just like daddy does." However, she quickly accepted the teacher's offer of just a helping hand.

> Paula's need for support and sympathy during this time are easily related to the father's move. Impressive again is that while previous modes of fragile functioning were returned to, signs of effective functioning in coping with the strain in the nursery, as well as continuation of growth in various skill areas, were still in evidence.

While her closeness to both the teacher and Joan continued after March 30th and during April and May, occurrences of extreme crying or clinging to the teacher were rare. Certain new behavior was also apparent. For the first two weeks of this period Paula manipulated and yelled at the children in a fierce and rejecting way. Thus, on March 30th Paula had again organized the play with the other girls in the doll corner. Suddenly, with Paula as their leader, they were all shouting at the boys to "Get out." The boys were returning the verbal volley, but were obviously stopped by Paula's fierceness. Paula then insisted that everyone must go to bed. When Jennifer refused, Paula literally dumped her into bed.

> The above types of play do suggest Paula's defensive identification with a mother who might well have yelled, "Get out." To deal both with her own and the mother's sense of loss, she actively excludes others both from her house and her bed. Although the above sequences were repeated many times it was not possible to interpret them more exactly. Of particular interest is the fact that Paula and Joan between them made the best contributions during book time on this same day. Her ability to perform effectively in academic-like tasks, despite environmental stress, is shown again. It was tentatively concluded that though the impact of the parental separation was clearly noticeable, it had by the end of the first year of nursery school not seriously interfered with Paula's development.

D. Paula's Response to Task Situations at the End of the First Year of Nursery School

Paula's response to the listening comprehension task of book time was ranked as follows (a rank of one indicates she is highest in a group of ten children): Engagement (1); Compliance (1); Productivity (1); Pride and Pleasure (1); Creativity (1); and Regression (9). Thus in general she was very high in all dimensions but did show some signs of regression while listening to reading from a book. As will be seen in illustrative observation from June 5th, signs of regression mainly took the form of sucking her thumb.

Observations made on June 5th illustrate Paula's qualities both in relation to tasks chosen by herself and those planned by the teacher as part of the curriculum. Paula made a quick entrance into nursery school, and was soon cooking in the doll corner with Joan. While somewhat controlling in her play, her concentration, persistence, and creativity was marked. She and Joan enjoyed themselves for a whole hour. Most important, after the cooking (mud mixing) Paula requested that she be allowed to mix colors; as before, she created a beautiful set of colors.

Paula was all ready to get more water when she heard the teacher calling the children to book time; she quickly reversed field, washed her hands, and settled down. She was soon correctly answering questions about which of the children were missing, about various titles in the *Harry the Dog* series, and so forth. In association to a discussion of the animals in the story, Paula volunteered that her dog's name was Sarah. The link to her favorite student teacher and her mother's name was obvious; but the personal determinant did not disrupt the group.

Paula listened carefully as the next activity, gluing pieces of wood, was explained to the children. Although again settling down quickly, she slowly put little dabs of glue in certain places on the board. She was concentrating as she carefully and with obvious enjoyment made her first "arrangement." All observers agreed that the result was creative as well as practical. She produced one design after another until ultimately she had made six. Both shapes and color were actively employed to create a total effect. She had not only enjoyed her work but was proud of it and was making sure that each piece was labeled and saved. Moreover, she taught Jennifer how to glue certain pieces together.

E. Paula's Behavior in the Special Assessment Situations at the End of the Second Year of Nursery School

Of the total assessments made at the end of the second year of nursery school, those derived from the play interview and the administration of the WPPSI are of special interest.

Her manner of approaching these two tasks repeated in essential form the way Paula had made her entrance into nursery school. She was reluctant and sucked her thumb, but as her mother quietly made it clear that she wanted her to go, she quickly picked up her interest and was soon highly engaged in a most appropriate manner. In both the play and testing situation she quickly sized up the situation, chose certain of the possible alternatives, and proceeded along those lines. Her engagement and degree of self-motivation were again impressive. Of all the children observed, she played with the doll house in the most articulate manner. She rearranged the house to suit her purposes and then enacted a story. Confronted with the WPPSI test items one could see her mentally consider various alternatives and then act confidently. Her excellent capacity for observation and attention to detail made this approach effective. Taken together, the above qualities all suggested an excellent capacity for learning. Her actual performance in basic mathematical skills and perceptual motor functioning was high. On a visual motor task which involved a little chick finding its way through a maze to its mother (Maze Subtest), Paula did extremely well. Many children at this age are still disturbed by this presentation of mother-child separation. Her verbal capacity and level of information was also consistent with her general functioning in the Bright-Normal Range of Intelligence.

It also emerged, however, that Paula's ability to sort out experiences was sometimes under pressure and tended then toward a disruptive and even irritating perfectionism. Discussions with her mother revealed that the mother's own self-expectations, especially in the areas of orderliness and academic achievement, had always been high. Paula's ability to confine her feelings and yet experience the presence of their potential explosion was shown in a story that she enacted. A family is going to the zoo while the father goes to work in an office looking much like a cage. In constructing the first scene involving the cage of the hippopotamus, Paula spent a long time arranging the cage so that the huge animal could both be seen and not get away.

> This and other material suggested two major interpretations: (1) she wants to keep and see her father, not let him get away, but also accepts the fact of separation, and (2) she wants to express her feelings about the separation but curtails them, feeling they will go too far. All this would lead to great care in "getting it just right" and would not only produce some impatience in the male adult observer and interviewer, but, of course, also hold onto him.

In the testing situation Paula also at times pushed herself to the point of actually failing an item. Thus, on the Block Design subtest, rather than accepting the correct but not perfectly square design, she scattered the blocks and refused to continue. As already stressed, however, most of the time she was very competent in reaching her self-defined goals.

F. Interpretive Summary of Paula's Adaptation to Nursery School

Of great importance to Paula's development in the nursery school was her existing and continuing relationship with her mother. The nature of this relationship allowed for internalization of a maternal representation connoting both affection and a clarity as to when her wishes were or were not likely to be satisfied. Paula's inner situation was such that while knowing the limits of her at times distant and controlled mother, she could trust in her availability. She could, therefore, both psychologically and literally return to her mother. Having internalized a sufficiently nonambivalent representation of her central caretaking person, she approached new relationships with the expectation that she would be cared for again. In this move she was helped by a mother who encouraged the development toward self-reliance and ego competency. Although caution must be exercised in these conclusions, even less is known about the relationship to the father. Very likely he provided much of the more demonstrative affection that Paula missed in her relationship to the mother.

It is clear that the meeting of this very deficit in the new relationship to the openly affectionate teacher, Sarah, constituted an essential element in allowing Paula's excellent adaptation in the nursery. If a present and comforting mother had been the initial external person to assist Paula in coping with her longing and emerging anxieties about going too far in making a mess, or in expressing derivatives of her angry feelings toward her brother, so Sarah and Molly supplemented and to some extent replaced the mother in these functions, only to be in turn replaced by the head teacher and one peer in particular, namely Joan. If Sarah could provide a level of demonstrative affection probably not previously experienced, and give Paula the "home base" from which she could move toward engagement, so teacher Molly provided the quiet understanding and encouragement allowing Paula to turn to play involving defensive identi cations with aspects of the longed-for maternal role. Following these relationships, the head teacher became of increasing importance and this relationship now had a more varied meaning to Paula than those to the student teachers. Paula experienced her as a person who could provide organization, affection, direct help, encouragement, and effective limits. This more inclusive relationship turned out to be of great importance in helping Paula through the period when her "home base" was threatened by the parental separation and her longing for comfort was again intense.

Other sequences of coping methods could be noted and are closely related to the above. Paula's thumb-sucking was initially intense, and in fact never quite disappeared. From controlled doll play involving various defensive maternal identifications, she increasingly shifted to peer play and, most important, identification with the teacher's expectations allowing her not only to help the teacher but to grow in curriculum areas like singing and book time. Paula's persisting tendency to deal with the psychological separation from the parents in an active way is highlighted by the specific tendency to turn the passively experienced psychological separation into an actively controlled event. Its initial form involved running away from the teacher and returning. As if punctuating the implied resolution of the psychological issue of separation from her mother, Paula did extremely well on a visual-motor task (the Maze Subtest on the WPPSI) which can potentially be disrupted by association to issues of mother-child separation.

Similarly, one can trace in her development the various steps Paula took to deal with her fear of going too far in messing and of being overwhelmed by an aggressive boy. In both instances, the nursery-school environment allowed conditions in which she could pace herself in approaching the feared area. She ranged here from reading to a small friendly boy, Bob, to eventually being able to tolerate first the presence of aggressive boys, and then being able actually to retaliate the aggression of one impulsive child.

What is striking about each of these sequences is that in Paula's development the successive modes of coping with certain drives, such as the longing for the mother, and conflicts such as her aggressive feelings toward her brother, moved in a progressive direction so that new expressions were found for the drives, and the conflict areas often disappeared from view. Furthermore, as part of this progressive alteration of derivatives, one saw the increasing development of new ego functions.

It was the freedom from conflict interference that impressed one as she engaged in tasks and confidently moved toward goals. The essentially gratifying and clear availability of her relationship world with its corresponding inner expectations of trust toward that world, was reflected in her readiness to engage in and pursue to termination tasks set by that adult world. Her total experience had been such that previously experienced external demands had by the age of five become self-motivations. In this regard, internalized expectations derived from the mother's standards for control of aggression, orderliness, and academic achievement had very likely interacted with the experience of the partial loss of the father to lead at times to excessive control and perfectionism. At the age of five these determinants had, however, not interfered with her high level of functioning.

II. DESCRIPTION OF JEAN'S DEVELOPMENT IN NURSERY SCHOOL

A. Background and Parent-Child Relationships

Jean is a sturdily built girl with dark curly hair and dark eyes. Jean was just approaching her third birthday when entering nursery school and had one sister approximately one year older.

In the inital home visit with Mrs. L. it quickly became apparent that despite her friendliness she was extremely afraid of the potential judgments of the observer-interviewer. Though not disorganized, there was a flightiness in her movements that could also be observed in her daughter. The mother rarely spoke of her child, and though Jean was in the house, interaction with her mother was not observed. It was also learned that Mr. L. found it hard to give affection to Jean. It was noticed that the two sisters were dressed alike. Mrs. L. explained that she felt it was most important for the children to develop a strong attachment to each other. In subsequent interviews she stressed how she had had many close girlfriends all her life. One of these had developed a serious illness when Jean was seven months old. Mrs. L. spent much time with this friend until she died a year later. It was also learned that ever since Jean was six weeks old, much of her care was in the hands of a devoted maid. She treated Jean like a princess, but about a year before Jean's entrance into school, she left to be married and "to have a son."

> Striking at this point was Jean's isolation in the family. Jean very
> likely experienced an early physical, as well as psychological,

separation from her mother with the death of Mrs. L.'s friend. Potentially adding to the mother-child distance was the fact that Jean's primary caretaker till approximately age two seemed to be a maid. Given the possible early deprivation Jean experienced, and what seemed like a present lack of closeness between Jean and her parents, there was concern about the problems which might arise in Jean's meeting the requirements of adjustment to the nursery.

It also became apparent in the early interviews that Mrs. L. had high expectations about cleanliness. She was concerned about the "messiness" at the school and made her children feel that they must be ready at almost any time to be shown to company. Gradually it emerged that the disarray seen in parts of her house was congruent with serious inconsistencies in the messing which she did allow her children. There was in general a lack of consistent limits, but by contrast the mother made it very clear that she wanted the children to succeed academically and had no difficulty in encouraging Jean's entrance into the new relationships of the nursery school.

Although in the initial home visit the mother said she anticipated no problems with Jean in the nursery, in the first week of school she mentioned that she was concerned about Jean's tendency to withdraw and her excessive "independence." As an example of this independence Mrs. L. remarked that Jean had toilet trained herself around the age of two, even before her older sister had been trained. But Jean also entered the nursery school with two blankets which she had become very attached to.

B. Jean's Initial Adaptation to Nursery School

1. Jean enters nursery school by engaging in isolated activities but avoids relationships with all people, including her mother. September 19th to 26th. Days 1-6.

On Jean's first day of nursery school neither she nor Mrs. L. seemed to look for the other or desired any close contact. Striking near the end of the day was Jean's active avoidance of contact with the mother. Mrs. L. got up from her chair, walked toward Jean and called to her a number of times, with no visible response from Jean. At this point a student teacher told Jean her mother was going out and would be right back. Jean looked at the student teacher but quickly went back to the activity she was engaged in. The observer noticed that while the student teacher was talking to Jean, she would stare off into space or close her eyes tightly. When the mother returned to the room, she went to Jean and said, "I'm back now." Still Jean did not look up at her mother or answer in any way.

For the most part Jean's distance from her mother continued the entire first period. She rarely was in the vicinity of her mother and it was not uncommon for her to turn away from her mother when being talked to by her. For her part, Mrs. L. engaged in much socializing with the other mothers and rarely seemed to look in Jean's direction. This pattern was reversed on Day 4, when at the end of the day Jean wandered into the next yard. Mrs. L. went after her, picked her up and held her like a baby. For the first time Jean seemed content.

> Most impressive during this time was the distance in the mother-child relationship, and its possible consequences. Jean not only actively avoided her mother, but did this to the point of seemingly trying to shut out reality. Having experienced involvement as leading to rejection, all contact was hesitant or avoided all together. Two other factors noted were Jean's use of turning the passive experience into an active one (i.e., wandering into the next yard), and the strong infantile dependent wishes which were denied during this first week. Mrs. L. seemed physically available to Jean, but maintained her own emotional distance. It was speculated that Mrs. L. was unable to give to Jean except in prescribed ways.

Jean's characteristic manner of relating to the teachers and other children during this first period was very similar to the way she reacted to her mother. She rarely responded to the teacher's questions and most often ignored and avoided her. She could allow the head teacher to give her a ride but after 30 seconds Jean bolted from the wagon, leaving the teacher just standing in the middle of the yard.

In group activities, where one of the teachers would be reading a story or singing to the other children, Jean would approach the group and then veer away toward something else. When other children approached she would either leave the area or ignore them.

During this first period the extent of Jean's avoidance of others contrasted with her involvement in certain carefully selected tasks. For example, on the second day she sat for 25 minutes engrossed in painting. Jean was not concerned with the colors; she was just concerned with putting on thick layers of paint. Here, as in all of her activities, she concentrated a great deal on what she was doing, seemed purposeful in her movements, but rarely showed any type of pleasure or emotion. Occasionally her desperation broke through. On Day 5 she suddenly got up from her chair and said, "I'm lost." She then pointed to her chair and said, "She's lost." Similarly, her seeming unawareness contrasted with her obvious assimilation of much that was going on. For example, on Day 5 it was observed that she was singing to herself in accurate fashion, a song that the teacher had taught the children earlier in the morning.

   2. Jean begins a relationship with the teacher but the mother's departure sets off a serious regression to auto-erotism to which the mother in turn reacts by returning to the school. September 27th to 30th. Days 7-10.

During this period Jean's mother departed from the nursery. In some ways Jean became more involved in the nursery school, particularly in her relationship to the main teacher. The nature of this relationship fluctuated greatly, however. The range of behavior included a complete lack of eye contact, oppositional behavior, and wanting to be retrieved and held like a baby. Also her isolation from her peers continued. Rather than engaging in solitary activity she now moved frantically from one activity to another.

Particularly striking, however, was the sudden turn to various forms of self-stimulation. Jean now insisted on having one particular blanket. The importance of this blanket was seen in that the only time she cried in the nursery school situation was once when she could not find it. She used this blanket in a variety of ways. At times it was for regressive purposes, as she would lie down with it and suck on her thumb. At other times she moved from the security provided by it toward adaptive activities. Thus, she would leave the blanket for an activity, then go back to her blanket and then enter another activity.

During this period Jean also began to display her genital area a great deal and showed an excessive attachment to a frilly slip. The two occurrences were related in that when she would put on her slip, she resisted having any other article of clothing on. When sitting in a chair she would lift up her slip so that her bare bottom was on the chair, and often times her genitals would be exhibited.

> It would seem that Mrs. L.'s leaving the nursery at this point had various effects. Jean became more involved with the head teacher, but in a highly ambivalent fashion. Her previous task involvement was disrupted by anxiety. While at times using her blanket, for adaptive purposes, autoerotic behavior dominated and was Jean's maladaptive means of coping with the anxiety generated by mother's departure.

As Jean's inclination to regression was enhanced, Mrs. L. showed increasing concern. Her approaches to Jean were warmer, but there was a quality to these encounters of "who is this peculiar child?" Although not admitting any discomfort from Jean's regressive behavior, behaviorally Mrs. L. became increasingly anxious and flighty. A striking uncertainty about her own ability to mother her children was seen in her need to label herself as either perfect or bad. In this situation she insisted on evaluations and advice from the expert. In response to discussion, she herself suggested that she remain with Jean in the classroom during the morning and try to minister to Jean's needs as indicated.

For her part, Jean showed a growing need for her mother in the nursery.

> During this time Mrs. L.'s distance from Jean, not only in terms of ability to give warmth but also in understanding what Jean was all about and her uncertainty in the mothering role, was prominent. It was impressive, then, that from this stance Mrs. L. could see Jean's difficulty and move back to the nursery. Not surprisingly, an awkward, stilted quality characterized Jean's and Mrs. L.'s new-found contact with each other.

3. Jean is ill. October 3rd through 11th day. Days 11-17.

Jean was not in school during this period because of illness. Mrs. L. reported that both her children were sick at this time.

4. As her mother remains in the school, Jean is more affectionate with her than ever before and also more involved with the activities, peers, and teachers in the school. October 12th through 28th. Days 18-30.

On Jean's first day back in the nursery her avoidance was similar to that of the first period. However, this return to previous modes of behavior soon dissipated and she became increasingly involved in all aspects of the school experience.

This was the period when Mrs. L. was the only mother still spending a good part of the morning in the nursery school. Although Jean would still occasionally strain from her mother's hug, most of the time she would express her longing. For her part, Mrs. L. showed a variety of reactions to her daughter. At times she seemed anxious and concerned over Jean's isolation and at other times she seemed aloof and distant. Sometimes she treated Jean in a disorganized rush fashion and sometimes she was very affectionate.

Most striking during this period were Jean's positive moves toward individual children. The first instance of cooperative play with another child came on Day 22, when Jean went to sit on the teeter-totter with Ethel. Later that day in a song game where the children were to choose friends, Jean chose Ethel and Paula as friends, and was chosen as a friend by Joan. However, most of Jean's approaches to the other children were not that successful. Frequently when she approached a group she was either ignored or rejected, occasionally for no apparent reason. But there were times when she was rejected for specific reasons such as her determination to get her way, or because she entered a group in a provocative fashion. Jean's usual way of reacting to rejection was to withdraw to another area with little affectual expression. At other times she would make a positive approach to the girls, only to withdraw if this approach was reacted to favorably.

Uppermost in her contacts with the head teacher was a provocative, determined, oppositional behavior, especially during lunchtime. Jean would refuse to wash her hands, continually run away from the table and had to be stopped from various peculiarities in her eating habits. A great fluctuation in her attitude toward messing was consistent with this oppositional behavior.

> It seemed likely that Jean's greater involvement in the school was related to the greater affectionate closeness with her mother. However, Mrs. L.'s involvement with Jean as observed in the nursery was still highly ambivalent. Similarly, the ambivalence in Jean's relationship to other children and the head teacher was marked. Although it seemed a positive sign that she could approach other children, this was often done in a provocative manner that invited rejection. Also, positive overtures from other children would, at times, frighten her. Thus, although moves toward involvement were being made by Jean, these seemed highly colored by the anxiety that she would again be rejected.

During this period the mother reported a dramatic change in Jean's behavior at home. Mrs. L. felt that in contrast to her previous aloofness from the rest of the family, Jean was now more outgoing and affectionate. She herself felt closer to Jean than she ever had before, and became increasingly discouraged about the way her daughter was rejected by Ethel and Paula, even when Jean made an adequate positive approach. That she experienced this very personally was supported by her once more mentioning the importance of her friendships, and particularly her friendship to the woman who became ill when Jean was 7 months old. Although she was also very vulnerable to any possible rejection by the interviewer, and needed the constant reassurance of a "good report on Jean," her increasing trust of her own judgment was paralleled by her increasing comfort in talking to someone about her child. From this position of greater inner comfort the mother now decided gradually to shorten her time in the nursery. By the 31st day she was completely absent.

That her decision was not only governed by consideration for Jean's development is supported by her informing the head teacher that she was planning a trip in a few weeks and would be gone from Jean for one week. Mrs. L. stressed that Jean was used to the idea of her going and coming back. In relation to this Mrs. L. brought out how her own mother and father were always going places. It was unclear at the time what the reasons were for the mother's trip, but the interviewer had the feeling that the trip was not crucial.

> The question must be raised as to why Mrs. L. chose to leave at this particular time. It was the time when Jean was showing a greater reliance on her mother. Was Mrs. L. repeating with Jean the same

pattern of behavior her parents followed with her, and was it that Mrs. L. could not tolerate the growing closeness with her daughter and had to withdraw via the trip, in the same way as Jean withdrew from positive relationships?

Some further insights into Mrs. L.'s leaving may be possible from her interview on Day 29. Mrs. L. came into the patio area when the interviewer was talking to one of the mothers. She became visibly disturbed and more fidgety. She rushed into the office to make a phone call and soon a phone call came for her, which caused the office staff to go to great lengths to find her. She then went into the outside play area rather than waiting for the interviewer in the office.

Mrs. L.'s reaction in this situation was remarkably similar in many ways to what had been seen in Jean. There is the flight with perceived rejection from the interviewer into some seemingly purposeful activity. Then Mrs. L. runs away to another area where the person will have to find her and fetch her back. We wondered, at this point, about the role of the interviewer in Mrs. L.'s trip.

5. *As mother again leaves and simultaneously announces a trip out of town, Jean regresses in the form of experiencing a threat to her self-concept.* October 31st through November 4th. Days 31-35.

In this week before Mrs. L.'s departure, when the mother was no longer present in the nursery, Jean's relationship to her peers and the head teacher was not very different from the previous period. She maintained her contacts with the other children even though she continued to invite rejection. Not unexpectedly, the children reacted to her with a wary eye.

At this time of anticipating the mother's departure, it was no doubt of great importance that Jean could express her ambivalence as part of her relationship to the teachers. On Day 33 a number of girls were sitting around Sarah singing songs, when Jean entered the group and sat on Sarah's lap. She sat there contentedly singing but then abruptly tried to change the record. Sarah was forced to stop her and she promptly took off to another area.

We would infer that in identification with her mother and also to control actively what she had experienced passively, Jean first makes a very positive contact but then as if anticipating rejection, provokes that rejection and when disciplined "runs away" before being abandoned.

Twice on Day 31 it was noticed that she retreated into one of the wagons with her blanket and masturbated. On Day 33, after her pleasant and then provocative interaction with Sarah, Jean frantically began spilling water out of a kettle while holding her genitals.

> It would seem that, as in period 2, Jean again reacted to the mother's pending departure by a reliance on auto-erotism.

Further underlining a regressive trend is behavior observed on Day 32. The record of that day follows: "Jean wandered around from one activity to another, and suddenly she was in the sandbox screaming and crying in a terrified fashion. She was cringing against the back wall of the sandbox and crying something that was difficult to understand. It turned out to be: 'I'm a bunny, I'm a bunny.' As soon as this happened, Sarah went over to Jean and tried to comfort her, but this was impossible. She would not move from the back wall and it seemed as if she were having a hallucinatory experience in which she was being attacked and could not move. The head teacher now assured Jean that she wasn't a bunny, that she was Jean and a little girl, but she kept on crying. It turned out that she wanted her blanket, although once again it was very difficult to understand her because of the terrified screaming. The teacher tried to get her to walk with her to get the blanket, but she would not move unless she was carried."

> What was it that suddenly terrified her? Was the cry "I am a bunny" an expression of the fear of the loss of a fragile self? Or was it the defense against still another fear? Some light was thrown on this by Mrs. L.'s comment that the only time Jean cried was when her sister said something like, "You're not a duck," or "You're not a bunny." Thus it seems that it is not alone the fear of being a bunny that upsets her, but rather the taking away from her the notion that she is a "bunny." It was also noticed that Mrs. L. seldom called Jean by name, but said things like, "Give me a bunny kiss," or "you're my little bunny-honey." Often Jean brought carrots to school. Clearly one of her favorite stories was: *The Bunny that Ran Away.* In this story the bunny runs from her mother but is finally retrieved by her. Although obviously overdetermined, this incident suggested a breakdown in the reality-testing function of the ego accompanied by hallucinatory-like experiences. It raises questions about the adaptive and integrative function of Jean's ego.

While other evidence of regression has already been cited, in various areas Jean was capable of high-level functioning. On Day 31 it was reported that she showed a clarity of speech and happily engaged in a number of activities. On Day 32 it was noticed that she was able both to count out a quantity of crackers for herself, and subtract to get a desired amount. On Day 33 it was seen that her drawings showed the flow and structure of a child three to four years older.

> Thus, it is important to note that the intense conflicts that had led to serious distortions in self-representation did not encroach on the above areas of ego functioning.

6. As mother is out of town, Jean makes little progress in her relationship to the teacher but can use it to clarify the nature of her self concept. November 7th through 18th. Days 36-45.

This two-week period was the time when Mrs. L. was on her trip. As it turned out, her expected absence of one week ended up being a little over two weeks. While in school Jean made no mention of her mother's absence. However, on Day 43 she ran away four times and had to be brought back by the teacher. When the teacher responded to this and asked her if she missed her mother, Jean responded "yes."

> Here, once again, we see the passively experienced abandonment by the mother turned into the active running away.

During mother's absence gross signs of regression were no longer in evidence. There were indications even in her provocativeness with other children that Jean, sensing her lack of acceptance, made her moves more assertively and with less anticipation of being rejected. Also important was the first observed attempt by another child to actively seek contact with Jean. That Paula should ask her to join her in the sandbox was especially important since she previously shrank from Jean's approaches.

> It seems likely that Paula had picked up a noticeable difference in her, and that the absence of extreme regression on Jean's part was related to her increasing involvement with the head teacher and peer-group activity.

Jean's relations with the teachers and observers during this period was highly focused around one particular idea—Jean's being a bunny. It started on Day 38 when Kurt brought some food into the play area and she went to him saying, "I want some. I want some." Although Kurt was giving out food to a number of the other children, he did not give any to Jean. At this point, with an anxious smile on her face, she went running to the head teacher saying, "I'm a bunny."

> Here, as in the previous period, one can see how in the face of rejection she retreated to her bunny identification. However, in

contrast to the previous terrified screaming affirmation of her being a bunny, Jean turned to one of the adults and seemed to be asking: Do I have to be a bunny to be loved or can I be loved as a girl? The above examples as well as the other behavior indicated that Jean did imagine that particularly "boy bunnies" get more love. This would be consistent with her experience of losing her favorite maid who went to get married and "have a son."

In her play she still vascillated between active involvement in group activities like Play-doh, withdrawal into painting with dark paints, or lying somewhere with her blanket, and daydreaming.

7. Her mother's return is marked by some renewed emotional distance between them but Jean's relationship to the teacher and one friend, Gloria, progresses further. November 21st through December 2nd. Days 46-54.

This period was the two weeks following Mrs. L.'s return from her trip. When her mother returned there was no noticeable reaction on Jean's part and all went well. Despite this apparent easiness, some avoidance of feelings and the associated distance were again observed. The mother's account of Jean's reaction to her return home was quite limited, however, since she was far more interested in finding out from the interviewer how he felt Jean had been doing.

This and other evidence seemed to indicate that Mrs. L. anticipated that her departure might have seriously damaged her daughter.

During this period two striking developments occurred in Jean's relationships to adults in the nursery. First of all there was her increasing reliance on the head teacher. On numerous occasions it was noticed that she went to her for help. The second development was the almost complete disappearance of her remarks around her being a bunny. Gone was the frantic rushing from one adult to another with the seeming question, "Must I be a bunny in order to be accepted or can I be a little girl?" The importance of Jean's relationship to the head teacher in accounting for this change could be observed on Day 50. The mother came into school and Jean came running up to her and was held in her arms. The head teacher came over and Jean looked at her and said to her mother, "Mommy, Esther doesn't call me a bunny."

In this apparent plea to her mother, she seemed to be saying, "Look how the teacher can accept me and I don't have to be a bunny." Just as important, though, was the ease with which she approached her mother in a positive fashion, and her comfort in bringing up an area which was once extremely anxiety-provoking.

Jean both continued to be isolated from the other children, but also showed some progress in partaking in group activities. She would still for long periods of time lie passively on the floor with her thumb in her mouth and her blanket on her shoulder. By contrast, on Day 52 Jean for the first time joined the group in tricycle riding. She didn't know quite how to pedal but with the head teacher's help was soon doing quite well.

Further indicating Jean's willingness to make social contacts was the initiation of her first friendship in the nursery school. Observations from Day 51 are as follows: "Jean came in with her blanket over her shoulder, went directly toward Gloria and said, 'Come with me.' Gloria quite obediently followed her over to the sandbox where Jean handed her a shovel and they both started to dig in the sand. Although Jean said nothing to Gloria, or made any further overtures, Gloria continued to remain close to her."

> It is not surprising that Jean should choose this girl to make a first direct contact. Gloria was the most passive of the children and in comparison to the rest of the group, seemed much younger. After the repeated rejections from the other girls in the group, Gloria was a very safe, compliant choice as a playmate. That Jean was able to initiate contact with Gloria was an unquestionable positive move on her part. However, as in all previous interactions, she was initially unable to maintain the contact for any length of time, even though Gloria was obviously willing.

8. Jean is ill but maintains contact with her teacher. December 5th through 9th. Days 54-58.

Jean was out sick during this period. During a pleasant telephone conversation Jean asked her teacher whether she could come back to the nursery, paint on the floor, and lie on the floor with her blanket.

> Among various interpretations, these questions do seek reassurance in areas where the mother's response had been uncertain. She allowed messing but then became irritated. She was intensely available to her child but then had to run from her.

9. Jean's relationship to the teacher and Gloria continues to develop but her sustained involvement in an activity is still limited. December 12th through 15th. Days 59-62.

Upon her return to nursery school Jean initially showed an inordinate amount of lack of contact, and turned from the main teacher's attempt to greet her.

This initial lack of contact and its subsequent dissipation were reminiscent of Jean's behavior when returning after an absence on previous occasions.

Although Jean again made futile tentative approaches to both Joan and Ethel, her main contact among the children remained Gloria. Despite their lack of verbal interchange, a definite mutuality now characterized their play. However, when asked what they were doing, Jean immediately answered, "*I* am making mud-pies."

> It would seem that even while there is mutuality in her play with Gloria, a strong element of narcissistic isolation remains.

Most striking during this period was the continuation of her reliance on the head teacher. The continuing influence of this relationship and the initiation of one with the observer was shown on Day 62. Jean was climbing on the jungle gym where Bob was proclaiming that he was going to grow up to be a big man. Observer C. H. asked Jean, "What are you going to be when you grow up?" Very quickly she said, "A teacher." When asked, "You mean just like Esther?" she answered, "Yes."

> Unlike evidence for identification with the teacher seen in the other girls, Jean showed no spontaneous inclination to help the head teacher. But for Jean it was a big step. It was only six weeks before this that she had stood in terror against the wall in the sandbox saying, "I'm a bunny."

In general Jean still found it difficult to sustain her interest in any one activity. Rather than withdrawing, however, she shifted again to an impulsive meandering. But constantly being on the verge of leaving did not prevent her from absorbing much. For example, she was the only child who could accurately remember and retrieve the ornaments that she had placed on the Christmas tree.

> This distinction between Jean's excellent capacities on the one hand, and her inability to remain at a task constructively for any length of time, was again striking.

C. Jean's Development from the Fifth to the Tenth Month of Nursery School

Many important changes in Jean's adjustment took place from the fifth to the tenth month of nursery school. She showed more freedom both in her movements and affect expression. For the first time there was evidence of enjoyment and involvement in activities of various types. This is not to say that there were not many variations in the way Jean functioned. At times she still appeared to be a very peculiar child who was isolated and withdrawn from the group.

Some of the most striking changes during this period occurred in Jean's relations with other children. In the first two months after the Christmas holiday these changes were still barely perceptible and highly colored by the continuation of earlier patterns leading to lack of contact. Around the beginning of March, though, her whole pattern of interaction with the other children began to change. Again the important initial step was taken with Gloria.

By the middle of April Jean was seen to be talking and smiling with Gloria while playing with her. Soon afterwards Jean was observed in animated play and conversation with most of the other girls on a fairly consistent basis. Mrs. L. reported that in the car-pool Jean was able to engage in a give-and-take relationship with the other children. Also noticeable was the change in her reaction to rejection from the other children and aggressiveness in general. Rather than flee to another area or withdraw, Jean was usually able to stay and handle the particular incident in an adaptive fashion.

Occasionally her behavior was hardly adaptive and difficult to comprehend. For example, early in June Jean told Observer P.C. that she was putting on her shoes to "kick Kurt in the stomach." Later in the morning Jean did indeed go over to both Gloria and then Kurt, and tried to kick them.

There was also a definite change in her relationship to the adults in the nursery. In general she showed much greater warmth, directness and openness. She was observed in many animated conversations with the head teacher, and her relationships with both student teachers included many affectionate interchanges. In fact, for the first time one experienced the impression of Jean as a "very cuddly" girl. At times she did ignore all greetings upon entering in the morning, and was provocative or demanding, but at other times she was able to wait patiently for aid from one of the teachers, or justifiably speak up for herself in an appropriate fashion.

Mrs. L. reported that Jean was more affectionate at home and showed greater feeling towards all the family members. She felt more involved with Jean, enjoyed doing things with her, and reported that there was a considerable decrease in her provocative behavior at home. However, the mother also continued to express her uncertainty about how Jean was doing and how she was to handle her. Striking was the fact that when told of Jean's budding friendship with Gloria, the mother indicated that she had heard of Gloria but had never seen her.

The many positive changes in Jean's relationships at the nursery seemed to mirror those in the home. However, the distance and ambivalence in the mother-child relationship was still evident.

Jean's functioning in task oriented situations still varied a great deal. She showed great persistence and skill in certain tasks, even in the face of difficulty, and for the first time experienced enjoyment from these activities. However the one area in which Jean had the most trouble was in adapting to the task set by the teacher. This was especially noticeable during "book time" where the main teacher would read a story and ask the children various questions about it. Jean still rarely participated in this activity. She would either wander away from the group or lie passively with her blanket while her thumb was in her mouth.

> A serious question was raised at this point regarding encroachment of conflictual areas on academic functioning. The type of "give and take" necessary to perform well in something like "book time" is not unlike what is demanded in many school tasks. Thus Jean must "take" from the teacher reading the book certain directions, as well as the words of the story read. Then she is asked to "give" back certain responses. That this type of mutuality was a problem for Jean, both in the home and later at the nursery, was apparent.

Like her commitment to tasks, Jean's speech also varied a great deal. Sometimes it was clear though low, but at other times she was very hard to understand. Or her enunciation would be clear but her logic was difficult to follow. The one area in which Jean's speech was perfectly clear was when she made her demands known.

Certain residuals of former areas of conflict and Jean's typical mode of coping with these occurred throughout the last six months of the first year. It was not uncommon to hear her talk about "pooh-pooh" and say such things as, "I smell my own pooh-pooh."

> From this would be inferred Jean's anxiety around her anal explosiveness and self-representation of being a "dirty girl."

She also constantly played dress-up with a set of frilly Victorian clothes. One was reminded of her previous use of clothing for self-comfort.

> One could also infer in this her need to see herself as a Cinderella figure rather than an unkempt peculiar girl who cannot attract anyone, and certainly not a prince.

D. Jean's Response to Task Situations at the End of the First Year of Nursery School

Jean's response to task situations was categorized as showing low engagement, variable productivity and creativity, little pride and pleasure, and a striking tendency toward regression. There were moments when she could attend and demonstrate her excellent intelligence, but as often as not she would then either actively distract the group or more frequently withdraw all involvement, and show signs of regression.

As it happened, during the time that the response to task situations was studied, Jean had just experienced a loss of another maid. Thus, even though two of her girlfriends (Gloria and Jennifer) were both available to her in the initial free play time on the morning of June 5th, she made little contact with anyone, preferring to suck her thumb and hold her blanket.

> No doubt, Jean's tendency toward withdrawal was accentuated by the recent departure of the maid.

When it was time to have juice and listen to a book reading, Jean complied quickly but initially she did not eat any crackers or drink any juice. When Bob in answer to the teacher's question called the pineapple juice "pooh-pooh" juice, her affect momentarily changed and she too offered this as her answer. That she was attending well and could remember well could be inferred from her answer to questions as to who was missing, as well as one correct identification of the action in the story. Following this response it was more difficult to know what she was attending to. She sucked her thumb, clung to her blanket, seemed to be listening, but was in no way actively participating.

> We would infer that some disengagement had again taken place.

Yet she once more complied well with the instructions of the goal-directed motoric activity—gluing pieces of wood together. Working quickly, but with no pleasure, she piled a number of large pieces of wood together and then glued them. It was a practical design but most unimaginative. Most important, she only made one object and was the first to leave the table. Since most of the boys also left early and formed a "bicycle gang," and since the girls remained at the table, Jean's isolation was once more underlined. She took her blanket, seemed almost asleep, but then looked at a book.

> Again, in the goal-directed activity, a quick and adequate engagement is followed by withdrawal. This seemed to characterize so much of Jean's functioning in the task situation, and was reminiscent of Mrs. L.'s manner of relating to Jean.

What is missing in this example is the fact that on other days she made excellent contributions during the listening-comprehension task, but could also become a distraction by suddenly and teasingly running away. Otherwise her reactions on this day are representative of the essential features of her adaptation.

E. Jean's Behavior in the Special Assessment Situations at the End of Second Year of Nursery School

Statements summarizing Jean's behavior in the WWPSI test situation one year later, even though made independent of the knowledge of the above description, are strikingly consistent with them: "Jean approached the testing situation in a rather distant manner with a vague look about her and her thumb wedged tightly in her mouth. Although tending to find each task initially interesting, she soon withdrew into her own inner thoughts, either because of difficulties with the task or sometimes for no other observable reasons. At these moments attention and approval would move her back to the task. Thus, she tended to be dependent on the regard of others rather than her own standards. Taken together, these characteristics made her performance very variable."

Jean's actual functioning was, nevertheless, well within the Bright-Normal range. Her capacity for dealing with abstractions was excellent and yet she was equally competent in dealing with "everyday" kinds of situations. Her level of vocabulary was also very good and her spoken language development was equally impressive. Were it not for the difficulties cited, her performance would clearly have fallen within the Superior range.

The most serious deterioration occurred on the Maze and Picture Completion subtest. When asked on the Maze subtest to get the chick to its mother, Jean literally froze, became disoriented, and then contrary. Her total score on this subtest was extremely low.

> In both this and the Picture Completion sub-test, Jean's performance seemed to be disrupted by stimuli suggestive of mother-child separation.

Jean's behavior in relation to the play interview did much to throw further light on these testing observations and those collected in the two years of her nursery-school development. Before the play interview the observer had been looking at an illustrated booklet that Jean had composed the day before. The dominant question portrayed again was: Would Snow White attract the prince? Or was she really an ugly, stupid stooge? And if she did get the prince, would the wicked witch of the North swoop down on her and would she then be destined to die? Just then indeed Jean swooped in, not unlike her mother. She claimed to have a baby in her stomach and promptly pulled her favorite teddy out from under her dress.

Jean had been playing with Play-doh in the classroom and then initially continued with this play in the play interview room. Both the degree of control and the perseverance of producing one "nice" object after another produced feelings of boredom in the observer. This was interrupted by truly capturing associations; thus, an L-shaped piece quickly became a sofa. All this time she avoided eye contact with the observer and often indeed seemed in another world.

> We would infer from this initial behavior Jean's continued preoccupation with messy things, and her simultaneous and desperate effort to prove that she is a clean girl. There also appeared to be a defensive function being served in her seeming concentration and distance.

Next, a flood of ideas suddenly swept away the monotony. A house she had built became Dorothy's house, and as in *The Wizard of Oz*, a tornado swept it away and took her to another land.

> The temporary loss of a sense of self as linked to a tornado-like disappearance of "home base" is again suggested.

Much like her mother, she for a while became again an anxious, swooping little girl as she shifted quickly from one activity to another. Both a short sequence of doll play and her subsequent drawing of a Queen were done in the context of a good grasp on reality.

> It also showed, however, her inability to move developmentally beyond an oedipally tinged identification with the Queen. As her teacher observed, Jean had enacted these dramas for a whole year. Much evidence in turn pointed to the interpretation that a mother experienced as suddenly vanishing would seriously undermine her confidence in attracting any person, including her daddy. The mother noted at that time that Jean is afraid actively to approach her father for fear of being rejected. It is then safer to be the Queen in fantasy.

When asked to tell a story, in a high-pitched, punishing Victorian voice she told about the ducks who were commanded not to get their clothes dirty, but wallowed in the mud anyway. This turned out to be disastrous because the mother was expecting company. When she returned from the hair dresser they were isolated in their rooms and no excuses were accepted.

> In this story still another reason was revealed why it was difficult for Jean to feel attractive and why she had to turn to being the fantasy

Queen. Jean suggests that she can never really be pretty and clean enough to gain power over her mother. Also impressive, however, was her excellent use of language and the creative development of a dramatic story. Frustrating therefore was the very low volume of certain of her sentences.

Returning to the classroom she tried immediately to provoke her teacher. The teacher responded firmly. Joining some girls, Jean next concentrated on making herself beautiful. But this obviously again did not satisfy her and very secretly she now moved around like a fairy putting flour in the children's hair. Interestingly, only one child discovered her magic "snow" and reacted very negatively.

> In this one can see how, having had a man all to herself, Jean now needs to be punished. She then attempts to attract the man who had been nice to her, but feeling rejected, we infer that she uses magic and denial of her feelings as she moves back to her beautiful dream world. At the same time she proves that her peers and not herself are in fact the ugly ducklings.

Interpretive Summary of Jean's Adaptation to Nursery School

By contrast to Paula, Jean had in the past experienced and once more reexperienced during entrance into nursery school, a set of relationships leading to an inner expectation that people make an initial engagement but then depart. Her mother had psychologically left her infant to a maid and turned to a sick friend. The maid had treated her like a princess only to get married "in order to have a boy." The mother during entrance into nursery school first stayed with her faithfully, then left her, then returned, only to leave her again to go on a trip. Nor was the relationship to the father initially likely to ameliorate this condition. He very much preferred Jean's sister. The relationship to the sister was positive and was very likely important in helping Jean to make a positive relationship to Gloria in the nursery school.

Yet, much transpired before this new-found relationship was possible. In the first few days it became clear that Jean's defensive need to avoid all contact was extensive. Only the paints seemed a secure outlet. Yet her intense longing as well as her general tendency to turn the passively experienced desertion into an active running away, could be seen when she wandered into the next yard only to be carried back like an infant, first by her mother and then by the teacher.

By Period 2 her isolation was augmented by clear-cut regressive trends in reaction to the mother's departure from the nursery. Her attachment to certain clothing concerned the staff and obviously frightened the mother. That the regressive trend was Jean's reaction to separation from the mother is demonstrated by the fact that this behavior disappeared once her mother decided again to remain in the nursery and reappeared when she felt it would be best to let Jean adjust on her own. Comparison of Jean's and Paula's reaction to the stress of entrance into nursery school underlines the difference between this regression and that in the service of further progression. Unlike Paula, Jean did not turn directly to her mother nor even to the teacher, but remained essentially isolated, and regressed to autoerotic types of gratification.

During Period 4, with the mother there, Jean made a greater number of direct affectionate contacts with her. The mother was herself more affectionate, but most important for Jean, the essential sequence of maternal interest and affection followed by absence (whether psychological or an actual separation) was once more repeated as mother then left town. Very likely for both mother and daughter this sequence of events was associated with the fundamental fantasy that any intense involvement is likely to lead to a helpless state of abandonment, and must therefore be avoided altogether or be cut prematurely.

Jean's primary reaction to her mother's second departure from the school in Period 5 was to return once more to the comfort of her blanket and masturbation. One aspect of her former libidinal regression was missing. The intense attachment to a silken or frilly piece of personal clothing was not observed. However, an instance of ego regression was now observed as she stood in terrified fashion insisting she was a bunny. It would seem that intense feelings of helplessness associated with fantasies of being abandoned were in turn related to the insistent thought that she might be loved if she were a "bunny." It is likely that the terror of the disintegration of a self-representation was tied to the question of what do I have to be in order to be fed and loved. Jean gave much evidence that she felt she was not accepted because she was a girl. She talked about her maid's leaving her to have a boy. Particularly during the period under discussion (Period 5) did she attack certain passive boys and take things from them. She paraded around with her carrot and on one occasion insisted she was a bunny when Kurt refused to give her one of his carrots. (See Period 6).

If the mother's withdrawal from nursery school during Period 5 had made the question "Can I be loved as a girl?" one of disruptive intensity, so during her mother's absence from home because of her trip, Jean could increasingly answer the above question in the affirmative. It is suggested that two primary factors combined to make this successful reality testing possible. Jean's relationship to the teacher had developed sufficiently to make her reassurance that she was a pretty girl and not a bunny, a powerful one, and the impact of this reassurance was no doubt strengthened when the mother's constant, "Hi, honey-bunny" was no longer present. Jean herself sorted things out further when the mother returned by confronting her with: "Esther [the teacher] doesn't call me a bunny."

While the relationship to the teacher continued to grow and Jean subsequently could sustain a relationship to one quiet little girl, the residuals of past wishes and anxieties had not been as adequately transformed or resolved as in the case of Paula. Her wish to mess and lie on the floor like a baby was still evident. The slight reluctance of another person frightened her into anticipations of abandonment and so she withdrew first. Similarly her basic task orientation was one of some initial commitment but little follow-through. For example, she typically either disrupted the book time or removed herself altogether. That is, rather than showing self-motivation she relied on others to demonstrate that they were interested in her performance. One had to give a great deal to Jean before she could give in return. Even her successes were undermined by her conviction that she really couldn't attract anyone. Further follow-up is needed, however, to see how indeed she will learn in the early grades.

CONCLUDING REMARKS

The above descriptions give the step-by-step process whereby a three-year-old adapts to nursery school and, in particular, to certain tasks which are part of the curriculum. The methods of data collection and data analysis that have been illustrated focus on depicting the balance and quality of the child's progressive and regressive developments and how certain environmental events influence that development. Of these events the descriptions have concentrated on the existing family relationships and new and supplemental relationships in the nursery. To summarize certain aspects of the contrasts in development, Paula had internalized and continued to experience a care-taking situation that led to the expectation that she would be cared for again. There is no doubt, however, that the initial supplemental affectionate relationship to Sarah greatly enhanced Paula's eventual commitment to the new relationships and tasks of the nursery.

By contrast, Jean had in the past experienced and once more reexperienced during entrance into nursery school, that people make an initial engagement but then depart. All her commitments including those to the task reflected the expectation that abandonment would follow. Characteristically she would flee the situation first. It was particularly through the reassurance that she would not be abandoned and could be loved as a girl, that teacher Esther could in important ways enhance her development.

Both the nature of the regressions that developed and the manner in which the conflict derivatives were or were not altered highlights once more the contrast in the two girls and allows us to make more general inferences about the balance of progressive and regressive trends. When experiencing the stress of separation from her parents, Paula sucked her thumb but retreated mainly to a person and specifically to Sarah's warm lap, only to emerge again into activity. By contrast, Jean turned for comfort to her body and to certain pieces of clothing. At one point the regression in her ego-functioning went to the point of experiencing extreme helplessness.

Similarly, whereas Paula could gradually master her anxiety of making too big a mess or being attacked by a boy, Jean continued to be preoccupied with making messes and lying on the floor like a baby. More generally, many factors combined to make Paula's functioning less subject to conflict interference.

It must again be stressed that the differential adaptation of the two children was obviously influenced by many factors not studied in this report. What we have done is to describe in process detail how the children did adapt to nursery school and what important current events were influencing that adaptation. Many more children will have to be studied to permit more specific generalizations concerning the association between parent-child relations, adaptation to nursery school, and the child's task orientation. We do believe that the method illustrated provides promise in this regard.

ACKNOWLEDGMENT

We wish to thank the staff of the Reiss-Davis Child Study Center and the Center for Early Education and especially the parents and children for making this study possible. The devoted assistance of Dr. Joel Liebowitz was particularly invaluable. We also gratefully acknowledge the financial support of the Foundation for Research in Psychoanalysis, Los Angeles, and that given by the Office of Child Development Grant No. OCD-CB-48.

REFERENCES

Attwell, A. A., Orpet, R. E., and Meyers, E. C. (1967). Kindergarten behavior ratings as a predictor of academic achievement. *Journal of School Psychology,* **6**, 43-46.

Baumrind, D. (1967). Child care practices anteceding three patterns of preschool behavior. *Genetic Psychology Monographs,* **75**, 43-88.

Cohen, T. B. (1963). Prediction of underachievement in kindergarten children. *Archives of General Psychiatry,* **9**, 444-450.

Freeberg, N. E. and Payne, D. T. (1967). Parental influence on cognitive development in early childhood: A review. *Child Development,* **38**, 67-87.

Freud, A. (1965). *Normality and pathology in childhood.* New York: International Universities Press.

Heinicke, C. M. (1968). Parent-child interaction and the child's approach to task situations. In *Approaches to and applications of the study of parent-child interaction.* Symposium presented at the American Psychological Association, San Francisco. E. E. Maccoby (Chm.).

Kagan, J. and Moss, H. A. (1962). *Birth to maturity.* New York: Wiley.

Mahler,   M.   (1963).   Thoughts   about   development   and   individuation. *Psychoanalytic Study of the Child,* **16**, 332-351.

Westman, J., Rice, D. and Bermann, E. (1967). Nursery school behavior and later adjustment. *American Journal of Orthopsychiatry*, **37**, 725-731.

CHAPTER 10

Differences in Cognitive Style and Birth Order

Irving D. Harris

Casualties from the educational arenas—grade and high-school failures, college dropouts, and doctoral depressions—are coming increasingly to the attention of the clinician. He is well able to understand many of these through his knowledge of psychodynamics and his awareness of the role played by intellectual endowment and cultural background. However, he tends to be much less aware of the influence of cognitive style on success or failure in the educational system.

My objective here is to describe certain styles of thinking which may arise out of certain family experiences. More specifically I hope to indicate how two different kinds of minds of equal intelligence and equal cultural advantage may arise from within the *same* family. The educational repercussions of this contrast are familiar to all: the mind which is book-wise and attracted to abstractions is rewarded by academia, whereas the mind which is playground and street-wise and interested in practical reality tends to be penalized by the system.

Much of what I have to say revolves around the repercussions of birth order or family position, a subject rarely mentioned in the psychoanalytic literature, although Sigmund Freud (1933) wrote: ". . .a child's position in the sequence of brothers and sisters is of very great significance for the course of his later life, a factor to be considered in every biography". Furthermore, Ernest Jones (1953) referred to birth order in describing Freud's personality, "He was the eldest child, at least of his mother, and for a time thereafter of what may be called the inner family. This in itself is a fact of significance, since an eldest child differs, for better or worse, from other children. It may give such a child a special sense of importance and responsibility."

In contrast to the lack of attention given to birth order by psychoanalysts, there have been abundant studies of this factor by psychologists. The investigations, however, have not produced unequivocal findings, and the result has been a low-keyed debate over the value of birth order as a determinant of personality differences. Difficulties in replication caused discouraging literature reviews some 30 years ago in experimental social psychology by Murphy, Murphy, and Newcomb (1937), who flatly stated that the results of studies attempting to find a relationship between birth order and intelligence, personality traits, and other factors, were inconsistent and contradictory. While replicatory difficulties are often understandably a deterrent to further investigation, they also can constitute a challenge. This kind of challenge may be seen in the review made by H. Jones (1946) in the *Manual of child psychology.* He wrote:

> In an earlier critique of research in this field, evidence has been given that when. . .methodological difficulties are properly controlled. . . no birth order differences in intelligence occur in normal samples. . . atypical results, however, have been encountered in certain highly selected samples. . . Studies of gifted children by Terman and of eminent men by Ellis, Cattell, and Huntington has shown a distribution of birth order different from chance expectation and strongly favoring the first born. . . No satisfactory explanation of this finding has been given.

The foregoing considerations, and in particular the review by Jones, persuaded me to take seriously the possible value of birth order. With the question in mind "Were first borns indeed more gifted or creative?", and following the lead of Ellis, Cattell, and Huntington, I chose for my subjects a large number of men who had been eminent in Western civilization since 1600. Because biographical information was frequently lacking as to the exact birth position these eminent men had in relation to older and younger brothers and sisters, my compromise solution was to concentrate on whether the eminent man was the first or only surviving male offspring of the mother or whether he was a later male offspring. Of the thousand eminent men investigated, there was an almost equal division between first sons and later sons.

Needless to say, the first direction of the inquiry ran almost immediately into an insuperable obstacle. There was no way of measuring whether one eminent man was more creative than another. And one would be hard put even to estimate whether first son Einstein was more gifted than later son Darwin or first son Jefferson than later son Hamilton. Consequently the assumption was made that the superior intellects of these men were of equal quantity and that any discoverable differences between first and later sons would reside in the directions their creativities took. The difficulties involved in evaluating these directions were only slightly less formidable. But by recourse to some original writings and especially to the authorities in the various fields, it was possible to discern what appeared to be polar divergences in the thinking, feeling, and behavior of eminent first and later sons. This does not mean that every first son thought similarly to every other first son and differently from every later son. It means rather that on certain issues first sons appeared to be clustered toward one side of an issue, and later sons toward the other. Examples of this clustering will be given later.)

In summary, then, the study of eminently creative men (Harris, 1961) was completely unenlightening as to any relationship between birth order and the quantity of creative intelligence. Quite apart from birth order, it was equally unenlightening as to the baffling question of what makes a man highly creative. But the study did persuade me that, (given creativeness, there appeared to be some kind of relationship between family position and style of creativity, a relationship which would be premature at this point to spell out.)

Let me approach this point gradually by summarizing my reflections in the form of a thesis that can be applied not only to the eminently creative but also to more "typical" samples. The thesis conceives of two psychological types which arise out of different early experiences in the family. I shall call them the *adult-civilized* and the *peer-civilized*. How much and how little the parents have been energetically involved in nurturing, civilizing, and grooming the child will decide to which type he belongs.(If it has been much—more likely to be the case with the only child, the first born, or the first son—the offspring will bear the sobering mark of the previous generation and its values and can be thought of as adult-civilized.)If it has been little—more likely to be the case, say, with the fifth child of 10—the transplant of adult values is less likely to become a permanent and influential component in the child's personality. This offspring can be regarded as peer-civilized inasmuch as older brothers and sisters, roughly of the same generation, have participated in raising him and serving as his models. The thesis rests on family experience and not simplistically on family position. The position is only important to the extent that it influences family experience.

(What I am describing is, I am sure, not unfamiliar to most readers. I am pointing in a systematic way to the adult-civilized child—most frequently the first son—who has learned the logical language and thought processes of his parents, has absorbed with his milk their values and traditions which he internalizes, assimilates, and makes his own. His serious, high self-expectation is conditioned by the fact that he provides the first vehicle whereby the parents can continue their own identities and realize their frustrated hopes and ambitions.) Also I am calling attention to the peer-civilized child—most frequently a later son—who is not as intensely nurtured since his parents are more relaxed or weary by the time of his arrival or content that their ambitions are safely harnessed to the shoulders of the older child. As he is not often enlisted as a parent surrogate or as a model for younger siblings, he tends to be more lighthearted and carefree, more "childlike" and less reverent of authority than his eldest brother.

How will these two species fare in the educational system? As might be expected, the adult-civilized does much better than the peer-civilized. His serious, conscientious characteristics along with his verbal skills serve him well in an academic milieu. Thus there are many studies showing that first borns and first sons are overrepresented among National Merit Scholars and among college and graduate students (Schacter, 1963). This does not seem entirely attributable to family size nor to the fact that the smaller, more advantaged families have more first sons. MacArthur (1956) in a study of *two-son* Harvard families, found that when the Harvard graduate and son were first male offspring, the adult-civilized characteristics of being serious and studious were significantly more frequent, whereas when they were later sons, the peer-civilized traits of being carefree and nonstudious were most prominent.

Whether "seriousness" is to be considered an attribute of cognitive style or of achievement drive or of general character structure is of course open to argument. Much less debatable is the postulate that possession of such a characteristic—the taking of things seriously—helps greatly in moving up the educational ladder. There is little doubt in my mind that it is found much more frequently in the adult-civilized first of sex than in the peer-civilized later of sex.

I have been persuaded in this direction by my *clinical* experience, by studies such as MacArthur's, and by two quantitative studies in which I was involved. The earlier one—made on a child-guidance clinic sample—disclosed that first borns (in contrast to last borns) were much more often described as "serious" by the school teacher (Harris, 1964).

The later study—done in conjunction with K. I. Howard (Harris, 1968)—took for its sample 1200 normal subjects, of which two-thirds were high school seniors and one-third law and dental students. A questionnaire elicited from them their opinion as to how early in life a child should begin to assume serious responsibilities (e.g., do chores, the earning of spending money) and how early he should begin to have certain freedoms (e.g., stop going to Sunday school, have car for a date). The results disclosed that the first of sex—whether they were high-school males or high-school females, or professional-school males—significantly more often (in comparison to the later of sex) chose an earlier age for the assumption of serious responsibility.

Along with "seriousness" the adult-civilized first of sex tend to possess another characteristic more directly related to cognitive activity, and again very helpful in academic success. I refer to what is known as verbal skills. By this I do not mean verbal facility which can manifest itself as a gift of gab; rather I mean a special predilection to language, a sensitivity to its structure and meaningful use.

It is not surprising that the first born would tend to have this characteristic. His verbal skills would appear to stem from the fact that he tends to be talked to more frequently by the parent, to be more often a participant in an adult-child dialogue. In this dialogue, he would have to understand what is said to him, and he would have to respond in a fashion meaningful to the parent. In short, in verbal intercourse with the parent, the first born would have to adopt the viewpoint of the parent. He would more quickly leave the stage of monologue which Piaget has described as characteristic of child language even beyond entry to school.

Indications of this language proclivity were seen in the eminent men. There was, for example, a noticeable over-representation of first sons among the major poets—Shakespeare, Goethe, and Pushkin being prime examples. There were also signs among first sons of the studious absorption in words and meaningful language—illustrative creative products being Samuel Johnson's *Dictionary of the English Language,* Roget's *Thesaurus,* H. L. Mencken's *The American Language,* and George Bernard Shaw's devising of a new alphabet. The flavor of this kind of absorption can be seen in what first son Edmund Wilson (1963) wrote in a *New Yorker* article entitled "My Fifty Years with Dictionaries and Grammar":

> I have always been greedy for words. . . .I love Elizabethan plays, dictionaries of slang and argot. . . .I suppose that it is partly that I like to recapture the excitement I felt in childhood when attacking for the first time on my own a greenish-gray primer, I found that the sentences ran on with meaning.

The principal pertinent experimental evidence can be found in the work of Helen Koch (1956) whose investigation of five- and six-year olds from two-children families is perhaps the most carefully controlled experimental study on birth order. She found in relation to understandable speech that "first born children articulate consistently better than second born children." She also found that those first born sons who were two to five years older than their siblings scored significantly higher on the verbal subtest of the SRA primary mental abilities test. This verbal subtest according to Koch (1954) "is heavily saturated with Thurstone's factor V (verbal meaning)."

The basic issue stemming from language and the necessity for meaningful connected dialogue centers around how much and how soon the child adopts the adult viewpoint. The first born, for reasons described, must adopt this viewpoint in order to engage in dialogue with the parent. In so doing he makes a synthesis between his own world and the adult world. Additionally, he receives the first full impact of the parent's indoctrination of prohibitions and values. The first born or first son is more likely then to be connected with the past, with the older generation and its traditional values. He stands midway as a connecting link between the older generation and his own. The later born or later son is less involved with the older generation or the past. His companions are more often his older siblings of the same generation or his peers. He can remain longer in the stage of expressive monologue and can address himself to the tasks of the present, to those of his own generation.

A basic way of describing these differences is to say that the first born, due to his experience in meaningful dialogue and his link with the past generation, is prone to see things in connection, to try to make connections by relating one thing to another, he is, so to speak, *connectedness prone.* On the other hand, the later born, due to his experiences in premeaningful language and his less intense link with the past, is prone to see things as not necessarily connected, in fact actually to disconnect the part from the interrelated whole; he is, so to speak, *disconnectedness prone*. Both mental activities—connecting the parts in a whole and disconnecting the part from the whole—are quite necessary for the optimum exercise of the intellect. But, although superior intellects employ both activities, frequently—and this is the point of the communication—one activity characteristically predominates over the other.

Thus, intellectual styles can emerge from variation in parental involvement: a proneness in first borns toward connectedness, toward a synthesis of the whole, and in later borns toward disconnectedness, toward an analysis of the isolated part. The former would tend to see fence posts as assuming a continuous connection and call the assemblage a fence; the latter would tend to regard each fence post as disconnectedly discrete and to say that there are just 10 fence posts, each one of which needed accurate description. These different styles correspond to the two kinds of intellect described by Pascal (1947)—the intellect which can entertain many interrelating premises without confusing them and the precise intellect which accurately probes the part.

Evidence supporting the foregoing trends is not as clear cut as was the case in language proclivity. Yet, in the writer's view, there are certain trends which do suggest that the first born's creative style is manifested in synthesizing connectedness, the later born's style in analyzing disconnectedness. There is, for example, a list of some 20 eminent mathematicians given by Bell (1937) and divided by him into those who made special contribution in the interconnected "continuous" aspects of mathematics (e.g., calculus) and those who made particular contributions in the disconnected "discrete" aspects (e.g., algebra). First sons predominated in the "continuous" category, later sons in the "discrete" category.

A first son and later-son polarity can also be detected among those philosophers and scientists who have theorized about how much connected order there is in the real world. The most outstanding philosophic advocate of disconnectedness is later son David Hume, who was skeptical not only about causal connections but also about the existence of a continuous self. Earlier, another later son, Francis Bacon (1947), in his argument for a scientific method based on accurate particulars rather than on synthetic generalities, stated that "the human understanding is of its own nature prone to suppose the existence of more order and regularity than it finds."

It is well known that despite Bacon's strictures, scientific discoveries continue to be made by generalization and speculation as well as by analytic methods. And the great generalizers, the great finders of regularity and connected order, have tended to be first sons, such as Galileo, Newton, and Einstein. Einstein's (1950) connectedness tendency can be seen in his statement, "It is the aim of science to establish general rules which determine the reciprocal connection of objects and events in time and space." An aversion to disconnectedness is also evident in Einstein's comment regarding indeterminism in physics that God does not play at dice.

As might be expected, experimental evidence concerning such complex intellectual differences is not easily forthcoming from a study of normal samples. However, an investigation by Stein and Heinze (1960) of creativity in a highly selected sample does have considerable pertinence to what has been just discussed. Stein took a large group of intellectually superior chemists and endeavored to separate them into two groups on the basis of their creative ability. Utilizing the evaluations of the particular chemist's superiors, peers, and subordinates, he was able to set up two groups: the creative and the not-as-creative. He could find no relationship between birth order and creativity as so defined. However, in response to the present writer's query, Stein kindly went over his data and noted that there were significant differences between first borns and later borns as to their score on the Miller Analogy Test. On this test, used to ascertain abstract verbal ability and the facility in making connective analogies, first borns scored significantly higher than later borns. Stein's findings appear to support not only the verbal ability and connectedness trends in first borns but also the general observation that birth order has no discernible relationship to quantity of creativity.

Perhaps at this point the general characteristics of the two styles have been sufficiently portrayed. I would like now to approach the matter more clinically and describe certain problems in learning and living which arise from each cognitive style and from the associated personality.

The adult-civilized are certainly not immune to difficulties in academia. Their problems, however, tend to occur more often in college than in high school. They have usually achieved enough in the secondary schools that they enter college with at least a surface confidence. Their Achilles heel is the need to maintain or escalate self-worth by producing grand achievements. They may use their connectedness-prone minds to put forth all embracing syntheses which are impressive in the first years of college but which may be too speculative for the solid work of the departmental and graduate levels. Sooner or later their conceptions of self-worth are liable to be non-endorsed by their professors. As C. P. Snow wrote about this intellectual type in his novel *The Search* "at their best. . . .they are the great generalizers, at their worst they are infantilely fantastic and removed from all reality."

Thus, severe identity crises can develop in the adult-civilized, in the over-ambitious first sons. Their fervent wish is not merely to be adequate and have society recognize them as such, but rather to be idolized "somebodies." When society does not endorse them, their omnipotent feeling of self-identity is threatened. They suffer depressive episodes of nonfunctioning self-doubt which are interspersed with hopeful periods during which they envisage new, over-ambitious goals.

One young man, the eldest of three sons, while in a Midwestern suburban high school, had achieved in athletics but not academically. His ambitious mother pressured him into entering an Eastern university, where his inability to compete brought on a confused, agitated state marked by depression. He felt he had let his parents down. Returning to the Midwest, he languished for about three months until he hit on the notion of distinguishing himself in law and went back to his studies. Another, the eldest child with a younger sister and brother, had been valedictorian of his high-school class. His father and a cousin had made Phi Beta Kappa. In his freshman year, he was convinced he would make Phi Beta Kappa without too much exertion; in his sophomore year he realized it would take some effort and in his junior year he realized he would not make it at all. After that he studied desultorily, turned to marijuana, and finally dropped out of school. He submerged himself in philosophical and historical readings which extolled Nietzsche and Hitler and revisited the college dormitory, posing as a sophisticated superman. Finally, imagining himself to be a computer wizard who would amass a fortune, he pulled himself together.

First daughters exhibited similar tendencies. Their high self-expectations, ability, and good work habits led them, much more frequently than later daughters, to achieve master and doctoral degrees, and they held teaching or administrative positions at the college level. But when their ambitions outstripped their ability and patience, like the first sons, they fell victims to disturbing symptoms. Often the ambitions were transferred to the sexual realm. Two varieties of behavior were evident. They became involved in affairs in which they were romantically overestimated. The overestimations endorsed their inordinately high opinion of themselves.

Or, they were determined to set sexual records, motivated by the combined desires to conquer males and to punish themselves. One first daughter, during her college years, had sexual relations with 17 men within two months. Four years later, when in treatment and doing well in her work, she complained that she was not receiving enough recognition and said, "I can appreciate how Speck must have felt when he killed those nurses. I have to do something outstanding now, either very good or very bad."

The peer-civilized are not as likely to be plagued by the necessity to live up to an exaggerated self-worth. Their problem is frequently just the opposite: an abiding sense of inferiority which is not quickly alleviated by success. Thus, one younger later son, a Ph.D. at 23, referred to himself as an utter incompetent. He pictured his mind as a battlefield in which rotting corpses were buried, each corpse a humiliating memory of himself. While the same kind of feeling of unworthiness may depress a first son to the point of debilitation, this later son continued to function. He wrote articles throughout his depression and kept abreast of ideas and events, secured committee assignments and managed, though not without considerable anxiety, to conceal his real and imagined inadequacies from the "right people."

From reading his articles and listening to him during the therapeutic hour, I gained the impression that he had an excellent analytic mind but was afraid to display *any* ignorance because of the hazing he had sustained at the hands of an older brother. He expected of himself that he read *every* book in his and related fields. He equated, "I don't know," with total inadequacy. This anxiety hampered his teaching ability as he tried to avoid asking his students questions which he himself might not be able to answer.

Other later sons, not as able as the young Ph.D., were equally dubious of their competence. One, whose academic record was spotty, aimless, and undistinguished, managed to hold a job in a family firm. He visualized his inner self as a weak nucleus in a cell which is in constant danger of inundation by a shift in cellular water balance. A more competent later son, similar to the Ph.D., who had a keen analytic mind, was not bolstered by his Harvard Law School degree nor by the fact that he had a successful law practice. He maintained that "you are what people say you are," and whenever he was not given the best table at a restaurant or was bumped from a plane in favor of a V.I.P., he was overcome by feelings of inferiority. Not until he had been in analysis for more than a year was he able to give up his habit of refusing to surrender his driver's license when picked up for speeding. He regarded his driver's license as his card of identity, concrete proof that he was an adult citizen entitled to equal rights.

Exhibiting feelings of inferiority and an overweening concern for social identity, later-of-sex patients, male and female, tend to place considerable emphasis on two questions: "What will people say about me," and "Am I normal,"–both of which can perhaps be reduced to one question, "Do I conform to expected social norms?"

In the sensitivity of the peer-civilized to external approval they are eager for any psychological food from external objects which does not decrease their status. In contrast to the first of sex who tend *not* to ingest anything from the outside that is not relevant to their self-system or does not mesh with their own ideas, the later of sex will take whatever is offered if it is introduced in a nonpatronizing, nonhumiliating manner which demonstrates basic acceptance and interest in them. Thus, they frequently ask for advice in therapy and follow it without much personal revision. The more they add to their fund of knowledge, the more adequate they feel. What these later-of-sex patients mostly seek is how-to-do-it knowledge, which aids in current self-preservation, rather than abstract interpretations of why they are as they are.

The contrast between the adult- and peer-civilized may be noted in two brothers who underwent therapy with me. I saw the elder, a first born of professional parents (followed in the sibship by a sister and then a brother) when he was 18, shortly after he had recovered from a paranoid episode which required hospitalization. Possessing a keen mind and verbal skills, he was interested in literary composition and gave me many of his poems to read. The only academic problem he had was that stemming from his opinion that the university had little to teach him. Though bored with many of his college courses, he passed them easily and took each academic hurdle as it came.

Most striking was his feeling of self-importance, the feeling Jones alluded to as derived from being the center of the inner family. Not only did it make him depreciate what college had to offer: more important, it led to a therapeutic impasse in which he, asserting that his time was as valuable as mine, demanded that I see him without fee and be available for telephone calls at any time of the night, a practice he indulged in with his *real* friends. When I declined his terms, he discontinued therapy. Due to my later contact with his younger brother, I was able to follow his career. Some of the self-importance appears to have been warranted, for he went on to become a poet and an editor of a literary magazine.

A few years after he stopped treatment, his younger brother, now 18, consulted me because of a severe learning problem. He had failed in his college freshman year and was in a state of confusion and depression. Though he had not done well in high school he had applied to this particular school in order to keep up with his brother's intellectual achievements. Many of his opinions were more than derived from his brother—they were frankly imitative. Self confidence was chronically at low ebb, largely due to his brother's domination and intellectual hazing. He was anxious to please me, a technique which had proved successful with his domineering father who was at swords points with his self-important son. Prolonged therapy over many years did little to increase his capacity for systematic learning. Although becoming able to think, as he described it, in sentences rather than in words, he was never able to master the embracing connections of a paragraph, let alone an entire article. Not only was he unable to finish any of the occasional courses he took at night, he was not up to learning what was offered in the on-the-job training program.

Of particular interest was this young man's dependence on physical closeness. Several incidents strongly suggested that he was unable to perform any sustained intellectual task unless there was a supporting object concretely near. This other human being need not supply him with answers nor with constant promptings. All that was required of the object was that it not be at a distance, that it be within the range of sight and touch.

One such incident occurred in childhood when he was called upon in the third grade to spell words. He was only able to do so if the teacher stood next to him and put her hand on his shoulder. A similar incident took place in therapy when I suggested that a written plan for an agenda for the week might reduce the chaotic confusion he experienced in establishing priorities. Several months passed without his bringing in a written agenda. Finally I suggested that he write it during the therapy session. It was only then that he was able to set down on paper a connected plan for the week, an effort that once begun flowed without fits and starts.

Illustrated here is the kind of learning difficulty experienced by the peer-civilized. This is not to say that they will necessarily have learning problems. A superior intelligence can overcome many scholastic obstacles. But, as the vignette indicates, their particular cognitive style will not be facilitated by an educational system which throws the individual entirely on his own, a practice increasingly engaged in on the college levels. The system appears to favor the adult-civilized person who by virtue of deep internalizations can think abstractly and connectedly and can work by himself. It operates, I believe, to hamper the more practical peer-civilized mind insofar as it does not supply a supporting and connecting framework of objects who are near in space and time.

The impression may have been given that the advantages are all with the adult-civilized. If personality is considered narrowly, if academic achievement is made synonymous with ego strength, there is no doubt that the adult-civilized are the more advantaged. But this narrow perspective fails to take into account the psychological price paid for educational gigantism. Pressured from within by their deep internalizations, the adult-civilized may be forced to give their all to achievement, and to be subject to melancholia if the impossible goal is not realized.

Moreover, one should not forget that there is more to life than cloistered academia. One need not be cynical to appreciate the realistic fact that in any society—and especially in an other-directed society—what one knows frequently has to yield precedence to who one knows. Here the peer-civilized, sensitive to fluctuations in exterior power and status have the advantage. Outside the academic subculture, they tend to come into their own. Their goals are more modest than those of the adult-civilized, they address themselves in a practical way to the here and now, and their need for supporting objects attracts support from those whose self-esteem depends on being needed.

Although there is much more that could be said about the adult and peer-civilized, any further amplification would be beyond the scope of this essay. Perhaps enough has been set forth that the clinician has gained some increased appreciation of the repercussions of family position and of the interaction between cognitive style and the educational system.

REFERENCES

Bacon, F. (1947). Novum organum. In *Philosophers of science,* S. Cummins and R. N. Linscott (Eds.). New York: Random House. P. 91.

Bell, E. T. (1937). *Men of mathematics.* New York: Simon and Schuster.

Einstein, A. (1950). *Out of my later years.* New York: Philosophical Library. P. 27.

Freud, S. (1933). *A general introduction to psychoanalysis.* New York: Liveright. Pp. 289-290.

Harris, I. (1961). *Emotional blocks to learning.* New York: The Free Press of Glencoe.

Harris, I. (1964). *The promised seed.* New York: The Free Press of Glencoe.

Harris, I. D. and Howard, K. I. (1968). Birth order and responsibility. *Journal of Marriage and The Family,* **30,** No. 3.

Jones, E. (1953). *The life and work of Sigmund Freud, Vol. I.* New York: Basic Books. Pp. 13-14.

Jones, H. (1946). The environment and mental development. In *Manual of child psychology,* L. Carmichael (Ed.). New York: Wiley. P. 628.

Koch, H. (1954). The relation of "primary mental abilities" in five and six year olds to sex of child and characteristics of his sibling. *Child Development,* **25,** 219.

Koch, H. (1956). Sibling influence on children's speech. *Journal of Speech and Hearing Disorders,* **21,** 322-28.

MacArthur, C. (1956). Personalities of first and second children. *Psychiatry,* **19,** 47-54.

Murphy, G., Murphy, L., and Newcomb, T. (1937). *Experimental social psychology.* New York: Harper and Brothers.

Pascal, B. (1947). *Pensees in the speculative philosophers.* New York: Random House. P. 209.

Schacter, S. (1963). Birth order, eminence and higher education. *American Sociological Reviews* **28,** 757-767.

Stein, M. and Heinze, S. (1960). *Creativity and the individual.* New York: The Free Press of Glencoe.

Wilson, E. (1963). My fifty years with dictionaries and grammar. *New Yorker Magazine,* April 20. P. 165.

Part IV

RESEARCH MODELS

"Science is nothing but the determination to establish differences."

HERMAN HESSE

INTRODUCTION

As is true with any science, psychological research on personality has suffered from the lack of satisfactory theoretical models from which strategies and methods naturally flow. This section includes three prototype models: behavioral, psychoanalytic, and animal. These three have been selected to illustrate the range of possibilities for comparing individuals and because each contains motivational, developmental, and interactional capabilities.

In Chapter 11, Lorna Benjamin calls attention to the need for the rigorous organization of behavioral information. She has devised a chart of social behavior permitting the construction of a precisely defined profile for an individual child and, also, for his parent. Although each personality profile stands alone, it is clearly related to the reflected images of significant others. Of particular importance is the fact that she employs only commonly understood language, rendering her system both easily applicable and intelligible.

The usefulness of Dr. Benjamin's behavior chart has been demonstrated through clinical trials. As an example, the application of the chart to a vignette of family life is given, showing how the parentlike, childlike, and introject surfaces of the chart actually can be used to analyze the interaction of mother, father, and child.

The chart is designed so that numerically corresponding points on each chart surface represent complementary behaviors for two persons conducive to the stability of that particular relationship. An unstable relationship results when noncorresponding points on two surfaces occur together at the same point in time. In addition, then, to offering a tool for describing interpersonal transactions, this chart can be used for predicting the stability or consistency of interaction between people over time.

In the following chapter, Christoph Heinecke draws upon the theoretical system of psychoanalysis and describes the methodology employed in the nursery-school project reported in Chapter 9. However, he also sets forth a replicable method that ingeniously relates data about the parent-child relationship collected in the home to longitudinal behavioral observations of the child by nursery-school based observers. With this data he then defines periods of critical development for the child and uses this information to explain observed life experiences. Of particular note is his technique of separating objective behavioral observations from inferences, thereby permitting the testing of alternative explanations in order to maximize validity.

Although painstakingly complex in its execution, Dr. Heinecke's method achieves understandable simplicity through its clearly differentiated categories of direct observations and indirect inferences collated at periodic intervals for each child. He relies upon participant observers who capture vignettes of a child's natural life experiences both in nursery school and at home. His work extends previous efforts to confirm psychoanalytic theory through the study of psychotherapy to the direct observation of young children.

In an entirely different vein, William McKinney draws attention in Chapter 13 to the availability of infrahuman subjects for personality research by first reviewing the feasibility of correlating knowledge of primate and human stages of development. As background information, he summarizes Harlow and Harlow's five affectional systems which lend themselves to behavioral and psychophysiological investigation. He next describes methods for experimentally influencing the personality development of monkeys both through partial and total social isolation of the animals and through producing specific stress situations in order to create predictable behavioral and affective effects. Of particular interest is the possibility of identifying biochemical factors that might predispose individuals to differing degrees of depressive reactions following identical deprivation experiences.

Each of the lines of experimentation described by Dr. McKinney yields variant responses in individual monkeys offering opportunities under laboratory conditions for exploring predisposing individual differences. The material in this chapter suggests that research in primate personality development has progressed to the point of permitting useful correlations with human behavior.

CHAPTER 11

A Biological Model for Understanding the Behavior of Individuals

Lorna Smith Benjamin

The search for order within the universe of behavior is hindered by the belief in free will. Philosophers have long debated whether human actions are predictable from knowledge of a sufficient number of antecedents. No one has yet quieted the question with a definitive answer. However, the problem can be approached pragmatically; if certain social conditions can be identified as antecedents to certain social attitudes and behaviors, that observation has uncontestable practical implications. Psychotherapists vary greatly in the extent to which they believe in social determinism (e.g., Freudians, Rogerians, Existentialists), but no matter what their philosophical persuasion, those who in good faith charge a fee for their services must necessarily believe that behavior can at least be influenced.

Freud (1959) was openly deterministic with his proposal that early childhood experiences at the oral, anal, phallic, and other stages had major influence on adult personality. Erikson (1959) extended Freud's ideas to suggest that early childhood experience at the stages of trust versus mistrust, autonomy versus control, initiative versus guilt, and so on shaped adult personality. Carrying Freud's idea further, Mahler (1968) proposed that major early childhood stages influencing adult personality include normal autism, normal symbiosis, and individuation-hatching, practicing, and rapproachement.

Although Freud clearly intended to create a "science" of human behavior by borrowing a fixed-energy model from physics, psychoanalysis has been repeatedly criticized for its failings as a science. Psychoanalysis is said to lack sufficient specificity, to be too phenomenological, too private, and too contradictory to be amenable to the objective operational scientific method. Despite its scientific "failings," psychoanalysis has survived—at times, even thrived—in a culture which is basically pragmatic. Probably its survival is due to its apparent effectiveness in relieving the psychological suffering of a considerable number of individuals. . .whether it is "scientific" or not. Nonanalytic psychotherapies have developed since Freud, and they too have helped individuals. Nevertheless, neither analytic nor nonanalytic psychotherapies have yet been defined as sciences in the usual sense; if they could be so defined, they might become even more useful.

As a contribution toward the development of a more scientific means of describing human behavior, this chapter describes a chart of primate social behavior. The chart is a rational description of dyadic human social relations, and it grew from a knowledge of the behavior of infrahuman primates, of factor analytic studies of children and adults, of the behavior of normal adults, and of adult psychiatric patients. The chart is highly specific in its descriptions and predictions of what social experiences are associated with what attitudes and behaviors. It specifies 54 logically opposite social behaviors, thereby offering clear definitions of ambivalences and double binds; it predicts what kinds of social behaviors are compatible; it specifies what kinds of social behaviors are antidotes to other behaviors. This specific, testable, theoretical model is proposed as a means by which individual differences, as they have long been conceived by clinicians such as Freud, Erikson, Sullivan, and many others, can now be researched and understood in a more objective, quantified, scientific manner.

The proposed chart of primate social behavior has been defined and tested by a questionnaire which allows an individual to rate his own social attitudes and behaviors and/or those of others. The questionnaire has been applied to hundreds of individuals including normal children, child psychiatry outpatients, normal adults, and adult psychiatric patients. Analyses of the resulting data by techniques of autocorrelation and of factor analysis have confirmed the hypothesized structure of the chart. Statistically significant differences among normal children of different ages can be interpreted in part by psychoanalytic theory, particularly as revised by Erikson (1959), and by Mahler (1968). Thus the chart questionnaire attempts to offer a means of testing and refining the interpersonal aspects of psychoanalytic and other theoretical principles which have proved to be clinically useful. In addition, the chart method intends to allow a statistical and geometric description of the social history and behavior of an individual. For example, a person can rate his social relations with his spouse, children, colleagues, therapist, and parents as remembered from childhood, with siblings as remembered from childhood, and so on. Contrasts and similarities can then be specified among these ratings. Examples of outcomes observed in ratings made to date include the discovery that a spouse resembles a particular sibling, that a spouse resembles the opposite- (or like-) sexed parent; that the spouse is the "negative image" of a parent, that a father's relation with his child parallels his memory of how his mother treated him, and so on, through all the patterns meaningfully but less rigorously described in many psychotherapies. The idea of comparing memory of early childhood experiences to current relations is, of course, associated with psychoanalysis.

The questionnaire uses everyday language rather than the relatively abstract professional terms like "object loss," "separation anxiety," "dependency," "castration anxiety," and "Oedipal complex." Yet the questionnaire does attempt to measure social behaviors which are related to these concepts. Thus, the method offers a logically rigorous, quantitative, and qualitative description of a person's perceived social relations with important others in terms that can be communicated to patients and interested laymen as well as to the psychiatrically sophisticated.

The purpose of this chapter is to briefly describe the structure of social behavior as described by the chart. Because of limits on space, this paper will not include a description of the questionnaire itself, of the computer analysis of the ratings of an individual, of the factor analytic and developmental data, of the chart's relation to the human and infrahuman primate literature, or of the scheme's attempt to distinguish normal from pathological social behavior. This information will be available elsewhere (Benjamin, in preparation).

The idea that there is an underlying structure to behavior has been proposed by many theorists in addition to Freud. Examples of persons proposing structural descriptions of human behavior include Foa (1961), Bierman (1969), Feiffer (1970), Chance (1966), and others, including Cattell (1957) and Eysenck (1957), who are among the more widely published modern structural theorists. Some structural theorists speak of personality in terms of *fixed traits.* However, the search for structure need not be accompanied by the attempt to classify people in terms of traits, or of *fixed* roles or styles of interpersonal interaction. It is perfectly possible to hold that behavior is lawful without also requiring that people have rigid character structure. The only restriction that the search for structure imposes is that behavior in a particular context must relate to that context in a lawful way according to structural principles. The observation that the same person is quite different in one situation than he is in another in no way vitiates the notion that lawful principles underlie his behavior. For example, the fact that a patient is submissive at work and tyrannical at home (or vice versa) would preclude a description of this person as a "dominating personality" or as a "weak personality." However, his behavior in these different contexts would nevertheless have "structure" and order; such an order might be found in the fact that his father was tyrannical whereas his mother was warm and submissive to the patient. In his current life, the patient is relating to his boss as to his father, and to his wife as to his mother. Further, the patient's dominance or submissiveness may even vary in relation to the same person, depending on the context. Maybe, for example, the patient dominates his wife in matters of money and rules of the household, but defers to her in matters related to the handling of children. This example is intended to illustrate that it is meaningful to speak of the structure of the patient's behavior without necessarily entering into a study of "fixed personality."

The proposed chart of social behavior incorporates major features from the interpersonal classifications of Freedman et al. (1951), and of Schaefer (1965). The system of Freedman et al. arranged interpersonal behaviors in a circle and included the categories: dominate, boast, reject, punish, hate, complain, distrust, condemn self, submit, admire, trust, cooperate, love, support, give, and teach. Love is placed opposite hate, and submit appears opposite dominate. Adjacent behaviors have some elements in common. For example, the behavior on the *hate* side of dominate is boast, and the behavior on the *love* side of dominate is teach. This theoretical system has been effectively applied to the study of the process of psychotherapy. For example, by rating patients' interactions with their therapists and patient reports of interactions with parents and others in terms of the interpersonal circle of this system, Mueller (1969) has been able to quantify the phenomenon of transference.

Schaefer's system also arranges interpersonal behaviors in a circle or circumplex. Schaefer's circumplex describes parental behavior and has been confirmed by factor-analytic studies in several different cultures. His circumplex is built on two dimensions: (1) psychological control versus psychological autonomy and (2) rejection versus acceptance (in an earlier version, Schaefer named the second dimension, hate versus love). Starting at the pole of psychological control, Schaefer's circle includes the points: satellitization, intolerance, hostile involvement (rejection pole), hostile indifference, indifference, detachment (psychological autonomy pole), emancipation, encouragement of divergence, acceptance of individuation (acceptance pole), loving involvement, protectiveness, and intrusiveness.

Thus, both Schaefer's system and that of Freedman et al. conceive of two-person interactions in terms of (at least) two* underlying dimensions: one ranging from hate to love, and the other ranging from dominate to its opposite. Schaefer places autonomy in opposition to dominate (control), whereas Freedman et al. place submission in opposition to dominate. Autonomy is a logical opposite to domination while submission seems more *complementary* to domination; Schaefer's system therefore specifies opposites more precisely than does that of Freedman et al. To illustrate, note the plausible oppositional relations between opposite points in Schaefer's circumplex: emancipation versus satellitization, intrusiveness versus detachment, protectiveness versus indifference, and loving involvement versus hostile indifference. By contrast, opposite points on the Freedman et al. interpersonal circle do not seem to be rigorously oppositional: punish versus cooperate, reject versus trust, boast versus admire, and teach versus condemn self. Thus Schaefer's system has a

---

* Schaefer also discusses a third dimension: firm control as opposed to lax control, but this has not yet been incorporated into his circumplex.

logical integrity not shared by the Freedman et al. interpersonal classification system.

THE AXES OF THE CHART

The proposed chart of primate social behavior, presented in Figure 1, builds on the logical integrity of Schaefer's circumplex by including in its top part, that is, on its first surface, a domain of parentlike behaviors described by two underlying dimensions: *dominate* versus *emancipate* and *murderous attack* versus *embrace, tender touch.* The vertical dimension described by the poles *dominate* versus *emancipate* is named "interdependence," and refers primarily to the amount of physical and psychological space which is mutually shared. At the domination pole, the dominator totally controls the available time, space, and supplies. The purest manifestation of dominance is found in the behavior of the dominant male monkey or human primate (e.g., administrator) who controls group movements and has absolute priority to everything and everyone. At the emancipation pole is the concept of separate psychological and/or physical territory (in the human primate: to quit a job; to get a divorce).

The horizontal dimension, described by the poles *murderous attack* versus *embrace, tender touch* is named affiliation. The dimension affiliation is defined in terms of touch rather than hate and love because touch is felt to represent the essence of what is usually meant by these concepts. Murder in the purest form is harsh, brutal, rhythmic touch to vital body parts; embrace, tender touch in its purest form is gentle, rhythmic touch to erogenous body parts. Conceiving of touch as the basis of affiliation defies psychoanalytic tradition, but is supported by Harlow and Harlow's (1965) finding that tender bodily contact has priority over nursing in the primate infant's attachment to its mother.

All points on the proposed chart of primate social behavior are conceived as consisting of complementary proportions of these underlying dimensions: affiliation and interdependence. For example, the point *stimulate, teach* consists of about equal amounts of affiliation and domination, and the point *explore, let discover* consists of about equal amounts of affiliation and emancipation. By contrast, the point *possessive* consists almost completely of domination and a little bit of affilation, while the point *starve, poison* consists almost completely of murderous attack and a little bit of emancipation. A more precise statement of the relation of each of the chart points to the underlying dimensions appears later in the section headed *Tracks.*

OPPOSITES AND COMPLEMENTS

In the proposed chart, as in Schaefer's circumplex, behaviors placed opposite to each other are logical opposites. For example, *possessive* is the opposite of

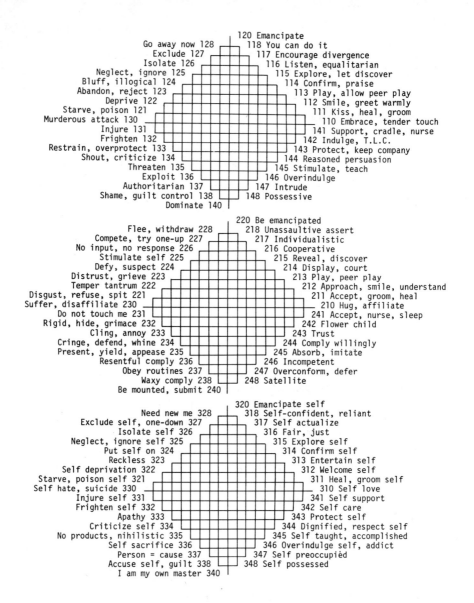

Figure 1. The chart of primate social behavior. The first surface describes parent-like behaviors; the second, childlike; and the third, introjected attitudes from significant others.

communicating *go away now, shame and guilt control* is the opposite of indicating *you can do it, authoritarian* is the opposite of *encourage divergence,* and so on. In Table 1, the opposite points on the parentlike surface appear in the rows marked "surface 1." Since there are 36 points on the surface, there are 18 pairs of opposites shown on that part of the chart, and in the rows marked surface 1 in Table 1.

The first surface of the chart, shown in the top of Figure 1, describes the domain of parentlike behaviors, and was an outgrowth of Schaefer's circumplex of parenting behaviors. Although the behaviors charted on the first surface are named "parentlike," they are by no means restricted to parents; nor are they all-inclusive of parental behavior. For example, submission is not included in Schaefer's system, nor does it appear on the first surface of the chart. Nevertheless, in real life, parents quite often submit to children. The Freedman et al. interpersonal circle does have the advantage of including the important set of interpersonal behaviors called submissive. In recognition of this advantage of their system, the second surface of the chart, shown in the middle of Figure 1, includes the point *be mounted, submit* at the bottom of the vertical axis. *Submit* appears at a place on the second surface of the chart which matches the location of *dominate* on the first surface of the chart. Submit is conceived as the *complement* (not the opposite) of dominate. Similarly, every other point on the second surface of the chart is the *complement* of the corresponding point on the first surface.

On the second as well as the first surface, the horizontal axis represents affiliation, and the vertical axis represents interdependence. Specifically, the horizontal axis ranges from *suffer, disaffiliate* to *hug, affiliate* and these are the respective complements to *murderous attack* and *embrace, tender touch.* The vertical axis ranges from *be mounted, submit* to *be emancipated,* and these points are the respective complements of *dominate* and *emancipate.*

Further examples of complementary relations between the first and second surfaces are: *possessive-satellite; intrude-overconform, defer; overindulge-incompetent;* and so on, around the chart, with the 36 points on the second surface specifying the complements of the respective 36 points on the first surface. When two individuals exhibit complementary behaviors, they are *matched* with respect to affiliation and interdependence. They form a *stable social compound* in the sense that each is exhibiting the same amounts of the underlying dimensions of interpersonal behavior in complementary relation. Without change in external or internal conditions being described at the moment, the social relation between matched individuals is not likely to change. For example, if one person happens to be possessive (148)* and the second person is a satellite (248), they remain in a stable symbiotic relation. However, if

* The numbers in parentheses refer to code numbers of chart points; the rationale of code numbers is presented subsequently.

Table 1.

Surface Point	Opposite Point

Track 0—Chart Axes

1. Dominate (140)
2. Be mounted, submit (240)
3. I am my own master (340)

Emancipate (120)
Be emancipated (220)
Emancipate self (320)

1. Murderous attack (130)
2. Suffer, disaffiliate (230)
3. Self hate, suicide (330)

Embrace, tender touch (110)
Hug, affiliate (210)
Self love (310)

Track 1 (8/9 affiliation; 1/9 interdependence)

1. Injure (131)
2. Do not touch me (231)
3. Injure self (331)

Kiss, heal, groom (111)
Accept groom, heal (211)
Heal, groom self (311)

1. Starve, poison (121)
2. Disgust, refuse, spit (221)
3. Starve, poison self (321)

Support, cradle, nurse (141)
Accept, nurse, sleep (241)
Self support (341)

Track 2 (7/9 affiliation; 2/9 interdependence)

1. Frighten (132)
2. Rigid, hide, grimace (232)
3. Frighten self (332)

Smile, greet warmly (112)
Approach, smile, understand (212)
Welcome self (312)

1. Deprive (122)
2. Temper tantrum (222)
3. Self deprivation (322)

Indulge, tender loving care (142)
Flower child (242)
Self care (342)

Track 3 (6/9 affiliation; 3/9 interdependence)

1. Restrain, overprotect (133)
2. Cling, annoy (233)
3. Apathy (333)

Play, allow peer play (113)
Play, peer play (213)
Entertain self (313)

1. Abandon, reject (123)
2. Distrust, grieve (223)
3. Reckless (323)

Protect, keep company (143)
Trust (243)
Protect self (343

Track 4 (5/9 affiliation; 4/9 interdependence)

1. Shout, criticize (134)
2. Cringe, defend, whine (234)
3. Criticize self (334)

Confirm, praise (114)
Display, court (214)
Confirm self (314)

Table 1 (continued)

Surface Point	Opposite Point

Track 4 (5/9 affiliation; 4/9 interdependence) (continued)

1. Bluff, illogical (124)	Reasoned persuasion (144)
2. Defy, suspect (224)	Comply willingly (244)
3. Put self on (324)	Dignified, respect self (344)

Track 5 (4/9 affiliation; 5/9 interdependence)

1. Threaten (135)	Explore, let discover (115)
2. Present, yield, appease (235)	Reveal, discover (215)
3. No products, nihilistic (335)	Explore self (315)
1. Neglect, ignore (125)	Stimulate, teach (145)
2. Stimulate self (225)	Absorb, imitate (245)
3. Neglect, ignore self (325)	Self taught, accomplished (345)

Track 6 (3/9 affiliation; 6/9 interdependence)

1. Exploit (136)	Listen, equalitarian (116)
2. Resentful comply (236)	Cooperative (216)
3. Self-sacrifice (336)	Fair, just (316)
1. Isolate (126)	Overindulge (146)
2. No input, no response (226)	Incompetent (246)
3. Isolate self (326)	Overindulge self, addict (346)

Track 7 (2/9 affiliation; 7/9 interdependence)

1. Authoritarian (137)	Encourage divergence (117)
2. Obey routines (237)	Individualistic (217)
3. Person = la cause (337)	Self actualize (317)
1. Exclude (127)	Intrude (147)
2. Compete, try one-up (227)	Overconform, defer (247)
3. Exclude self, one-down (327)	Self preoccupied (347)

Track 8 (1/9 affiliation; 8/9 interdependence)

1. Shame, guilt control (138)	You can do it (118)
2. Waxy compliance (238)	Unassaultive assert (218)
3. Accuse self, guilt (338)	Self-confident, reliant (318)
1. Go away now (128)	Possessive (148)
2. Flee, withdraw (228)	Satellite (248)
3. Need new me (328)	Self-possessed (348)

a third person intrudes (147) in a way which leads the possessive person (148) to exclude (127) his satellite (248) in any way, then the satellite may match the exclusion (127) with the new response of competing (227) or fleeing (228). Again, it should be noted that since the chart does not describe chronic traits, the concept of "stability" and "matching" is restricted to the particular set of circumstances being described at the moment. The same person might alternate between intrusion (147) and exclusion (127) with respect to another depending on internal and/or external states; momentary stability is achieved, however, when he intrudes (147) and his dyadic partner is deferential (247).

In Table 1, behaviors indexed by the second surface of the chart appear in the row marked "surface 2." Behaviors charted on surface 2 appear in Table 1 directly below the surface 1 behavior which they complement. The table is divided into sections labeled *tracks,* and this term will be precisely defined in a section headed *Tracks.* For the present, it is useful to note that all points on a given track consist of the same relative amounts of interdependence and affiliation, and thus the arrangements of points by tracks allows complements and opposites to be discerned in a glance. For example, in the section of Table 1 marked Track 1, the second surface chart point named *do not touch me* is listed as the complement of *injure;* its opposite, named *accept groom, heal* appears as the complement of *kiss, heal, groom.*

The set of points presented in the second surface of the chart are named the childlike group, because prototypically they are characteristic of children in complementary relation to parents. Just as parentlike points are not descriptions of fixed roles, so the childlike points are neither restricted to nor exhaustively descriptive of children. For example, children dominate parents even though this is often thought to be a parental prerogative. Incidentally, data obtained by maternal rating of pediatric outpatients suggest that the childrens' dominance (140, in the sense of controlling mutual use of time, space, and supplies) is maximal during the first 6 months of life! The idea of children "parenting parents" is underdeveloped in the literature, but mothers of normal children did endorse items on the chart questionnaire suggesting their children would direct parentlike behaviors toward them including protect and keep company (143), support, cradle, and nurse (141), kiss, heal, and groom (111). Interview follow-up of these ratings revealed explanations like: "Well, the other night I was laying on the couch crying and he (three-year old) came over and brought me Kleenex and kissed me; he said: 'Don't cry, Mom!' " R. Q. Bell (1971) has recently presented more formal arguments in support of the idea that children actively influence parents' behavior as well as the more familiar idea that parents actively influence children.

In general, behaviors charted on the parentlike surface are *initiating* whereas behaviors charted on the childlike surface are *reactive.* Although the parentlike surface includes points like *intrude, possessive, dominate, shame, guilt control,* and *authoritarian,* the parentlike group is not restricted to this sort of interpersonal domination. The parentlike surface *also* includes many initiating behaviors which are not so close to the dominate pole. Examples of parentlike points which are not dominating include: *encourage divergence; listen, equalitarian; explore, let discover; confirm, praise; go away now; exclude.* The reader may object that "go away now" and "exclusiveness" can be extremely powerful communications. However, if these words are powerful, then they must be in service of shame and guilt control (138), rather than genuinely representing communications at the highly independent points *go away now* and *exclude.* If go away now (128) and exclude (127) effect much interpersonal power, then they must mean: "I won't have anything to do with you unless you do it my way; or . . . until you say you're sorry, etc." In other words, in the context of power, these messages are calling for waxy compliance (238) and/or submission (240), and, as such, they represent shame and guilt control (138). The misunderstanding of go away now (128) as shame and guilt control (138) would be an example of within-track generalization, a term defined in a later section.

Just as behaviors charted on the parentlike surface are not always powerful, so behaviors charted on the childlike surface are not necessarily submissive or passive. An example of the common belief that submissiveness is synonymous with being childlike is the insistence that college and/or graduate curricula should not be structured because the students are *adults* and not *children.* In other words, it would be "childlike" to submit to structures imposed by faculty; that is, the points *obey routines, waxy compliance, be mounted, submit,* might be thought to "define" childlike behaviors. They do not. For example, their opposite points shown in Figure 1 and Table 1 are *individualistic, unassaultive assert,* and *be emancipated,* and these refer to behaviors which are "childlike" without being submissive. The chart suggests that for social stability, such assertive behaviors would have to be respectively matched by the faculty with the parentlike group of behaviors: encourage divergence (117), you can do it (118), and emancipate (120). The acceptance of such a high degree of independence would raise the question of whether there is a need for faculty at all. Further discussion of the curriculum problem is beyond the scope of this paper. The example is used primarily to show that in contrast to popular usage, in the chart system parentlike is not synonymous with domination, and childlike is not synonymous with submission.

CODE NUMBERS OF CHART POINTS

To make the logical relations among points on the chart more explicit, code numbers are assigned to each of its points. All of the points on the first surface (parentlike) are coded in the 100s, and those on the second surface (childlike), in the 200s. For each surface, the tens digit in the code number refers to the quadrant of the chart point, following the mathematical convention of assigning the first quadrant to the region ranging from 0 to 90 degrees (12 to 3 o'clock); the second, from 90-180 degrees (9 to 12 o'clock); the third, from 180-270 degrees (6 to 9 o'clock); and the fourth, from 270-360 degrees (3 to 6 o'clock). Thus on the parentlike surface all points between *embrace, tender touch* (0 degrees) and *emancipate* (90 degrees) have a 1 in the tens digit of their code number; points between *emancipate* and *murderous attack* (180 degrees) have a 2 for their tens digit; all points between *murderous attack* and *dominate* (270 degrees) have a 3 for a tens digit; and between *dominate* and *embrace, tender touch* (360 degrees) points have a 4 for a tens digit.

The units digit of the code number of the chart point refers to the subdivision of the quadrant. Thus, the units digit of the polar point *embrace, tender touch* (110) is a 0. The point *kiss, heal, groom* (111) is 1 step in the direction of *emancipate* (120) and it has a 1 in the units column; the point *smile, greet warmly* (112) is two steps in that direction, and has a 2 in the units column; this continues through 3,4,5,6,7,8 in the units column of succeeding points until the boundary of the quadrant, *emancipate* (120) is reached. Here, the units column reverts to 0, a characteristic of points marking the boundaries of the quadrants, and the axes of the chart.

One use of code numbers is that opposites can be specified exactly. Opposites must be on the same surface of the chart; for example, if a point is on the parentlike surface, its opposite must also be on that surface. In terms of code numbers, this means both points must begin with a 1 in the hundreds column. Opposites must also be in opposite quadrants; this means the tens digit must be 2 versus 4 or 1 versus 3. Exact opposites must meet the first two conditions, and must also have the same units digit. Thus the point 147, *intrude,* is the opposite of the point 127, *exclude.* Near opposites are defined by points which are adjacent to exact opposites. Thus the points 148, *possessive,* and 146, *overindulge,* are adjacent to 147, *intrude,* and they are near opposites to 127, *exclude.* Similarly, the points adjacent to 127, *exclude,* are 128, *go away now,* and 126, *isolate;* these are nearly opposite to 147, *intrude.* The specification of opposites and near opposites is useful when describing social conflicts, and looking for antidotes to social behaviors. Applications of the concept of opposites will be presented in the section headed *Antidotes.*

TRACKS

Another logical implication of the chart made clear by the code-numbering system is found in the concept of tracks. All points of a given surface having the same units entry in their code number belong to the same *track.* Thus the points

147, *intrude;* 127, *exclude;* 117, *encourage divergence;* and 137, *authoritarian,* belong to the same track, namely track 7. This track includes all points ending with the units digit 7, and this necessarily means that they consist of the same proportions of the underlying dimensions, affiliation and interdependence. The points on track 7 are shown in Figure 2; there, and in Figure 1, it can be seen that the point 147, *intrude,* has +2 units of maximal affiliation (i.e., of 110, *embrace, tender touch*) and +7 units of maximal interdependence (i.e., of 140, *dominate;* or −7 units of 120, *emancipate*). The opposite of 147, *intrude,* is 127, *exclude,* which has +2 units of 130, *murderous attack* (i.e. −2 units of 110, *embrace, tender touch)* and +7 units of 120, *emancipate* (or −7 units of 140, *dominate*). Since each quadrant is divided into 9 parts, the coordinates for the point 147, *intrude,* are (+2/9, −7/9); and for 127, *exclude,* the coordinates are (−2/9, +7/9). For example, the point 147, *intrude,* is 2/9 of the way toward

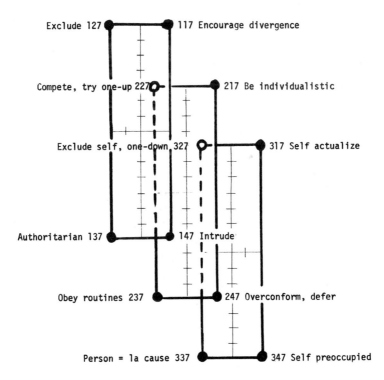

Figure 2. Track 7. All points from Figure 1 consisting of two units (±) of affiliation and seven units (±) of interdependence belong to track 7. As in Figure 1, the top group of chart points describe parent-like behaviors; the middle group, childlike; and the bottom, introjected behaviors.

maximal affiliation, and −7/9 of the way toward emancipation. The point 127, *exclude,* is 2/9 of the way toward murderous attack, and 7/9 of the way toward maximal emancipation. Figures 1 and 2 show the points *intrude* and *exclude* to be located exactly opposite each other. The values of the coordinates of these points indicate that they have the same amounts of interdependence (7/9) and affiliation (2/9), but the sign of each component is opposite.

The requirement that each point of the chart can be specified in terms of complementary proportions of the underlying dimensions means that the sum of the absolute values of the coordinates of each point on the chart must equal +1. If the affiliation axis is assigned the conventional variable name X, and the interdependence axis, the name Y, then the diamond shape of the chart shown in Figure 1 is specified by the equation $|X| + |Y| = 1$. For example, the coordinates for the point 147, *intrude,* are of the form (X, Y) and satisfy the relation $|X| + |Y| = 1$. That is, the absolute value of 2/9 plus the absolute value of −7/9 does = 1.

The other two members of track 7 in the parentlike group of points are the opposites *encourage divergence* (117) and *authoritarian* (137). They, too, consist of 7 units of interdependence, and 2 units of affiliation, and have opposite signs. Thus *authoritarian* (137) has the coordinates (−2/9, −7/9) indicating it includes much *domination* (140), and some *murderous attack* (130). *Encourage divergence* (117) has signs opposite to those for *authoritarian* (137); the coordinates for *encourage divergence* (117) are (+2/9, +7/9), indicating it has much *emancipation* (120), and some *embrace, tender touch* (110).

GENERALIZATION WITHIN TRACKS AND AMONG ADJACENT POINTS

The four points on a given track have the same proportions of affiliation and interdependence, and differ only in sign of the coordinates; apparently it is easy to confuse the sign of the coordinates, since there are often discrimination failures resulting in confusions or generalizations among points within a track. For example, in the process of encouraging divergence (117), it is possible to be perceived as excluding (127). Suppose a six-year-old child is coloring a picture, and asks his mother if it is "the right way." The mother might say "do it any way you like" intending to encourage him to develop his own coloring style (i.e., encourage divergence from her, 117). The child may perceive her remark as exclusion (127), particularly if at the moment when he asked the question, the mother was busily engaged in conversation with his father. As a further illustration of generalization within track 7, the child's question at that moment may have actually represented an attempt to intrude (147) into the conversation between the mother and father. Still another side of the interaction might emerge if the mother had actually wished to encourage divergence (117) with respect to coloring style, but first wished to explore what the child had "in mind" (explore, let discover, 115). Then she might have said: "Did you want to outline the picture before coloring it in?" Depending, among other things, on the amount of maternal domination in their interpersonal history, the child could misinterpret the mother's efforts at encouraging divergence (117) as other track 7 behaviors. If her questions strike him as "nosy," then she would be perceived as intruding on him (147). On the other hand, if he has been taught that the question "Do you want to . . . " really means "I want you to . . . ," her question "Did you want to outline the picture before coloring it in?" will be perceived as "I want you to outline the picture first . . ." which would be authoritarian (137).

In addition to generalization among points within a track, generalization to points adjacent on the chart are frequently observed. Generalization to adjacent points probably occurs because they differ very little in proportion of underlying dimensions affiliation and interdependence. For example, in describing his mother's domination, a normal adult professional man said: "My mother always holds everybody in judgment. . . .She had unreasonable control over my father (140). She thought of rigidity as stability (137, authoritarian). I think if she didn't have such a tight hold on everyone, she would have fallen through the slats (136, exploit)." Inspection of Figure 1 shows that his description of his mother included some adjacent points in the region of hostile power. Another example of generalization among adjacent chart points is found in a mother's description of intrusion (147) as she explained her rating of her two-year five-month-old daughter as dominating (140): "If I'm talking to someone on the phone, she always wants to know who I am talking to and what they are saying. . . .When I am getting my allergy shots, she always has to be let in on what is going on." The common association of hugging (110) and kissing (111) is another example of covariation of behaviors appearing at adjacent points on the chart. A mother described an instance of support (141) leading to hugging (110) and kissing (111) from her 10-year-old daughter: "The day before school was out, her class went to visit the State Historical Society. . .at 10:30 I discovered her lunch in the trunk of the car. I hunted her up, and finally found her group in the Historical Society. I said: 'Here's your lunch; did you miss it?' She said: 'Oh Mommy!' There, right in front of everyone, she reached up and gave me a big hug and a kiss."

Generalization among adjacent points on the childlike surface occurs as on the parentlike surface. For example, the behaviors described by the points *submit* (240), *satellite* (248), *overconform, defer* (247), and *incompetent* (246) are observed to covary just as much as their respective parentlike complements *dominate* (140), *possessive* (148), *intrude* (147), and *overindulge* (146).

ANTIDOTES

Since the parentlike and the childlike surfaces specify opposites within themselves and complements between each other, the two surfaces describe behaviors which are antidotes to each other. The antidote to behavior described at any chart point is found in the behavior charted 180 degrees away on the complementary surface. To illustrate, by referring to points on track 7 shown in Figure 2, consider the antidote to behavior described by the point *overconform, defer* (247). Deferential behavior is charted on the childlike surface and its complementary surface is the parentlike surface. The point on the parentlike surface directly opposite the coordinates for point 247 ($+2/9$, $-7/9$) is the point *exclude* (127) with coordinates ($-2/9$, $+7/9$). Thus the person who is showing behavior overconform, defer (247) will, if exposed to exclusion (127), begin to exhibit the opposite of overconform, defer (247), namely compete, try one up (227). A more or less "classical" illustration of this sequence would be the three-year-old male child who is docile and "good" (i.e., conforming, deferring, 247) in relation to his father; on approaching age 4, he comes to notice that his father is more involved with his mother than with himself (i.e., the father excludes, 127, the son); matching this exclusion with complementary behavior, the son begins to compete with and try to outdo his father (227). Thus, paternal exclusion (127) of the son is the (albeit unknowing) antidote to deferential behavior (247), and yields competitive behavior (227).

For another example of antidotes, suppose a female patient tells a male therapist he has not "helped" her enough; that he should give her more or different medicines "because" under his care, she is suffering. The therapist who responds by changing the medications *without objective* reason to do so would be responding to her shame and guilt control (138) with waxy compliance (238). The antidote to shame and guilt control (138) would be unassaultive assert (218). Such highly independent behavior might take the form of simply saying: "I'm doing what I think is best right now." The message is that the therapist lives in his own life-space, and will neither mount, crowd, attack, submit to, nor "love" the patient around the issue of medications. If pressed for prescribing a certain medication when he was not inclined to do so, the therapist might add something like: "If you feel strongly about this, I could refer you to Dr. Y, whom I understand uses that medication quite a bit; perhaps you and he could work something out." However, with changes in the sign of affiliation and/or interdependence, this remark could slip into behaviors charted at other track 8 points. In this case, the therapist might be perceived as saying go away now (128) which the patient might match with flee, withdraw (228) rather than positively approaching the potential new therapist. Similarly, the therapist's response might be heard as shame and guilt control (138) should the patient get the message: "If you don't do things my way, I won't like you, and I won't have you with me anymore." If the therapist does counter the patient's shame and guilt control (138) with more of the same, the result would be a maximally unstable relation in the form of a power struggle.

Less primitive examples of antidotal behaviors are found on tracks 3,4,5, which are located midway between the polar points of power (140, −240), murder (130, −230), sexuality (110, −210) and territory (120, −220). These middle points, consisting of approximately equal proportions of the underlying dimensions, describe behaviors generally considered to be more "civilized" in contrast to the more "primitive" behaviors charted near the axes. For example, on the affiliative side of the chart, points on these middle tracks include *explore, let discover* (115); *reveal, discover* (215); *confirm, praise* (114); *display, court* (214); *play, allow peer play* (113); *play, peer play* (213); *protect, keep company* (143); *trust* (243); *reasoned persuasion* (144); *comply willingly* (244); *stimulate, teach* (145); *absorb, imitate* (245). An example of antidotes within these tracks would be the handling of a defiant child (224) through reasoned persuasion (144). Because of discrimination failures within tracks, it is not simple to accurately communicate reasoned persuasion (144) to a child who expects bluff, illogic (124). The task is to communicate 6/9 affiliation, and 3/9 interpersonal power; a person who doesn't have a warm "touching" (110) relation with the child probably can't communicate enough affiliation, and therefore can't "persuade" him reasonably (144).

Another example of an antidote within this middle, civilized domain of behaviors is the use of protect, keep company (143) as an antidote to depression (223). Milieu therapy recognizes the antidotal relation when it designs a program of maximal social interaction (company keeping) for depressed patients. Similarly, the child who has lost a parent is not left alone; he is given lots of affiliative "attention" as an antidote to his loss.

ILLUSTRATION OF COMPLEMENTS, OPPOSITES, ANTIDOTES, AND GENERALIZATIONS

One procedure for understanding the descriptive power of the chart is to personally try it out on everyday interactions. To illustrate, a brief family interaction will be presented. Although they did not have the chart "in mind" when behaving, the adult participants agree that the recapitulation in terms of chart points is accurate. The vignette describes a family problem solving situation which primarily involved behaviors charted near the interdependence axis. Basically, the issue was one of individualism versus submission; there were four assertive family members with differing preferences for how to spend a Sunday. At first, there was little matching, but as the resolution was reached, members began exhibiting behaviors which are charted at complementary points. The sequence also illustrates that parents exhibit childlike as well as parentlike behaviors, and that movement within tracks, between surfaces, and among adjacent points is rapid.

The family lives in the suburbs of a city, and has recreational land about 30 miles from the home. On this land, they are building a small cottage by themselves.

Father:	"I'm going out today and start putting in the electricity."	He is declaring his independence in a mildly affiliative way with behavior charted at individualistic, 217.
	"What do you guys want to do?"	He initiates an exploration of the wishes of other family members without specifying any particular outcome: Explore, let discover (115).
Two Children:	"We wanna stay here and play with our friends."	The children assert their independence in a comparable individualistic fashion (217).
Mother	(sulking): "Oh, all right."	She shows resentful compliance to the children (236).
	"But I was hoping to go out and see what new signs of spring I could find."	In a sense, she is asserting her wishes in an unassaultive fashion (218). However, there is also the possibility of shame and guilt control (138) since she may be hinting at personal sacrifice and potential disaffiliation in order to get the children to comply with her wishes. Note the confusion between two antidotal points on track 8: 138 vs 218.
Father	"Well, you have the right to have your way some of the time."	He encourages his wife to assert herself (218) with his "You can do it" (118). The "You have a right" part is

also somewhat moralistic in tone, and therefore implies some shame and guilt control (138) too. Thus his communication contains opposite implications that she is free to define her own psychological territory (118), but also she "ought" to define it in a way which conforms to his wish (understood through past exchanges) that the family join him out at the country place.

"Just say what you want and I'll back you up."

He continues the affiliative independent communications with a listen, equalitarian (116) message, indicates he will cooperate with her decision (216). His now unequivocal message of affiliative independence (encourage divergence, 117 and listen, equalitarian, 116) provides strong antidotes to the wife's potential resentful compliance (236) to either the children or to him.

Mother   "I don't know what I want to do."

Here she expresses a feeling of interpersonal incompetence (246) which is a "call" for the complement of over-indulgence (146). In this instance, such over-indulgence would be obtained if the husband were to take over and "solve" the problem.

Father   No response.

He gives 226, no input, no response, which is the antidote to overindulgence (146), thereby closing off that possibility to his wife.

Mother	(angrily): "I just don't want another hassle with somebody squawking no matter what choice I make."	She is having a temper tantrum (222) in response to his failure to provide the desired indulgence (142). In reality, she was asking for *over*-indulgence (146) but perceived her request as for appropriate indulgence (142), or behavior charted at the adjacent point, support (141). She also has assumed she can read her husband's mind (possessive, 148) in that on the basis of past experience, she has concluded that he will be angry if she does not go. Similarly, she has assumed the children will be angry if she does go. Such "mind reading" (148) has created a dilemma which might *or might not* actually develop on this day.
Mother	(continues angrily): "I wish you would give me some support."	She declares she has been deprived (122) of the requested indulgence (142) and support (141). However, since the husband has in fact explicitly offered his support, her claim of no support appears to be nonsense, or bluff, illogic (124). The discrepancy in perception as to whether he is supporting her or not lies in the fact that the wife feels the husband should "solve it" (146) to support

		her, whereas he is asking her to make her own decision, and *then* he will support her (116-216).
Father	(angrily): "Now don't you start giving me a hard time."	This is a threat of some sort (135).
	"I *said,* just say what you want, and I'll back you up."	The husband resumes his initiating, parentlike role with independent, affiliative behaviors: explore, let discover, 115; listen, equalitarian, 116. Again, this is antidotal to resentful compliance (236).
Mother	"You're right. Just because I'm in an impossible spot of not being able to please everyone is no reason to put you in one too."	She accepts the responsibility of solving the anticipated dilemma, and matches his affiliative independence with cooperation (216).
Father	"Well, why don't you go by your own wishes once in a while; these kids have their way often enough."	Here, he encourages divergence (117) from the children. Possibly he is also competing (227) with them for the wife's company. This would be an example of within-track 7 generalization.
Mother	"Well, I'd like to go out there for lunch and for a hike. I really would."	She continues to match his affiliative independence; she asserts herself (218).
	"Kids, we are going out there for lunch, and to stay a while in the afternoon if the weather stays nice."	Now she takes total control of the children's physical location for the day (dominate, 140).
Child #1	"Can I bring a friend?"	The child asks in a pleasant way, indicating a cooperative, bargaining approach (216).

Mother	"Yes."	Mother returns cooperation (116).
Child #2	"I want to look for a bird's nest to take to Show and Tell."	The child asserts (218).
Mother	"O.K., I know where there is an old one which wasn't used last year."	She says You can do it (118), matching the child's assertiveness (218). By suggesting that the nest will not be used again, she teaches (145) the family ethic that nature should not be unduly disturbed.

Thus, the family disagreement was resolved after a good deal of assertive independence; some sheer power; and a fair amount of cooperation. The husband was the prime mover through his steady adherence to the parentlike independent, affiliative responses. With these communications, he provided a strong antidote to the wife's tendency to yield to the children's initial demands. Nor was the outcome to be interpreted in terms of both parents agreeing to dominate the children without regard to how they would feel; there was a favorable history of experience at the country place for the children. However, in the immediately preceding trips, the weather had been bad, and the children had had atypically unpleasant experiences with discomfort and boredom. On this day, the weather was splendid, and that was taken into account when the mother decreed they were going (140). At the end of the day, she asked the children: "Were you glad you went today?" (Explore, let discover, 115.) Both children enthusiastically answered to the effect that they had a very good time and were glad they went (215, reveal, discover).

Of course the above sequence does not prove anything. It is intended merely to illustrate some of the postulated interpersonal relations (complements, opposites, antidotes, generalizations) and to show how the chart might ultimately be used to code and study interpersonal interactions. For proof of the postulated relations, such an analysis would have to be obtained by independent observers.

RELATION OF INDIVIDUAL'S BEHAVIOR TO EXPERIENCE WITH SIGNIFICANT OTHERS

The development of personality is hypothesized to consist of thousands of everyday interactions like the one just described. Around the issue of how to spend that Sunday, the children observed the parents disagreeing and ultimately complementing each other to reach a cooperative decision without either "losing" or "suffering in silence." In addition, the children had the experience of submitting to the general parental plan for the day which indicated they were wanted as participants. Nor were they required to passively and helplessly go along with the parental plans without being able to shape the day according to their own wishes. They had some bargaining power as individuals in that they were allowed to bring a friend and received help in getting a bird's nest. If such give-and-take were the general experience of the children in the home, they would take this way of interacting to the peer group, and, if sufficient rewards accrued there, they would maintain cooperativeness as an interpersonal propensity in adult life.

Imitation (245) of parental behavior is known in psychoanalytic terms as identification. *Behaving as one behaved in relation to parents* is also common, and is easiest to discern in families which do not allow flexibility of interpersonal role. For example, the child who must chronically submit (240), be a satellite (248), and show waxy compliance (238) without regard for his own wishes may continue in that role in relation to others; he may seek dominating associates. The child who is chronically neglected (125) and develops a pattern of chronic self-stimulation (225) is unlikely to change this self-orientation as an adult. Similarly, the child who is able to tyrannize over a submissive mother may select meek friends so that he can continue his habit of always "being on top" (140). It is suggested that this tendency to recreate what has been experienced previously with significant others be named *recapitulation*; it is an interpersonal form of repetition compulsion. The tendency to react to others in a manner *opposite to that of the parents* is also commonly observed. For example, if the father were chronically critical (134), the child might cultivate becoming a praiser (114); if the parent were unyielding in his domination (140), the child may take pains to become extremely emancipating (120). This pattern of being the 180-degree opposite of the parent is an interpersonal version of the psychoanalytic idea of reaction formation, and has been observed relatively frequently in the response of psychiatric residents to the chart questionnaire. It is suggested that this tendency be named *imitation in reversal. Recapitulation in reversal* is also observed. For example, the child required to chronically comply (238), and obey routines (237) may develop a posture of chronic assertiveness (218) and individualism (217). It is not known what variables determine whether a child will imitate the parent, recapitulate his role in relation to the parent, become the negative image of the parent (imitation in reversal), or become the negative image of himself in relation to his parents (recapitulation in reversal), or none of these. However, by making rigorous distinctions among many types of social opposites and complements, the chart contributes to efforts to solve the problem of objectively and systematically exploring the relation of early childhood experience to adult personality.

RELATION OF EXPERIENCE WITH SIGNIFICANT OTHERS TO THE INDIVIDUAL'S ATTITUDES TOWARD SELF

Not only do the child's experiences with parents and important others affect his adult social behavior; these experiences also affect his attitudes *toward himself*. The alternatives in this domain are specified by the third surface of the chart, which appears at the bottom of Figures 1 and 2. Whereas the first two surfaces of the chart describe *inter*personal behavioral tendencies, the third surface describes *intra*personal attitudes. Borrowing a psychoanalytic term, this surface which describes a person's attitudes toward himself is named the *introject* surface. The idea is that the child takes the behaviors and attitudes of the parent toward him, and turns them inward on himself. In simplest form, this phenomenon can be observed in the toddler's acquisition of conscience. For example, children who are told "no no" when they reach for an electric plug or a forbidden object are observed to *tell themselves* "no no" when they look at the electric plug or forbidden object. Those who are slapped when they reach are more likely to slap themselves as they contemplate the plug or object. This widely observed phenomenon in toddlers is presumed to be the prototype of the development of attitudes toward the self. The idea that the child's feelings about himself reflect the way he has been treated by significant others has been proposed by many others, including H. S. Sullivan (Jersild, 1968, pp. 172).

The third surface of the chart, the introject surface, organizes attitudes toward the self in terms of the underlying dimensions of interdependence and affiliation. Code numbers are the same as for the first two surfaces, except they begin with 3. As the first and second surfaces, the third surface specifies 18 pairs of opposite attitudes and behaviors. All of the attitudes described on the third surface of the chart are hypothesized to represent the turning inward of parentlike behavior experienced from important others.

Some points on track 7, shown in Figures 1 and 2, may be used to illustrate the introjection of attitudes toward the self. The child who has an intrusive, nosy (147) parent may come to turn this behavior on himself, and be constantly asking himself questions such as "What am I doing this for? Is this what I really want to do?" and may become self-preoccupied (347). The patient in psychotherapy who perceives the therapist as intrusive and who introjects the therapist, likewise may become preoccupied with self. The child who introjects a parent who insists on order, structure, punctuality, neatness, and obedience for the sake of some principle (authoritarian, 137) begins to define himself in terms of some structured plan or cause (religious, political, academic, personal) and develops the attitude named person = la cause (337). The person who introjects exclusion from a significant other (127) arranges things so that he will continue to be excluded, and consistently come out "one-down" (exclude self, one down, 327). A child who introjects the parental attitude opposite to shame and guilt control

(138), namely encourage divergence (117), will be able to develop himself in whatever direction his own potential and inclinations suggest, and this situation is described by the point self-actualize (317).

For different examples of introjected behaviors, consider the child who has experienced bodily harm at the hands of important others (injure, 131). Such a child will turn this inward and have an undue number of accidents, or deliberately hurt himself (injure self, 331). The person who *perceives* that significant others would like to murder him (murderous attack, 130) will, if he likes them well enough to introject their attitudes, commit suicide. This interpretation makes explicit the clinical principle that suicide is a "two-person event"; someone else is always implicitly "in the background" and the therapist does well to help find out who it is, and why. The significant other "wanting" the death of the victim can range in subtlety from previous outright mortal assault to a misunderstanding of the murmurings of an harrassed mother to the effect that: "I'd like to kill you for that." Another example would be in the spouse who wants divorce, but can't accept it on moral or religious grounds; in this case, the victim's suicide would provide an "acceptable" way out, and so the "second person" is unconsciously facilitating the suicide. The chart is not intended to describe "unconscious" phenomena in general. However, the theory of the chart does allow the specification of what "unconscious" attitudes and behavioral propensities "ought" to be uncovered. Thus, on observing self-destructive behaviors, the therapist should help the patient uncover memory of overtly destructive behaviors experienced in the past, and/or the perception (misperception) of current destructive attitudes from important others. The question of suicide is not simple, and the above analysis is not intended to be comprehensive. It is suggested, however, that in the matter of suicide (chart point 330) and all the other self-directed attitudes described by the third surface, the chart offers a means of more logically rigorous study of these attitudes and their relations to early as well as current experiences.

The self-directed attitudes are specified in Table 1 in the rows marked surface 3. Because oppositional relations apply in the third surface as in the first two, therapist behaviors which would serve as antidotes for introjected attitudes are also specified. For example, the self-critical person (334) is hypothesized to have introjected a criticizing significant other person (134), and needs someone who will praise and confirm him realistically (114). Because of within-track generalization, therapist praise might be perceived as (or actually be) bluff, illogic (124) which would be expected to elicit the complementary behavior, defy, suspect (224) and/or the introjected attitude put self on (324). The therapist's task is to get enough positive affiliation (110), and enough emancipation (120) into his communication to create praise (114) which could serve as a maximally oppositional force to the patient's introjection of shout, criticize (134). Reasoned persuasion (144) may also help in this effort.

SUMMARY

The preceding discussion outlines the structure of the proposed chart of primate social behavior. Some of the interpersonal applications have been briefly described. The chart is offered as a step in the direction of more rigorous, objective, logical understanding of interpersonal behavior. The chart questionnaire describes the social meaning of the chart points, and offers a means of measuring individuals' perceptions of their past, present, and anticipated social relationships with specific other persons. Neither the chart nor its questionnaire refer exclusively to traits which require the notion of generalized rigidity in interpersonal interactions. Some individuals are in fact inflexible in their relations with others and therefore could be described in terms of traits, but the chart is intended to apply to moment to moment interactions as well as to chronic ways of relating. The proposed chart of primate social behavior describes oppositional, complementary, and antidotal social relations as well as specific antecedents of 36 different attitudes toward the self. Because of its high degree of specificity in behavioral terms, the model may serve as a tool with which the problem of individual differences can be researched more objectively and rigorously.

ACKNOWLEDGMENTS

Many friends and colleagues have contributed to the development of the chart. Special thanks go to Robert Benjamin, Ph.D., Carl Whitaker, M.D., William Lewis, M.D., Marjorie Klein, Ph.D., Robert Sears, Ph.D., Joseph Kepecs, M.D., David Graham, M.D., Sherwyn Woods, M.D., Jack Westman, M.D., William McKinney, M.D., and Gene Abroms, M.D. for their encouragement and for their patient reading of manuscripts overloaded with data and statistics. Their comments led to the present attempt to describe the chart without burdening the reader with all the technical detail.

REFERENCES

Benjamin, L. S. A chart of primate social behavior. In preparation.

Bell, R. Q. (1971). Stimulus control of parent or caretaker behavior by offsprings. *Developmental Psychology* **4**, 63-72.

Bierman, R. (1969). Dimensions of interpersonal facilitation in psychotherapy and child development. *Psychological Bulletin*, **72**, 338-352.

Cattell, R. (1957). In chapter on Factor Theories, *Theories of personality*, C. S. Hall and G. Lindzey (Eds.). New York: Wiley.

Chance, E. (1966). Content analysis of verbalizations about interpersonal experience. In *Methods of research in psychotherapy*, L. Gottschalk, A. Auerbach (Eds.). New York: Appleton-Century, Crofts.

Erikson, E. (1959). Identity and the life cycle. *Psychological Issues*, Vol. 1.

Eysenck, H. J. (1957). In chapter on Factor Theories. *Theories of personality*. C. S. Hall and G. Lindzey (Eds.). New York: Wiley.

Feiffer, M. (1970). Developmental analysis of interpersonal behavior. *Psychological Review,* **77**, 197-214.

Foa, U. G. (1961). Convergences in the analysis of the structure of interpersonal behavior. *Psychological Review*, **68**, 341-353.

Freedman, M., Leary, T., Ossorio, A. G., and Coffey, H. S. (1951). The interpersonal dimension of personality. *Journal of Personality*, **20**, 143-161.

Freud, S. (1959). *Sigmund Freud. Collected papers*. E. Jones (Ed.). New York: Basic Books.

Harlow, H. F. and Harlow, M. K. (1965). The affectional systems. In *Behavior of nonhuman primates,* Vol. II, Schrier, A., Harlow, H., Stollnitz, F. (Eds.), New York: Academic Press.

Jersild, A. (1968). *Child psychology*. Englewood Cliffs, New Jersey. Prentice Hall.

Mahler, M. (1968). *On human symbiosis and the vicissitudes of individuation. Volume 1. Infantile Psychosis*. New York: International University Press.

Mueller, W. J. (1969). Patterns of behavior and their reciprocal impact in the family and in psychotherapy. *Journal of Counseling Psychology*, **2**, part 2.

Schaefer, E. S. (1965). A configurational analysis of children's reports of parent behavior. *Journal of Consulting Psychology*, **29**, 552-557.

Schaefer, E. S. Development of hierarchical configurational conceptual models for parent behavior and child behavior. *Minnesota Symposium on Child Psychology*, Vol. 5, E. Hill (Ed.). In press.

CHAPTER 12

A Methodology for the Intensive Observation of the Preschool Child

Christoph M. Heinicke

Fred Busch

Phyllis Click

and Estelle Kramer

The methods described here are part of a series of projects studying variations in the child's development as he moves from the exclusive involvement with his family to functioning in some form of group setting such as nursery school, day care, or residential care. Given our impression that previous methodologies had not addressed themselves sufficiently to the process of development and the context of specific behavioral sequences, methods were chosen that maximized knowledge of the individual child's development and his significant environment through intensive observations made by professionals, all of whom had had extensive experience with children of this age.

The particular constellation of methods used to observe the preschool child developed out of our previous experience with a method designated by Wright (1960) as a field unit analysis system. Categorizations of the child's behavior sequence were done in the nursery room or play-yard in terms of a predetermined set of categories. Following the observation period the most significant global behavioral sequences were highlighted; we also attempted to provide an integrated first-level interpretation of the total data (Heinicke and Westheimer, 1965).

It was from the global observations dictated after doing the categorizations that we developed a method of characterizing the child's successive periods of development and called it the period analysis. (See Heinicke and Westheimer, 1965, and the description of it given below.) Most important, more relevant knowledge was gained from this procedure than from the analysis of categorization done on the spot. We therefore dropped the categorization and

243

took steps to intensify the observations on child and environment that are used in the period analysis. Not that the categories were useless, but it became a matter of priorities in relation to the problem being studied.

The decision to concentrate on the global observations of the child and his environment was also made on the basis of an opinion gathered from reading the literature. Too often essential and specific behavioral nuances are lost if the categorizations reduce the data too quickly, if certain categories are used in isolation, and if the context is lost in both these ways.

One part of our methodology can be further described by relating it to Wright's (1960) summary of methods of observational study. Our observations of the child in the room or play-yard environment come closest to what has been called specimen description. This consists of scheduled and continuous observing and narrative descriptive recording under chosen conditions of time and life settings. Everything the child does and says is potentially included and the impact of the environment is also carefully studied. The most important difference lies in the fact that our observers do select certain aspects of behavior on the basis of broadly defined areas of interest. These are described below. Anything may be potentially relevant but not everything is of interest.

As will be seen, we have not confined ourselves to a method of observational child study. Some of the additional techniques used have been grouped by Mussen (1960) under the study of personality and cognitive development: the play interview, projective dollplay, and the standardized ability test such as the WPSSI. In one area (the child's dealing with a task like listening to a book), we did retain the specific field-unit categorizations. Finally, both the observation and interviewing of the parents provided the necessary information for what is listed in the Mussen volume as "family life variables."

The very factor which may give greater precision in understanding the individual child, namely intensive observation by the experienced person, may also introduce greater subjective and theoretical bias. The above-mentioned standard techniques guard against individual bias and facilitate child-to-child comparison. That the total pool of observations and initial inferences about them are contributed to by the parents, teachers, diagnostic psychologists, and various psychotherapeutically trained child observers further insures the reliability of the observations. But most important, we have during both the observing and data analysis separated the descriptions from the interpretation of that description.

The comparison and grouping of children is facilitated not only by the way the observations are made, but also by the methods of data analysis that have been developed. Two types of comparison have been made. Cross-sectional comparisons at a given time point have been facilitated by a method of profile construction (Freud, 1965) and ratings based on that profile. Longitudinal descriptions and comparisons have been organized through the period analysis.

Again, important in these introductory remarks is the fact that reliability of this type of data analysis has been checked.

The methods described in detail below were first used in a pilot study of ten intact, middle-class families and their three-year-olds entering a half-day nursery school in a large urban area. Here it suffices to state that the observations were directed toward those variations in the 3-year-old's development and his environment that are related to his task orientation; that is, his ability to engage in, produce in, persist in, and enjoy nursery-school tasks.

Since completion of this study, the methodology has been developed further and is being used to study the child's entrance into a day-care center. It is the present version of the constellation of methods that we will describe, but we will also indicate what specific aspects of it were used in the pilot study. Before moving to this level of detail it is useful to have a quick view of the total procedure.

AN OUTLINE OF THE TOTAL PROCEDURE

The initial approach to the families is made through the nursery school. In seeking their long-term cooperation we are guided by the consideration that the families and their children as well as the investigator must benefit from the project. All families entering a beginning class in September of a specific year agreed to participate and were studied in the pilot project.

Once permission is granted, both the worker who will talk to and observe the family in the home and the teacher who will have the child in her room now make one or more visits before the child enters school. The interviewer typically talks to the mother in one part of the house while the teacher plays with and observes the child in another part of the house.

The major longitudinal *information on the parent-child relationships* is provided by and continues to be confined to the interviews and observations of parents and child in the home. These occur about every two weeks until the end of the first year of nursery school. This data is supplemented by the many observations made on the parent in the nursery school, and especially so during the first two weeks when they are asked to remain in the vicinity of the child. In the first pilot study two interviewers each dealt with five of the families.

The major longitudinal *information on the child* is provided by the intensive observations made in the nursery school by three different observers. These are scheduled to provide representative and fairly constant samples of behavior. During the first five months, daily observations are available. After this, until the end of the first year of school, a minimum of one observation period per week is planned for. The above longitudinal data gathered by the observers is supplemented by conversations with the teachers and by recorded staff conferences in which the teachers participate. Taken together, all of the above data provide the basis for later formulating the various *periods of development* that the child and family go through during the first year.

In order to provide sufficient information for formulating *cross-sectional* assessments, other procedures of data collection are added to the above basic observations at certain time points. Considerations of what the child and classroom can tolerate and at which points a certain stability is typically reached, governed these choices. The cross-sectional points chosen are: after six weeks, after five months, and at the end of the first and second year of nursery school. In addition to the ongoing observations in the room and play-yard, the following data are available on all four time points: written categorized observations of the child's task orientation and his performance on an intelligence test. For the last three time points, the following data are also available: an extensive standard teacher's report on the child's development, a play interview with each child, and films of the child's general behavior, but particularly of his task orientation. What data are available both from the current work and from the Pilot Project are given in Table 1. This can clearly be changed to suit different problems.

Consistent with the above outline, the description of the details of our methodology is divided into longitudinal process and the cross-sectional data.

Table 1. Data Available for Cross-Sectional Assessments

| Sources of Data | Point in Nursery School Stay | | | |
	After 6 wks.	After 5 mo.	After 1 yr.	After 2 yrs.
1. Ongoing observation in room and play-yard	Available	Available	Available	Available
2. Categorized observation of task orientation	Available[a]	Available	Available	Available
3. Performance on intelligence test	Available[a]	Available[a]	Available[a]	Available
4. Extensive standardized teacher's report	Not available	Available	Available	Available
5. Standardized play interview	Not available	Available[a]	Available[a]	Available
6. Filming focused on task orientation	Not available	Available[a]	Available[a]	Available[a]

[a] Available in current work but not available in Pilot Project.

LONGITUDINAL PROCESS DATA

Observations of the Child in the Nursery School

As indicated previously, three people observe the child in the nursery school. Each observer stays in the room for about half an hour and then goes to another part of the building to dictate his observations into a tape recorder. The time of beginning and ending the observation is recorded. Care is taken to separate observation of behavior from inference about that behavior. If the observer wishes to interpret a specific piece of behavior he instructs the typist to indent the interpretation of it. An interpretive "Overall Evaluation" is given at the end of the observation.

During the first four months of the pilot study, at least one observer was present at all times, and approximately 30% of the time more than one of the observers was present. Schedules were worked out to allow focus on certain children and to maximize coverage of all the children during the 9 a.m. to 12 noon stay in the nursery. That is, we attempted to achieve reliability not so much by having two observers focus on the same child but rather by having several observers follow the child's development during a given time span.

In making the daily and continuous observations of the child, the primary orientation was to describe all behavior likely to be important to understanding his development in the nursery school. Insofar as the child's immediate environment made a significant impact on him, this was also recorded. While specific categorization was not attempted as part of this narrative observation, and while there was of course a readiness to note new phenomena, a number of foci of observation were developed in order to facilitate the later period analysis.

1. Approach to Each Nursery-School Day. In view of our interest in the child's psychological move from the home to nursery school, his initial adaptation at the beginning of each day was thought to be particularly revealing. We asked ourselves to what extent the child became involved in new relationships and new activities, and what modes of alternate adaptation he pursued if his engagement did not increase during the morning.

2. Relationships. The child's relationships to the various people in his life were noted with great care. Influenced particularly by Anna Freud's developmental line concept of moving from dependency to self-reliance (1965), we asked how changes in past relationships and formation of new ones tended either to represent the continuation of the past or tended toward greater self-reliance and adaptive exchange.

3. Expression of Affects. While many affects, such as sadness, cheerfulness, hate, and love, would most easily be studied as part of the observations of the child's relationships, we also followed the child's development in expressing affects independently of those relationships.

4. Anxiety. Anxiety was also most frequently observed in the context of relationships. Those anxieties relating to separation, messing, and the expression of aggression were especially noted. Wherever possible, observations and inferences were also made about related present and past conflicts. In general we were, however, cautious about inferring underlying dynamics.

5. Defenses and Modes of Coping. Defenses seen in the nursery school include such things as turning a passively experienced event into an actively manipulated one, a great variety of defensive identifications, and various forms of avoidance of painful situations.

6. Ego Development. This included what Anna Freud (1965) has conceptualized in her Developmental Profile as *ego functions,* as well as those considerations involved in her concept of *lines of development.* Ego functions include attentiveness, frustration tolerance, memory, and reality testing. Many of these functions and their effective integration were best studied in relation to certain tasks and special assessment procedures which are discussed in subsequent sections. Observations on such lines of development as reliability in bladder and bowel control and the attitude toward food could readily be made in the everyday nursery setting. Similarly, the learning of certain skills such as tricycle riding or holding a pencil proved to be sensitive reflections of ego development. We also noted any indications of the child's identification with persons in the environment.

7. Superego and Superego Representations. In this regard we observed any indications of guilt or shame, the cognitive elaboration associated with such affects (superego representations), and the underlying conflicts which possibly are associated with such phenomena.

8. Self-Representations and Ideal Self-Representations. We were interested in how the child sees himself and whether or not this representation is fairly accurate or distorted. Sometimes one observed the child's enactment of what he might want to be.

9. Fantasy. While we have been cautious in inferring fantasies from the child's overt behavior, there were instances when the operation of an underlying fantasy could be inferred with considerable confidence.

Of the various foci noted above, the child's relationship to the observer needs elaboration. The observers did not initiate or even encourage interaction with the child. When the child became too involved with the observer, steps were taken to shift the relationship to the teacher. Despite this stance, the children did react to the observers and the nature of this reaction became one of the most sensitive indices of the child's development. Thus, one little girl first turned to the observer asking for her mother, later actively avoided the observer, and then both rejected and invited him.

Before moving to the description of the method of analyzing the data on the child, the method of obtaining the longitudinal process data on the parent-child relationship will be described.

Observations of the Parent-Child Relationship

The visits made to the home about every two weeks provided an opportunity for direct observation of parent and child and also allowed interviewing of the parents. The methods used followed the procedure described by Heinicke and Westheimer (1965). The primary orientation is to follow the parents' initiative in discussing what they feel to be important about the development of their child and their understanding and handling of him. The focus was not psychotherapeutic but, rather, one of facilitating the development of the child and his family.

As in the observations of the child in the nursery, an effort was also made to obtain certain kinds of information. Before the child's entrance into nursery school, the interviewer obtained the following data: an initial developmental history, his relationship to members of his family and peers, how the child reacts to new people and situations, his favorite play, food, clothing, and so on, and his special possessions. Four general areas served as foci for the further data collection. In regard to the parent-child relationship, the interviewer was asked to gather information relevant to certain dimensions, such as the level of parent-to-child affection. These dimensions will be defined below. In regard to the child's development in the home, the observers were guided by the same foci used in the nursery. The interviewer was also asked to attend to data relevant to the marital relationship and those character traits of the parents which have a less direct though important impact on the child. For example, Jean's mother approached many different things in a flighty manner.

As already indicated, the presence of the parent in the nursery during the first weeks as well as the occasion of daily pick-up and visits provided very important opportunities for observing the parent-child relationship.

From an extensive working manual of definitions, we list the headings of those ratings relating to the parent-child relationship. In many instances, we have followed definitions outlined by Baumrind (1967) and Heinicke and Westheimer (1965). Wherever appropriate, we rate mother and father separately. Each rating is carefully defined and includes many subheadings.

1. The quality and quantity of the parent's affection for and liking for his child. Warmth has also been used to refer to this dimension. It involves the love and compassion for the child as expressed in a variety of ways.

2. The extent of time and energy that the parent has available for his child. Although related to affection and liking, it is important to describe just how often the parent is affectionate and available.

3. The parent's capacity to maintain an organized environmental sequence. Even if affectionate and capable of setting limits, can the parent organize an effective set of routines to which the child can adapt?

4. The clarity with which the parent defines his availability. The parent may be affectionate and spend considerable time with the child, but he is often uncertain as to just when he can expect the parent.

5. The extent and consistency of the limits set by the parents. Can the parent confront the child's challenge of power and manipulation in order to insure consistent directives?

6. The standards set and the sanctions used by the parents in regard to the areas listed below. It is important to recognize that certain sanctions work best for a given child. Where the parent expects greatest compliance with standards, these sanctions will be used with insistence.

(a)   Aggression control
(b)   Cleanliness
(c)   Self-reliance
(d)   Adult role behavior
(e)   Achievement in preacademic areas

7. The extent of clarity in parent-child communication. To what extent does the parent use reason to persuade, encourage verbal give-and-take, and in general openly confront issues?

8. The extent of the parent's active instruction. How effectively does the parent instruct the child in large motor skills, in fine perceptuo-motor skills, and in conceptual distinctions such as word meaning and naming of objects?

9. The extent to which the parent actively encourages the child to move toward new experiences and new relationships. Does the parent encourage his child to go to a different house or meet with a new friend?

10. The frequency with which the parent is involved in a conceptual exchange with the child. How often does the parent read to the child, tell him a story, and talk to him in the sense of giving and seeking information?

Analysis of the Longitudinal Process Data: The Period Analysis

In attempting to grasp the essential aspects of a young child's development, we assume that the strength as well as direction of the progressive over the regressive forces is one of the key considerations. The period analysis breaks a defined developmental span into subperiods. Examination of the nature of each period and their relation to each other then provides a way of assessing his progressive trends at the moment and of estimating the child's future development. This method of developmental analysis can be applied separately to the longitudinal process data on the child and the parent-child relationship. We have initially concentrated on the observations made in the nursery during the first five months. These data are sufficiently continuous to make such efforts productive. Most important, they make it possible to determine whether a specific type of behavior persists long enough to be abstracted as a particular period of development within a certain aspect of behavior.

In applying the method to the child's initial four or five months of nursery school, the first step is to read the total observations available on a given child. The purpose of this reading is to become very familiar with the child's development and to begin to organize it around certain specific categories. Notes are made on how to develop more specific distinctions and categories in relation to the guidelines previously outlined. The second step is to reread the material, classifying the important aspects of it in terms of the categories and knowledge generated in the first step (see Table 2). The third step is to attempt to delineate periods of development, first within each of the most significant subcategories, and then by visual examination of the tabulation, determining at what point in time a great number of the most important subcategories showed a change and thus indicated major shifts in the child's development. The reliability of this procedure has been checked previously (Heinicke and Westheimer, 1965). The fourth step is to depict each of the major periods of adaptation during the first four or five months of the child's entrance into nursery school. An effort is made to separate the description from inferences drawn and to discuss the overall implications of the observations in a final section. Without the same degree of detail, essentially the same procedure is used to describe development from the fifth to the tenth month.

This same method can be applied to the longitudinal process data on the parent-child relationship and is now being experimented with. The data on the parent-child relationship is an integral part of the period analysis of the child. Without this data on their family, Paula's and Jean's development would be hard to comprehend.

CROSS-SECTIONAL DATA

Observations of the Child Added for the Cross-Sectional Assessment

The distinctions between longitudinal and cross-sectional data become less sharply defined when one asks: What is the data base for a particular cross-sectional assessment? It is, however, meaningful to speak of the development status of a child and the profile of parent-child relationships at a *given moment*. Thus, in assessing the child's development after five months in nursery

Table 2. Showing Paula's Entrance into Nursery School

Categories	Days in Nursery School		
	Sept. 19th--1st Day (Mother there)	Sept. 20th--2nd Day (Mother there)	Sept. 21st--3rd Day (Mother sometimes gone)
Reaction to Entrance			
Major approach	Anxious then controlled play	Anxious, then many activities	Sad, isolated, sits alone
Engagement	Limited--in doll play only	Fleeting	Limited--with teacher
Sucking	Very little; some biting	Very little; some biting	Considerable
Swinging	None	None	None
Relationships to			
Mother	Seeks affection and moves out	Seeks affection and moves out	Seeks attention; longing
Student teacher	None evident	None evident	Jumps with Molly
Teacher	Points to Ethel's spilling	Asks permission to play	None evident
Peers	Parallel play in doll corner with Ethel	Parallel play in doll corner with Ethel and Donna	None evident
Transitional objects	None evident	None evident	None evident
Defenses			
Defensive identification	Maternal: feed dolls	Maternal: feed dolls	Maternal: feed, clothe dolls
Passive to active	Refuse to leave school	None evident	None evident
Affects			
Sadness versus cheerful	Some pleasure in Play-doh	Vicariously enjoy mess	Mostly sad
Anxiety in relation to			
Separation	Control by turning to mother	Near tears	Near tears
Messing	Concerned about spilled water	Concerned about mess	Concerned about mess
Aggression	None evident	None evident	None evident
Ego Development			
Identification with teacher	None evident	None evident	None evident
Passivity versus assertiveness	Active--defends toy	Active--on move	Passive--often sits

252

Table 2. Showing Paula's Entrance into Nursery School (continued)

Categories	Days in Nursery School		
Learn singing; story	None evident	None evident	None evident
Ride tricycle	None evident	None evident	None evident
	Sept. 22nd--4th Day (Mother sometimes gone)	Sept. 23rd--6th Day (Mother mostly gone)	Sept. 27th--7th Day (Mother mostly gone)
Reaction to Entrance			
Major approach	Cautious--then retreat	Very controlled, less anxious	Great longing; immobolized
Engagement	Some engagement; retreat from mess	Limited	Limited--teacher facilitates
Sucking	Considerable	Considerable	A great deal
Swinging	None	None	None
Relationships to			
Mother	Seeks reassurance after mess	Some longing	Longing; fretting
Student teacher	Molly attends; accepts help	Jump with: sit next to	Follow Sarah, Molly
Teacher	Attends: changes clothes	None evident	Follow and sit close
Peers	Parallel play in doll corner. Read book to Bob	Parallel play in doll corner	Parallel play in doll corner; defends right
Transitional objects	None evident	None evident	None evident
Defenses			
Defensive identification	Maternal: feed dolls	Maternal: feed dolls	Clean-up excessive
Passive to active	None evident	None evident	Not go to mother
Affects			
Sadness versus cheerfulness	Cheerful when mess	Cheerful when mess	Sad except when mess
Anxiety in relation to			
Separation	Whines at end of morning	Near tears	Near tears or crying
Messing	Greatly concerned	Great concern; very clean	Considerable concern
Aggression	None evident	None evident	None evident
Ego Development			
Identification with teacher	None evident	None evident	Helps: Distributes toys

253

Table 2. Showing Paula's Entrance into Nursery School (continued)

Categories	Days in Nursery School		
Passivity versus assertiveness	Passive--often sits	Passive and active	Immobile and defends
Learn singing; story	None evident	None evident	Attend actively
Ride tricycle	None evident	None evident	None evident
	Sept. 28th--8th Day (Mother mostly gone)	Sept. 29th--9th Day (Mother doesn't stay)	Oct. 3rd--11th Day (Mother doesn't stay)

Reaction to Entrance			
Major approach	Great longing then cheer up a little	Great longing; turn to teacher	Great longing; turn to teacher
Engagement	Limited--teacher facilitates	Very limited--teacher facilitates	Limited--teacher facilitates
Sucking	A great deal	A great deal	A great deal
Swinging	Sarah swings some	None evident	None evident

Relationships to			
Mother	Longing. Seeks affection when hit	Great longing. Frets	Great longing
Student teacher	Seeks lap and swing: Sarah	Sarah: lap; Molly: play	Sarah: lap
Teacher	Seeks lap. Little response otherwise	Seeks comfort	Seeks comfort for hurt
Peers	Limited: not tolerate aggression; jealous of swing	Limited: not share	Parallel play in doll corner: defend rights
Transitional objects	None evident	None evident	Special gift from father

Defenses			
Defensive identification	Clean-up excessive	Cry when can't help teacher	Maternal: comforts doll
Passive to active	None evident	None evident	Sarah: runs away

Affects			
Sadness versus cheerfulness	Very sad	Very sad	Very sad, Play-doh cheers

Anxiety in relation to			
Separation	Near tears	Near tears; barely holds on	Near tears
Messing	Considerable concern	Considerable concern	Some concern
Aggression	Not tolerate bump from Bob	None evident	Not tolerate attack

Table 2. Showing Paula's Entrance into Nursery School (continued)

Categories	Days in Nursery School		
Ego Development			
Identification with teacher	None evident	Helps: set table	None evident
Passivity versus assertiveness	Passive: stares	Passive: subdued	Passive and defends
Learn singing: story	None evident	Can attend	Can attend
Ride tricycle	None evident	None evident	None evident
	Oct. 4th--12th Day (Mother doesn't stay)	Oct. 5th--13th Day (Mother doesn't stay)	Oct. 6th--14th Day (Mother doesn't stay)
Reaction to Entrance			
Major approach	Great longing: cries	Great longing	Happier after swing
Engagement	Limited--teacher facilitates	Limited--teacher facilitates	Considerable--teacher facilitates
Sucking	A great deal	A great deal	A great deal
Swinging	Some from Sarah, teacher	Some from teacher	Extensive Sarah
Relationship to			
Mother	Great longing	Cling plus longing	Some longing
Student teacher	Sarah: lap; Molly: play	Sarah: lap excessive	Sarah: swing
Teacher	Seeks swing, lap	Swing eases entrance	Sarah: swing
Peers	Limited: not tolerate aggression: Kurt	Limited: little contact	Parallel play in doll corner: Ethel
Transitional objects	Special gift from father	Special gift from father	None evident
Defenses			
Defensive identification	Maternal: feed, brush hair	None evident	None evident
Passive to active	None evident	None evident	Teacher: run away and back
Affects			
Sadness versus cheerfulness	Very sad; cries	Very sad	Smiles at teacher Cheers up with play
Anxiety in relation to			
Separation	Cries: seeks mother	Near tears	Cry when can't swing
Messing	None evident	None evident	None evident
Aggression	Not tolerate attack: Kurt	None evident	None evident

Table 2. Showing Paula's Entrance into Nursery School (continued)

Categories	Days in Nursery School		
	Oct. 4th–12th Day (Mother doesn't stay)	Oct. 5th–13th Day (Mother doesn't stay)	Oct. 6th–14th Day (Mother doesn't stay)
Ego Development			
Identification with teacher	Help: set table	None evident	Help Sarah clean
Passivity versus assertiveness	Passive: does little	Passive: does little	Active, can't assert self
Learn singing: story	Can attend	None evident	Can attend
Ride tricycle	None evident	None evident	None evident

school, we have drawn on our knowledge of his development up to that point, but have nevertheless queried what his status is at that moment.

To provide further cross-sectional focus and information, certain additional observations were made. The details of these are described below.

Observation of the Child's Response to Task Situations

To provide more intensive data on behavior likely to be particularly relevant to future adaptation to academic requirements, observation of the child's reactions to two kinds of task situations, one involving a goal-directed motor activity and the other listening to and comprehending something from a book, were included.

During the pilot study the teacher was asked to plan a variety of art and book activities during the third-to-last week of the first year of school. Activities were chosen that would elicit a wide range of responses and appeal to both sexes. An example of the type of book used was *Harry the Dog and the Sea Monster;* one art activity was gluing wood, bolts, and other materials on a panel to form a collage. The juice-and-book time started at about 9:45 a.m. and was followed immediately by the goal-directed motor activity. There was free play before and after these activities.

The child's activity during free play was observed as before. During the two task activities the observers took verbatim notes. They were guided by an outline of areas to cover and specific subcategories which they were to note, but the final coding of the observations was done afterwards. Three of the authors observed; there were at least two observers on any one day, and each child was observed on at least five different days.

The choice of the aspects of the child's adaptation on which to focus was determined both by our previous experience and the distinctions suggested in the literature. Consistent with the total emphasis on the child's engagement in new relationships and new activities, we focused initially on the child's engagement in the particular task being observed. *Engagement* in the listening comprehension task was judged by the child's ability to attend and volunteer actively as opposed to withdrawing. In this situation as well as in the goal-directed motor activity, we paid particular attention to the child's ability to persist in the activity. We saw this persistence as one index of the child's ability to tolerate frustration.

Closely related, but focusing more on the child's ability to tolerate anxiety, is his *compliance with the definition of the task situation.* Can the child follow the teacher's instructions and respond to her efforts at control? Does he disrupt by interfering with others, either by making personal demands or by hitting other children or running from the group?

The child's *productivity* was also assessed. How frequently was he able to answer the teacher's question and how appropriate were his answers? In the goal-directed motor activity, did he produce what was called for, and if so, how extensive was his production? What *pride* and what *pleasure* did the child show in appropriate answers to certain requests or the production of certain articles? We also assessed the child's capacity for *creativity and imagination.* Were his answers unique and fresh without becoming bizarre? Did he combine material in a new way without losing integration? We also noted whether the child was sucking his thumb, holding a blanket, or masturbating, and so forth, as evidence of the child's tendencies toward *regression*.

Examination of the observations obtained in the pilot study led to some revisions and additions in the subcategories. It was this revised list that was used for categorizing. For example, the following subcategories are assumed to be relevant to the child's level of engagement: (1) listens actively, (2) withdraws attention, (3) volunteers appropriately, (4) volunteers inappropriately, (5) wants activity continued, (6) withdraws appropriately, and so on. The subcategories could be analyzed individually or combined with others relating to a given dimension. The resulting summary scores could serve as a basis for ranking the children on a given dimension for each of the two types of task situations. The ten children of the pilot study were also ranked on each dimension by two observers without using the summary scores in each category. Not surprisingly, these ranks correlated highly with the ranks based on the summary scores. The Spearman Rank Order Correlation Coefficients of the association between the rankings of the two observers range from .64 to 1.00 with a median coefficient of .95.

Filming of the Child's Response to Task Situations

The value of observations, namely film records that can be viewed repeatedly by observers of different theoretical persuasion, has long been recognized. In a longitudinal study trying to anticipate what factors lead to later learning, films can be invaluable in going back to see what may have been missed.

Since the pilot study had indicated that the child's task orientation in nursery school is likely to be predictive of later intellectual functioning, his response to that task situation has been chosen as the focus of the filming. Two broad considerations are kept in mind. Films are made of the child's involvement in a task that he chooses from a variety of tasks laid out by the teacher, such as Playdoh, puzzles, block building, painting, and so forth. Films are also made of the child's orientation to a task in which all children are supposed to participate. As described in the previous section, we have used one involving a goal-directed motor activity (the wood gluing) and the other involving listening to and comprehending something from a book. Since the responses to the task situation are also observed by at least one observer, it is possible to compare scores derived from his protocol with those derived from the film.

Psychological Testing of the Child

Consistent with the research of several investigators (e.g., Hunt, 1961), our own psychotherapy assessment research (Heinicke, 1969) had shown that performance on the Stanford Binet intelligence test is associated with a cluster of personality ratings which we named the *extent of ego integration.* Included in this cluster were such ratings as the capacity to sublimate, the level of self-esteem as a function of the child's achievement, the ability to assert himself, the extent of academic ambition, the ability to persist in a task, realistic concern about his academic progress, and so forth. We therefore anticipated that the child's task-orientation scores at about four years would be related to certain aspects of his tested intellectual functioning at age five. The pilot study gave some support to this hypothesis (Heinicke, 1968).

Our present methodology therefore includes the administration of the Stanford-Binet test after six weeks and five months, and also at the end of the first and second year of nursery school. In addition, and this because of its differentiation of verbal and performance items, we administer the WPPSI at the end of the second year.

During the pilot study, we also administered the Bender Gestalt at the end of the second year. Examination of the responses indicated to us as it has to others (Keogh, 1969) that children who have just turned five cannot as yet respond adequately to this test.

The intelligence testing is done by an experienced clinical psychologist (Dr. Joel Liebowitz), who analyzes the test scores without having access to other information. Since the testing is done individually in a room away from the classroom, ample opportunity is afforded to observe the conditions which will permit the child to leave his familiar surroundings and how he reacts to being alone with a less well-known person.

The Play Interview

A diagnostic play interview was included in our total battery to enable us to formulate what seemed to be the child's major preconscious concerns at the time of assessment. For example, much of Paula's play could be understood in terms of her concern of how to get closer to a father who had separated from her mother.

To maximize both the familiarity with the child and the diagnostic skill of the interviewer, one of the observers, who is also an experienced child psychotherapist, conducts the interview. In the pilot study the author did all these interviews.

To facilitate comparison of the children's reaction, the play materials used are held constant. These include a doll house with a family of dolls (Heinicke and Westheimer, 1965), a family of large hand puppets, a variety of rubber animals, packets of soldiers, Indians and cowboys, a variety of cars and airplanes, two large dolls, one of which could be bottle-fed, a Play-doh factory set, and crayons and paper.

In the initial part of the play interview an effort is made to allow the child to express himself and to encourage what he wishes to communicate. Only if the child becomes too anxious does the observer-diagnostician make an explicit intervention. After about thirty-five minutes some structure is provided. Various authors have found that the young child's ability to tell a story, recognize letters, and write his name is highly predictive of later reading ability (de Hirsch, Jansky, and Langford, 1966). Accordingly, the observer ends the interview by first asking the child to tell a story. If he can't think of one he is prompted by the suggestion that he tell the story of "The Three Bears." After this he is asked to draw a person and encouraged to talk about it. Finally he is asked to write his name on the picture. If the child cannot do this he is asked what letters make up his name. We have found these procedures actually facilitate the child's return to the classroom.

Both this play interview and the intelligence testing is tape recorded. In addition, the observer-diagnostician gives a full description of the chronology of events and then adds his own evaluation of the salient aspects of his observations.

The drawing of the person, the telling of the story, and the writing of the name can be evaluated using the guidelines developed by de Hirsch, Jansky, and Langford (1966). The other observations have so far not been processed further, but are used as such in the writing of the Developmental Profile.

Analysis of the Cross-Sectional Data: The Developmental Profile

The procedure and outline developed by Anna Freud (1965) is used to integrate the information available for a child at the following points: five months after the beginning of school and at the end of the first and second year. Our experience suggests that at these points our knowledge is sufficient to permit such profiles. Even so, it is immediately recognized that the Profile procedure has to be modified because of the age group and because inferences based on observational material have a different status than those based on the extensive data of a child psychoanalysis. Below we discuss such modifications as were made in the use of the Profile.

The first sections of the Profile deal with the description of the child, certain broad background factors, and the developmental history of the child. No changes are involved here.

The section entitled "Significant Environmental Events" has in our usage been expanded. The first part is a qualitative description of the salient environmental events that impinge on the child. Because this section is written by the interviewer, the primary emphasis is on the family environment. Included in this are the adult-to-child and child-to-adult relationships, the marital relationship, the sibling relationship, outstanding parental characteristics which impinge on the child, and so forth. The impact of other adults, teachers, peers, and other events is integrated into this summary as again seen from the vantage point of the interviewer.

The second subsection includes the rating of the various dimensions of the parent-child relationship listed previously. The resulting set of ratings is then interrelated and a profile of these ratings is tabulated.

In the pilot study, ratings of the mother-child couples in terms of the single dimensions were done after the child had been in the nursery school for six weeks. A second step involved examination of the profile of ratings. Seven different profiles were initially distinguished. Given the small size of the sample, it is premature to report these in detail. It is important to stress, however, that the formulation of these typical profiles is open-ended; families studied in the future will very likely require the addition of new profiles.

In the pilot study the two interviewers independently placed each of the families in one of the profiles with 80% agreement. Further grouping of the agreed-upon results revealed two major groupings of mother-child dyads: (1) those where the mother shows an adequate level of affection and acceptance, where her psychological availability to the child is fairly clearly defined, where new relationships are encouraged, where she definitely sets limits to the demands and experiences of the child, and where she actively encourages the child's development toward independent achievement, particularly in preacademic subjects; and (2) those where in some respect the above is not the case.

The remaining sections of the Profile are written by one of the nursery observers. All the observations previously listed are available to this observer. Again, it must be stressed that we have taken care not to over-interpret the observations that are available. Nevertheless, we expect those formulations that are made are of sufficient specificity and accuracy to anticipate later development.

Some checks on the reliability of this procedure have been carried out. Reliability studies of profile-making and ratings based on profiles have been undertaken as part of an assessment of psychotherapeutic outcome (Heinicke, 1969). The 46 ratings used in this psychotherapy research can be applied to the nursery-school child. Certain ratings which expand and define the ego section are particularly relevant: the extent to which the child's defenses are balanced, the child's capacity to express a variety of affects, the child's ability to elaborate imaginatively, and so forth.

Another initial reliability check consisted of having three different child psychotherapists not involved in the observations read the material on Paula and independently formulate profiles on her. Although no systematic reliability assessments were made, there was agreement on the main conclusions as well as on the choice of areas where judgment was not possible.

On one child in the pilot group, Bob, profiles were written not only during the time he was in nursery school, but a diagnostic profile was also constructed by a team of clinicians when Bob began child psychoanalytic treatment at the age of six (Heinicke, 1970). These diagnostic clinicians and the therapist did not have access to the previous observational and profile material. Comparison of the various profiles suggests that the profiles made from the data collected in the nursery school are particularly strong in tracing the specific impact of the family interactions on the child and in delineating the details of the child's ego development. A great deal can also be concluded about the child's pattern of fixations and regressions, but it is in this and some other areas that the additional information provided by the psychoanalysis of the child is also needed to come to firmer conclusions.

CONCLUDING REMARKS

We have presented a methodology that combines various approaches to the study of the individual child and family. A high specificity and intensity of observation enhances the possibility that the environmental and developmental variables anticipating future academic learning can be isolated. Cross-sectional analyses complement longitudinal ones so that grouping of children is possible and meaningful. The emphasis on the period analysis recognizes the importance of studying the process and balance of progression and regression. By stressing the context of a piece of behavior, the profile analysis avoids groupings of it that hide rather than elucidate relationships. By collecting and analyzing the data in this manner it can be more easily related to the treatment data available on some of the children. Having both developmental and psychoanalytic treatment data available on the same child should provide a unique perspective.

We see as a further value the use of observers who have a great deal of experience with children and who are trained to infer from manifest behavior to generalizations about personality functioning; for example, how the child relates to the observer. That is, the interpretation of this behavior becomes one of the best indices of the changes in the child's general status.

A potential weakness lies in this very step of inferring underlying constructs. Use of many observers and techniques goes some way of insuring the reliability of the data. Separation of observation and inference allows persons of different persuasion to infer other constructs. Further work is needed in checking the reliability of the data analysis. Many more children need to be studied before the power of grouping children can be tested adequately. Follow-up studies need to be completed, including data from treatment, in order to assess the predictive power of the earlier observations. Some will also object to the time-consuming nature of this methodology and the expense of training the observers who are involved. We are, however, sufficiently encouraged by the knowledge yielded by these methods to continue to develop and use them further.

ACKNOWLEDGMENT

We wish to thank the staff of the Reiss-Davis Child Study Center and the Center for Early Education, and especially the parents and children for making this study possible. The devoted assistance of Dr. Joel Liebowitz was particularly invaluable. We also gratefully acknowledge the financial support of the Foundation for Research in Psychoanalysis, Los Angeles, and that given by the Office of Child Development Grant No. OCD-CB-48.

REFERENCES

Baumrind, D. (1967). Child care practices anteceding three patterns of preschool behavior. *Genetic Psychology Monographs, 75*, 43-88.

de Hirsch, K., Jansky, J., and Langford, W. (1966). *Predicting reading failure: A preliminary study of reading, writing and spelling disabilities in preschool children.* New York: Harper and Row.

Freud, A. (1965). *Normality and pathology in childhood.* New York: International Universities Press.

Heinicke, C. M. (1970). In search of supporting evidence for reconstructions formulated during a child psychoanalysis. To be published in *Reiss-Davis Clinic Bulletin.*

Heinicke, C. M. (1969). Frequency of psychotherapeutic session as a factor affecting outcome: Analysis of clinical ratings and test results. *Journal of Abnormal Psychology,* **74,** 553-560.

Heinicke, C. M. (1968). Parent-child interaction and the child's approach to task situations. In *Approaches to and applications of the study of parent-child interaction,* E. E. Maccoby (Chm.). Symposium presented at the American Psychological Association meetings, San Francisco.

Heinicke, C. M. and Westheimer, I. (1965). *Brief separations.* New York: International Universities Press.

Hunt, J. McV. (1961). *Intelligence and experience.* New York: Ronald Press Co.

Keogh, B. K. (1969). The Bender Gestalt with children: research implications, *Journal of Special Education,* **3,** 15-22.

Mussen, P. H. (Ed.) (1960). *Handbook of research methods in child development.* New York: Wiley.

Wright, H. F. (1960). Observational Child Study. In *Handbook of research methods in child development,* Mussen, P. H. (Ed.). New York: Wiley.

CHAPTER 13

Methods and Models in Primate Personality Research

William T. McKinney, Jr.

Stephen Suomi

and Harry Harlow

Monkeys are attractive subjects for controlled research on personality development and psychopathology. Paralleling past trends in child development research, the University of Wisconsin Primate Center has placed major emphasis on studying and influencing the normative development of affectional systems in rhesus monkeys. As a result, a series of generalizations have emerged regarding stages and lines of affectional development with continuous awareness of individual variance, sometimes obscured by statistical analysis and sometimes highlighted as an entrée to fresh understandings.

Until recently, unexpected deviant states resulting from social isolation and mother-infant procedures have received limited attention and have been regarded as unexplained variants. The potential value of relating human deviance to primate deviance, however, has led to a shift in emphasis to the production and study of induced abnormal states in monkeys, particularly those resembling human psychopathology.

Although knowledge of individual differences in monkeys is limited, the methodology applicable to infrahuman subjects is available and adaptable to the study of individuality. This chapter sets the stage for such pursuit by first reviewing the body of knowledge generated regarding primate affectional systems. Next the behavioral aberrations noted in social isolation and mother-infant separation studies are summarized. Finally, several techniques devised for manipulating personality and producing precise forms of stress are described to illustrate the possibility of experimentally controlling both the past life experience and the current state of monkey subjects.

THE AFFECTIONAL SYSTEMS

Total social isolation from mother and peers is a rare occurrence among humans. Most human psychopathological traits develop in a context where there has been some kind of relationship between the infant or child and these groups, though its quality may have been variable. We are currently conducting studies designed to produce psychopathological states after normal or near-normal maternal and/or peer affectional bonds have been formed. For this reason, an understanding of the normal development of the affectional systems is necessary.

Affectional systems, as defined by Harlow and Harlow (1965), are "those systems which bind together various individuals within a species in coordinated and constructive social relations." Harlow and Harlow have postulated five affectional systems to serve as an effective basis for behavioral and psychophysiological investigation. In order of development these are: (a) the mother-infant or maternal affectional system; (b) the infant-mother affectional system which binds the infant to the mother; (c) the infant-infant, age-mate, or peer affectional system through which infants relate to each other and develop persisting affectional ties; (d) the sexual and heterosexual affectional system culminating in adolescent sexuality and finally in those adult behaviors leading to procreation; and (e) the paternal affectional system broadly defined in terms of positive responsiveness of adult males toward infants, juveniles, and other members of their particular social group. Systematic papers concerning the first four systems have appeared in the literature (Harlow, 1962a; Harlow, 1962b; Harlow, 1969; Harlow, Harlow, and Hansen, 1963) and the following discussion is a summary of current knowledge about these affectional systems. It is important to understand these affectional systems prior to the discussion concerning separation experiments.

Maternal Affectional System

The development of the mother-infant affectional system goes through a series of orderly stages involving both maturation and learning. It is best described in terms of three stages: (a) maternal attachment and protection, (b) maternal ambivalence or transition, and (c) maternal separation and rejection.

In the case of most mother monkeys the stage of *maternal attachment and protection* begins at the time of birth or within a few minutes after the baby is born. It is characterized by protective, maternal responses including cradling, nursing, grooming, bodily exploration, restraining the infant when it attempts to leave, and retrieving the infant when it does escape. Gradually the cradling pattern, for example, changes to a maternal pattern of loose physical attachment in which the infant is not closely attached to the mother's ventral surface but sits on or near her haunches with the mother's arms easily available. The change from close cradling to loose attachment serves as an important role in providing the baby with enough contact and comfort to impart a sense of security while denying a bond of physical attachment that would be so strong as to impair interaction of the infant with other members of its age group. Nutritional and nonnutritional contacts with the nipple follow a developmental course similar to clinging. Initially the mother restrains the infant when he attempts to leave and immediately retrieves him if he should get away. With recurring attempts of the infant the mother gradually gives him more freedom; however, the maternal protective response persists long after the maternal attachment response has allowed the infant more freedom. The maternal protective response may be restrained after the protection stage and even after the separation stage if the infant is threatened.

As the initial stage of attachment and protection wanes, a transitional or *ambivalent maternal* stage develops characterized by increasing indifference and occasional comparatively harsh punishment of the infant by the mother. Punishment of her own infant begins toward the end of the third month and reaches a maximum during the fourth and fifth months. During this stage the mother's rejecting responses become progressively harsher, consisting of vigorously shaking the infant from her body or even stiff-arming the infant when it attempts to initiate bodily contact. There is considerable individual variation in the development and intensity of these negative punishing responses.

The experimental situation in the laboratory makes it difficult to see the complete normal development of *maternal separation* and *rejection*. However, from field study reports it is known that a primary variable contributing to physical separation of the mother and child is the advent of the next infant. Apparently there are both sex and species differences; female macaques and baboons remain in proximity with their mothers after the male juveniles have departed.

The Infant-Mother Affectional System

The infant is tied to the mother by a very powerful system, probably less variable than any of the others, which appears and develops in four stages. This system continues with great strength even in the face of strong punishment by unfeeling mothers.

The nature of the infant's affectional responses to the mother throughout these developmental stages is a function of many variables, including the species, the nature of the mother, the characteristics of the total environment, and individual inherent infant differences, making it difficult to assign exact days or weeks when one developmental stage ends and another begins. Stages gradually blend from one to another and transitions are made in terms of weeks or months rather than in terms of hours or days. There is considerable overlapping of stages, with the possible exception of the reflex stage, and all stages can be modified by special experimental procedures. The four developmental stages of the infant-mother affectional system are: (a) a reflex stage, (b) a comfort and attachment stage, (c) a security stage, and (d) a separation stage.

(a) Reflex Stage. In rhesus monkeys the reflex stage is present during the first 15 to 20 days of the infant's life, depending on the reflex selected and the maturity of the infant at birth. During this period, reflexes associated with nursing and intimate physical contact operate to maximize the chances for the early survival of the infant. Fundamental reflexes at this stage include the rooting reflex, forced upward climbing, clinging reflex, the righting reflex, and the grasp reflex. The reflex stage comes closer than any of the other stages to having a sharp temporal cut off. However, even with this stage there are considerable individual differences between infant monkeys. The presence of a reflex stage does not mean that all responses of the infant are determined by reflex during the first 20 days; during the 10th-20th day of life the rhesus monkey develops effective locomotor abilities and may actually break contact with the mother for brief periods of time both in the wild and in the laboratory. Gradually the reflex pattern of attachment subsides and is supplemented by and subverted to voluntary activities.

(b) Stage of Comfort and Attachment. This stage in the monkey may be relatively brief, ending at about 60 to 80 days. During this time the infant receives from the mother satisfaction of its basic bodily needs, that is, nursing, contact, warmth, appropriate stimulation, and protection from danger. During this period the mother is highly protective. Tight reflex clinging gradually diminishes, and the infant monkey spends a considerable amount of time either loosely cradled in the mother's arms exploring her body or exploring the adjacent physical world. Available evidence suggests that intimate physical contact is the variable of primary importance enabling the infant to pass from this stage to a stage of security, that is specific security from a specific maternal figure.

In this regard experiments with surrogate mothers should be mentioned. Eight infant monkeys were raised with a cloth surrogate and a wire-surrogate mother always available. Four of the infants were fed on demand by the cloth surrogate and four by the wire surrogate. This difference turned out to be relatively unimportant because each group of four infants averaged over 15 hours a day in contact with the cloth surrogate. Much of this time was devoted to ventral clinging, a response that normally disappears with the stage of comfort and attachment, but which persists in this experimental situation long after the stage of security can be demonstrated in infants with biological mothers. The explanation of this peculiar situation lies in the nature of the artificial cloth surrogate, which from the ethological point of view is not only a good, but a "super-normal," monkey mother in that it was always available, it never moved away, and it never punished.

(c) Stage of Security. In this stage of the infant-mother affectional system the infant learns to explore strange stimuli and strange environments but needs the mother as a secure base from which to operate and to which he can return periodically. The mother imparts feelings of security to her infant by being present while he explores the environment around him. Real mothers are the most effective in this regard. Cloth-surrogate mothers are not quite so useful as a security base but are more so than wire mothers. The development of the security stage of infants in the wild is a function not only of the presence of its mother but also a function of her social role. For example, if the mother is a highly dominant female, the infant has little or nothing to fear since he can treat other infants and even other mothers with a certain degree of impunity. On the other hand, if the mother is a low-dominant female the infant must be careful since his mother cannot guarantee security from other infants or from other mothers.

(d) Separation Stage. The dissolution of the affectional relationships between a particular infant and its mother is in part a function of the infant's behaviors and in part a function of the mother's allowing the infant to separate. There is a certain amount of ambivalence and resistance to separation on the part of both infant and mother. Much data attests to the enormous power and persistence of the infant-mother bond, and it is easy to see how this bond in both rhesus monkeys (and human beings) could become so intimate and prolonged as to disrupt seriously other affectional relations such as those between peers. However, the fact remains that eventual physical and psychological separation is a general rule in all primate species.

Age-mate or Peer Affectional System

This third affectional system has been relatively neglected in both animal and human studies. Like the other affectional systems, the peer affectional system is characterized by several developmental stages, each stage being dependent on maturation and influenced by learning experiences.

(a) The Reflex Stage. This is illustrated by behavior of infants under 20-30 days of age and is characterized by close, group-oriented, contactual relationships. Infants keep close to each other. In a play-room situation if one monkey leaves the group the others are quick to follow; the animal that has left returns to the group if they do not.

(b) The Stage of Object Exploration. This phase consists of gross bodily

contact and oral and manual manipulation of all animate and inanimate objects in the environment. There is some evidence to suggest that this kind of object exploration precedes more complex social exploration.

(c) Interactive Play. The stage of object exploration is followed by the development of interactive play either of the rough-and-tumble variety or of an approach-withdrawal variety. Late in the first year or early in the second, a stage of aggressive play develops. This supersedes the more gentle rough-and-tumble play. In a stage of aggressive play the animals wrestle and roll and bite and the manual contact can be physically painful. However, monkeys are seldom permanently injured during these play contacts with long time associates, and aggressive play leads to the establishment of firm peer relationships and to dominance hierarchies.

Heterosexual Affectional System

This system is of less relevance to the theme of this chapter and is mentioned only for the sake of completeness. It refers to that body of behaviors which enables adult males and female primates to reproduce their kind, and, like the other affectional systems, it goes through a series of maturational stages with the behaviors evoked in each stage being constantly subjected to minor modifications. The stages of heterosexual affectional development are: (a) the reflex stage, (b) the infantile heterosexual stage, (c) the preadolescent heterosexual stage, and (d) the adult heterosexual stage.

There are many variables which influence the development of heterosexual behavior in primates. There can be no question, for example, that hormonal influences affect the differential nature of the heterosexual affectional system in male and female monkeys, even though most normal male and female monkeys have demonstrated an adult pattern of heterosexual behavior before the advent of gonadotropins. The appearance of these gonadal hormones no doubt affects the frequency of sexual behavior and makes possible the culmination of sexual congress including insemination and fertilization of the female by the male. A large body of observational data from the Wisconsin Laboratory and other places indicates that heterosexual behavior is also greatly influenced by early experience. Failure of infants to form effective infant-infant affectional relations delays or destroys adequate adult heterosexual behavior.

Paternal Affectional System

The primate paternal affectional system expresses itself in the behavior of the adult male to the members of his social group, whether this group is a monogamous family, polygamous family, clan, herd, or tribe. It involves care and protection of the female and her offspring.

THE IMPACT OF SOCIAL ISOLATION ON MONKEYS

Human social isolation in all its multiple forms is recognized as a problem of great importance. The effects of such isolation are almost certainly damaging to the individual, particularly when the isolation occurs at various critical developmental stages and impairs an individual's ability to relate on an interpersonal level, such as in the modulation of aggressive behavior. Isolation in our country can result from a breakdown in family structure, which often results in orphaned or semi-orphaned children, and it can also result from isolation of certain subgroups from the mainstream of societal life. There has been considerable difficulty in studying scientifically the full impact of culturally produced social isolation, and ethical considerations prohibit extensive manipulation of several key variables. This does not mean that naturalistic observations of the effects of various kinds of social isolation in humans have not been useful; they certainly have.

There is every reason to believe that the research which will be reviewed here concerning the effects of social deprivation in rhesus monkeys has application to human behavior, even though human behavior is considerably more complex, variable, and subtle, than that of subhuman primates. Despite these differences one should still be able to gain insight into the problems created by human social isolation from studies of social isolation in monkeys.

There are two basic kinds of social isolation techniques used at the Wisconsin Primate Laboratories, partial social isolation and total social isolation (Cross and Harlow, 1965; Griffin and Harlow, 1966; Harlow, Dodsworth, and Harlow, 1955; Mitchell et al., 1966; Seay et al., 1964). Under partial social isolation the monkeys are raised in bare wire cages as illustrated in Figure 1 so that they can see and hear other monkeys but cannot make physical contact with them. Total social isolation involves placing the animals, usually at birth, in an enclosed steel cage for some predetermined time such as 3, 6, 9, 12, or 18 months. It is illuminated and is not sound-shielded so that the monkey's sensory deprivation is held to a minimum.

Data from numerous studies indicate that prolonged partial social isolation has deleterious effects upon development of appropriate monkey social, sexual, and maternal behaviors. By one year of age, partial-isolate subjects exhibit more self-orality and self-clasping, and less locomotion and exploration than similar-age monkeys reared with mothers and/or peers. When placed in a social situation, these monkeys exhibit few appropriate social behaviors, most of their activity being directed toward avoiding rather than initiating social contact with peers. Instead they spend the majority of their time self-clutching or huddling in a corner of the playroom.

This lack of social sophistication in young partial isolates generalizes as the monkeys mature. When placed in social situations the older animals exhibit few

Figure 1.   Infant monkeys in social isolation cages.

appropriate social behaviors such as grooming. They do show considerable aggressive behavior, but most of it is ill-directed. Sexually, partial-isolate adults leave much to be desired. The best that can be said for females is that they are incompetent, while males are absolutely hopeless. It has been possible to impregnate some partial-isolate females, chiefly by artificial methods, and with few exceptions, their initial maternal behaviors have been inadequate.

As partial-isolate monkeys get older, locomotion and exploration in their home cage gradually decline. In addition, the disturbance patterns seen earlier in life, such as self-mouthing, self-clasping, and huddling, seem to drop away. They are replaced, however, by other abnormal behavior patterns.

An abnormality which appears late is one to which we, partly in jest, gave the name "schizophrenic stare." In this situation the monkey sits at the front of the cage vacantly staring outward or paying no attention to the activities of monkeys or people in the external environment.

More recently another strange behavior pattern has been observed in some of the partial-isolate monkeys. While they are staring with their gaze averted to the left, their right arm gradually raises as if it did not belong to the body. The wrist flexes and the fingers form a tight fist. The monkey may then stare at the "phantom arm" and try to retreat from it as if it were a threatening object that had no connection with his real body. It is tempting to compare this to the phenomenon of depersonalization as seen in some psychotic patients. One must, of course, guard against being excessively anthropomorphic at this stage of our knowledge. The same caution would also hold for many other seemingly clinically familiar behaviors. However, it is as fallacious not to make a correct analogy as to make one which is erroneous.

Another pattern, which was originally thought to be rare but which is now known to be quite common in monkeys subjected to prolonged partial social isolation, is self-aggression. We have conducted experiments which enable one to plot the frequency of self-aggression as contrasted to externally directed aggression in terms of the animals' age and duration of partial social isolation. Externally directed aggression appears in the isolate-raised male in the second year of life and in the female about a year later, indicating a sex-determined variant. The development of self-aggression usually appears later than externally directed aggression in partial-isolate monkeys, but follows similar developmental trends for males and females. Ordinarily the monkeys do not break the skin of their hands, arms, or legs during the self-aggressive displays, but under stress or provocation they can inflict wounds that rend skin and muscle and inflict dangerous or lethal hemorrhage.

The effects of total social isolation on the behavior of rhesus monkeys has also been studied extensively. Isolation periods have begun a few hours after birth and have lasted for 3, 6, 9, 12, or 18 months. Oddly enough these isolate monkeys show relatively few abnormal behaviors during the term of total social isolation, but the devastating effects of this early life experience become obvious when the monkeys must enter into and engage in social communication with more normally raised, age-mate associates. Furthermore, since the period of total isolation has been varied, it is possible to evaluate the effect of the progressive duration of total social isolation on the production of abnormal or psychopathological behaviors. In general the findings show that the longer the animal is in isolation, the more severe and irreversible are the psychopathologic effects.

No monkey has died during isolation. When first removed from total social isolation, they usually go into a state of emotional shock characterized by self-clutching and rocking as illustrated in Figure 2. Release from three months of total social isolation is occasionally lethal to monkeys who fall victims to self-induced anorexia, but if this does not occur or is prevented by forced feeding, the 90-day total social isolates rapidly adjust to age-mate peers. The

Figure 2.   Infant monkey following three months of total social isolation.

data indicate that the debilitating effects of three months of total social isolation are dramatic but reversible. Furthermore, there is no indication that long-term behavioral deficits develop in terms of social, sexual, or maternal adjustment.

A very different picture appears after six months of total social isolation. This period of isolation severely impairs the potentiality for socialization as indicated by playroom data comparing six-month isolates with their controls and with three-month isolates and their controls. When placed with equal aged peers, the six-month isolates display almost no social responsiveness. Even after 32 weeks such social behavior as has gradually evolved is almost entirely limited to interchanges with the isolate partner rather than with the controls After six months of isolation sexual behavior at first appears to be obliterated. Later males and females may show signs of conjugal interests, but if these desires exist they are blocked by the appearance of completely inadequate patterns of sexual positioning, such as the pattern of sidewise posturing and thrusting.

Despite the sexual inadequacy or reluctance shown by monkeys socially isolated for six months, it was possible eventually to impregnate about half of the females, thanks in part to persistent breeding-stock male monkeys and in part to a specialized apparatus. These reluctant mothers, termed motherless-mothers since they had entered motherhood without the benefits of having a mother of their own or early play experience with age-mates or peers, were completely inadequate maternally. They were either totally indifferent to their own infants or were abusive to their infants, as is the mother in Figure 3 who is crushing the face of her baby against the steel mesh floor of the cage.

We have also traced the long-term effects of total social isolation during the first half year of life, and two of the results are particularly noteworthy. Adequate social interaction does not develop, even 3 or 4 years after removal

Figure 3.   Behavior of motherless-mother, raised in total social isolation for six months, toward her own infant.

from total social isolation, as illustrated by the behavior of the isolate huddled in a corner (Figure 4) while normal monkeys half his age play about him, inspect his body, and eventually attack him with savage ferocity. Secondly, although the six-month isolate monkeys showed no signs of aggression when first placed with age-mates, certain forms of aggression developed later. If at one year of age they were placed with even more socially damaged 12-month isolates, some of the half-year isolates attacked the helpless, more socially emasculated monkeys. Furthermore, when the six-month isolates were tested for aggression after they were three to four years of age, they frequently attacked infant monkeys—a kind of behavior never seen in normal adolescent or adult monkeys. Finally, rhesus monkeys socially isolated for six months would occasionally make a suicidal attack against a normal adult animal—attesting to the power of aggression when it matures and to the social stupidity of the six-month social isolates even after they had entered maturity.

Figure 4.   Permanent isolate behavior of male raised in total social isolation for six months.

It should be mentioned that six months of total social isolation occurring during the second half year of life produced a radically different syndrome than that occurring in the first half year of life, again indicating the importance of the developmental stage at which the social isolation occurs. Within a relatively short period of time after release from isolation, these six-month, late isolates adjusted adequately to the equal-aged playmates. The six-month, late-isolates made more approaches than the controls, perhaps reflecting somewhat greater aggressiveness of the isolates and the consequent caution of the controls. Observational data showed the six-month, late-isolate group were hyperaggressive compared with its control group, whereas both the six- and twelve-month, early isolate subjects were characterized by a lack of aggression compared with their controls.

It is as though the early socializing experience prior to isolation had enabled the late-isolates to resume social contact without much fear following their release from isolation. However, aggression was not very well modulated.

Although six months of total social isolation produced a dire, devastating, endurable pattern of social destruction or pattern of permeating and permanent psychopathology, the effect of twelve months of total social isolation was even more severe. The simplest play patterns were eradicated in these monkeys, and the twelve-month social isolate animals and their controls had to be terminated because the controls became increasingly aggressive toward the helpless isolate animals and would have killed them had social testing continued.

Although we have been extremely successful in producing psychopathological monkeys by early social isolation, it is obvious that this method has severe limitations as a monkey model for human psychopathological states. The devastating effects of total social isolation probably result from denial of any opportunity to form the basic early affectional attachments of maternal and peer or age-mate love. It is the formation of these early attachments at appropriate developmental stages which prepares the monkey for mature social adjustments including heterosexual and maternal responsiveness and aggression control.

Denial of age-mate or peer social security leaves the infant for all practical purposes a social isolate. Maternal affection from an animate or even from a good inanimate mother provides the infant monkey with a sense of basic security and trust which enables him to explore the inanimate and animate world about him. Important as it is for the infant to gain mastery over the inanimate world, it is even more important that he gain mastery over the world of animate objects, particularly his age-mates or peers. Given maternal social security the infant is free to interact with his age-mates, and primarily through acts of vigorous physical interacting play he develops age-mate affection which probably generalizes to include affection for all members of his social group.

Not only do normal socializing forces follow a natural maturational course, but so also do traits that can inhibit or block normal affectional development.

Two of these are fear and aggression, which commonly develop in the monkey after 3 and 12 months of age, respectively. Normally, maternal security holds fear within reasonable bounds when the monkey matures, and normally both maternal and age-mate affection keep aggression from becoming a social destructive force at least within integrated social groups.

EXPERIMENTAL STUDY OF DEPRESSION

It is apparent that by subjecting monkeys to total or partial social isolation we have inadvertently raised monkeys who exhibit profound behavioral abnormalities. As previously mentioned, the focus of work in this laboratory has been on studying and influencing the normative development of rhesus monkeys. Only recently have we begun a systematic study of psychopathological states in monkeys. The specific disorder which we are attempting to simulate first is depression. The purpose of the research, which is being done jointly with the Department of Psychiatry, is to create experimental primate models for depression. Such models could provide systems in which the social and biological variables believed to be important in the etiology and treatment of depression could be systematically manipulated and their relationship to depression clarified. The implications of the creation of such a model have recently been discussed by McKinney and Bunney (1969).

The first step in the creation of an experimental animal model of depression is to develop techniques which will produce a predictable, stable, and intense depressive syndrome in rhesus monkeys. Depression is a disorder of affect or mood and such feelings are obviously not verbally reportable by monkeys as they are in human beings. However, it is believed that enough behavioral manifestations analogous to those seen in humans who report they are depressed can be produced and measured in primates to make a very strong case for the existence of a depressive syndrome in nonhuman primates. Such behaviors could include anorexia, weight loss, decreased responsiveness to the external environment, an increase in self-directed behaviors, decreased play activity, decreased motor activity, huddling posture, and self-mutilation.

The feasibility of an animal model of depression comes largely from separation experiments and anecdotal evidence. The separation experiments have consisted largely of mother-infant separation and the anecdotal evidence consist largely of case histories of individual animals.

The human literature clearly establishes that mother-infant separation in the second half of the first year of life produces a syndrome termed anaclitic depression by Spitz (1946). Robertson and Bowlby (1952) studied a similar condition in older children, and described three progressive stages as part of the infant's response to separation: (a) a stage of protest, (b) a stage of despair, and

(c) a stage of detachment when mother and child were reunited. These stages will be further described in the discussion of specific separation experiments. A variety of studies show that mother-infant separation in monkeys is a traumatic experience for both mother and infant, especially the latter. The changes seen following monkey mother-infant separation occur in phases similar to those described by Spitz and Bowlby and Robertson in human infants except that the detachment response has seldom been observed.

The initial studies (Seay et al., 1962; Seay and Harlow, 1965) on mother-infant separation at Wisconsin used groups of four monkeys that had lived with their mothers and had been allowed to interact with each other. Separation from the mothers when the infants were six months of age gave rise to Bowlby's first two stages, those of protest and despair as illustrated in Figure 5. The initial disturbance (protest stage) took the form of agitation and consisted of disoriented scampering around, high pitched screeching, and crying. The second phase was characterized by increased viewing of the mother, decreased infant-infant interaction, and decreased play activity.

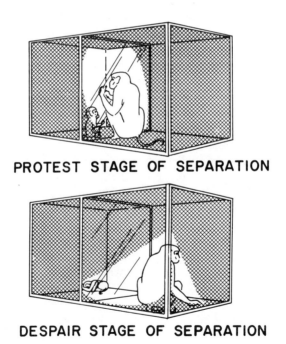

PROTEST STAGE OF SEPARATION

DESPAIR STAGE OF SEPARATION

Figure 5. Stages of protest and despair following separation of six-month-old monkey from mother.

Several investigators at different laboratories have studied mother-infant separation (Hinde et al., 1966; Jensen and Tolman, 1962; Kaufman and Rosenblum, 1967a; Kaufman and Rosenblum, 1967b) and all have obtained results similar to those described above. The focus of most of the studies of mother-infant separation has not actually been on depression itself, but on the nature of the mother-infant relationship. Kaufman and Rosenblum studied the reaction of four, group-living, pigtail monkey infants to removal of the mother and tried to integrate their observations with the clinical reports of Spitz and Bowlby. All animals showed distress, and profound behavioral changes followed in three of the four. The syndrome consisted of three phases: (a) a phase of "agitation" lasting 24-36 hours, (b) a phase of decreased activity and decreased social interaction lasting 5-6 days, and (c) spontaneous recovery in stages alternating with "depression." Each stage was viewed as part of the infant's adaptation to the loss of the mother. Undoubtedly significant, but unexplained, was the lack of a persistent behavioral response in one subject. Despite these useful reports, no one has systematically focused on the experimental production and study of depression.

The mother-infant separation model has been a useful one in understanding the nature of the mother-infant tie and in confirming many of the observations about anaclitic depression in human beings. A comprehensive study of depression and its experimental production, however, must go beyond the anaclitic or the mother-infant separation model. For example, the question remains as to whether one can produce in nonhuman primates a syndrome comparable to the depression of adult humans. Would separation experiments utilizing peers and juvenile or even adult monkeys, rather than mother and infants, produce a depressive-like syndrome?

In this regard a series of studies conducted over the last several years indicate that monkey infant-infant or peer affection formed under favorable circumstances is at least as strong, if not stronger, than maternal affection. There is reason to believe that by the time the infants are 6 months of age peer separation may be a technique at least as effective as maternal separation in the production of depression and might be used as a model system which would enable one to move beyond the mother-infant model. Bowden and McKinney at NIMH and Suomi, Harlow, and Domek at Wisconsin conducted early studies on peer separation.

A number of studies involving repetitive infant-infant separations are now being conducted at the Wisconsin Primate Laboratories. In the first study the monkeys were raised as a group of four for the first three months of life and were subsequently subjected to a series of 12 separation sessions followed by 6 weeks of being housed together as a group of four before undergoing a second series of 8 separation sessions (Hinde et al., 1966). Each session involved a 7-day test period when the 4 monkeys lived together in a group for periods of 3 days followed by a 4-day period of separation. The data show very clearly that the monkeys went through the conventional stages of protest, which characterized the next 48 hours of separation, and later despair. In effect the data indicate that repetitive periods of peer separation produce repetitive states of depression. Whether or not these repetitive depression periods could "fuse" to produce a profound and protracted depressive state remains open for investigation.

Depression is undoubtedly related to multiple variables and any model system to study the depressive syndrome must take this fact into account. For example, any comprehensive research program analyzing depression should involve a consideration of both social and biological factors.

A current biochemical explanation of depression is the catecholamine hypothesis. This hypothesis is based on a considerable amount of indirect evidence relating lowered functional levels of norepinephrine and/or other biogenic amines with depression and elevated functional levels with mania (Bunney, Jr. and Davis, 1965; Prange, 1964; Schildkraut, 1965; Schildkraut and Kety, 1967). While the catecholamine hypothesis has had considerable heuristic value, its validity in terms of the *direct* relationship of biochemical changes to depression remains largely untested. An additional useful experimental model would be one in which the biochemical theories about depression could be directly tested in an animal who exhibited behaviors akin to those seen in depressed patients. The question also remains whether it might be possible by biochemical means to sensitize a monkey so that he would be more likely to develop a depressive response to separation experience.

The most common psychiatric theories about depression emphasize the importance of object loss or separation experiences of some kind. It is not the loss *per se* that causes depression but the individual's perception of and response to this loss. Such considerations as the presence of unresolved ambivalent feelings toward the lost object or prior traumatizing separation experiences are thought to predispose to the development of a more intense depressive-type response. Unexpressed hostile or aggressive feelings which are turned inward in a self-punitive manner are also thought to play a key role in the etiology of many depressions. We are currently attempting to create experimental paradigms for some of these theories.

Most attempts to produce psychopathological states experimentally in animals have failed because insufficient attention has been paid to the importance of multiple variables. For this reason a variety of concepts are being tested in a study of depression, and several pieces of apparatus have been designed to assess the relative contribution of many of these variables (Suomi and Harlow, 1969). For example, recently we have been studying the effects of social isolation in a special apparatus, a *vertical chamber*. Depression has been characterized by some as a state of helplessness and hopelessness, and the vertical chambers were designed to produce such a state experimentally. The chambers do not produce physical discomfort or disability. Vertical chambers are designed so that they can be combined with various combinations of antecedent, simultaneous or subsequent social separation conditions.

In an exploratory study we placed four subjects reared in wire cages individually in chambers for a period of 30 days. When home-cage behaviors prior to incarceration were compared with behaviors for two months following emergence from the chambers, the alterations were precisely in the direction of what we would call depressed. Self-clasping, rocking, and huddling, that is, self-directed disturbance behaviors, rose dramatically, while locomotion and exploration, that is behaviors reflecting activity and responsiveness to the environment, dropped out.

A second, more formal study illustrates how powerful the effects of chamber confinement early in life can be (Harlow, Suomi, and McKinney, 1970). Previous research has firmly established that six months of total social isolation from birth produces relatively permanent deficiencies in social, sexual, and maternal behaviors in monkeys, but monkeys isolated for only three months quickly recover and develop normal behaviors. In the present study we placed four monkeys 45 days old individually in vertical chambers and confined them for six weeks so that upon emergence they were three months of age. Subsequently they were individually housed but given social experience in a play situation (playroom) with equal-age monkeys, some reared individually and some reared with peers.

Figure 6 shows the monkeys four days following removal from the chambers. Four months later they looked the same. There had been no recovery. Comparing the home-cage behaviors of these subjects with cage-reared and peer-reared controls of the same age, it is obvious that their depressive syndrome was profound and stable over time. At ages 5-7 months and also at ages 9-11 months, chambered monkeys self-mouthed, self-clasped, and huddled significantly more and locomoted and explored significantly less, than either control group. Even more striking were their behaviors in the social playroom situation. Here, at both ages, the above differences were even more extreme. In addition, the complete absence of social behavior, either in the form of contact or play, was powerful evidence that these chambered subjects were depressed in their behavior. We have concluded from this study that chamber confinement produces destructive behavioral effects more striking, in less time, and with fewer individual differences among subjects than total social isolation, previously the most powerful psychopathological behavior producing technique employed with monkey subjects. Furthermore, the psychopathological behaviors produced are of a depressive nature.

A third study has combined the manipulations of multiple peer separation and vertical chamber confinement. Infants were reared with each other as a group of four from birth to three months, then separated from each other a total

Figure 6. Monkeys four days after removal from six weeks confinement in vertical
chambers after forty-five days of age.

of 20 times, four days for each separation, in precisely the same sequence as
previously described for the multiple peer-separation study. The difference in
this study was that the infants, when separated, were confined to vertical
chambers rather than housed in individual cages. As in the previous study,
protest and despair reactions to the separations were noted and maturational
arrest of development was clearly observed. However, for chamber-separated
monkeys this arrest took a slightly, but significantly, different form from that of
the cage-separated monkeys. As in the previous study baseline behaviors
following separation were typified by abnormally low levels of locomotion,
exploration, and play, and high levels of self-mouthing. However, the chambered

monkeys showed significantly lower levels of social clinging and higher levels of self-clasping than the cage-separated monkeys. In other words, immature *socially* directed behavior was being "replaced" by immature (and depressive) *self*-directed behavior. These and other data from the study lead us to suspect that in these subjects we have been observing Bowlby's detachment stage of reaction to separation, a phenomenon never before seen in monkey subjects. It is apparent that chamber confinement coupled with separation produces depressive effects beyond those produced by separation alone.

On the basis of this and ongoing research, we are now convinced that we can reliably produce many of the behavioral manifestations of depression in monkeys under one year of age, regardless of their early rearing experience. At present we are extending these procedures to older subjects, while modifying them by including such manipulations as presentation of intense fear-producing stimuli and alternation of circadian rhythms. Concurrently we are developing procedures to measure biochemical consequences of these behavioral manipulations by analysis of catecholamine and corticosteroid levels.

Behavioral assessment of the effects of our depression-inducing manipulations is currently done in two situations. The first is within specially designed living-experimental home cages, termed "quad cages," which house four subjects apiece (Figure 7). Monkeys can be separated within quad cages by wire, Plexiglas, or movable opaque slides, or may be allowed to interact freely in any combination the experimenter desires. Social interaction behavior is the simplest behavior situation that can be stuided. With this apparatus the dichotomy of home care versus the social test situation is eliminated because the unit provides both. One of its chief advantages is that group social living is maximized with the subsequent opportunity to study disruptions or abnormal behavior produced by separation experiences.

In addition, much of our social testing is done in a playroom. The playroom situation has already been highly standardized for studying normative development of infant-infant affection and for studying recovery from social loss following various antecedent events. In the present context an experimenter can study interaction patterns between depressed subjects and whatever type of stimulus animals he desires. This enables him to scale the degree of behavioral abnormality shown by depressed subjects in comparison to that exhibited by monkeys who have been reared under conditions (e.g., total social isolation, partial social isolation) for which a wealth of normative data already exists.

The initial emphasis in this field needs to be on the establishment of methodologies for producing depressed animals which could serve as experimental models. It is probably important to use animals that form social bonds because within the animal kingdom "depression" seems to occur most frequently in such animals. The depression induced within such a social system would then be available for a variety of biochemical and behavioral studies. One

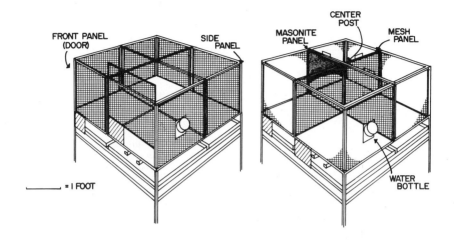

FRONT PANEL (DOOR) — SIDE PANEL — MASONITE PANEL — CENTER POST — MESH PANEL — WATER BOTTLE — ___ = I FOOT

COMBINED LIVING EXPERIMENTAL CAGE

Figure 7. Combined living experimental cage permitting manipulation of social interaction.

could explore the significance of object loss in relation to depression and could study such issues as the effects of separation at varying stages of bond formation and attachment and the effects of reunion with the lost object at varying times following the separation.

Also, what is the effect of age on the response to separation? Is there a critical time beyond which reunion has no effect, as suggested in humans by the work of Spitz? It would be a mistake to view such studies as definitively confirming or negating current theories about depression; rather, a more reasonable viewpoint would be that work in this area would provide a more complete understanding of many poorly understood concepts about human depression. There is the potential for a system in which variables relevant to depression could be manipulated or held constant as one chose, and areas in which additional research is needed relevant to depression could be highlighted.

The question has been and will probably continue to be asked, "How do you tell a monkey is depressed and not schizophrenic?" This question can only be responded to in the context of the situations used to produce the psychopathological state at hand and careful evaluation and rating of the total constellation of behaviors thus produced.

That is, to make the situation as close as possible to depression, one would need to invoke such core concepts as separation and object loss and construct rating scales which include behaviors commonly associated with the depressed mood in humans. We are using rating scales that do this. In any event, the experimental production of psychopathological states has value regardless of what diagnostic label one chooses to use. Even more important is the possibility of relating different responses to standardized stresses to previous life experience which is more readily traced for individual experimental monkeys than for humans.

REFERENCES

Bunney, W. E., Jr. and Davis, J. M. (1965). Norepinephrine in depressive reactions. *Archives of General Psychiatry,* **13**, 483-494.

Cross, H. A. and Harlow, H. F. (1965). Prolonged and progressive effects of partial isolation on the behavior of Macaque monkeys. *Journal of Experimental Research in Personality,* **1**, 39-49.

Griffin, G. A. and Harlow, H. F. (1966). Effects of three months of total social deprivation on social adjustment and learning in the Rhesus monkey. *Child Development,* **37**, 533-547.

Harlow, H. F. (1962a). The heterosexual affectional system in monkeys. *American Psychologist,* **17**, 1.

Harlow, H. F. (1962b). Development of the second and third affectional systems in Macaque monkeys. In *Research approaches to psychiatric problems,* T. T. Tourlentes, S. L. Pollock, and H. E. Himwich (Eds.). New York: Grune & Stratton. Pp. 209-229.

Harlow, H. F. (1969). Age mate or peer affectional system. In *Advances in the study of behavior.* New York: Academic Press, Inc.

Harlow, H. F., Dodsworth, R. O., and Harlow, M. K. (1955). Total social isolation in monkeys. *Proceedings of the National Academy of Sciences,* **54**, 90-97.

Harlow, H. F. and Harlow, M. K. (1965). The affectional systems. In *Behavior of non-human primates,* A. M. Schrier, H. F. Harlow, and F. Stollnitz (Eds.). New York: Academic Press, Inc.

Harlow, H. F., Harlow, M. K., and Hansen, E. W. (1963). The maternal affectional system of Rhesus monkeys. In *Maternal behavior in mammals,* H. L. Rheingold (Ed.). New York: Wiley. Pp. 254-281.

Harlow, H. F., Suomi, S., and McKinney, W. T. (1970). Experimental production of depression in monkeys. *Mainly Monkeys,* **1**, 6.

Hinde, R. A., Spencer-Booth, Y., and Bruce, M. (1966). Effects of 6-day maternal deprivation on Rhesus monkey infants. *Nature,* **210**, 1021-1023.

Jensen, G. D. and Tolman, C. W. (1962). Mother-infant relationship in the monkey, Macoca Nemestrina: The effect of brief separation and mother-infant specification. *J. Comp. Physiol. Psychol.,* **55**, 131-136.

Kaufman, I. C. and Rosenblum, L. A. (1967a). Depression in infant monkeys separated from their mothers. *Science,* **155,** 1030-1031.

Kaufman, I. C. and Rosenblum, L. A. (1967b). The reaction to separation in infant monkeys: Anaclitic depression and conservation-withdrawal. *Psychosomatic Medicine,* **29,** 648-675.

McKinney, W. T. and Bunney, W. E. (1969). Animal model of depression. Vol. I. Review of evidence: Implications for research. *Archives of General Psychiatry,* **21,** 240-248.

Mitchell, G. D., Raymond, E. J., Ruppenthal, G. C., and Harlow, H. F. (1966). Long-term effects of total social isolation upon behavior of Rhesus monkeys. *Psychological Reports,* **18,** 567-580.

Prange, A. J. (1964). The pharmacology and biochemistry of depression. *Dis. Nerv. System,* **25,** 217-221.

Robertson, T. and Bowlby, J. (1952). Responses of young children to separation from their mothers. *Cours du Centre International de l'Enfance,* 2, 131-142.

Schildkaut, J. J. (1965). The catecholamine hypothesis of affective disorders: A review of supporting evidence. *Amer. J. Psychiat.,* **122,** 509-522.

Schildkraut, J. J. and Kety, S. S. (1967). Biogenic amines and emotion. *Science,* **156,** 21-37.

Seay, W., Alexander, B. K. and Harlow, H. F. (1964). Maternal behavior of socially deprived Rhesus monkeys. *Journal of Abnormal and Social Psychology,* **69,** 345-354.

Seay, W., Hansen, E., and Harlow, H. F. (1962). Mother-infant separation in monkeys. *J. Child Psychol. Psychiat.,* **3,** 123-132.

Seay, W. and Harlow, H. F. (1965). Maternal separation in the Rhesus monkey. *J. of Nervous and Mental Disease,* **140,** 434-441.

Spitz, R. A. (1946). Anaclitic depression: An inquiry into the genesis of psychiatric conditions in early childhood. Vol. II. *Psychoanal. Stud. Child.,* **2,** 313-342.

Suomi, S. and Harlow, H. F. (1969). Apparatus conceptualization for psychopathological research in monkeys. *Behavioral Research Methods and Instrumentation,* **1,** 1-12.

Suomi, S., Harlow, H. F., and Domek, C. J. Effect of repetitive infant-infant separation of young monkeys. *Journal of Abnormal Psychology* (in press).

Part V

CLINICAL APPLICATIONS

*"If a man does not keep pace with his companions,
perhaps it is because he hears a different drummer. Let
him step to the music he hears, however measured or far
away."*

HENRY DAVID THOREAU

INTRODUCTION

The preceding chapters have contained hints and some direct illustrations of practical applications of their authors' work. As this section discloses, however, there is a paucity of knowledge about the actual use of information about individual differences in the fields of practice. Knowledge of individuality is of obvious value to the school teacher and undergirds much educational planning. Clinicians, however, have had less exposure to these ideas.

The first two chapters of this section are deliberately restricted to the extended application of the work of Thomas and Chess in order to provide "case histories" of what actually happens when one shifts from research to practice.

This is of interest not only to the practitioner, but, hopefully, to researchers who increasingly bear the responsibility of relating the ultimate usefulness of their work to the issues that beset the practitioners who make use of their output.

This section illustrates the complex task of applying research findings, even those arising from so-called applied as contrasted with basic research, to the daily work of practicing clinicians. Practical problems and delays accompanied the introduction of such a clearcut discovery as penicillin into the routine management of infectious disease. It is to be expected that the application of less tangible and more subjective information about personality will encounter even greater practical obstacles.

In Chapter 14, William Carey adapts the concepts and approaches of Thomas and Chess to the office practice of pediatrics. He graphically describes the pressures of time, expense, and immediate payoff as he developed and tested a condensed instrument for use with the mothers of infants. His experience disclosed that the chief value of the questionnaire was to screen for the "difficult child" in Chess's terminology. He further calls attention to the potential use of the questionnaire in parent counseling, both through its sensitivity to discrepancies between maternal attitudes toward a child and the more objective information gained from their specific ratings of that child and its usefulness in sketching a profile of the child, permitting an individualized and detailed knowledge of his personality and behavior.

Applying Carey's questionnaire for mothers to children with specific problems—those infants who sustained physical abuse, those who survived intrauterine transfusions, and those with Down's syndrome—Grace Gregg in Chapter 15 further probes the instrument's strengths and weaknesses. She adds information that can be gained from direct observation of the child's behavior in the office through a standard checklist—in effect extending the physical examination of the child into the personality and behavioral realm. Because some parents are unable to complete a questionnaire and even provide accurate information in an interview, the clinician must accumulate his own firsthand data. Although direct observation adds an important dimension, Gregg outlines its limitations and misleading aspects. Recognizing these drawbacks, she calls attention to the value of both historical information and direct observation as sources of data for enhancing the clinician's comprehensive diagnosis and management of both the physical and psychological aspects of children.

Dr. Gregg also notes that the process of completing a temperament questionnaire can be a useful experience in itself for parents who are placed in the position of thinking about their child in behavioral and emotional terms. The pediatrician is also stimulated to examine himself as he records behavioral observations of his patients, since the responses are in part a reflection of his manner and personality.

The concluding chapter reviews the fruits and style of individual difference research and places them in perspective, suggesting that this field of interest, in fact, is the heart of current efforts to scientifically study man in his emerging form—the child.

CHAPTER 14

Measurement of Infant Temperament in Pediatric Practice

William B. Carey

The observant pediatrician soon learns that babies are not all alike physiologically or psychologically, even at birth. In helping mothers take care of their infants and children, he should make allowance for these various behavioral styles. Yet, any judgments he may make about his patients' temperaments are usually based on their mothers' reports, which are sometimes biased, or on his own limited observations in his office. No practical clinical method had yet been made available for obtaining information that is both objective and comprehensive.

Aware of its potential theoretical and practical importance, I developed an instrument to measure temperament in the clinical setting. The process involved three phases: (1) selecting an established method that could be adapted to pediatric use, (2) setting up and running the instrument through a trial sample in pediatric practice, and (3) evaluating its validity and reliability. These steps could shed light on the clinical usefulness of the instrument.

1. A review of the literature revealed only one technique that seemed appropriate for this purpose, the New York Longitudinal Study research interview of Thomas, Chess et al. (1963, 1968.) This method, however, presented several obstacles to practical pediatric use: (1) two hours or more are needed for the interview, dictation, and rating; (2) various interpretations are possible in the scoring process; and (3) some uncertainties exist in the conversion of category ratings into diagnostic labels and the use of these labels for classifying babies into diagnostic groups.

An acceptance of, and close adherence to, the NYLS method meant, of course, that a technique derived from it would share its weaknesses. However, an examination of their conceptualization and statistical methods offered considerable reassurance that the risk was small.

2. By taking the material directly from the NYLS interview protocol, it was

possible to set up a multiple-choice questionnaire with 70 items, yielding 76 ratings in the 9 categories of reactivity (Appendix I). The total ratings in each category were reduced to a single score between 0 and 2 for that category (for example, between 0 for highly active and 2 for very inactive), just as with the NYLS interview. The questionnaire was then given to the mothers of 101 infant subjects, a generally middle-class group in private practice, all being between 4 and 8 months of age or the equivalent in the prematurely born. The average time required for completion of the questionnaire was 21 minutes, short enough to be practical in a clinical setting.

A scoring sheet was devised so that the questionnaire could be rated quickly (Appendix II). The usual time for this procedure was 8-10 minutes. A more complete description of the questionnaire and scoring process is available elsewhere (Carey, 1970; 1972).

Thus, the professional time required for the process is small. The mother was given the questionnaire at the conclusion of an office visit, or it was sent to her by mail. A cover letter described the purpose and gave directions. She completed the questionnaire at home at her convenience and returned it to the office. An office assistant can easily learn to rate the questionnaire. The results are, therefore, ready for the next monthly office visit or earlier if there is a problem.

3. The evaluation of the validity of the questionnaire consisted of a comparison of the results obtained by it and from NYLS interviews designed to elicit the same information. The questionnaire and interview material were evaluated in three ways: (a) by comparing the average category scores obtained from my questionnaires and the NYLS interview, (b) by contrasting the incidence of concurrent signs of a particular syndrome, the difficult child, and (c) by using both techniques simultaneously on a subsample.

On the basis of the average category scores (see Table 1), using 1.00 as the dividing line, we can conclude that by both techniques the average baby at 4-8 months of age is active, regular, adaptable, high in initial approach, low in threshold, mild, predominantly positive in mood, distractible, and persistent.

Table 2 compares the frequency of concurrent signs of the difficult child: irregularity, slow adaptability, initial withdrawal, high intensity, and negative mood. In other words, it shows the incidence of difficult temperament components found in the Thomas and Chess series by their interviews and the incidence in this questionnaire group. Using their figures for babies at one year (Korn, 1969), since those at six months are not available, we find a very close resemblance in these two separate, but similar, populations.

The third comparison was made between interviews and questionnaires completed by three mothers at the same time. In each case the interview, scored by NYLS raters, was immediately followed by the questionnaire. On the ratings above or below the means in the five major categories, there was disagreement

Table 1. Average Category Scores

Category	Questionnaire (N-101)	NYLS Interview (Period 1: mean age 5.9 months) (N-80)
Activity	0.52 ± 0.32	0.80
Rhythmicity	0.53 ± 0.46	0.56
Adaptability	0.35 ± 0.26	0.50
Approach	0.48 ± 0.35	0.67
Threshold	1.08 ± 0.39	1.20
Intensity	1.05 ± 0.32	1.21
Mood	0.40 ± 0.25	0.83
Distractibility	0.57 ± 0.32	0.59
Persistence	0.69 ± 0.38	0.40

Table 2. Concurrent Signs of the Difficult Child

	Questionnaire (4–8 mos. N-101)	NYLS Interview (at 1 yr. N-108)
5 signs	8%	10%
4 signs	15%	17%
3 signs	23%	20%
2 signs	22%	27%
0–1 signs	32%	26%

only for one of these for one baby. For statistical validity, a larger series would be needed.

By these methods, then, the questionnaire appears to be reasonably valid in that it produces results similar to those of the interview. The differences are attributable to several possible causes such as: (1) small variations in material covered, or in emphasis in reporting, in the interview, (2) differences in scoring technique, and (3) the possible repeated choice by a mother of one of the three questionnaire options as a matter of habit.

The same subsample was employed to estimate the reliability of the questionnaire. The three mothers unexpectedly received and completed the form a second time two weeks later. On rating above or below the means in the five major categories there was complete agreement for these three.

CLINICAL APPLICATION

It is very important to explore the usefulness of this questionnaire in pediatric practice. I find that its chief value is in identifying the *difficult baby syndrome* (see Chapter 5). Eleven of the 101 subjects could be so designated, using the revised criteria of four or five difficult category ratings with two or more greater than one standard deviation from the mean. Forty-one were rated as *easy babies* and 49 fell somewhere between, designated *intermediate.*

Nine fulfilled the criteria for the *slow-to-warm-up* syndrome. This was not a helpful concept in this series since these babies were heterogeneous, ranging from one who barely crossed the line from an easy baby diagnosis to two who qualified as difficult babies by the above redefinition. Furthermore, while the syndrome accounted for part of the intermediate group, it left over 40% with no further diagnostic designation.

An evaluation of the physical background of the difficult babies, a subject not reported by Thomas, Chess et al., has begun but has not yielded conclusive data as yet.

Knowing which babies are difficult is of value since mothers' general descriptions are sometimes inaccurate. It is true that the more difficult the baby is, the more likely the mother is to complain about him: 73% complain about difficult babies in contrast with 13% about easy ones. There were, however, important distortions in the mothers' general impressions of their babies. As part of the initial study they were asked to rate their babies as high, medium, or low in each of the nine categories. In a quarter of the instances when a baby was more than one standard deviation on the difficult side of the mean in five major categories, the mother actually rated him as on the easy end. Misinterpretations in the opposite direction, toward difficulty, were much less common.

One can illustrate these discrepancies by two examples. On the one hand, there was a 41-year-old mother of her first born who was delighted to have even a difficult baby and willing to overlook the trouble he gave her. In contrast, a young career woman, unready for the responsibilities of child care, reported feeling exasperated by an easy baby. In such cases the questionnaire was exceedingly valuable in providing more objective evidence about the babies' actual performance.

The pediatrician should be wary of superficial impressions of a baby's functioning, whether his own or the mother's. If he really wants to know what is going on, he must obtain descriptions of the baby, either by questionnaire or some sort of interview, and then make his own comprehensive diagnosis.

The areas of application of the questionnaire could be several. In addition to (1) defining the characteristics of infants routinely, and (2) trying to determine the contribution of the infant to reported behavior problems, it might be employed (3) to help pediatric residents become acquainted with the concept and importance of temperament, and (4) for research purposes (Carey, 1970).

Until further experience has accumulated, it seems wise to look upon this questionnaire as a screening device for the *difficult temperature* syndrome. It should be supplemented by interviewing to clarify the extent of the problem and its impact on the parents. Surely the instrument can be improved with further experience.

It will be noted that only five of the nine categories have been included in the determinations of difficult, intermediate, and easy babies. The dimensions of activity level, distractibility, and persistence can be of significance in behavioral problems at a later date but are evidently not of major importance in early infancy. High or low sensory threshold has not seemed to predispose to problems in behavior. It is not surprising that 10 of the 15 very high threshold ratings were with easy babies. If these other four categories were eliminated from the questionnaire, it would take even less time to administer and score without losing its value. These other four are the least stable of the nine categories (Thomas, Chess et al., 1963) and, therefore, would need to be redetermined at a later date when they have become more significant.

The usefulness of the questionnaire with groups other than middle-class American suburbanites has yet to be established, although some families of both upper- and lower-class status were included in this study.

Scarr and Salapatek (1970) of the University of Pennsylvania have also developed a temperament questionnaire based on the material of Thomas, Chess et al. It has 159 true or false statements. While this instrument has been useful in their research, it has not been used in a clinical setting.

Further work with the questionnaire will be in two principal directions: (1) to reduce methodological problems, and (2) to explore the significance of temperament in infancy and, therefore, the potential usefulness of the instrument in pediatric care. Beside the areas of well child care and behavior problems suggested by Chess (1966), temperamental differences may be of clinical significance in development, growth, psychosomatic problems, and reactions to physical disease.

SUMMARY

This chapter has reviewed the process of devising a questionnaire for assessing temperamental characteristics of babies in the 4 to 8 month age range. It was derived directly from the research technique of Thomas, Chess et al., but can be completed and rated more rapidly in the clinical pediatric setting. The practicality, validity, reliability, and usefulness of the instrument were discussed.

REFERENCES

Carey, W. B. (1970). A simplified method for measuring infant temperament. *Journal of Pediatrics,* **77**, 188.

Carey, W. B. (1972). Measuring infant temperament. *Journal of Pediatrics*, **81**, 414.

Carey, W. B. (1972). Clinical applications of infant temperament measurements. *Journal of Pediatrics*, **81**, 823.

Chess, S. (1966). Individuality in children, its importance to the pediatrician. *Journal of Pediatrics,* **69**, 676.

Korn, S. (1969). Personal Communication.

Thomas, A., Chess, S., Birch, H. G., Hertzig, M. E., and Korn, S. (1963). *Behavioral individuality in early childhood.* New York: New York University Press.

Thomas, A., Chess, S., and Birch, H. G. (1968). *Temperament and behavior disorders in children.* New York: New York University Press.

Scarr, S. and Salapatek, P. (1970). Patterns of fear development during infancy. *Merrill-Palmer Quarterly of Behavior and Development,* **16**, 53.

APPENDIX I.   SURVEY OF TEMPERAMENTAL CHARACTERISTICS

Sleep

1. (a) Generally goes to sleep at about same time for night and naps (within ½ hour).
   (b) Partly the same times, partly not.
   (c) No regular pattern. Times vary 1-2 hours or more.
2. (a) Generally wakes up at about same time from night and naps.
   (b) Partly the same times, partly not.
   (c) No regular pattern. Times vary 1-2 hours or more.
3. (a) Generally happy (smiling, etc.) on waking up and going to sleep.
   (b) Variable mood at these times.
   (c) Generally fussy on waking up and going to sleep.
4. (a) Moves about crib much (such as from one end to other) during sleep.
   (b) Moves a little (a few inches)
   (c) Lies fairly still. Usually in same position when awakens.
5. With change in time, place or state of health:
   (a) Adjusts easily and sleeps fairly well within 1-2 days.
   (b) Variable pattern.
   (c) Bothered considerably. Takes at least 3 days to readjust sleeping routine.

Feeding

6. (a) Generally takes milk at about same time. Not over 1 hour variation.
   (b) Sometimes same, sometimes different times.
   (c) Hungry times unpredictable.
7. (a) Generally takes about same amount of milk, not over 2 oz. difference.
   (b) Sometimes same, sometimes different amounts.
   (c) Amounts taken unpredictable.
8. (a) Easily distracted from milk feedings by noises, changes in place, or routine.
   (b) Sometimes distracted, sometimes not.
   (c) Usually goes on sucking in spite of distractions.
9. (a) Easily adjusts to parents' efforts to change feeding schedule within 1-2 tries.
   (b) Slowly (after several tries) or variable.
   (c) Adjusts not at all to such changes after several tries.
10. (a) If hungry and wants milk, will keep refusing substitutes (solids, water, pacifier) for many minutes.
    (b) Intermediate or variable.
    (c) Gives up within a few minutes and takes what is offered.
11. (a) With interruptions of milk or solid feedings, as for burping, is generally happy, smiles.
    (b) Variable response.
    (c) Generally cries with these interruptions.
12. (a) Always notices (and reacts to) change in temperature or type of milk or substitution of juice or water.
    (b) Variable.
    (c) Rarely seems to notice (and react to) such changes.
13. (a) Suck generally vigorous.
    (b) Intermediate.
    (c) Suck generally mild and intermittent.
14. (a) Activity during feedings—constant squirming, kicking, etc.
    (b) Some motion: intermediate.
    (c) Lies quietly throughout.
15. (a) Always cries loudly when hungry.
    (b) Cries somewhat but only occasionally hard or for many minutes.
    (c) Usually just whimpers when hungry, but doesn't cry loudly.
16. (a) Hunger cry usually stopped for at least a minute by picking up, pacifier, putting on bib, etc.
    (b) Sometimes can be distracted when hungry.
    (c) Nothing stops hunger cry.
17. (a) After feeding, baby smiles and laughs.
    (b) Content but not usually happy (smiles, etc.) or fussy.
    (c) Fussy and wants to be left alone.
18. (a) When full, clamps mouth closed, spits out food or milk, bats at spoon, etc.
    (b) Variable.
    (c) Just turns head away or lets food drool out of mouth.
19. (a) Initial reaction to new foods (solids, juices, vitamins) acceptance. Swallows them promptly without fussing.

       (b)   Variable response.

       (c)   Usually rejects new foods. Makes face, spits out, etc.

20.   (a)   Initial reaction to new foods pleasant (smiles, etc.), whether accepts or not.

       (b)   Variable or intermediate.

       (c)   Response unpleasant (cries, etc.), whether accepts or not.

21.   (a)   This response is dramatic whether accepting (smacks lips, laughs, squeals) or not (cries).

       (b)   Variable.

       (c)   This response mild whether accepting or not. Just smiles, makes face or no expression.

22.   (a)   After several feedings of any new food, accepts it.

       (b)   Accepts some, not others.

       (c)   Continues to reject most new foods after several tries.

23.   (a)   With changes in amounts, kinds, timing of solids does not seem to mind.

       (b)   Variable response. Sometimes accepts, sometimes not.

       (c)   Does not accept these changes readily.

24.   (a)   Easily notices and reacts to differences in taste and consistency.

       (b)   Variable

       (c)   Seems seldom to notice or react to these differences.

25.   (a)   If does not get type of solid food desired, keeps crying till gets it.

       (b)   Variable

       (c)   May fuss briefly but soon gives up and takes what offered.

Soiling and Wetting

26.   (a)   When having bowel movement, generally cries.

       (b)   Sometimes cries.

       (c)   Rarely cries though face may become red. Generally happy (smiles, etc.) in spite of having bowel movement (b.m.).

27.   (a)   Bowel movements generally at same time of day (usually within 1 hour of same time).

       (b)   Sometimes at same time, sometimes not.

       (c)   No pattern. Usually not same time.

28.   (a)   Generally indicates in some way that is soiled with b.m.

       (b)   Sometimes indicates.

       (c)   Seldom or never indicates.

29.   (a)   Usually fusses when diaper soiled with b.m.

       (b)   Sometimes fusses.

       (c)   Usually does not fuss.

30.   (a)   Generally indicates somehow that is wet (no b.m.)

       (b)   Sometimes indicates.

       (c)   Seldom or never indicates.

31.   (a)   Usually fusses when diaper wet (no b.m.)

       (b)   Sometimes fusses.

       (c)   Usually does not fuss.

32.   (a)   When fussing about diaper, does so loudly. A real cry.

       (b)   Variable.

(c)   Usually just a little whimpering.

33. (a)   If fussing about diaper, can easily be distracted for at least a few minutes by being picked up, etc.

      (b)   Variable.

      (c)   Nothing distracts baby from fussing.

Diapering and Dressing

34. (a)   Squirms and kicks much at these times.

      (b)   Moves some.

      (c)   Generally lies still during these procedures.

35. (a)   Generally pleasant (smiles, etc.) during diapering and dressing.

      (b)   Variable.

      (c)   Generally fussy during these times.

36. (a)   These feelings usually intense: vigorous laughing or crying.

      (b)   Variable.

      (c)   Mildly expressed usually. Little smiling or fussing.

Bathing

37. (a)   Usual reaction to bath: smiles or laughs.

      (b)   Variable or neutral.

      (c)   Usually cries or fusses.

38. (a)   Like or dislike of bath is intense. Excited.

      (b)   Variable or intermediate.

      (c)   Like or dislike is mild. Not excited.

39. (a)   Kicks, splashes and wiggles throughout.

      (b)   Intermediate—moves moderate amount.

      (c)   Lies quietly or moves little.

40. (a)   Reaction to very first tub (or basin) bath. Seemed to accept it right away.

      (c)   At first protested against bath.

41. (a)   If protested at first, accepted it after 2 or 3 times.

      (b)   Sometimes accepted, sometimes not.

      (c)   Continued to object even after two weeks.

42. (a)   If bath by different person or in different place, readily accepts change first or second time.

      (b)   May or may not accept.

      (c)   Objects consistently to such changes.

Procedures—Nail Cutting, Hair Brushing, Washing Face and Hair, Medicines

43. (a)   Initial reaction to any new procedure: generally acceptance.

      (b)   Variable.

      (c)   Generally objects; fusses or cries.

44. (a)   If initial objection, accepts after 2 or 3 times.

      (b)   Variable acceptance. Sometimes does, sometimes does not.

      (c)   Continues to object even after several times.

45.   (a)   Generally pleasant during procedures once established—smiles, etc.
         (b)   Neutral or variable.
         (c)   Generally fussy or crying during procedures.
46.   (a)   If fussy with procedures, easily distracted by game, toy, singing, etc., and stops fussing.
         (b)   Variable response to distractions.
         (c)   Not distracted. Goes on fussing.

Visits to Doctor

47.   (a)   With physical exam, when well, generally friendly and smiles.
         (b)   Both smiles and fusses: variable.
         (c)   Fusses most of time.
48.   (a)   With shots cries loudly for several minutes or more.
         (b)   Variable.
         (c)   Cry over in less than a minute.
49.   (a)   When crying from shot, easily distracted by milk, pacifier, etc.
         (b)   Sometimes distracted, sometimes not.
         (c)   Goes right on crying no matter what is done.

Response to Illness

50.   (a)   With any kind of illness, much crying and fussing.
         (b)   Variable.
         (c)   Not much crying with illnesses. Just whimpering sometimes. Generally his usual self.

Sensory—Reactions to Sounds, Light, Touch

51.   (a)   Reacts little or not at all to unusual loud sound or bright light.
         (b)   Intermediate or variable.
         (c)   Reacts to almost any change in sound or light.
52.   (a)   This reaction to light or sound is intense—startles or cries loudly.
         (b)   Intermediate—sometimes does, sometimes not.
         (c)   Mild reaction—little or no crying.
53.   (a)   On repeated exposure to these same lights or sounds, does not react so much any more.
         (b)   Variable.
         (c)   No change from initial negative reaction.
54.   (a)   If already crying about something else, light or sound makes crying stop briefly at least.
         (b)   Variable response.
         (c)   Makes no difference.

Responses to People

55.   (a)   Definitely notices and reacts to differences in people: age, sex, glasses, hats, other physical differences.

(b)   Variable reaction to differences.

(c)   Similar reactions to most people unless strangers.

56.   (a)   Initial reaction to approach by strangers positive, friendly (smiles, etc.).

(b)   Variable reaction.

(c)   Initial rejection or withdrawal.

57.   (a)   This initial reaction to strangers is intense: crying or laughing.

(b)   Variable.

(c)   Mild—frown or smile.

58.   (a)   General reaction to familiar people is friendly—smiles, laughs.

(b)   Variable reaction.

(c)   Generally glum or unfriendly. Little smiling.

59.   (a)   This reaction to familiar people is intense—crying or laughing.

(b)   Variable.

(c)   Mild—frown or smile.

Reaction to New Places and Situations

60.   (a)   Initial reaction acceptance—tolerates or enjoys them within a few minutes.

(b)   Variable.

(c)   Initial reaction rejection—does not tolerate or enjoy them within a few minutes.

61.   (a)   After continued exposure (several minutes) accepts these changes easily.

(b)   Variable.

(c)   Even after continued exposure, accepts changes poorly.

Play

62.   (a)   In crib or play pen can amuse self for half-hour or more looking at mobile, hands, etc.

(b)   Amuses self for variable length of time.

(c)   Indicates need for attention or new occupation after several minutes.

63.   (a)   Takes new toy right away and plays with it.

(b)   Variable.

(c)   Rejects new toy when first presented.

64.   (a)   If rejects at first, after short while (several minutes) accepts new toy.

(b)   Variable.

(c)   Adjusts slowly to new toy.

65.   (a)   Play activity involves much movement—kicking, waving arms, etc. Much exploring.

(b)   Intermediate.

(c)   Generally lies quietly while playing. Explores little.

66.   (a)   If reaching for toy out of reach, keeps trying for 2 minutes or more.

(b)   Variable.

(c)   Stops trying in less than ½ minute.

67.   (a)   When given a toy, plays with it for many minutes.

(b)   Variable.

(c)   Plays with one toy for only short time (only 1-2 minutes).

68.   (a)   When playing with one toy, easily distracted by another.
      (b)   Variable.
      (c)   Not easily distracted by another toy.
69.   (a)   Play usually accompanied by laughing, smiling, etc.
      (b)   Variable or intermediate.
      (c)   Generally fussy during play.
70.   (a)   Play is intense: much activity, vocalization or laughing.
      (b)   Variable or intermediate.
      (c)   Plays quietly and calmly.

Appendix II. Temperament Questionnaire—Scoring Sheet (x = no score; * = score in two categories). The responses on the questionnaire are transposed to this score sheet providing a total score of high, medium, or low for each dimension of temperament.

Item	Activity H	M	L	Rhythmicity R	V	I	Adaptability A	V	N	Approach A	V	W	Threshold H	M	L	Intensity I	V	M	Mood P	V	N	Distractibility D	V	N	Persistence P	V	N
1				a	b	c																					
2				a	b	c																					
3																			a	b	c						
4	a	b	c																								
5							a	b	c																		
6				a	b	c																					
7				a	b	c																					
8																						a	b	c			
9							a	b	c																		
10																									a	b	c
11																			a	b	c						
12													c	b	a												
13	a	b	c																								
14	a	b	c																								
15																a	b	c									
16																						a	b	c			
17																			a	b	c						
18																a	b	c									
19										a	b	c															
20																			a	b	c						
21																a	b	c									
22							a	b	c																		
23							a	b	c																		
24													c	b	a												
25																									a	b	c
26*																a	b	c	c	b	a						
27				a	b	c																					
28													c	b	a												
29																			x	b	a						
30													c	b	a												
31																			x	b	a						
32																a	b	c									
33																						a	b	c			
34	a	b	c																								
35*							a	b	c										a	b	c						
36																a	b	c									
37																			a	b	c						
38																a	b	c									
39	a	b	c																								

Appendix II. Temperament Questionnaire—Scoring Sheet (x = no score; * = score in two categories). The responses on the questionnaire are transposed to this score sheet providing a total score of high, medium, or low for each dimension of temperament. (Continued)

	Activity			Rhythmicity			Adaptability			Approach			Threshold			Intensity			Mood			Distractibility			Persistence		
	H	M	L	R	V	I	A	V	N	A	V	W	H	M	L	I	V	M	P	V	N	D	V	N	P	V	N
40										40 a	x	c															
							41 a	b	c																		
							42* a	b	c				42* a	b	c												
										43 a	b	c															
							44 a	b	c																		
																			45 a	b	c						
																						46 a	b	c			
							47* a	b	c										47* a	b	c						
																48 a	b	c									
																						49 a	b	c			
50																			50 c	b	a						
													51 a	b	c												
																52 a	b	c									
							53 a	b	c																		
																						54 a	b	c			
													55 c	b	a												
										56* a	b	c							56* a	b	c						
																57 a	b	c									
																			58 a	b	c						
																59 a	b	c									
60										60* a	b	c							60* a	b	c						
							61 a	b	c																		
																									62 a	b	c
										63 a	b	c															
							64 a	b	c																		
	65 a	b	c																								
																									66 a	b	c
																									67 a	b	c
																						68 a	b	c			
																			69 a	b	c						
																70 a	b	c									
TOTAL																											

CHAPTER 15

Clinical Experience with Efforts to Define Individual Differences in Temperament

Grace S. Gregg

The role of the pediatrician has undergone drastic change. Today he is less often called on to perform the traditional duties of diagnosing and prescribing for children with life-threatening organic illnesses than in previous times; more of his time is devoted to parents who question the normalcy of their children's growth, intellectual and emotional development, and their personal adequacy in child rearing. This role change has been attributed to the loss of cultural guidelines usually available to young families in more stable societies, and as a consequence they require much professional counseling in regard to parenting. Since the situation will in all likelihood intensify, the pediatrician cannot anticipate relief from the role of family counselor unless he chooses to relegate this responsibility to other professionals, a complicated and questionable solution.

Traditional pediatric training prepares the pediatrician to manage the problems of sick children; his reference point is the clinical laboratory, which provides the biochemical data required to solve the problems with which he is comfortable. In this respect, pediatric training programs fail to adequately prepare young physicians for practices that will consist largely of normal children and their concerned parents. When the pediatrician deals with normal children the clinical laboratory is of very little value except to confirm what he already knows, since screening tests are notoriously unproductive. As he moves further into the behavioral area, less and less data is available, and often he founders pitifully or forges ahead unwittingly in a sincere desire to fullfil his unexpected role. Since watered-down psychiatric approaches usually are a failure in his hands, other methods are urgently needed to give him a better grasp on his counseling role with mothers and infants.

It has been our impression that the young pediatrician will respond to formal training in the behavioral sciences. For this reason we were intrigued with the research of Thomas, Chess, and Birch (1963) who first systematically measured the temperamental individuality of infants. Here, we felt, was an opportunity to develop "a measure" of the child along another dimension. Physical condition, growth, intelligence, and temperamental individuality might be handled as equally important data which the pediatrician could understand and learn to use effectively in counseling parents.

First we will describe our experience with the Thomas, Chess, and Birch research interview in The Infant Accident Study. Then we will mention the use of the direct-observation method in two clinical studies of children who survived fetal transfusion and children with Down's Syndrome. Finally we will describe our efforts to refine a direct-observation technique for use in the pediatrician's office.

THE INFANT ACCIDENT STUDY

In 1964 a group at the Children's Hospital of Pittsburgh began to study mother-infant pairs in a research project, The Infant Accident Study (1964). The project was a continuation of a retrospective study of the families of children who had sustained multiple skeletal injuries in infancy. In the second phase of the study we concentrated on babies 13 months of age or younger who had been injured either by accident or by abuse, or who were failing to thrive because of deprived environments.

The children in the first study were evaluated years after the injuries occurred. The influence of intracranial trauma, deprivation, and removal from the home, in addition to the effect of time made it impossible to even speculate about their temperament at the time of the injuries in infancy. Their physical condition was documented in old medical records, and their retarded development was apparent when they were reevaluated, but without a method to study infant temperament, only anecdotal material was available for judging their behavior. The description of the child who cried excessively, whose appetite never was satisfied, who regurgitated everything he ate and then demanded refeeding, who was perceived as "evil" or "mean" by his mother raised important unanswered questions: Were these the "difficult babies" described by Thomas, Chess, and Birch? Might they have been so difficult that their mothers in nurturing them assumed deviant child-care patterns? The Thomas, Chess, and Birch formulations appealed to us as a possible method of measuring the temperamental characteristics of neglected and abused babies in an effort to answer these questions.

We set out to identify the temperamental characteristics of each baby who entered The Infant Accident Study using the interviewing technique and scoring the results according to the method used by the original Thomas, Chess, and Birch group. We hypothesized that the abused infants would be outstandingly "difficult" and that the babies who had maneuvered themselves into accidents would display high activity levels. We then began to question whether the abusive mother perceives her baby realistically and if not, whether the interview would be valid. Was it possible that the abused baby was no more difficult than most babies but was merely perceived by his mother as more harassing? In order to answer this question, we developed an observation rating of each baby at the time of the pediatric examination to compare with the interview results. If there were discrepancies between how the mother described the baby and how he was when we observed him, a difficult mother-infant relationship leading to neglect and abuse might have existed. Furthermore, as a spin-off, it might be possible to refine a simple observational method, side-stepping the lengthy interview which we are certain the pediatrician could never put to practical use in a clinical setting.

The categories of behavior which we assessed by the clinic observational method were activity, mood, approach, and distractibility. Adaptability and rhythmicity were not applicable since they depend on behavior rated over a time period. We found that threshold to stimuli was too difficult to measure in an unpredictably noisy clinical setting; and we were unable to consistently and reliably differentiate between persistence and distractibility. Intensity seemed so closely correlated with mood that we decided to score them together. All such decisions were made after considerable clinical trial and error. Three behavioral appraisals were derived for each child: one which resulted from interviewing the mother within two weeks of the time of the injury, another from observation of the baby as close to the time of the injury as was feasible considering his physical condition, and a follow-up observation at the time of the pediatric reevaluation one year later. Interobserver reliability was established for scoring the interview material as well as for the observation.

The sequences during which we assessed the baby's behavior by observation in the clinic were:

1. In the research coordinator's office.
2. When the mother and baby first entered the examining room of the pediatrician.
3. On the mother's lap while she was interviewed by the pediatrician.
4. When the baby was placed in the infant seat or feeding table.
5. When the baby was presented with a toy.
6. During the pediatric examination.
   a. Examination of the abdomen.
   b. Examination of the thorax.
   c. Examination of the head and neck including the oral cavity and ears.
7. During weighing.
8. During redressing by the mother.

The conditions for the observations were as nearly as possible the same for all: each of the eight sequences was designed to last no less and no more than a specified period of time, and one pediatrician performed all examinations, utilizing the same examining room and maintaining uniform lighting and furniture arrangements.

In the analysis of data, we compared nonabused boys with girls as to predominant mood. Roughly half the boys were predominantly positive, and half were predominantly negative. At the time of the second evaluation when the children were a year older, the mood distribution of the boys had not changed, while that of the girls showed a sharp swing to positive mood.

When we compared the mood of the abused boys with that of the nonabused, we found a marked preponderance of negative mood. When the mood of the abused girls was compared with the nonabused, we found a predominance of positive mood. However, the abused girls were significantly more advanced developmentally, and thus, we might have been measuring an effect of increasing age on mood rather than the effect of abuse on mood. Distractibility seemed associated throughout with developmental retardation, raising the question of the effect of negative mood and distractibility on test scores. Since some of these babies were black, one might also speculate about the reaction of the black child to a white woman examiner as well as to the unaccustomed environment of the hospital. This effect might explain the racial differences in approach-withdrawal scores, also, since the white babies scored predominantly positive in approach while the black babies of both sexes were observed to withdraw.

The nonabusive mothers usually described their babies as positive, and in most instances the observational scores were concordant with the interview scores. However, some mothers whose babies were described by them as positive were found by our observational method to be predominantly negative. The white mothers appeared to be invested in presenting their babies in the most favorable light. By contrast, 5 of the 14 abusive mothers described their babies as predominantly negative. We scored only 2 of these as negative by the observational method; the other 3 by observation were positive, thus suggesting that their mothers were less inclined to present their babies positively and possibly were less perceptive to their true temperament.

All the children who were positive in both mood and distractibility were also positive in approach. This constellation of traits fit the "easy baby" description. Their comparatively high mental scores may have resulted in part from their interested involvement in the testing situation and their eagerness to perform well. In contrast, the negative babies tended to score lower. Negativity adds to the difficulty in testing a young baby and may obscure his true potential. However, a baby who spends most of his day in reacting negatively to life experiences is depriving himself of many of the learning opportunities available to the more positive baby.

We analyzed the babies' temperamental characteristics in relation to the accident history. A large group of babies had maneuvered themselves into accident situations. They had collided with objects, fallen down stairs, and climbed to dangerous heights. These babies tended to be highly active, negative, and difficult to distract, as we had hypothesized. In general, their mothers perceived them as active as they truly were, but they still were unable to completely protect them from injury. The other accident babies seemed to vary through the range of activity, mood, and distractibility; their accidents seemed to be more a function of developmental age than of a unique temperamental pattern. Even the babies who accidentally rolled off elevated surfaces were not more active than other babies, either by interview or observation.

Several of the babies of The Infant Accident Study were predominantly neglected rather than abused. They were chronically ill, having failed to thrive in both growth and development. Many had been premature by weight, and their growth had not caught up. Some may have suffered from intrauterine growth retardation and thus were born with a lower potential to grow and develop. As a group they were less active, less intense, and their moods were bland. In such cases, it is impossible to know whether one is tapping poor physical and mental status rather than temperamental characteristics. Interestingly, many of their mothers described the babies in very negative terms, perhaps expressing personal disappointment in the baby's failure to thrive rather than his real temperament.

Our experience with the interviewing method convinced us that drastic modification unquestionably was necessary before it could be used as a clinical tool. The busy practitioner must utilize his working hours to the best advantage. As Carey points out, the interview consumes more than an hour under the most favorable circumstances, and scoring the protocol is a major chore, hardly a task for a clinician (Carey, 1970). Hiring a scorer would elevate the cost of the method prohibitively.

Over and above these very real physician-economic problems, we found that the less intelligent mothers could not describe their babies in words which could be scored since their own language skills were remarkably impoverished. Although our interviewers were skilled in psychiatric interviewing and in the special technique of the behavioral interview, in many instances we could not elicit sufficiently rich scorable responses. Therefore, we concluded that the interview method is not applicable to all mothers.

Another problem arose when we encountered babies whose natural mothers shared the care of the baby with others. Many babies had several part-time mothers—sometimes a grandmother, a teen-age aunt, or a girlfriend of the mother. No one person could supply a total picture of the baby, therefore limiting the use of the interview in another dimension.

On the other hand, the observation method seemed more promising, especially since it could be carried out by the pediatrician when performing his traditional duties. Even here, however, we were aware that the scoring method would require simplification so that an office aide could use it without much training. Eventually we hoped to restrict the time of observation to the segment of the pediatric visit which was most likely to reveal the baby's characteristic temperament.

CHILDREN WHO SURVIVED INTRAUTERINE TRANSFUSIONS

A group of 15 babies who had survived fetal transfusions performed as a life-saving procedure in serious hemolytic disease of the newborn secondary to Rh-factor incompatibility were seen in follow-up and their temperamental characteristics were scored by the observational method described above (Gregg and Hutchinson, 1969).

We rated activity, mood and intensity, and approach. We did not attempt to interview the mothers in depth but merely asked them to rate their babies in regard to activity, mood, intensity, approach, rhythmicity, adaptability, threshold, persistence, and distractibility. All babies were living in middle-class families, with two exceptions. The mothers, by virture of their decision to undergo the obstetrical procedures necessary to produce a baby who otherwise would have died, had registered their personal value for the child. They were deeply invested in the child's development and all were experienced in child care since each had more than one other living child.

We were interested in studying the children to learn the effects of severe antenatal and perinatal stress on growth and development. If there were no "hard" neurological signs, no mental retardation, and no epilepsy, we expected the children would show "soft" neurological signs combined with the hyperkinetic brain dysfunction syndrome. Both from the mothers' report and by our observation, the children as a group tended to be "easy" babies; only two of the children were clearly "difficult." Interestingly these two were boys who had evidence of brain damage manifested by "soft" neurological signs. In spite of massive perinatal stress, the children had done well. Temperament in general seemed not to have been affected.

In this study it was necessary to use a measure of behavior which would add depth to the classic developmental neurological examination and formal psychological testing, since we were searching for subtle central nervous system dysfunctioning. It was our impression that the combination of parent interviewing and direct observation was successful in eliciting information which was replicable, since it was based on data rather than on subjective global impressions.

DOWN'S SYNDROME STUDY

A group of 12 mothers of babies with Down's Syndrome ranging in age from 6 to 24 months were asked to respond to the Carey questionnaire (Baron, 1971). It was our hypothesis that these babies would be "easy babies" based on time-honored indoctrination that the Down's Syndrome child is affable, pleasant, easy-going, and of low activity. Among these 12 babies, there seemed to be no common behavioral profile which sets them apart as a group and the range of temperament is much like that of normal middle-class babies. We assume that there is no personality type characteristic of Trisomy 21 that can be distinguished by the Carey questionnaire. From our clinical experience with many Down's Syndrome babies, we would speculate that this is a valid result rather than questionnaire insensitivity to subtle temperamental differences.

DEVELOPMENT OF A DIRECT CLINICAL OBSERVATIONAL METHOD

Our goals were directed toward simplifying the observational method by working with a homogeneous healthy middle-class population of infants and later to correlate the results of the observational method with the results obtained from the Carey questionnaire completed by the mother at the time of the pediatric visit (Laufman, 1971). Therefore, we continued our work with the observational method through two medical students who studied the temperament of well babies brought to their private physicians for a routine physical examination. The methodology and recommendations for further study are presented here as a preliminary note pending later publication.

Clinical Observation Rating Scale

All observations were made by one of two observers during a routine pediatric examination. Each observation consisted of four segments which routinely occurred despite variable office procedures among pediatricians. These segments consisted of the following: *undress* (two-minute period while mother undresses infant), *initial contact* (pediatrician's first contact with infant), *examination* (physical examination, divided into subsegments of thorax, abdomen, ears, and mouth), and *dress* (two-minute period while mother dresses infant after examination). Because variation occurred among the office routines of different pediatricians the *examination* segment was the observation period that was most consistently structured.

NAME _____ SEX ___ BIRTHDATE _____ OBSERVER _____

PEDIATRICIAN _____ AGE _____ HISTORY _____

			UNDRESS	INITIAL CONTACT	EXAM				EXAM TOTAL	DRESS
					THORAX	ABDOMEN	EARS	MOUTH		
ACTIVITY	HIGH	CLIMB								
		LUNGE								
		ROLL OVER								
		SQUIRM								
		KICK								
		BANG, HIT								
		GRAB								
		TOTAL HIGH (H)								
	MODERATE	SIT UP								
		FIDGET								
		TURN HEAD								
		GRASP								
		PUSH, PULL								
		WAVE, REACH								
		TOTAL MODERATE (M)								
	LOW	FINGER								
		HAND TO FACE								
		EXPRESSION								
		STILL								
		TOTAL LOW (L)								
		ACTIVITY RATING $\frac{2L+M}{L+M+H}$								
MOOD		POSITIVE (P)								
		NEGATIVE (N)								
		MOOD RATING $\frac{2N}{P+N}$								
DISTRACTIBILITY		DISTRACTIBILITY (S)				DISTRACTIBILITY (U)				
		DISTRACTIBILITY RATING $\frac{2U}{S+U+1}$								

Figure 1. Clinical Behavioral Observation Scoresheet.

A copy of the scoresheet identical to the sample is provided (Figure 1). The column headings denote the segments and subsegments of observation. The first grid is used for activity. The second grid is used for facial and vocal expressions of mood. If the infant receives an injection immediately before the dress segment, he is usually very negative unless the mother intervenes and successfully distracts him. For this reason mood was not observed during dress. Distractibility observations were recorded at the bottom of the score sheet. Unlike mood and activity, distractibility was observed continuously and was not limited to the segments defined. The observer scores distractibility only when an attempt has been made to divert the infant's attention or redirect his actions. When an attempt is made to distract the baby, the observer checks either the distractibility positive or negative column.

All ratings range from 0 to 2, the same scales used by Thomas and Carey. A rating is developed as the weighted average of the checkmark totals of each classification relative to that behavioral characteristic.

Activity

Each infant receives four activity ratings, one for each observation segment. High, moderate, and low activity totals are calculated for each segment and are weighted by factors of 0, 1, and 2, respectively. Each weighted total is divided by the total number of events recorded in that segment, yielding the activity rating.

Mood

Each infant receives two mood ratings, one each for the undress and examination segments. The examination subsegment ratings are calculated separately and then averaged. For each subsegment or segment, the positive and negative totals are calculated and are weighted by the factors of 0 and 2, respectively. Each weighted total is divided by the total number of mood indications observed during the subsegment or segment, yielding the mood rating. A rating of 1.0 is arbitrarily assigned any segment or subsegment in which no mood indication was given.

Approach/Withdrawal

This rating is calculated from the mood indications of the initial contact segment, using the same procedure described for mood.

Distractibility

One overall rating is obtained. The successful and unsuccessful distractions are totaled and weighted by the factors of 0 and 2, respectively. The weighted total is divided by the number of distraction attempts plus one. This factor of one is added to the denominator so that ratings derived solely from unsuccessful distraction attempts may be differentiated.

The Sample

The sample consisted of 81 infants, 47 males and 34 females, ranging in age from 8 to 12 months. Infants with a history of serious illness, hospitalization, or prematurity were not included. Observations were made in the offices of 18 pediatricians. The distribution was unequal, with 19 infants examined by one pediatrician and only one by each of seven pediatricians.

Results

Effects of Variables

In the analysis of variables, the activity and mood ratings of the examination segment were used because this segment was the most consistently structured.

Interobserver reliability was found to be highly positive. Average ratings for each behavioral characteristic were calculated by one-month age groupings, and each age group was found to differ from all other groups and from the whole sample by only random variation (see Figure 2).

Separate averages were calculated for males and females within the same one-month age groupings. With the exception of the nine-month-old approach ratings where the male/female difference was significant, the differences between male and female ratings were found to represent chance variation for all characteristics and ages.

When the data were analyzed in regard to individual pediatricians, a significant difference was found among the approach/withdrawal ratings, indicating that each pediatrician must compute average values for his own infant population.

Frequency Distributions

Figure 3 shows the frequency distributions for ratings of the four behavioral characteristics for all infants, again using the examination ratings for activity and mood.

The frequency distribution for activity ratings shows a unimodal curve with a mode between 1.0 and 1.25. Such ratings correspond to moderate activity scores. Note that relatively few ratings are above 1.25, e.g., low activity. The distribution of the mood ratings is skewed to the left, showing a high proportion of very negative ratings. This finding should not surprise anyone who has observed a howling 8-12 month old infant subjected to the rigors of a pediatric

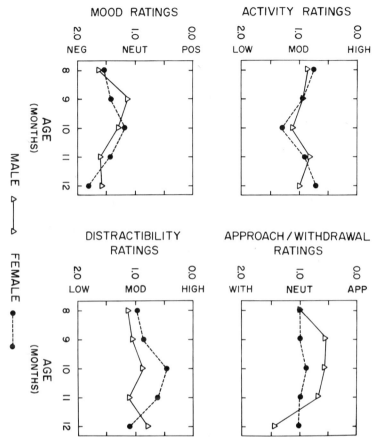

Figure 2. Average ratings on Clinical Behavioral Observation instrument indicating little variation because of age and sex.

examination. The approach/withdrawal rating distribution is polymodal with modes at 0.0, 1.0, and 2.0, corresponding respectively to approach, neutrality, and withdrawal. Since approach/withdrawal is observed only during the physician's initial contact with the infant, only one reaction is generally seen. The highest mode is at 1.0, showing that more infants react neutrally. The distractibility frequency shows a unimodal curve, with mode between 1.0 and 1.25, indicating moderate distractibility.

The examination activity rating was compared to the three other activity ratings. Generally the examination rating was higher than the initial contact rating and lower than the undress rating. Examination and dress ratings were equal. Thus one should expect an infant's highest activity as the mother undresses him, and the lowest as the pediatrician first approaches him.

A comparison of the infant's two mood ratings shows, as expected, more negative mood during examination than during undress.

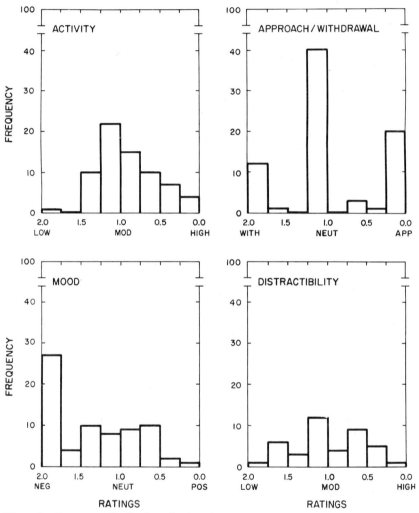

Figure 3.   Frequency distribution of ratings for each characteristic on Clinical Behavioral
Observation instrument.

318

Just as Thomas and Carey discovered the clustering of several traits, we discovered relationships among our four characteristics. Generally, negative mood, withdrawal, high activity, and low distractibility were found in the same children. One can readily picture the screaming child who lunges away from the pediatrician's first contact, and who cannot be soothed or distracted.

We have continued to refine the observational method. Recently we sent questionnaires to 84 mothers of healthy babies asking them to complete the questionnaire within a few days of a scheduled well-baby visit. We modified the questions in an attempt to circumvent built-in bias and to fit the developmental age of 8-12 months. The babies were observed with their mothers while in the same office undergoing routine physical examination by the same pediatrician. Thus, we hope to minimize the effect of variables created by individual pediatrician differences. The analysis of data has not been completed. However, preliminary study shows a trend also followed in The Infant Accident Study for middle-class white mothers to present a rosy picture of infant behavior which could not always be substantiated by direct observation. Also, many babies sharply reduced the amount of physical activity when the pediatrician approached the examining table. It is possible they were searching an unfamiliar face hoping to find a memory match, as has been described by many observers studying looking behavior in infancy. Most babies, however, became more active and intensely negative as the physical examination proceeded. The final analysis of the data will take into consideration variables such as mother's level of education and previous experience in mothering with the expectation that further light will be shed on the confusing results of the first analysis.

DISCUSSION

The observation technique has several advantages. It is easy to use and does not disrupt the pediatrician's office routine. The time necessary for rating an observation is usually one to two minutes, making the results immediately available for counseling. The source of the behavioral information is the infant himself. No allowances need be made for middleman misinterpretations, and the mother's cooperation in completing or returning a questionnaire is not required. Usually the pediatrician sees the child frequently enough in the first two years to obtain several ratings, thus minimizing the chance of overestimating a rating obtained on a single "cranky" day. In essence the child creates his own longitudinal study. The observation segments undress and examination appear to be most valid since by virtue of their structure, they produce comparable data in both content and quantity.

There are also disadvantages to the observation method. It is often difficult to know whether the child who rates very negative by the observational method is by temperament a highly negative child or simply reacting intensely and negatively to a strange environment. Also, certain behavioral characteristics which depend on change over time cannot be rated by a short observation. At least one of these, adaptability, is considered to be crucial in the "difficult child" profile. Yet material to rate this characteristic can be derived only from the interview or questionnaire. The questionnaire is at present applicable to only the four to eight month age group. Also the options for parental response to the questions often imply a "good" or "bad" judgment so that internal bias may be operating.

Additional study will be necessary before either method can be adapted as a standard office procedure. Probably the best assessment of infant behavior will be obtained from the use of a combination of questionnaire and observation.

We recommend that the pediatrician try out both the Carey questionnaire and the observational method. The questionnaire provides considerable useful information about the baby which the pediatrician can utilize in counseling. It also organizes the mother's perception of the baby's behavior. Most intelligent mothers profit from the type of structure imposed by the questions and they then begin to view the baby's reactions along a continuum. In regard to the observation, the pediatrician using the check list also will profit from its structure by specifically noting the baby's reactions at comparable stages of the physical examination. We observed that some pediatricians provoke more negative and intense reactions than others. Thus, it will be necessary for each pediatrician to study his own population in order to judge how he is effecting baby behavior.

In our own work with retarded and handicapped children we have been impressed with the value of rating temperamental individuality in addition to performing a developmental neurological examination. The wide range of behavior in infants with Down's Syndrome has been described above. Some mothers disbelieved the diagnosis because they had been told by professionals that their babies would be listless, unresponsive, and placid. When they did not conform to the prototype, they shopped from one facility to another hoping to find a more favorable prognosis. Also, some mothers with severely brain-damaged infants, who were hypotonic and unresponsive and for whom the outlook was virtually hopeless, were overstimulating the babies to the detriment of their personal emotional well-being and the functioning of the family unit. Such mothers were able to relax their efforts and lower their frustration when a realistic interpretation of the baby's behavior was made. Other examples become clear to the pediatrician as he applies the techniques.

SUMMARY

How the observational method or the interview method or a combination of the two ultimately will be utilized depends on whether a pediatrician is concerned about his limitations in dealing with behavioral disorders and recognizes the need for a simple method for assessing the temperament of young babies for counseling purposes. Generally, pediatricians are becoming more aware of the need for behavioral as well as growth and developmental norms.

If the physician shortage further shifts the role of the pediatrician to supervision of paraprofessionals who are administering actual care, counseling of parents will become more directive. A method based on temperamental individuality can be applied by mental health workers of all derivations in dealing with families who do not have access to more involved methods of remediation. If applied to young families as anticipatory mental health guidance, later serious emotional problems occurring when interactional styles are difficult to alter might be circumvented.

In order to successfully fulfill his role, the pediatrician must understand that it is by early counseling that mutual respect between parent and child is established and maintained. Such counseling to be truly effective must be based on meaningful interpretation of the behavioral style of the infant. Psychotherapy rarely changes parents quickly enough to be beneficial to the rapidly developing infant.

The pediatrician must be convinced that individual differences in infants are present and can be consistently measured. Refined inventories are needed for this purpose. Probably the research oriented practicing pediatrician is the key person to develop them. Furthermore, the pediatrician must be convinced that the mother-infant dyad forms an inseparable interactional system, the least modifiable component of which is the infant. On the other hand, if wisely counseled, the intelligent parent often can monitor his emotional reactions to the infant as well as child-care practices in order to allow for individual differences.

REFERENCES

Baron, J. (1972). Temperament profile of children with Down's syndrome. *Developmental Medicine and Child Neurology*, **14**, 640.

Carey, W. B. (1970). A simplified method for measuring infant temperament. *The Journal of Pediatrics,* **77**, 188-194.

Gregg, G. S. and Hutchinson, D. L. (1969). Developmental characteristics of infants surviving fetal transfusion. *Journal of the American Medical Association*, **209**, 1059.

Laufman, L. and Klein, A. (1971). *A practical method of rating infant behavior.* In preparation.

Thomas, A., Chess, S., and Birch, H. G. (1963). *Temperamental individuality in early childhood.* New York: New York University Press.

"The infant accident study" (1964). Continuation of "Neglected and abused children and their families," Public Health Service Research Grant No. 5 R 01 MH 14739-06, The National Institute of Mental Health.

CHAPTER 16

Significance of the Individual Difference Approach

Jack C. Westman

At this point in time three powerful forces spur general interest in the life courses of individual persons. The most compelling is a public desire to prevent mental illness and promote mental health. The second is the knowledge gained from psychoanalysis linking problems in later life with experience during the early years. The third is the influence of existential philosophy stressing the unique way in which each person views himself and his world. The combined effect, then, of public interest in preventing mental disorder, of scientific recognition of the importance of childhood, and of philosophical emphasis on individual experience creates an unusually favorable climate for research on individuality in children.

Broadly examining the currents of Western civilization, we now find ourselves in an epoch which stresses the similarities among members of the human race. We have moved from class-conscious stress on human superiority and inferiority to a current emphasis on universal human needs and capacities. In fact, at the present time, mention of innate differences may evoke fear of regression to the prejudices of previous times. Nonetheless, it is likely that we are on the threshold of a new era which, having established human similarities, can now proceed to identify the unique qualities of each individual.

From another point of view, any developing science first establishes common features in any population whether it be a population of molecules or of human beings, in order to distinguish categories of things that resemble each other. After finding clusters reflecting similarities, the science moves to the next stage of predicting change in individual units resulting from known interventions by learning how to describe these units and follow them over time. It is possible that child-development research has moved past the first phase of a science by achieving the base needed in understanding the common ingredients of being human. The theoretical contributions of Piaget (Phillips, 1969) and Erickson

(1963) have refined the observations of Gesell and Ilg (1946), and others and now provide a coherent framework for the application of psychoanalytic and child development knowledge.

As the authors of this volume have demonstrated, there also is a range of methodologies which makes it possible to apply psychophysiological, participant observational, and inferential techniques to the study of children in real-life situations, whether it be in a newborn nursery, in a nursery school, or in a home. We are now prepared to describe behavior at the present and predict to behavior at a later time. In the past we have been able to do this for groups of individuals, for example, the maternally deprived and the prematurely born; now we stand on the threshold of predicting to the future of individuals.

BREAKTHROUGHS IN THE STUDY OF INDIVIDUALS

The recent contributions of research and clinical experience with individual differences flow from a growing tendency to abandon the mind-body dichotomy, which for so long has hindered the study of children as they naturally live. The mind-body distinction was a pragmatic philosophical device which led to the separate development of the behavioral sciences and the biological sciences. However, the blind alleys resulting from the study of fragments of people are now apparent, and the time is ripe for the holistic study of naturally occurring human events.

Because of awareness that observer bias is an important contaminant in the behavioral sciences, great efforts in the past were made to achieve objectivity through testing, examining, and obtaining historical information on individuals in vitro, either in clinical, laboratory, or child-study-center settings. Furthermore, the tenor of early work on individual differences in children implied that only innate differences between individuals could be studied because of the extreme complexity of experiential factors. Past research also tended to focus on normal characteristics as distinct from pathological characteristics and attempted to achieve precise, detailed descriptions of personalities and behavior.

By and large, the focus over the years has shifted away from in vitro studies to in vivo studies, using participant observers, who are parts of living systems, in order to develop naturalistic pictures of actual life situations. As illustrations, in vivo studies, particularly those of Escalona and Heinecke, now permit us to describe transactions between children and their mothers. This capacity to deal with in vivo material represents a significant step forward from the use of artificially devised screening and testing procedures which have characterized most research in differential psychology and child development. The major limitation of previous research was the lack of transfer from testing in a clinic or child-study institute to behavior encountered in real life. We now, in effect, have moved from the laboratory to life situations.

In addition there has been a decline by age in research attention to small children and infants, recognizing that the longer a person lives, the more complicated his cognitive structure, personality, and life situation become. As Escalona (1969) points out, individual differences in infants were ignored for a long time. They ultimately were studied because infants are accessible for research purposes, as in neonatal nurseries; infants are less complicated than older children, and the form of biological givens are potentially more obvious because less time has elapsed for the appearance of experiential influences.

Two breakthroughs, then, have occurred in research on individual differences in the form of increased confidence in *participant observers* as reporters of that which they are experiencing and the direct study of *early life*. All of this leads to the characterization of recent studies of individual differences as follows: a specific individual is described in his natural life setting using a range of methods for the purpose of obtaining naturalistic pictures of that individual of sufficient precision to permit predictions about future behavior patterns.

A third theoretical breakthrough has been the ability to link behavioral *observations* with behavioral *determinants*. This capacity has breathed life into hitherto sterile and voluminous recordings of unrelated and isolated pieces of behavior. As the work of Heinicke reflects, the ability to make interpretive statements about observed behavior in a developmental framework sets the stage for connecting both intrapsychic and manifest behavioral phenomena over time.

CURRENT TRENDS IN INDIVIDUAL DIFFERENCE RESEARCH

The recent studies of individual differences in personality rest on the assumptions that an individual child is a subject suitable for scientific study, that he is unique in both his constitution and experience, and that his personality maintains continuity in time as he passes through successive developmental stages.

The methods employed rely upon direct observation by participant-observers of behavior in natural contexts and solicitation of information about behavior from persons who are part of the individual's natural context (e.g., parents and teachers).

The purposes of the studies are fourfold:

1. Descriptive. The first is to generate a description of an individual which is recognizable as the behavioral equivalent of a portrait. The goal of the description is to capture the uniqueness of the individual, not his resemblance to other individuals at that particular maturational phase or in that particular experiential context. The features sought as elements in the description may well be common to many individuals, but in the gestalt aspect of their integration may be found the particularization. In other words, behaviors or patterns of behaviors that serve as a "signature" of the individual are sought. One of the early goals of this kind of research is to develop economical ways to create descriptions based upon objective observation rather than conjecture--how much, what kind, and in what form information must be presented to convey a picture of the individual.

2. Predictive. From the description, which is the external form of the understanding of what that individual is, it should be possible to predict the behavior or state of that individual in probable future settings and relationships. It is in the nature of this kind of study that each description can be related to a later description, the validity of the experiment resting upon the success of these predictions.

3. Clinical Application. One of the desires of our society, improved mental health for particular individuals, may be served by this process. Since the description and prediction deliberately apply to only one individual in his own context, it should be possible to prevent, avoid, or minimize future difficulties by altering the context and setting of that individual person (cf. the implications of Escalona's work for day-care programs).

4. Cultural Spin Off. If the assumptions of uniqueness are accepted, and the values of uniqueness (i.e., unequalness) nurtured, there can be changes in the treatment of children by those influential figures who move in their orbit—parents, siblings, teachers, therapists, and others (cf. the utility of Chess's formulations in parent counseling). We suspect that, in sum, such changes could alleviate suffering, enhance development of some individuals or some traits of some individuals, and provide a general cultural setting in which a wider range of behavior is acceptable and, hence, tolerated.

WHAT IS MEANT BY INDIVIDUAL DIFFERENCES?

The whole thrust of interest in individual differences rests on identifying qualities, or *dimensions,* upon which differences between children can be measured. Arriving at a useful definition of what is meant by individual differences, or variations, is not as easy as it might seem. The critical question is *variation in what?* One way to clarify this question is to adopt a multilevel general system scheme which permits a coherent description of structures and functions at the molecular, cell, organ, organism, interpersonal, and societal levels. If these levels are not recognized, one is bogged down in reconciling descriptions of genetic variations in molecular structure with descriptions at another system level of interactions between a mother and child. With a multilevel conception we can sensibly limit comparisons of factors to those operating on the same system level. We can talk about variations in skin sensitivity in infants, body physique, facial appearance, genital size, differences in approach-withdrawal behavior between an infant and mother, and even differences in separation anxiety between two girls and their mothers in a nursery-school experience. Each of these phenomena represents a different system level of concern.

A general system theory model which takes into account both change over time and multilevel factors in space is required. From the point of view of development, one can identify predispositions, using Escalona's framework, and dispositions in subsequent stages. From the spatial point of view one can range from ecological considerations through social, psychological, individual, and organ systems. In so doing we can focus our attention on naturally occurring transactional units, whether they are at the molecular or interpersonal level. To illustrate, let us consider individual variations at the molecular level.

At the moment of human conception a unique array of gene material is combined, and encoded in its sequence of submolecular units as the basic information that will be expressed in the human being that is to be. Our present knowledge of genetic codes, the enormous number of bits of information in each molecular strand within the chromosome, and the number of possible, viable variations of any gene locus make it evident that a fertilized ovum is unique. Human biological individuality is present from the first instant (Dobzhansky, 1962).

The extraordinary power of molecular biology has revealed many of the elements and processes by which information is stored in molecules of desoxyribonucleic acid and expressed in the multitude of molecular entities that are organized in the functioning organism. The precision and complexity of the process that translates the genetic code is such that it unerringly proceeds to develop a species-specific organism. It ultimately influences structure at each level of organization—whether molecular, subcellular, tissue, organ, or organism. Only human morphology and activity can derive from human biochemical machinery. Thus, it is not within the repertoire of human biochemistry to synthesize vitamin B_{12}, because the requisite enzymes are not present; neither is it within the human range to consciously perceive differences in magnetic field or to regenerate a lost limb. These constraints can be detected in statistical universals—no human being shows these structures or functions.

With careful progression up the system ladder, molecular differences can be related to organ dysfunction, organism defects, and behavioral effects. Those human features characteristic of the species are equally universal within the species, whether it is an enzyme pathway, upright stature, affective drive, or smiling. Within these limits is a wide range of qualitative and quantitative differences resulting from known chromosomal variations, as in the presence or absence of skin melanin (black versus albino), an enzyme lack (phenylketo-nuria), or the Y chromosome (male versus female).

The problem in establishing logical stepwise links between system levels is illustrated by the historically important concept of constitution. Montague's (1962) definition merits direct quotation:

> Constitution is the sum total of the structural, functional, and psychological characteristics of the organism. It is in large measure an integral of genetic potentialities influenced in varying degrees by internal and external environmental factors. . .there is little that is final about constitution as a process rather than an unchanging entity. In brief, it is important to understand at the outset that constitution is not a biological constant, a structure predestined by its genotype. The manner in which the genotype functions is determined by the interaction of the genotype with the environment in which it undergoes development. The outcome of this interaction will be expressed as the organism's constitution.

FINDING DIMENSIONS ON WHICH TO MEASURE VARIATIONS

After establishing the system level of concern, the next step, then, is to identify a dimension that can be described at one point in time and related to another dimension or to itself at another point in time. This permits prediction. The dimension may be either *structural* (morphological-static) or *functional* (action-changing), although distinguishing structure-static and function-changing is, strictly speaking, inaccurate and overlooks the actual unity of time, space, and matter. In fact, the properties of structure and function are inseparable in any living organism, divisible only as we arbitrarily, or of necessity, choose to consider one or the other feature. As an illustration, hormone action can be studied and thought about independently of glandular structure, but when the gland itself is intact and operating, its function of producing hormones is inevitable. Similarly, mental activity, the function of the central nervous system, does not exist apart from its structural basis. Viewed in this light, separating function from structure, an operation which is possible conceptually as one can think of its engine apart from an automobile's motion, does not alter the unity of both. Structural makeup alone is sufficient cause for individuality; however, the story does not end here, for each structure has a function within its system level of organization.

We find that biochemical knowledge can provide some of the keys to variance in human personality and behavior, but only pieces, not the whole picture. Furthermore, information about static pieces actually is not accurate because transactions constantly take place between that which lies within the skin of the individual and his external world. Dimensions can be devised at the organism level devoid of interpersonal connotations (for example, Chess's threshold of responsiveness). However, extending that dimension to an interpersonal level strengthens its predictive power. For example, the study of individual differences has focused inevitably on the mother-child unit where we no longer can ignore the presence of interacting individual differences. In her work, Escalona examines infant responses in transaction with environmental events with the mother.

The relationships between structure and function at different system levels involve both obstructing physical barriers and facilitating communication channels. Organisms and their subunits, from the one-cell stage onward, are bounded by membranes, and the only milieu that is real to an organism is that which can be internalized. The nutrient supply to a fetus is not a reality until it crosses the semipermeable membrane that bounds the fetal cells; the sound of the bell rung by the infant's ear is not part of the infant's reality unless it is perceived, that is, until it impinges on receptive internal sound transmitting equipment. For some phenomena the appropriate sensory receptors are not present, or the membrane boundary is impermeable (such variations are subsumed in the concept of thresholds of sensitivity). Toward some stimuli humans display either voluntary procurement or exclusion. For example, one can alter incoming stimuli by masking (turning up the volume on the radio), filter incoming stimuli by obstructing (closing one's eyes), or eliminate stimuli by withdrawing from an area. By these modes and others each human organism can define its own environment, the degree varying among individuals and increasing in complexity and extent with age and resources. Thus, while there is an external environment, in part uncontrollable and unpredictable, its existence is only significant insofar as it crosses the body's boundaries, becoming part of the internal environment and, thereby, becoming a part of the organism itself.

Operational descriptions are and will continue to be found to capture fragments of life experience so that they can be compared with each other and with themselves over time. The descriptions chosen generally reflect the formal characteristics of behavior rather than its continuously changing content. The emphasis is on the study of *style* rather than the developmental process itself (Korner, 1964). In Chapter 11 Benjamin's chart of behavior is an example of a precise, yet easily applied, coding system for this purpose. Until now, the novelist has been the only one capable of conveying the essence of vital life situations with any degree of authenticity. However, students of behavior are now developing word pictures, or vignettes, as descriptive tools. Progress is being made in developing specific descriptions, not using new words or neologisms, but through adapting common language to permit generalizations and communication with other workers. With the capacity to process prodigious amounts of data through computers, new coding systems, then, are needed and are emerging.

It may be possible to develop a coding language tailored to each research project to describe structures and functions as a dimension in naturally occurring situations. In order to carry this out it is necessary to synthesize viable transactional units, such as a daughter clinging to her mother in nursery school, from basic behavioral and intrapsychic units. In much the same way as symbolic language evolved, it may be possible to develop a coding key using models such as the one in Table 1. In this mother and daughter situation in nursery school, it is apparent that focusing on one piece as a dimension upon which to measure differences, for example, merely the approach behavior of a child in nursery school (the "syllable" equivalent), is not sufficient or useful. But when combined with other "syllables" the pieces of information blend into meaningful "sentences" or "paragraphs." This is an example of a relatively simple and valid set of behavioral observations, coded for comparative or predictive uses. Explanatory inferences, such as separation anxiety, can be included also. This particular example is at the two-person system level, the simplest naturally occurring interpersonal unit.

WHAT ARE VARIATIONS ON A DIMENSION?

The next question that arises, once a dimension upon which variation can occur is identified, is what constitutes a "just noticeable difference?" Actually, this point is fraught with theoretical and practical implications. The most striking feature is that one can refer to differences on a dimension without resorting to averages, means, normal ranges, and abnormal extremes. All that is necessary is to identify the fact that a difference exists between two individuals. This aspect

Table 1. Model for Constructing a Two-Person Unit Dimension

Language Equivalent	Behavioral Elements
Letter of alphabet	Child
Syllable	Child's approach behavior
Word	Child's approach behavior + separation anxiety
Sentence	Child's approach behavior + separation anxiety + mother + nursery school
Paragraph	Daughter persistently clinging to mother in nursery school

offers technical and scientific support for a public attitude shift toward acceptance of the fact that individuals vary.

In child-development research the interest is in what the variations imply for the future of the individual and what they imply in comparison with other individuals. Some decision obviously must be made about what constitutes a significant difference within the dimension. For example, comparing the threshold of response to sound requires a measurement of the sound and the response of the organism to the sound with a quantitative judgment about the relationship of the sound to the response: whether mild, moderate, or severe in terms of one's expectations at that particular time, in that particular place, and in that particular set of interpersonal relationships. The measurement of *quantity* of stimulus needed to exceed the threshold of response tells us how much; the *frequency* tells us how often it occurs; the *timing* tells us when it occurs; the *sequence* tells us in what order it occurs; and the *system level* tells us where it occurs. Without these details we are unable to meet the most important aspects of the dimension, namely, that its description be precise enough to be replicated and complete enough to accurately portray a naturally occurring life event. Applying these criteria to the mother-daughter nursery-school vignette, we can say that the child intensely, frequently, and at the beginning of the nursery school experience desired to be in her mother's arms. Once a pattern, or vignette, has been described it can be compared with patterns evoked in other children under similar conditions in order to discern significant variations.

THE IMPLICATIONS OF INDIVIDUAL DIFFERENCE RESEARCH

As summarized by Escalona (1969), among its significant products, work on individual difference has pioneered the field of relationships between physiological states and behavior, demonstrated that normal infants differ in excitability, shown that learning takes place at a very early age, found that maturational advances are proportional to self-generated activities (for example, responsiveness to invited perceptual stimulation of the special senses), suggested that reciprocal processes and structures demonstrate a relationship between inner growth and input, and pointed to motivation arising from the need to master novelty and complexity, a drive which is independent of primary need states.

An intriguing aspect of developmental research is seen in the finding that early influences may not appear in observable behavior until later life. For example, the influences of early minimal brain injury only become manifest later when perceptual and cognitive development proceed to the point where defects become obvious. It is also likely that the results of stimulation, or its lack, during early life experiences produce subtle changes which cannot be observed until later life. These predispositions, however, could be detected earlier if we knew how to identify them. This is one of the exciting prospects of further research.

In broad terms the notion of individual differences is not limited to variations arising from chance or random factors, but relates to structural defects, disease processes, trauma, under, over, or inconsistent sensory stimulation or mismatching of receptors and input with abrasive effects, for example, in the combination of a mother and infant with high activity-level dispositions. Furthermore, any group of social animals recognizes the existence of individual differences in its members through establishing hierarchies, as with pecking orders among fowls. In a similar vein differences between people in both naturally occurring and artificially contrived groups are intuitively recognized on many dimensions, ranging from power through physical attractiveness and intelligence.

The study of individual differences has forced a reassessment of the contrasting ideas of "pathology" and "individuality." Increasing sophistication has appeared in identifying those who present problem behavior for various aspects of our social system. We can predict the number of emotionally disturbed children in a typical school system and predict psychiatric casualty rates among Peace Corps volunteers. One prominent repercussion of this mass identification of people who are different has been defining *difference* as *deviance*. The underlying assumption is that most people fall into a normal range with the others bearing the label of abnormal or deviant.

For the clinician the evolving language of child-development research permits a shift away from the classification of behavior on a pathological-normal axis and provides a new way of describing children in clinical situations (Group for the Advancement of Psychiatry, 1966). One no longer must rely solely upon such concepts as anxiety and depression with the current availability of operational descriptions of the child's actual behavior, such, for example, as the Thomas and Chess concepts of persistence and threshold of responsiveness.

From the clinical point of view, the question is regularly raised, "Why is this child disturbed?" That question more appropriately becomes, "How do this child's unique qualities result in impairment of his functioning?" and "What can be done to alter his state and lead to a predictable improvement in functioning?" Interest in individual differences can, in this way, bypass etiology when necessary, obviating the need to blame causative factors or find "guilty" parties. The implications for taxonomy are obvious. The opportunity to free ourselves from the behavioral labels of mental illness, mental retardation, and emotional disturbance is enhanced by thinking of variations in an individual child's mental, cognitive, affective, and behavioral styles.

Variations between individuals are greater for humans than lower animals not only because homo sapiens is a more complicated organism. Also important is the fact that lower animals, even primates, ordinarily are less able to compensate for major individual differences, thereby tending to breed out differences of significance between members of the group through natural selection. As has been pointed out by Wolff, the lower the animal form in phylogeny, the less the range of variability among adult members of the species, based largely on the greater reliance upon the preformed nature of those central nervous system structures which are relatively less sensitive to feedback than man's. In contrast, in human society one can survive with significant differences, particularly when social supports exist, for example, in special education for the retarded and rehabilitation services for the handicapped.

PROSPECTS

As the preceding chapters carry us through the range of studies on individual differences in children, it becomes increasingly obvious that we, in fact, have traced trends in the scientific study of the individual. Stated another way, much attention has been devoted to the psychological study of *men* in the past, but the work on individual differences has inevitably sharpened the focus to the study of a *man*, specifically in his emerging form as a *child*. In this light, our current interest in individual differences is a critical step toward a scientific understanding of the human being—a logical sequel to working out our knowledge of similarities among people during life stages.

To paraphrase Piaget, the latency period of childhood is characterized by concrete thinking with a simple cause-effect basis. It is later during early adolescence that the appearance of formal operations permits thinking in abstract terms. For the child, the concrete relationship between cause and effect matures to a more realistic operational sense which recognizes complicated interplay between stimuli and responses. From this point of view, the individual difference approach may well be the entrée to formal operational thinking for the behavioral sciences, the clinician, and society. A major attitude change may be produced by the shift from the level of attempting to assign simple causes to behavior to the level of accepting multifactorial, transactional determinants. This trend may be reflected in our society's movement away from vertical thinking of parallel, but isolated, pieces comprising the world to horizontal thinking in which the "big picture" of interrelationships between systems is recognized.

We find, then, that we actually are dealing with the psychology of the individual as an outgrowth of a more restricted concern about differences between individuals. More accurately, we are dealing with the psychology of different individuals rather than the psychology of individual differences.

Certainly, a basic shift in values from an expectation of uniformity to an expectation of variability follows an acceptance of individuality. The shift to an acceptance of differences rather than consternation because of them, or the older view of expecting and hoping for homogeneity, could be followed by child-rearing and educational goals that would sharpen adaptive differences rather than minimize them in children. Perhaps our society stands on the brink of shifting from an emotionally laden "deviance" attitude toward differences between people to a more objective "variance" attitude.

REFERENCES

Bertalanffy, L. von (1968). *General system theory.* New York: George Brazillar.

Dobzhansky, T. (1962). *Mankind evolving.* New Haven: Yale University Press.

Erikson, E. H. (1963). *Childhood and society.* New York: W. W. Norton. 2nd ed.

Escalona, S. K. (1969). *The roots of the individual.* London: Tavistok Publications.

Group for the Advancement of Psychiatry (1966). *Psychopathological disorders of childhood: Theoretical considerations and a proposed classification.* Vol. 6, Report No. 62. New York: Group for the Advancement of Psychiatry.

Gesell, A. and Ilg, F. L. (1946). *The child from five to ten.* New York: Harper.

Korner, A. F. (1964). Some hypotheses regarding the significance of individual differences at birth for later development. *Psychoanalytic Study of the Child.* **19**, 58-72.

Montague, A. (1962). *Prenatal influences.* Springfield, Illinois: C. C. Thomas.

Phillips, J. L. (1969). *The origins of intellect—Piaget's theory.* San Francisco: W. H. Freeman.

EPILOGUE

In their southernmost range, certain Cecropia moths have two breeding cycles in a season, as described by Worth.* The caterpillars of the usual spring and summer group are almost sure to survive by wintering over in their cocoons. The exceptional second later crop is endangered because few find enough food during the short autumn days to develop rapidly or attain the size of maturity necessary to spin a cocoon and pupate successfully over the winter. Most of the second crop dies. One asks the obvious survival question—why would a species adopt what seems to be a suicidal pattern? Why would some individuals maintain over generations a difference which is so clearly selected against by survival factors? The suggested, but not proven, answer is that biological variability, even when deleterious to individuals, may provide security for the species—namely, the flexibility of the species to adapt to changing environmental conditions. So that, if their environment became warmer or if they migrated to a warmer climate, the moths which complete their metamorphosis in one season and lay a second batch of eggs would have an advantage and be the most successful members of their species. Even though a remote analogy, the Cecropia moths suggest another reason why protecting individual differences is important for society—that which is maladaptive for the individual today may be of advantage to the species at a later time.

*Worth, C.B., The last days of Polyphemus. *Audubon Magazine*, **72**, 22-30, March, 1970.

Author Index

Adkins, G., 41
Adler, A., 11, 23, 143
Adrian, E. D., 33, 40
Alexander, B. K., 287
Allen, L., 48, 62, 102
Alpert, A., 84, 101
Altman, S. A., 35, 40
Amatruda, C. S., 24
Ambrose, J. A., 34, 40
Ames, L. B., 23, 102
Anastasi, A., 17, 23, 45, 48, 59
Anderson, E. V., 36, 40
Anthony, E. J., 48, 59
Anokhin, P., 29, 40
Apgar, V. A., 47, 59
Arganian, M., 7, 45–59
Attwell, A. A., 159, 161, 196
Asmussen, E., 48, 59
Avis, V., 28, 44

Bacon, F., 204, 209
Bacon, M., 50, 59
Baldwin, H. H., 9–23
Barry, H., 50, 51, 59
Baron, J., 211, 313
Baumgartner, L., 47, 59
Baumrind, D., 159, 196, 249, 262
Beach, F. A., 37, 40
Becker, W. C., 62
Beiser, H. R., 100, 101
Bekesy, G. V. von, 32, 40
Bell, E. T., 204, 209
Bell, R. Q., 36, 40, 48, 58, 60, 224, 240
Benjamin, J., 70, 76, 80, 141

Benjamin, L. S., 53, 60, 211–212, 215–
    240, 240, 329
Bentzen, F., 48, 60
Bergman, P., 77, 80
Bertalanffy, L. Von, 334
Bierman, R., 217, 240
Biller, H., 57, 60
Birch, H. G., 24, 58, 63, 85, 87, 98, 101,
    102, 103, 157, 298, 307–308, 321
Birns, B., 69, 76, 81
Bock, R. D., 40
Bower, T. G. R., 32, 40
Bowlby, J., 7, 34, 40, 278, 279, 280, 284,
    287
Brackbill, Y., 15, 23
Brandt, E. M., 54, 62
Bricker, W., 57, 62
Bridger, W., 99, 101
Bronfenbrenner, U., 55, 60
Bronson, W. C., 15, 23
Broverman, D. M., 37, 40
Broverman, I. K., 40
Bruce, V. G., 43
Bruce, M., 286
Bruch, H., 90, 101
Bunney, W. E., Jr., 278, 281, 286, 287
Bunning, E., 33, 40
Burks, B., 25
Busch, F., 159–196, 243–262

Cahell, R. B., 24
Carey, W. B., 290, 293–306, 294, 296, 297,
    298, 311, 315, 319, 321
Cattell, R., 23, 200, 217, 240

Chance, E., 217, 241
Chess, S., 20, 24, 58, 63, 66–67, 83–101, 87, 90, 96, 99, 101, 102, 103, 157, 289, 290,293,296,297,298,307–308,321,326, 329, 332
Child, I. L., 50, 59
Childs, B., 47, 60
Click, P., 159–196, 243–262
Cloudsley-Thompson, J. I., 33, 40
Coffey, H. S., 241
Cohen, T. B., 161, 196
Costello, N. S., 36, 40, 48, 60
Cross, H. A., 271, 286
Crowell, D. H., 48, 60

Damarin, F. L., 15, 23
D'Andrade, R. G., 50, 51, 60
Darwin, C. R., 34, 40
Davidson, A., 114, 116
Davis, J. M., 281, 286
deHirsch, K., 259, 262
De Lucia, L. A., 36, 43, 48, 63
De Vore, I., 35, 41, 44
Diamond, M., 46, 60
Dobzhansky, T., 334
Dodsworth, R. O., 271, 286
Domek, C. J., 280, 287

Ehrhardt, A., 37, 43
Eibl-Eibesfelt, I., 35, 41
Eimas, P. D., 32, 41
Einstein, A., 204, 210
Eisenberg, R. E. J., 32, 41
Ekman, P., 35, 41
Elkind, D., 67, 105–116, 116
Emerson, P., 74, 82
Erikson, E. H., 51, 60, 215, 216, 241, 323–324, 334
Escalona, S. K., 15, 16, 23, 27, 70, 77, 78, 79, 80, 81, 85, 102, 141–142, 145–157, 150, 157, 324, 325, 329, 331, 334
Eysenck, H. J., 16, 23, 217, 241
Eysenck, S. B. G., 23

Fagot, B. I., 54–55, 57, 60
Fantz, R. L., 32, 41, 75, 81
Fay, J., 114, 116
Feiffer, M., 217, 241
Feshbach, S., 57, 60
Finch, S., 100, 102

Fitch, R. O., 40
Foa, U. G., 217, 241
Freeberg, N. E., 159–160, 196
Freedman, D. G., 35, 38, 41, 47, 60
Freedman, M., 218, 221, 241
Freeman, F. S., 17, 23
Freud, A., 21, 23, 160, 196, 259, 262
Freud, S., 20, 23, 69, 81, 84, 102, 116, 199, 210, 215, 241, 244
Fries, M. E., 16, 23, 70, 81, 84, 85, 102
Friesen, W. V., 41
Fuller, J. L., 36, 41

Gadpaille, W. J., 49, 60
Garai, J. E., 48, 49, 60
Gardner, R., 78, 81
Gautier, M., 42
Gesell, A., 14, 23, 24, 84, 102, 324, 334
Goldberg, S., 55, 56, 58, 60
Gosse, E., 109–110, 116
Gottesman, I. I., 36, 41
Goy, R. W., 44
Gregg, G. S., 290, 307–321, 312, 321
Griffin, G. A., 271, 286
Grobstein, R. I., 24, 81
Group for the Advancement of Psychiatry, 334
Gullickson, G. R., 48, 60

Haar, E., 20, 24
Halberg, F., 41
Hamburg, D. A., 36, 41, 48, 49, 60, 61
Hamilton, W. J. III, 34, 42
Hampson, J. G., 61
Hampson, J. L., 46, 61
Hansen, E. W., 266, 286, 287
Hanzik, M. P., 102
Harlow, H. F., 51, 52, 53, 58–59, 61, 63, 219, 241, 265–286, 266, 279, 280, 281, 282, 286, 287
Harlow, M. K., 219, 241, 286
Harper, L., 58, 61
Harris, I. D., 143, 199–209, 201, 202, 210
Hartman, H. I., 21, 24, 69, 80, 81
Hebb, D. O., 33, 41
Heeball-Nielsen, K., 48, 59
Heider, G. M., 23, 146, 157
Heinecke, C. M., 142, 159–196, 159, 196, 212, 243–262, 249, 251, 258, 259, 261, 262, 263, 324, 325

Heinze, S., 205, 210
Hellmer, L. A., 62
Hertzig, M., 102, 103, 157, 298
Hetherington, M., 48, 57, 61
Hinde, R. A., 35, 41, 280, 286
Holst, E. V., 33, 41
Honzik, M. P., 48, 62, 77, 81
Hooker, D., 30, 41
Howard, K. I., 202, 210
Hubel, D. H., 31, 41
Hull, C. L., 16, 24
Hume, D., 204
Humphrey, T., 30, 42
Hundleby, J. D., 16, 24
Hunt, J. McV., 46, 61, 258, 263
Hutchinson, D. L., 312, 321
Huxley, J., 28, 42

Ilg, F. L., 324, 334
Inhelder, B., 117
Irwin, O. C., 14, 24

Jackson, E. B., 102
Jansky, J., 259, 262
Jenkins, J. J., 17, 24
Jensen, D. Y., 25
Jensen, G. D., 280, 286
Jersild, A., 238, 241
Jones, E., 199, 210
Jones, H., 200, 210
Jusezyk, P., 41

Kagan, J., 59, 61, 77, 78, 81, 95, 102, 146,
    157, 159, 161, 197
Kallman, F. J., 49, 61
Kaufman, I. C., 35, 42, 280, 287
Keogh, B. K., 258, 263
Kessen, W., 32, 42
Kety, S. S., 281, 287
Klaiber, E. I., 40
Klatskin, E. H., 90, 102
Klein, A., 321
Koch, H., 203, 210
Kohlberg, L., 54, 61
Komisaruk, B. R., 33, 42
Korn, S., 103, 157, 294, 298
Korner, A. F., 21, 24, 65–66, 69–80, 71–
    72, 73, 75, 76, 81, 82, 99, 102, 329, 334
Kotinsky, R., 83, 103
Kraemer, H., 81

Kramer, E., 159–196, 243–262
Kretschmer, E., 12, 24
Kris, M., 95, 102
Kuffler, S. W., 31, 42

Landy, F., 57, 63
Langford, W., 259, 262
Lashley, K. W., 33, 34, 42
Laufman, L., 313, 321
Lawick-Goodall, J. V., 35, 41, 42, 52, 63
Leary, T., 241
Lehman, H. C., 54, 61
Lehrman, P. R., 110, 117
Lejeune, J., 36, 42
Lenard, H. G., 43
Lenneberg, E. L., 28, 33, 42
Letch, M., 102
Lettvin, J. Y., 31, 42
Levine, S., 49, 61
Levy, N., 48, 62
Lewis, M., 49, 55, 56, 58, 60, 61
Liebowitz, J., 258
Lipsitt, L. P., 48, 62
Lipton, E. I., 99, 102
Littman, R. A., 57, 62
Lord, E. E., 23
Lorenz, K., 34, 42
Loring, C. B., 60
Lund, 36
Lunde, D. T., 41, 48, 49, 61
Lustman, D. L., 24
Lyles, T. B., 49, 62

Maccoby, E., 36, 42
MacArthur, C., 202, 210
McClearn, G. E., 48, 62
McCullough, W. S., 42
Macfarlane, J. A., 48, 62, 95, 102
McKinney, W., Jr., 212, 213, 265–286,
    278, 282, 286, 287
Mahler, M., 160, 197, 215, 216, 241
Marler, P., 34, 42
Marshall, W. A., 126, 130, 140
Martin, R. M., 60
Matthews, B. C. H., 33, 40
Matwrana, H. R., 42
Mead, M., 50, 62
Mednick, S., 77, 82
Meili-Dworetzki, G., 78, 79, 82
Meyers, E. C., 159, 161, 196

Minkowski, M., 30, 42
Mirsky, I. A., 84, 102
Mischel, W., 46, 62
Mitchell, G. D., 53–54, 58–59, 62, 271, 287
Money, J., 37, 43, 46, 62
Montague, A., 19, 24, 328, 334
Morris, D., 51, 62
Moss, H. A., 56, 58, 59, 61, 62, 73, 82, 95, 102, 146, 157, 159, 161, 197
Mueller, W. J., 218, 241
Murphy, G., 200, 210
Murphy, L. B., 84, 95, 102, 103, 146, 200, 210
Mussen, P. H., 57, 62, 137, 140, 244, 263

Neilon, P., 24
Neubauer, P. B., 101
Neuman, J. von, 29, 43
Newcomb, T., 200, 210
Niswander, K. R., 63

Ongue, G. C., 25
Opie, I., 106, 117
Opie, P., 106, 117
Orlansky, H., 90, 103
Ornitz, E., 77, 82
Orpet, R. E., 159, 161, 196
Ossorio, A. G., 241

Palmer, R. D., 40
Panofsky, H., 41
Parker, S., 59
Pasamanick, B., 19, 24
Pascal, B., 204, 210
Paterson, D. G., 24
Patterson, G. R., 54–55, 57, 60, 62
Pavlov, I., 77, 82
Payne, D. T., 159–160, 196
Peel, E. A., 108, 117
Peiper, J., 27, 30, 36, 43
Perl, R. E., 17, 24
Pessin, V., 59
Peterson, D. R., 48, 62
Phoenix, C. H., 44
Phillips, J. L., 323, 334
Piaget, J., 7, 28, 30–31, 43, 51, 62, 67, 70, 82, 105, 106, 110, 116, 117, 203, 323–324, 333
Pintner, R., 17, 24

Pittendrigh, C. S., 33, 43
Pitts, W. H., 42
Prange, A. J., 281, 287
Prechtl, H. F. R., 27, 43

Quay, H., 62

Rabban, M., 54, 62
Raph, J., 87, 103
Raymond, E. J., 287
Resier, M., 99, 101
Rhodes, P., 47, 62
Richmond, J. B., 21, 24, 102
Ritvo, E., 77, 82
Ritvo, S., 84, 103
Robbins, L. D., 87, 96, 103
Roberts, D. F., 137, 138, 140
Robertson, T., 278, 279, 287
Robson, K., 73, 82
Rorvik, D. M., 47, 63
Rosenberg, B. G., 57, 63
Rosenblith, J. F., 36, 43, 48, 63
Rosenblum, L. A., 35, 42, 280, 287
Ross, D. C., 99, 103
Rothney, J. W. M., 24
Rozner, L. M., 140
Ruppenthal, G. C., 287
Rutherford, E., 57, 62
Rutter, M., 20, 24, 97, 102, 103

Salapetek, P., 297, 298
Sauer, F., 34, 43
Scarr, S., 297, 298
Schacter, S., 210
Schaefer, E. S., 218, 219, 221, 241
Schaeffer, H., 74, 82
Schaller, G. B., 35, 43
Scheinfeld, A., 48, 49, 60, 63
Schildkraut, J. J., 281, 287
Schlegel, W. S., 49, 63
Seay, W., 271, 279, 287
Shaffer, H. R., 150, 157
Sheldon, W. H., 12, 13, 25
Shettles, L. B., 47, 63
Shirley, M. M., 14, 25, 84, 103
Shoemaker, D. J., 62
Siegel, F. S., 40
Singer, J. E., 47, 49, 56, 58, 63
Sigueland, E. R., 41
Skinner, B. G., 39, 43

Solberger, A., 33, 43
Solnit, A. J., 84, 103
Sorenson, E. R., 41
Spencer-Booth, Y., 286
Sperry, R. W., 29, 31, 43
Spitz, R. A., 9, 25, 278, 279, 280, 287
Stein, M., 41, 205, 210
Steinschneider, A., 102
Stevens, S. S., 25
Stevenson, I., 90, 103
Stolz, L. M., 57, 63
Stone, A. A., 25
Sullivan, H. S., 216, 238
Suomi, S. J., 52, 53, 59, 61, 63, 265–286, 281, 282, 286, 287
Sutton-Smith, B., 57, 63
Swan, A. V., 140
Swan, C., 15, 25
Szentagothai, J., 29, 43
Szilard, L., 47, 63

Takaishi, M., 122
Tamura, M., 34, 42
Tanner, J. M., 67–68, 119–139, 122, 123, 124, 125, 126, 128, 130, 135–136, 138, 140
Tecce, J. J., 20, 25
Tellgen, A., 40
Terestman, N., 87, 103
Terman, L. M., 16, 25
Thoman, E., 82
Thomas, A., 18, 24, 58, 63, 70, 77, 82, 83–101, 84, 87, 101, 102, 103, 146, 157, 289, 290, 294, 296, 297, 298, 307–308, 315, 319, 321, 332
Thomas, R. M., 25
Thomas, S. M., 25
Thompson, W. R., 36, 41
Thorpe, W. H., 34, 43
Tinbergen, N., 34, 43
Tisserand-Perrier, M., 137, 140
Tolman, C. W., 280, 286
Turpin, R., 42

Tyler, L. E., 25

Vandenberg, S. G., 40
Vigorito, J., 41
Vogel, W., 40

Waddinton, C. H., 28, 43
Wall, P. D., 32, 33, 44
Walker, R. N., 13, 25
Walter, W. Gray, 33, 44, 84, 103
Washburn, S. L., 28, 35, 44
Weil, A. P., 101
Weir, M. W., 108, 117
Weiss, P. A., 29, 30, 33, 44
Weller, G. M., 48, 63
Wenar, C., 96, 103
Wenger, M. A., 13, 25
Werner, H., 28, 30, 44
Wertheimer, M., 114, 117
Westheimer, I., 243, 249, 251, 259, 263
Westman, J. C., 9–23, 161, 197, 323–334
Westphal, M., 63
Whitehouse, R. H., 122
Whiting, J., 50, 63
Whitrow, G. S., 33, 34, 44
Wiener, N., 33, 44
Wiesel, T. M., 31, 41
Wilkin, L. C., 102
Williams, R. J., 13, 25
Williams, R. V., 84, 103
Wilson, E., 210
Windle, W. F., 30, 44
Witkin, H., 78, 82
Witmer, H. L., 83, 103
Witty, P. A., 54, 61
Wolfenstein, M., 111, 117
Wolff, P. H., 6, 7, 16, 27, 27–40, 30, 34–35, 36, 38, 44, 72, 76, 81, 82, 84, 85, 102, 150
Woltmann, A. G., 113, 117
Woolf, P. J., 23
Wright, H. F., 244, 263

Young, H. B., 123, 125, 140
Young, N. C., 37, 44

Subject Index

Abuse, child, 308
Adrenal hyperplasia, congenital, 37
Adult-civilized children, 201–203

Affectional systems, 266–270
  heterosexual, 270
  infant-mother, 267–269
  maternal, 266–267
  paternal, 270
  peer, 269–270
Affiliative behavior, 219
Antidotal behavior, 230–231
Anxiety, 248
Aphasia, 19
Assumptive realities, 108–115
Attachment behavior, 268
Attitudes toward self, 238–239
Authoritarian behavior, 221
Autonomic reactivity, 21

Behavior in context, 153
Birth order, creativity, 200
  intellectual style, 203–204
  personality, 200
Brain injury, minimal, 331

Catecholamine hypothesis, 281
Cecropia moths, 334
Cerebral palsy, 19
Cesarian section, 296
Childlike behaviors, 224–225
Cognitive conceit, 110–115
Complementary behaviors, 219–225
Concrete operations, 105–107
Conscience, external, 112

Constitution, definition, 328
Counseling, parent, 101, 297, 320–321, 326
Cytogenetics, developmental, 20

Day care programs, 155–156
Defense mechanisms, 248
Depression, behavioral manifestations, 284
  experimental model of, 278–286
  theories of, 281
Determinants, behavioral, 325
Developmental age, 133
Developmental lines, 21, 248
Developmental profile, 259–261
Deviance attitude, 334
Differential psychology, 15–16
Difficult child, 88–93, 295–297, 308
Dimensions, functional, 328
  individual differences, 326, 328–331
  structural, 328
Dispositions, 151
Dominating behavior, 219
Down's syndrome, 313
Dyslexia, developmental, 19

Easy child, 88–93, 296–297, 310, 313
Educational psychology, 17–19
Egocentrism, 107
Ego functions, 20, 248
Electroencephalographic acitvity, 33
Emancipating behavior, 219
Emotionally disturbed children, 332
Ethological studies, 35
Existential philosophy, 323

Family life variables, 244

Fantasy, 248
Field unit analysis system, 243
Formal operations, 105

General system theory, 326–327
Genetic code, 327
Genetic mechanisms, 19, 36

Homosexuality, 49
Hospitalization, effects on infants, 149–150
Hyperkinetic syndrome, 312

Individual differences, activity level, 86,
     295, 315
   adaptability, 86, 247, 295
   approach-withdrawal, 86, 295, 315
   attention span and persistence, 87, 295
   crying, 73
   deviance versus variance, 334
   dimensions of, 326–331
   distractibility, 87, 295, 315
   drive strength, 20, 75
   history, 10–14
   infancy, 28, 30, 31, 69–80
   intensity of reaction, 86, 247, 295
   mood, 87, 295, 315
   mother-oriented behavior, 73, 74, 86,
     150, 237
   nursery school adaptation, 195–196, 247
   pubertal growth rate, 127, 130, 135–137
   pubertal onset, 132
   pubertal physical size, 135
   racial, 38, 310
   reaction to sibling birth, 93
   rhythmicity, 86, 295
   sensory responsivity, 73, 75–79, 86, 295
   system level, 326–327
   toilet training, 92
   weaning, 91
Infant Accident Study, 308–312
Intellectual styles, connectedness prone,
     203
   disconnectedness prone, 204
Intelligence tests, 17, 258
Interpersonal behavior classifications, 218
Introjected attitudes, 238–239

Latency period, 105–116

Maternal deprivation, 9, 271–278, 278–
     280, 324

Mental illness, 332
   prevention, 323
Mental retardation, 332
Mind-body dichotomy, 324
Minimal brain dysfunction, 19
Molecular biology, 327
Mother-child unit, 146, 159, 216, 245,
     267–269, 296, 309, 330
Motor development, 29–31

Nature versus nurture, 1
Neuroembryology, 29, 31
Neurological examination, developmental,
     320
New York Longitudinal Study, 85, 293
   interview questionnaire, 294

Observation, participant, 324–325
Operation Headstart, 160
Opposite behaviors, 219–225

Para-professionals, 321
Parent-child profiles, 159, 237, 245, 249–
     250
Parentlike behaviors, 221–224
Parents, child rearing, 22, 250
Patterns of experience, 152
Pecking orders, 332
Pediatrics, changes in practice, 307
Peer-civilized, 201–203
Peer relations, influence of, 55, 106–107,
     160, 201, 269, 280
Period analysis, 243, 250–251
Periodicity, 33
Personality traits, 217
Play interview, 259
Prediction, infancy to later life, 145–147,
     324, 326
   nursery school to later life, 160–161
Predispositions, 151
Prefunctional structures, 28, 30, 31, 38
Premature birth, 324
Primate Center, University of Wisconsin,
     51, 265, 280
Primate social behavior, chart, 219–231
Psychoanalysis as a science, 215, 323
Psychological testing, 258, 324
Psychophysiology, 324
Psychosexual development, 21
Psychotherapy, 215, 230, 261

Puberty, changing trends, 137–139
onset of, 119–120

Questionnaire, New York Longitudinal
Study, 294
temperament, 297–304

Rating scales, child behavior, 251–258
clinical observation, 313–316, 325
depression, 285
newborn, 20
New York Longitudinal Study, 294
patients and therapists, 218
parent-child, 250, 260
social relations, 216
temperament, 294, 297–306, 309
Rehabilitation services, 333
Rh-factor babies, 312
Rights, individual, 22

Science, development of, 323
Self-attitudes, 238–239, 248
Sensorimotor development, 30
Sensory development, 31–32
Separation, in nursery school, 174–176,
193–195, 247
mother-infant, 278–280
Separation behavior, 269
Sex differences, anthropological evidence,
50–51
behavior, 36, 48, 57
cognitive, 36, 37
color sensitivity, 36
maternal behavior, 53, 56, 58

maturation rate, 49
play, 51–54
pubertal growth rates, 122–123
resistance to disease, 36, 47, 48
rhesus monkies, 51–54
sensory sensitivity, 36, 48
toy preference, 55
Sex reassignment, 46
Sexual dimorphism, 47, 124–132
Shame and guilt control behavior, 221
Slow-to-warm-up child, 89–93, 296–297
Smiling, 34, 153
Social isolation, impact of, 271–278
procedures, 271–272
Social roles, 217
Special education, 333
Superego, 248

Temperament and physique, 12–13
Temperamental styles, behavior problems,
96–100
the difficult child, 88–93, 295–297, 308
the easy child, 88–93, 296–297, 310, 313
the slow-to-warm up child, 89–93, 296–
297
Tracks, primate social behavior chart, 226–
230
Transactions, interpersonal, 324, 330
Transformation rules, 29, 32, 34
Transfusions, intrauterine, 312
Turner's syndrome, 37

Variability, observer, 9
Variance attitude, 334